The Works Of Adam Smith: The Nature And Causes Of The Wealth Of Nations

Adam Smith, Dugald Stewart

Nabu Public Domain Reprints:

You are holding a reproduction of an original work published before 1923 that is in the public domain in the United States of America, and possibly other countries. You may freely copy and distribute this work as no entity (individual or corporate) has a copyright on the body of the work. This book may contain prior copyright references, and library stamps (as most of these works were scanned from library copies). These have been scanned and retained as part of the historical artifact.

This book may have occasional imperfections such as missing or blurred pages, poor pictures, errant marks, etc. that were either part of the original artifact, or were introduced by the scanning process. We believe this work is culturally important, and despite the imperfections, have elected to bring it back into print as part of our continuing commitment to the preservation of printed works worldwide. We appreciate your understanding of the imperfections in the preservation process, and hope you enjoy this valuable book.

CHAP. II,

Of the Difcouragement of Agriculture in the ancient State of Europe after the Fall of the Roman Empire - - - 81

CHAP. III.

Of the Rife and Progrefs of Cities and Towns, after the Fall of the Roman Empire - - - - - - 99

CHAP. IV.

How the Commerce of the Towns contributed to the Improvement of the Country - 117

BOOK IV.

Of Syftems of Political Economy.

INTRODUCTION - - - Page 138

CHAP. I.

Of the Principle of the commercial, or mercantile Syftem - - - - 139

CHAP. II.

Of Reftraints upon the Importation from foreign Countries of fuch Goods as can be produced at Home - - - - 176

CONTENTS.

CHAP. III.

Of the extraordinary Restraints upon the Importation of Goods of almost all Kinds, from those Countries with which the Balance is supposed to be disadvantageous - Page 209

PART I. *Of the Unreasonableness of those Restraints even upon the Principles of the Commercial System.* ibid.

Digression concerning Banks of Deposit, particularly concerning that of Amsterdam - - - 219

PART II. *Of the Unreasonableness of those extraordinary Restraints upon other Principles* - - 235

CHAP. IV.

Of Drawbacks - - - - 252

CHAP. V.

Of Bounties - - - - - 261

Digression concerning the Corn Trade and Corn Laws 296

CHAP. VI.

Of Treaties of Commerce - - - 323

CHAP. VII.

Of Colonies - - - - - 343

PART I. *Of the Motives for establishing new Colonies* ibid.

PART II. *Causes of the Prosperity of new Colonies* 358

CONTENTS.

PART III. *Of the Advantages which Europe has derived from the Discovery of America, and from that of a Passage to the East Indies by the Cape of Good Hope* - 400

CHAP. VIII.

Conclusion of the Mercantile System - 485

AN
INQUIRY

INTO THE

NATURE AND CAUSES

OF THE

WEALTH OF NATIONS.

VOL. II.

AN
INQUIRY

INTO THE

NATURE AND CAUSES

OF THE

WEALTH OF NATIONS.

BOOK II.

CHAP. III.

*Of the Accumulation of Capital, or of productive
and unproductive Labour.*

THERE is one fort of labour which
adds to the value of the fubject upon
which it is beftowed : there is another which
has no fuch effect. The former, as it produces
a value, may be called productive; the latter,
unproductive * labour. Thus the labour of a
manufacturer adds, generally, to the value of the
materials which he works upon, that of his own

---

* Some French authors of great learning and ingenuity have
ufed thofe words in a different fenfe. In the laft chapter of the
fourth book, I fhall endeavour to fhow that their fenfe is an improper
one.

OF PRODUCTIVE AND UNPRODUCTIVE LABOUR.

BOOK
II.

maintenance, and of his mafter's profit. The labour of a menial fervant, on the contrary, adds to the value of nothing. Though the manufacturer has his wages advanced to him by his mafter, he, in reality, cofts him no expence, the value of thofe wages being generally reftored, together with a profit, in the improved value of the fubject upon which his labour is beftowed. But the maintenance of a menial fervant never is reftored. A man grows rich by employing a multitude of manufacturers: he grows poor, by maintaining a multitude of menial fervants. The labour of the latter, however, has its value, and deferves its reward as well as that of the former. But the labour of the manufacturer fixes and realizes itfelf in fome particular fubject or vendible commodity, which lafts for fome time at leaft after that labour is paft. It is, as it were, a certain quantity of labour ftocked and ftored up to be employed, if neceffary, upon fome other occafion. That fubject, or what is the fame thing, the price of that fubject, can afterwards, if neceffary, put into motion a quantity of labour equal to that which had originally produced it. The labour of the menial fervant, on the contrary, does not fix or realize itfelf in any particular fubject or vendible commodity. His fervices generally perifh in the very inftant of their performance, and feldom leave any trace or value behind them, for which an equal quantity of fervice could afterwards be procured.

The labour of fome of the moft refpectable orders in the fociety is, like that of menial fer-

vants,

OF PRODUCTIVE AND UNPRODUCTIVE LABOUR. 5

vants, unproductive of any value, and does not
fix or realize itfelf in any permanent fubject, or
vendible commodity, which endures after that
labour is paft, and for which an equal quantity
of labour could afterwards be procured. The
fovereign, for example, with all the officers both
of juftice and war who ferve under him, the whole
army and navy, are unproductive labourers.
They are the fervants of the public, and are
maintained by a part of the annual produce of
the induftry of other people. Their fervice, how
honourable, how ufeful, or how neceffary foever,
produces nothing for which an equal quantity of
fervice can afterwards be procured. The protection, fecurity, and defence of the commonwealth, the effect of their labour this year, will
not purchafe its protection, fecurity, and defence
for the year to come. In the fame clafs muft be
ranked, fome both of the graveft and moft important, and fome of the moft frivolous profeffions : churchmen, lawyers, phyficians, men of
letters of all kinds ; players, buffoons, muficians,
opera-fingers, opera-dancers, &c. The labour of
the meaneft of thefe has a certain value, regulated by the very fame principles which regulate
that of every other fort of labour ; and that of
the nobleft and moft ufeful, produces nothing
which could afterwards purchafe or procure an
equal quantity of labour. Like the declamation
of the actor, the harangue of the orator, or the
tune of the mufician, the work of all of them
perifhes in the very inftant of its production.

CHAP.
III.

B 2

Both

OF PRODUCTIVE AND UNPRODUCTIVE LABOUR.

BOOK II.

Both productive and unproductive labourers, and thofe who do not labour at all, are all equally maintained by the annual produce of the land and labour of the country. This produce, how great foever, can never be infinite, but muft have certain limits. According, therefore, as a fmaller or greater proportion of it is in any one year employed in maintaining unproductive hands, the more in the one cafe and the lefs in the other will remain for the productive, and the next year's produce will be greater or fmaller accordingly; the whole annual produce, if we except the fpontaneous productions of the earth, being the effect of productive labour.

Though the whole annual produce of the land and labour of every country, is, no doubt, ultimately deftined for fupplying the confumption of its inhabitants, and for procuring a revenue to them; yet when it firft comes either from the ground, or from the hands of the productive labourers, it naturally divides itfelf into two parts. One of them, and frequently the largeft, is, in the firft place, deftined for replacing a capital, or for renewing the provifions, materials, and finifhed work, which had been withdrawn from a capital; the other for conftituting a revenue either to the owner of this capital, as the profit of his ftock; or to fome other perfon, as the rent of his land. Thus, of the produce of land, one part replaces the capital of the farmer; the other pays his profit and the rent of the landlord; and thus conftitutes a revenue both to the owner of this capital, as the profits of his ftock;

and

OF PRODUCTIVE AND UNPRODUCTIVE LABOUR.

and to fome other perfon, as the rent of his land. C H A P.
Of the produce of a great manufactory, in the III.
fame manner, one part, and that always the
largeft, replaces the capital of the undertaker of
the work; the other pays his profit, and thus conftitutes a revenue to the owner of this capital.

That part of the annual produce of the land
and labour of any country which replaces a capital, never is immediately employed to maintain
any but productive hands. It pays the wages of
productive labour only. That which is immediately deftined for conftituting a revenue either
as profit or as rent, may maintain indifferently
either productive or unproductive hands.

Whatever part of his ftock a man employs as
a capital, he always expects it to be replaced to
him with a profit. He employs it, therefore, in
maintaining productive hands only; and after
having ferved in the function of a capital to him,
it conftitutes a revenue to them. Whenever he
employs any part of it in maintaining unproductive hands of any kind, that part is, from that
moment, withdrawn from his capital, and placed
in his ftock referved for immediate confumption.

Unproductive labourers, and thofe who do
not labour at all, are all maintained by revenue ;
either, firft, by that part of the annual produce
which is originally deftined for conftituting a
revenue to fome particular perfons, either as
the rent of land or as the profits of ftock; or,
fecondly, by that part which, though originally
deftined for replacing a capital and for maintaining productive labourers only, yet when it comes

B 3   into

OF PRODUCTIVE AND UNPRODUCTIVE LABOUR.

BOOK II.

into their hands, whatever part of it is over and above their neceffary fubfiftence, may be employed in maintaining indifferently either productive or unproductive hands. Thus, not only the great landlord or the rich merchant, but even the common workman, if his wages are confiderable, may maintain a menial fervant; or he may fometimes go to a play or a puppet-fhow, and fo contribute his fhare towards maintaining one fet of unproductive labourers; or he may pay fome taxes, and thus help to maintain another fet, more honourable and ufeful, indeed, but equally unproductive. No part of the annual produce, however, which had been originally deftined to replace a capital, is ever directed towards maintaining unproductive hands, till after it has put into motion its full complement of productive labour, or all that it could put into motion in the way in which it was employed. The workman muft have earned his wages by work done, before he can employ any part of them in this manner. That part too is generally but a fmall one. It is his fpare revenue only, of which productive labourers have feldom a great deal. They generally have fome, however; and in the payment of taxes the greatnefs of their number may compenfate, in fome meafure, the fmallnefs of their contribution. The rent of land and the profits of ftock are every-where, therefore, the principal fources from which unproductive hands derive their fubfiftence. Thefe are the two forts of revenue of which the owners have generally moft to fpare. They might both maintain indifferently

OF PRODUCTIVE AND UNPRODUCTIVE LABOUR. 7

ferently either productive or unproductive CHAP. III. hands. They feem, however, to have fome predilection for the latter. The expence of a great lord feeds generally more idle than induftrious people. The rich merchant, though with his capital he maintains induftrious people only, yet by his expence, that is, by the employment of his revenue, he feeds commonly the very fame fort as the great lord.

The proportion, therefore, between the productive and unproductive hands, depends very much in every country upon the proportion between that part of the annual produce, which, as foon as it comes either from the ground or from the hands of the productive labourers, is deftined for replacing a capital, and that which is deftined for conftituting a revenue, either as rent, or as profit. This proportion is very different in rich from what it is in poor countries.

Thus, at prefent, in the opulent countries of Europe, a very large, frequently the largeft portion of the produce of the land, is deftined for replacing the capital of the rich and independent farmer; the other for paying his profits, and the rent of the landlord. But anciently, during the prevalency of the feudal government, a very fmall portion of the produce was fufficient to replace the capital employed in cultivation. It confifted commonly in a few wretched cattle, maintained altogether by the fpontaneous produce of uncultivated land, and which might, therefore, be confidered as a part of that fpontaneous produce. It generally too belonged to the landlord, and

B 4   was

OF PRODUCTIVE AND UNPRODUCTIVE LABOUR.

BOOK
II.

was by him advanced to the occupiers of the land. All the reft of the produce properly belonged to him too, either as rent for his land, or as profit upon this paltry capital. The occupiers of land were generally bondmen, whofe perfons and effects were equally his property. Thofe who were not bondmen were tenants at will, and though the rent which they paid was often nominally little more than a quit-rent, it really amounted to the whole produce of the land. Their lord could at all times command their labour in peace, and their fervice in war. Though they lived at a diftance from his houfe, they were equally dependant upon him as his retainers who lived in it. But the whole produce of the land undoubtedly belongs to him, who can difpofe of the labour and fervice of all thofe whom it maintains. In the prefent ftate of Europe, the fhare of the landlord feldom exceeds a third, fometimes not a fourth part of the whole produce of the land. The rent of land, however, in all the improved parts of the country, has been tripled and quadrupled fince thofe ancient times; and this third or fourth part of the annual produce is, it feems, three or four times greater than the whole had been before. In the progrefs of improvement, rent, though it increafes in proportion to the extent, diminifhes in proportion to the produce of the land.

In the opulent countries of Europe, great capitals are at prefent employed in trade and manufactures. In the ancient ftate, the little trade that was ftirring, and the few homely and coarfe

manu-

OF PRODUCTIVE AND UNPRODUCTIVE LABOUR. 9

manufactures that were carried on, required but very small capitals. These, however, must have yielded very large profits. The rate of interest was no-where less that ten per cent., and their profits must have been sufficient to afford this great interest. At present the rate of interest, in the improved parts of Europe, is no-where higher than six per cent. and in some of the most improved it is so low as four, three, and two per cent. Though that part of the revenue of the inhabitants which is derived from the profits of stock is always much greater in rich than in poor countries, it is because the stock is much greater: in proportion to the stock the profits are generally much less.

That part of the annual produce, therefore, which, as soon as it comes either from the ground, or from the hands of the productive labourers, is destined for replacing a capital, is not only much greater in rich than in poor countries, but bears a much greater proportion to that which is immediately destined for constituting a revenue either as rent or as profit. The funds destined for the maintenance of productive labour, are not only much greater in the former than in the latter, but bear a much greater proportion to those which, though they may be employed to maintain either productive or unproductive hands, have generally a predilection for the latter.

The proportion between those different funds necessarily determines in every country the general character of the inhabitants as to industry or idleness. We are more industrious than our forefathers;

OF PRODUCTIVE AND UNPRODUCTIVE LABOUR.

BOOK
II.

forefathers; becaufe in the prefent times the funds deftined for the maintenance of induftry, are much greater in proportion to thofe which are likely to be employed in the maintenance of idlenefs, than they were two or three centuries ago. Our anceftors were idle for want of a fufficient encouragement to induftry. It is better, fays the proverb, to play for nothing, than to work for nothing. In mercantile and manufacturing towns, where the inferior ranks of people are chiefly maintained by the employment of capital, they are in general induftrious, fober, and thriving; as in many Englifh, and in moft Dutch towns. In thofe towns which are principally fupported by the conftant or occafional refidence of a court, and in which the inferior ranks of people are chiefly maintained by the fpending of revenue, they are in general idle, diffolute, and poor; as at Rome, Verfailles, Compeigne, and Fontainbleau. If you except Rouen and Bourdeaux, there is little trade or induftry in any of the parliament towns of France; and the inferior ranks of people, being chiefly maintained by the expence of the members of the courts of juftice, and of thofe who come to plead before them, are in general idle and poor. The great trade of Rouen and Bourdeaux feems to be altogether the effect of their fituation. Rouen is neceffarily the entrepôt of almoft all the goods which are brought either from foreign countries, or from the maritime provinces of France, for the confumption of the great city of Paris. Bourdeaux is in the fame manner the entrepôt of the wines

which

OF PRODUCTIVE AND UNPRODUCTIVE LABOUR. 11

which grow upon the banks of the Garonne, and C H A P. of the rivers which run into it, one of the richeft III. wine countries in the world, and which feems to produce the wine fitteft for exportation, or beft fuited to the tafte of foreign nations. Such advantageous fituations neceffarily attract a great capital by the great employment which they afford it ; and the employment of this capital is the caufe of the induftry of thofe two cities. In the other parliament towns of France, very little more capital feems to be employed that what is neceffary for fupplying their own confumption ; that is, little more than the fmalleft capital which can be employed in them. The fame thing may be faid of Paris, Madrid, and Vienna. Of thofe three cities, Paris is by far the moft induftrious: but Paris itfelf is the principal market of all the manufactures eftablifhed at Paris, and its own confumption is the principal object of all the trade which it carries on. London, Lifbon, and Copenhagen, are, perhaps, the only three cities in Europe, which are both the conftant refidence of a court, and can at the fame time be confidered as trading cities, or as cities which trade not only for their own confumption, but for that of other cities and countries. The fituation of all the three is extremely advantageous, and naturally fits them to be the entrepôts of a great part of the goods deftined for the confumption of diftant places. In a city where a great revenue is fpent, to employ with advantage a capital for any other purpofe than for fupplying the confumption of that city, is

probably

OF PRODUCTIVE AND UNPRODUCTIVE LABOUR.

BOOK II.

probably more difficult than in one in which the inferior ranks of people have no other maintenance but what they derive from the employment of such a capital. The idleness of the greater part of the people who are maintained by the expence of revenue, corrupts, it is probable, the industry of those who ought to be maintained by the employment of capital, and renders it less advantageous to employ a capital there than in other places. There was little trade or industry in Edinburgh before the Union. When the Scotch parliament was no longer to be assembled in it, when it ceased to be the necessary residence of the principal nobility and gentry of Scotland, it became a city of some trade and industry. It still continues, however, to be the residence of the principal courts of justice in Scotland, of the boards of customs and excise, &c. A considerable revenue, therefore, still continues to be spent in it. In trade and industry it is much inferior to Glasgow, of which the inhabitants are chiefly maintained by the employment of capital. The inhabitants of a large village, it has sometimes been observed, after having made considerable progress in manufactures, have become idle and poor, in consequence of a great lord's having taken up his residence in their neighbourhood.

The proportion between capital and revenue, therefore, seems every-where to regulate the proportion between industry and idleness. Wherever capital predominates, industry prevails: wherever revenue, idleness. Every increase or diminution

OF PRODUCTIVE AND UNPRODUCTIVE LABOUR. 13

diminution of capital, therefore, naturally tends to increafe or diminifh the real quantity of induftry, the number of productive hands, and confequently the exchangeable value of the annual produce of the land and labour of the country, the real wealth and revenue of all its inhabitants.

Capitals are increafed by parfimony, and diminifhed by prodigality and mifconduct.

Whatever a perfon faves from his revenue he adds to his capital, and either employs it himfelf in maintaining an additional number of productive hands, or enables fome other perfon to do fo, by lending it to him for an intereft, that is, for a fhare of the profits. As the capital of an individual can be increafed only by what he faves from his annual revenue or his annual gains, fo the capital of a fociety, which is the fame with that of all the individuals who compofe it, can be increafed only in the fame manner.

Parfimony, and not induftry, is the immediate caufe of the increafe of capital. Induftry, indeed, provides the fubject which parfimony accumulates. But whatever induftry might acquire, if parfimony did not fave and ftore up, the capital would never be the greater.

Parfimony, by increafing the fund which is deftined for the maintenance of productive hands, tends to increafe the number of thofe hands whofe labour adds to the value of the fubject upon which it is beftowed. It tends therefore to increafe the exchangeable value of the annual pro-

duce

14 OF PRODUCTIVE AND UNPRODUCTIVE LABOUR.

BOOK II.

duce of the land and labour of the country. It puts into motion an additional quantity of induftry, which gives an additional value to the annual produce.

What is annually faved is as regularly confumed as what is annually fpent, and nearly in the fame time too ; but it is confumed by a different fet of people. That portion of his revenue which a rich man annually fpends, is in moft cafes confumed by idle guefts, and menial fervants, who leave nothing behind them in return for their confumption. That portion which he annually faves, as for the fake of the profit it is immediately employed as a capital, is confumed in the fame manner, and nearly in the fame time too, but by a different fet of people, by labourers, manufacturers, and artificers, who re-produce with a profit the value of their annual confumption. His revenue, we fhall fuppofe, is paid him in money. Had he fpent the whole, the food, clothing, and lodging, which the whole could have purchafed, would have been diftributed among the former fet of people. By faving a part of it, as that part is for the fake of the profit immediately employed as a capital either by himfelf or by fome other perfon, the food, clothing, and lodging, which may be purchafed with it, are neceffarily referved for the latter. The confumption is the fame, but the confumers are different.

By what a frugal man annually faves, he not only affords maintenance to an additional number of productive hands, for that or the enfuing

year,

OF PRODUCTIVE AND UNPRODUCTIVE LABOUR. 15

year, but, like the founder of a public work-house, he establishes as it were a perpetual fund for the maintenance of an equal number in all times to come. The perpetual allotment and destination of this fund, indeed, is not always guarded by any positive law, by any trust-right or deed of mortmain. It is always guarded, however, by a very powerful principle, the plain and evident interest of every individual to whom any share of it shall ever belong. No part of it can ever afterwards be employed to maintain any but productive hands, without an evident loss to the person who thus perverts it from its proper destination.

The prodigal perverts it in this manner. By not confining his expence within his income, he encroaches upon his capital. Like him who perverts the revenues of some pious foundation to profane purposes, he pays the wages of idleness with those funds which the frugality of his forefathers had, as it were, consecrated to the maintenance of industry. By diminishing the funds destined for the employment of productive labour, he necessarily diminishes, so far as it depends upon him, the quantity of that labour which adds a value to the subject upon which it is bestowed, and consequently, the value of the annual produce of the land and labour of the whole country, the real wealth and revenue of its inhabitants. If the prodigality of some was not compensated by the frugality of others, the conduct of every prodigal, by feeding the idle with the bread of the industrious, tends not only

to

16 OF PRODUCTIVE AND UNPRODUCTIVE LABOUR.

BOOK II. to beggar himſelf, but to impoveriſh his country.

Though the expence of the prodigal ſhould be altogether in home-made, and no part of it in foreign commodities, its effect upon the productive funds of the ſociety would ſtill be the ſame. Every year, there would ſtill be a certain quantity of food and clothing, which ought to have maintained productive, employed in maintaining unproductive hands. Every year, therefore, there would ſtill be ſome diminution in what would otherwiſe have been the value of the annual produce of the land and labour of the country.

This expence, it may be ſaid indeed, not being in foreign goods, and not occaſioning any exportation of gold and ſilver, the ſame quantity of money would remain in the country as before. But if the quantity of food and clothing, which were thus conſumed by unproductive, had been diſtributed among productive hands, they would have re-produced, together with a profit, the full value of their conſumption. The ſame quantity of money would in this caſe equally have remained in the country, and there would beſides have been a reproduction of an equal value of conſumable goods. There would have been two values inſtead of one.

The ſame quantity of money, beſides, cannot long remain in any country in which the value of the annual produce diminiſhes. The ſole uſe of money is to circulate conſumable goods. By means of it, proviſions, materials, and finiſhed work,

OF PRODUCTIVE AND UNPRODUCTIVE LABOUR.

work, are bought and fold, and diftributed to their proper confumers. The quantity of money, therefore, which can be annually employed in any country, muft be determined by the value of the confumable goods annually circulated within it. Thefe muft confift either in the immediate produce of the land and labour of the country itfelf, or in fomething which had been purchafed with fome part of that produce. Their value, therefore, muft diminifh as the value of that produce diminifhes, and along with it the quantity of money which can be employed in circulating them. But the money which by this annual diminution of produce is annually thrown out of domeftic circulation, will not be allowed to lie idle. The intereft of whoever poffeffes it, requires that it fhould be employed. But having no employment at home, it will, in fpite of all laws and prohibitions, be fent abroad, and employed in purchafing confumable goods which may be of fome ufe at home. Its annual exportation will in this manner continue for fome time to add fomething to the annual consumption of the country beyond the value of its own annual produce. What in the days of its profperity had been faved from that annual produce, and employed in purchafing gold and filver, will contribute for fome little time to fupport its confumption in adverfity. The exportation of gold and filver is, in this cafe, not the caufe, but the effect of its declenfion, and may even, for fome little time, alleviate the mifery of that declenfion.

CHAP.
III.

VOL. III.   C   The

OP PRODUCTIVE AND UNPRODUCTIVE LABOUR.

BOOK II.

The quantity of money, on the contrary, muſt in every country naturally increaſe as the value of the annual produce increaſes. The value of the conſumable goods annually circulated within the ſociety being greater, will require a greater quantity of money to circulate them. A part of the increaſed produce, therefore, will naturally be employed in purchaſing, wherever it is to be had, the additional quantity of gold and ſilver neceſſary for circulating the reſt. The increaſe of thoſe metals will in this caſe be the effect, not the cauſe, of the public proſperity. Gold and ſilver are purchaſed every where in the ſame manner. The food, clothing, and lodging, the revenue and maintenance of all thoſe whoſe labour or ſtock is employed in bringing them from the mine to the market, is the price paid for them in Peru as well as in England. The country which has this price to pay, will never be long without the quantity of thoſe metals which it has occaſion for; and no country will ever long retain a quantity which it has no occaſion for.

Whatever, therefore, we may imagine the real wealth and revenue of a country to conſiſt in, whether in the value of the annual produce of its land and labour, as plain reaſon ſeems to dictate; or in the quantity of the precious metals which circulate within it, as vulgar prejudices ſuppoſe; in either view of the matter, every prodigal appears to be a public enemy, and every frugal man a public benefactor.

The

OF PRODUCTIVE AND UNPRODUCTIVE LABOUR. 19

CHAP. III.

The effects of mifconduct are often the fame as thofe of prodigality. Every injudicious and unfuccefsful project in agriculture, mines, fisheries, trade, or manufactures, tends in the fame manner to diminifh the funds deftined for the maintenance of productive labour. In every fuch project, though the capital is confumed by productive hands only, yet, as by the injudicious manner in which they are employed, they do not reproduce the full value of their confumption, there muft always be fome diminution in what would otherwife have been the productive funds of the fociety.

It can feldom happen, indeed, that the circumftances of a great nation can be much affected either by the prodigality or mifconduct of individuals; the profufion or imprudence of fome, being always more than compenfated by the frugality and good conduct of others.

With regard to profufion, the principle which prompts to expence, is the paffion for prefent enjoyment; which, though fometimes violent and very difficult to be reftrained, is in general only momentary and occafional. But the principle which prompts to fave, is the defire of bettering our condition, a defire which, though generally calm and difpaffionate, comes with us from the womb, and never leaves us till we go into the grave. In the whole interval which feparates thofe two moments, there is fcarce perhaps a fingle inftance in which any man is fo perfectly and completely fatisfied with his fituation, as to be without any wifh of alteration or im-

C 2

provement

20 OF PRODUCTIVE AND UNPRODUCTIVE LABOUR.

BOOK
II.

provement of any kind. An augmentation of fortune is the means by which the greater part of men propofe and wifh to better their condition. It is the means the moft vulgar and the moft obvious; and the moft likely way of augmenting their fortune, is to fave and accumulate fome part of what they acquire, either regularly and annually, or upon fome extraordinary occafions. Though the principle of expence, therefore, prevails in almoft all men upon fome occafions, and in fome men upon almoft all occafions, yet in the greater part of men, taking the whole courfe of their life at an average, the principle of frugality feems not only to predominate, but to predominate very greatly.

With regard to mifconduct, the number of prudent and fuccefsful undertakings is everywhere much greater than that of injudicious and unfuccefsful ones. After all our complaints of the frequency of bankruptcies, the unhappy men who fall into this misfortune make but a very fmall part of the whole number engaged in trade, and all other forts of bufinefs; not much more perhaps than one in a thoufand. Bankruptcy is perhaps the greateft and moft humiliating calamity which can befal an innocent man. The greater part of men, therefore, are fufficiently careful to avoid it. Some, indeed, do not avoid it; as fome do not avoid the gallows.

Great nations are never impoverifhed by private, though they fometimes are by public prodigality and mifconduct. The whole, or almoft the whole, public revenue, is in moft countries

OF PRODUCTIVE AND UNPRODUCTIVE LABOUR.

countries employed in maintaining unproductive hands. Such are the people who compose a numerous and splendid court, a great ecclesiastical establishment, great fleets and armies, who in time of peace produce nothing, and in time of war acquire nothing which can compensate the expence of maintaining them, even while the war lasts. Such people, as they themselves produce nothing, are all maintained by the produce of other men's labour. When multiplied, therefore, to an unnecessary number, they may in a particular year consume so great a share of this produce, as not to leave a sufficiency for maintaining the productive labourers, who should reproduce it next year: The next year's produce, therefore, will be less than that of the foregoing, and if the same disorder should continue, that of the third year will be still less than that of the second. Those unproductive hands, who should be maintained by a part only of the spare revenue of the people, may consume so great a share of their whole revenue, and thereby oblige so great a number to encroach upon their capitals, upon the funds destined for the maintenance of productive labour, that all the frugality and good conduct of individuals may not be able to compensate the waste and degradation of produce occasioned by this violent and forced encroachment.

This frugality and good conduct, however, is upon most occasions, it appears from experience, sufficient to compensate, not only the private prodigality and misconduct of indivi-

duals,

22 OF PRODUCTIVE AND UNPRODUCTIVE LABOUR.

BOOK
II.

duals, but the public extravagance of government. The uniform, constant, and uninterrupted effort of every man to better his condition, the principle from which public and national, as well as private opulence is originally derived, is frequently powerful enough to maintain the natural progress of things toward improvement, in spite both of the extravagance of government, and of the greatest errors of adminiftration. Like the unknown principle of animal life, it frequently reftores health and vigour to the conftitution, in fpite, not only of the difeafe, but of the abfurd prefcriptions of the doctor.

The annual produce of the land and labour of any nation can be increafed in its value by no other means, but by increafing either the number of its productive labourers, or the productive powers of thofe labourers who had before been employed. The number of its productive labourers, it is evident, can never be much increafed, but in confequence of an increafe of capital, or of the funds deftined for maintaining them. The productive powers of the fame number of labourers cannot be increafed, but in confequence either of fome addition and improvement to thofe machines and inftruments which facilitate and abridge labour; or of a more proper divifion and diftribution of employment. In either cafe an additional capital is almoft always required. It is by means of an additional capital only, that the undertaker of any work can either provide his workmen with better machinery, or

make

OF PRODUCTIVE AND UNPRODUCTIVE LABOUR. 23

make a more proper diftribution of employment C H A P.
among them. When the work to be done con- III.
fifts of a number of parts, to keep every man
conftantly employed in one way, requires a much
greater capital than where every man is occafionally employed in every different part of the work.
When we compare, therefore, the ftate of a nation at two different periods, and find, that the
annual produce of its land and labour is evidently
greater at the latter than at the former, that its
lands are better cultivated, its manufactures more
numerous and more flourifhing, and its trade
more extenfive; we may be affured that its capital muft have increafed during the interval between thofe two periods, and that more muft
have been added to it by the good conduct of
fome, than had been taken from it either by the
private mifconduct of others, or by the public
extravagance of government. But we fhall find
this to have been the cafe of almoft all nations,
in all tolerably quiet and peaceable times, even
of thofe who have not enjoyed the moft prudent
and parfimonious governments. To form a right
judgment of it, indeed, we muft compare the
ftate of the country at periods fomewhat diftant
from one another. The progrefs is frequently
fo gradual, that, at near periods, the improvement is not only not fenfible, but from the declenfion either of certain branches of induftry, or
of certain diftricts of the country, things which
fometimes happen though the country in general
be in great profperity, there frequently arifes a

c 4   fufpicion,

BOOK II. fufpicion, that the riches and induſtry of the whole are decaying.

The annual produce of the land and labour of England, for example, is certainly much greater than it was, a little more than a century ago, at the reſtoration of Charles II. Though, at preſent, few people, I believe, doubt of this, yet during this period, five years have feldom paſſed away in which fome book or pamphlet has not been publiſhed, written too with fuch abilities as to gain fome authority with the public, and pretending to demonſtrate that the wealth of the nation was faſt declining, that the country was depopulated, agriculture neglected, manufactures decaying, and trade undone. Nor have thefe publications been all party pamphlets, the wretched offspring of falfehood and venality. Many of them have been written by very candid and very intelligent people ; who wrote nothing but what they believed, and for no other reafon but becaufe they believed it.

The annual produce of the land and labour of England again, was certainly much greater at the reſtoration, than we can fuppofe it to have been about an hundred years before, at the acceſſion of Elizabeth. At this period too, we have all reafon to believe, the country was much more advanced in improvement, than it had been about a century before, towards the clofe of the diſſenſions between the houfes of York and Lancaſter. Even then it was, probably, in a better condition than it had been at the Norman conqueſt, and at the Norman conqueſt, than during the confuſion of of the Saxon Heptarchy. Even at this early period, it was certainly a more improved country than at the invafion of Julius Cæfar, when its inhabitants were nearly in the fame ftate with the favages in North America.

In each of thofe periods, however, there was, not only much private and public profufion, many expenfive and unneceffary wars, great perverfion of the annual produce from maintaining productive to maintain unproductive hands ; but fometimes, in the confufion of civil difcord, fuch abfolute wafte and deftruction of ftock, as might be fuppofed, not only to retard, as it certainly did, the natural accumulation of riches, but to have left the country, at the end of the period, poorer than at the beginning. Thus, in the happieft and moft fortunate period of them all, that which has paffed fince the reftoration, how many diforders and misfortunes have occurred, which, could they have been forefeen, not only the impoverifhment, but the total ruin of the country would have been expected from them ? The fire and the plague of London, the two Dutch wars, the diforders of the revolution, the war in Ireland, the four expenfive French wars of 1688, 1702, 1742, and 1756, together with the two rebellions of 1715 and 1745. In the courfe of the four French wars, the nation has contracted more than a hundred and forty-five millions of debt, over and above all the other extraordinary annual expence which they occafioned, fo that the whole cannot be computed at lefs than two hundred millions. So great a fhare of the annual

produce

OF PRODUCTIVE AND UNPRODUCTIVE LABOUR.

BOOK II.

produce of the land and labour of the country, has, fince the revolution, been employed upon different occafions, in maintaining an extraordinary number of unproductive hands. But had not thofe wars given this particular direction to fo large a capital, the greater part of it would naturally have been employed in maintaining productive hands, whofe labour would have replaced, with a profit, the whole value of their confumption. The value of the annual produce of the land and labour of the country, would have been confiderably increafed by it every year, and every year's increafe would have augmented ftill more that of the following year. More houfes would have been built, more lands would have been improved, and thofe which had been improved before would have been better cultivated, more manufactures would have been eftablifhed, and thofe which had been eftablifhed before would have been more extended ; and to what height the real wealth and revenue of the country might, by this time, have been raifed, it is not perhaps very eafy even to imagine.

But though the profufion of government muft, undoubtedly, have retarded the natural progrefs of England towards wealth and improvement, it has not been able to ftop it. The annual produce of its land and labour is, undoubtedly, much greater at prefent than it was either at the reftoration or at the revolution. The capital, therefore, annually employed in cultivating this land, and in maintaining this labour, muft likewife be much greater. In the midft of all the

exactions

OF PRODUCTIVE AND UNPRODUCTIVE LABOUR. 27

exactions of government, this capital has been silently and gradually accumulated by the private frugality and good conduct of individuals, by their univerfal, continual, and uninterrupted effort to better their own condition. It is this effort, protected by law and allowed by liberty to exert itfelf in the manner that is moft advantageous, which has maintained the progrefs of England towards opulence and improvement in almoft all former times, and which, it is to be hoped, will do fo in all future times. England, however, as it has never been blefled with a very parfimonious government, fo parfimony has at no time been the characteriftical virtue of its inhabitants. It is the higheft impertinence and prefumption, therefore, in kings and minifters, to pretend to watch over the œconomy of private people, and to reftrain their expence, either by fumptuary laws, or by prohibiting the importation of foreign luxuries. They are themfelves always, and without any exception, the greateft fpendthrifts in the fociety. Let them look well after their own expence, and they may fafely truft private people with theirs. If their own extravagance does not ruin the ftate, that of their fubjects never will.

As frugality increafes, and prodigality diminifhes the public capital, fo the conduct of thofe whofe expence juft equals their revenue, without either accumulating or encroaching, neither increafes nor diminifhes it. Some modes of expence, however, feem to contribute more to the growth of public opulence than others.

The

28 OF PRODUCTIVE AND UNPRODUCTIVE LABOUR.

BOOK II.

The revenue of an individual may be ſpent, either in things which are conſumed immediately, and in which one day's expence can neither alleviate nor ſupport that of another; or it may be ſpent in things more durable, which can therefore be accumulated, and in which every day's expence may, as he chuſes, either alleviate or ſupport and heighten the effect of that of the following day. A man of fortune, for example, may either ſpend his revenue in a profuſe and ſumptuous table, and in maintaining a great number of menial ſervants, and a multitude of dogs and horſes; or contenting himſelf with a frugal table and few attendants, he may lay out the greater part of it in adorning his houſe or his country villa, in uſeful or ornamental buildings, in uſeful or ornamental furniture, in collecting books, ſtatues, pictures; or in things more frivolous, jewels, baubles, ingenious trinkets of different kinds; or, what is moſt trifling of all, in amaſſing a great wardrobe of fine clothes, like the favourite and miniſter of a great prince who died a few years ago. Were two men of equal fortune to ſpend their revenue, the one chiefly in the one way, the other in the other, the magnificence of the perſon whoſe expence had been chiefly in durable commodities, would be continually increaſing, every day's expence contributing ſomething to ſupport and heighten the effect of that of the following day: that of the other, on the contrary, would be no greater at the end of the period than at the beginning. The former too would, at the end of the period,

be

be the richer man of the two. He would have a ftock of goods of fome kind or other, which, though it might not be worth all that it coft, would always be worth fomething. No trace or veftige of the expence of the latter would remain, and the effects of ten or twenty years profufion would be as completely annihilated as if they had never exifted.

As the one mode of expence is more favourable than the other to the opulence of an individual, fo is it likewife to that of a nation. The houfes, the furniture, the clothing of the rich, in a little time become ufeful to the inferior and middling ranks of people. They are able to purchafe them when their fuperiors grow weary of them, and the general accommodation of the whole people is thus gradually improved, when this mode of expence becomes univerfal among men of fortune. In countries which have long been rich, you will frequently find the inferior ranks of people in poffeffion both of houfes and furniture perfectly good and entire, but of which neither the one could have been built, nor the other have been made for their ufe. What was formerly a feat of the family of Seymour, is now an inn upon the Bath road. The marriage bed of James the Firft of Great Britain, which his Queen brought with her from Denmark, as a prefent fit for a fovereign to make to a fovereign, was, a few years ago, the ornament of an alehoufe at Dunfermline. In fome ancient cities, which either have been long ftationary, or have gone fomewhat to decay, you will fometimes

OF PRODUCTIVE AND UNPRODUCTIVE LABOUR.

BOOK II.

scarce find a fingle houfe which could have been built for its prefent inhabitants. If you go into thofe houfes too, you will frequently find many excellent, though antiquated pieces of furniture, which are ftill very fit for ufe, and which could as little have been made for them. Noble palaces, magnificent villas, great collections of books, ftatues, pictures, and other curiofities, are frequently both an ornament and an honour, not only to the neighbourhood, but to the whole country to which they belong. Verfailles is an ornament and an honour to France, Stowe and Wilton to England. Italy ftill continues to command fome fort of veneration by the number of monuments of this kind which it poffeffes, though the wealth which produced them has decayed, and though the genius which planned them feems to be extinguifhed, perhaps from not having the fame employment.

The expence too, which is laid out in durable commodities, is favourable, not only to accumulation, but to frugality. If a perfon fhould at any time exceed in it, he can eafily reform without expofing himfelf to the cenfure of the public. To reduce very much the number of his fervants, to reform his table from great profufion to great frugality, to lay down his equipage after he has once fet it up, are changes which cannot efcape the obfervation of his neighbours, and which are fuppofed to imply fome acknowledgement of preceding bad conduct. Few, therefore, of thofe who have once been fo unfortunate as to launch out too far into this fort of expence,

have

OF PRODUCTIVE AND UNPRODUCTIVE LABOUR. 31

have afterwards the courage to reform, till ruin and bankruptcy oblige them. But if a perfon has at any time; been at too great an expence in building, in furniture, in books or pictures, no imprudence can be inferred from his changing his conduct. Thefe are things in which further expence is frequently rendered unneceffary by former expence; and when a perfon ftops fhort, he appears to do fo, not becaufe he has exceeded his fortune, but becaufe he has fatisfied his fancy.

The expence, befides, that is laid out in durable commodities, gives maintenance, commonly, to a greater number of people, than that which is employed in the moft profufe hofpitality. Of two or three hundred weight of provifions, which may fometimes be ferved up at a great feftival, one-half, perhaps, is thrown to the dunghill, and there is always a great deal wafted and abufed. But if the expence of this entertainment had been employed in fetting to work mafons, carpenters, upholfterers, mechanics, &c. a quantity of provifions, of equal value, would have been diftributed among a ftill greater number of people, who would have bought them in penny-worths and pound weights, and not have loft or thrown away a fingle ounce of them. In the one way, befides, this expence maintains productive, in the other unproductive hands. In the one way, therefore, it increafes, in the other, it does not increafe, the exchangeable value of the annual produce of the land and labour of the country.

I would

32   OF PRODUCTIVE AND UNPRODUCTIVE LABOUR.

BOOK II. I would not, however, by all this be understood to mean, that the one fpecies of expence always betokens a more liberal or generous fpirit than the other. When a man of fortune fpends his revenue chiefly in hofpitality, he fhares the greater part of it with his friends and companions; but when he employs it in purchafing fuch durable commodities, he often fpends the whole upon his own perfon, and gives nothing to any body without an equivalent. The latter fpecies of expence, therefore, efpecially when directed towards frivolous objects, the little ornaments of drefs and furniture, jewels, trinkets, gewgaws, frequently indicates, not only a trifling, but a bafe and felfifh difpofition. All that I mean is, that the one fort of expence, as it always occafions fome accumulation of valuable commodities, as it is more favourable to private frugality, and, confequently, to the increafe of the public capital, and as it maintains productive, rather than unproductive hands, conduces more than the other to the growth of public opulence.

CHAP.

CHAP. IV.

Of Stock lent at Interest.

THE stock which is lent at interest is always considered as a capital by the lender. He expects that in due time it is to be restored to him, and that in the mean time the borrower is to pay him a certain annual rent for the use of it. The borrower may use it either as a capital, or as a stock reserved for immediate consumption. If he uses it as a capital, he employs it in the maintenance of productive labourers, who reproduce the value with a profit. He can, in this case, both restore the capital and pay the interest without alienating or encroaching upon any other source of revenue. If he uses it as a stock reserved for immediate consumption, he acts the part of a prodigal, and dissipates in the maintenance of the idle, what was destined for the support of the industrious. He can, in this case, neither restore the capital nor pay the interest, without either alienating or encroaching upon some other source of revenue, such as the property or the rent of land.

The stock which is lent at interest is, no doubt, occasionally employed in both these ways, but in the former much more frequently than in the latter. The man who borrows in order to spend will soon be ruined, and he who lends to him will generally have occasion to repent of his folly.

OF STOCK LENT AT INTEREST.

BOOK II.

folly. To borrow or to lend for fuch a purpofe, therefore, is in all cafes, where grofs ufury is out of the queftion, contrary to the intereft of both parties; and though it no doubt happens fometimes that people do both the one and the other; yet, from the regard that all men have for their own intereft, we may be affured, that it cannot happen fo very frequently as we are fometimes apt to imagine. Afk any rich man of common prudence, to which of the two forts of people he has lent the greater part of his ftock, to thofe who, he thinks, will employ it profitably, or to thofe who will fpend it idly, and he will laugh at you for propofing the queftion. Even among borrowers, therefore, not the people in the world moft famous for frugality, the number of the frugal and induftrious furpaffes confiderably that of the prodigal and idle.

The only people to whom ftock is commonly lent, without their being expected to make any very profitable ufe of it, are country gentlemen who borrow upon mortgage. Even they fcarce ever borrow merely to fpend. What they borrow, one may fay, is commonly fpent before they borrow it. They have generally confumed fo great a quantity of goods, advanced to them upon credit by fhopkeepers and tradefmen, that they find it neceffary to borrow at intereft in order to pay the debt. The capital borrowed replaces the capitals of thofe fhopkeepers and tradefmen, which the country gentlemen could not have replaced from the rents of their eftates. It is not properly borrowed in order to be fpent, but in order

OF STOCK LENT AT INTEREST.

order to replace a capital which had been spent before.

Almost all loans at interest are made in money, either of paper, or of gold and silver. But what the borrower really wants, and what the lender really supplies him with, is not the money, but the money's worth, or the goods which it can purchase. If he wants it as a stock for immediate consumption, it is those goods only which he can place in that stock. If he wants it as a capital for employing industry, it is from those goods only that the industrious can be furnished with the tools, materials, and maintenance, necessary for carrying on their work. By means of the loan, the lender, as it were, assigns to the borrower his right to a certain portion of the annual produce of the land and labour of the country, to be employed as the borrower pleases.

The quantity of stock, therefore, or, as it is commonly expressed, of money which can be lent at interest in any country, is not regulated by the value of the money, whether paper or coin, which serves as the instrument of the different loans made in that country, but by the value of that part of the annual produce which, as soon as it comes either from the ground, or from the hands of the productive labourers, is destined not only for replacing a capital, but such a capital as the owner does not care to be at the trouble of employing himself. As such capitals are commonly lent out and paid back in money, they constitute what is called the monied interest. It is distinct, not only from the landed, but from the trading and

OF STOCK LENT AT INTEREST.

BOOK II.

manufacturing interefts, as in thefe laft the owners themfelves employ their own capitals. Even in the monied intereft, however, the money is, as it were, but the deed of affignment, which conveys from one hand to another thofe capitals which the owners do not care to employ themfelves. Thofe capitals may be greater in almoft any proportion, than the amount of the money which ferves as the inftrument of their conveyance; the fame pieces of money fucceffively ferving for many different loans, as well as for many different purchafes. A, for example, lends to W a thoufand pounds, with which W immediately purchafes of B a thoufand pounds worth of goods. B having no occafion for the money himfelf, lends the identical pieces to X, with which X immediately purchafes of C another thoufand pounds worth of goods. C in the fame manner, and for the fame reafon, lends them to Y, who again purchafes goods with them of D. In this manner the fame pieces, either of coin or of paper, may, in the courfe of a few days, ferve as the inftrument of three different loans, and of three different purchafes, each of which is, in value, equal to the whole amount of thofe pieces. What the three monied men A, B, and C, affign to the three borrowers, W, X, Y, is the power of making thofe purchafes. In this power confift both the value and the ufe of the loans. The ftock lent by the three monied men, is equal to the value of the goods which can be purchafed with it, and is three times greater than that of the money with which the purchafes are made. Thofe loans, however, may be all per-

fectly

OF STOCK LENT AT INTEREST. 37

feᶜtly well fecured, the goods purchafed by the different debtors being fo employed, as, in due time, to bring back, with a profit, an equal value either of coin or of paper. And as the fame pieces of money can thus ferve as the inftru-ment of different loans to three, or for the fame reafon, to thirty times their value, fo they may likewife fucceffively ferve as the inftrument of repayment.

A capital lent at intereft may, in this manner, be confidered as an affignment from the lender to the borrower of a certain confiderable portion of the annual produce; upon condition that the bor-rower in return fhall, during the continuance of the loan, annually affign to the lender a fmaller portion, called the intereft; and at the end of it, a portion equally confiderable with that which had originally been affigned to him, called the repayment. Though money, either coin or pa-per, ferves generally as the deed of affignment both to the fmaller, and to the more confiderable portion, it is itfelf altogether different from what is affigned by it.

In proportion as that fhare of the annual pro-duce which, as foon as it comes either from the ground, or from the hands of the produᶜtive la-bourers, is deftined for replacing a capital, in-creafes in any country, what is called the monied intereft naturally increafes with it. The increafe of thofe particular capitals from which the owners wifh to derive a revenue, without being at the trouble of employing them themfelves, naturally accompanies the general increafe of capitals; or,

C H A P.
IV.

OF STOCK LENT AT INTEREST.

BOOK II.

in other words, as stock increases, the quantity of stock to be lent at interest grows gradually greater and greater.

As the quantity of stock to be lent at interest increases, the interest, or the price which must be paid for the use of that stock, necessarily diminishes, not only from those general causes which make the market price of things commonly diminish as their quantity increases, but from other causes which are peculiar to this particular case. As capitals increase in any country, the profits which can be made by employing them necessarily diminish. It becomes gradually more (and more difficult to find within the country a profitable method of employing any new capital. There arises in consequence a competition between different capitals, the owner of one endeavouring to get possession of that employment which is occupied by another. But upon most occasions he can hope to justle that other out of this employment, by no other means but by dealing upon more reasonable terms. He must not only fell what he deals in somewhat cheaper, but in order to get it to fell, he must sometimes too buy it dearer. The demand for productive labour, by the increase of the funds which are destined for maintaining it, grows every day greater and greater. Labourers easily find employment, but the owners of capitals find it difficult to get labourers to employ. Their competition raises the wages of labour, and sinks the profits of stock. But when the profits which can be made by the use of a capital are in this manner diminished,

OF STOCK LENT AT INTEREST. 39

nifhed, as it were, at both ends, the price which can be paid for the ufe of it, that is, the rate of intereft, muft neceffarily be diminifhed with them.

CHAP. IV.

Mr. Locke, Mr. Law, and Mr. Montefquieu, as well as many other writers, feem to have imagined that the increafe of the quantity of gold and filver, in confequence of the difcovery of the Spanifh Weft Indies, was the real caufe of the lowering of the rate of intereft through the greater part of Europe. Thofe metals, they fay, having become of lefs value themfelves, the ufe of any particular portion of them neceffarily became of lefs value too, and confequently the price which could be paid for it. This notion, which at firft fight feems fo plaufible, has been fo fully expofed by Mr. Hume, that it is, perhaps, unneceffary to fay any thing more about it. The following very fhort and plain argument, however, may ferve to explain more diftinctly the fallacy which feems to have mifled thofe gentlemen.

Before the difcovery of the Spanifh Weft Indies, ten per cent. feems to have been the common rate of intereft through the greater part of Europe. It has fince that time in different countries funk to fix, five, four, and three per cent. Let us fuppofe that in every particular country the value of filver has funk precifely in the fame proportion as the rate of intereft; and that in thofe countries, for example, where intereft has been reduced from ten to five per cent., the fame quantity of filver can now purchafe juft half the quantity of goods which it could have purchafed

D 4 before.

OF STOCK LENT AT INTEREST.

BOOK II.

before. This suppofition will not, I believe, be found any-where agreeable to the truth, but it is the moft favourable to the opinion which we are going to examine ; and even upon this suppofition it is utterly impoffible that the lowering of the value of filver could have the fmalleft tendency to lower the rate of intereft. If a hundred pounds are in thofe countries now of no more value than fifty pounds were then, ten pounds muft now be of no more value than five pounds were then. Whatever were the caufes which lowered the value of the capital, the fame muft neceffarily have lowered that of the intereft, and exactly in the fame proportion. The proportion between the value of the capital and that of the intereft, muft have remained the fame, though the rate had never been altered. By altering the rate, on the contrary, the proportion between thofe two values is neceffarily altered. If a hundred pounds now are worth no more than fifty were then, five pounds now can be worth no more than two pounds ten fhillings were then. By reducing the rate of intereft, therefore, from ten to five per cent., we give for the ufe of a capital, which is fuppofed to be equal to one-half of its former value, an intereft which is equal to one-fourth only of the value of the former intereft.

Any increafe in the quantity of filver, while that of the commodities circulated by means of it remained the fame, could have no other effect than to diminifh the value of that metal. The nominal value of all forts of goods would be greater, but their real value would be precifely the

the fame as before. They would be exchanged for a greater number of pieces of filver; but the quantity of labour which they could command, the number of people whom they could maintain and employ, would be precifely the fame. The capital of the country would be the fame, though a greater number of pieces might be requifite for conveying any equal portion of it from one hand to another. The deeds of affignment, like the conveyances of a verbofe attorney, would be more cumberfome, but the thing affigned would be precifely the fame as before, and could produce only the fame effects. The funds for maintaining productive labour being the fame, the demand for it would be the fame. Its price or wages, therefore, though nominally greater, would really be the fame. They would be paid in a greater number of pieces of filver; but they would purchafe only the fame quantity of goods. The profits of ftock would be the fame both nominally and really. The wages of labour are commonly computed by the quantity of filver which is paid to the labourer. When that is increafed, therefore, his wages appear to be increafed, though they may fometimes be no greater than before. But the profits of ftock are not computed by the number of pieces of filver with which they are paid, but by the proportion which thofe pieces bear to the whole capital employed. Thus in a particular country five fhillings a week are faid to be the common wages of labour, and ten per cent. the common profits of ftock. But the whole capital of the country being the fame

as

OF STOCK LENT AT INTEREST.

as before, the competition between the different capitals of individuals into which it was divided would likewife be the fame. They would all trade with the fame advantages and difadvantages. The common proportion between capital and profit, therefore, would be the fame, and confequently the common intereft of money; what can commonly be given for the ufe of money being neceffarily regulated by what can commonly be made by the ufe of it.

Any increafe in the quantity of commodities annually circulated within the country, while that of the money which circulated them remained the fame, would, on the contrary, produce many other important effects, befides that of raifing the value of the money. The capital of the country, though it might nominally be the fame, would really be augmented. It might continue to be expreffed by the fame quantity of money, but it would command a greater quantity of labour. The quantity of productive labour which it could maintain and employ would be increafed, and confequently the demand for that labour. Its wages would naturally rife with the demand, and yet might appear to fink. They might be paid with a fmaller quantity of money, but that fmaller quantity might purchafe a greater quantity of goods than a greater had done before. The profits of ftock would be diminifhed both really and in appearance. The whole capital of the country being augmented, the competition between the different capitals of which it was compofed, would naturally be augmented along with it.

OF STOCK LENT AT INTEREST.

it. The owners of thofe particular capitals CHAP. would be obliged to content themfelves with a IV. fmaller proportion of the produce of that labour which their refpective capitals employed. The intereft of money, keeping pace always with the profits of ftock, might, in this manner, be greatly diminifhed, though the value of money, or the quantity of goods which any particular fum could purchafe, was greatly augmented.

In fome countries the intereft of money has been prohibited by law. But as fomething can every-where be made by the ufe of money, fome-thing ought every-where to be paid for the ufe of it. This regulation, inftead of preventing, has been found from experience to increafe the evil of ufury; the debtor being obliged to pay, not only for the ufe of the money, but for the rifk which his creditor runs by accepting a com-penfation for that ufe. He is obliged, if one may fay fo, to infure his creditor from the penalties of ufury.

In countries where intereft is permitted, the law, in order to prevent the extortion of ufury, generally fixes the higheft rate which can be taken without incurring a penalty. This rate ought always to be fomewhat above the loweft market price, or the price which is commonly paid for the ufe of money by thofe who can give the moft undoubted fecurity. If this legal rate fhould be fixed below the loweft market rate, the effects of this fixation muft be nearly the fame as thofe of a total prohibition of intereft. The cre-ditor will not lend his money for lefs than the ufe

of

OF STOCK LENT AT INTEREST.

BOOK II.

of it is worth, and the debtor muft pay him for the rifk which he runs by accepting the full value of that ufe. If it is fixed precifely at the loweft market price, it ruins with honeft people, who refpeét the laws of their country, the credit of all thofe who cannot give the very beft fecurity, and obliges them to have recourfe to exorbitant ufurers. In a country, fuch as Great Britain, where money is lent to government at three per cent. and to private people upon good fecurity at four, and four and a half, the prefent legal rate, five per cent., is perhaps, as proper as any.

The legal rate, it is to be obferved, though it ought to be fomewhat above, ought not to be much above the loweft market rate. If the legal rate of intereft in Great Britain, for example, was fixed fo high as eight or ten per cent., the greater part of the money which was to be lent, would be lent to prodigals and projeétors, who alone would be willing to give this high intereft. Sober people, who will give for the ufe of money no more than a part of what they are likely to make by the ufe of it, would not venture into the competition. A great part of the capital of the country would thus be kept out of the hands which were moft likely to make a profitable and advantageous ufe of it, and thrown into thofe which were moft likely to wafte and deftroy it. Where the legal rate of intereft, on the contrary, is fixed but a very little above the loweft market rate, fober people are univerfally preferred, as borrowers, to prodigals and projeétors. The perfon who lends money gets nearly as much

intereft

OF STOCK LENT AT INTEREST.

intereſt from the former as he dares to take from the latter, and his money is much ſafer in the hands of the one ſet of people, than in thoſe of the other. A great part of the capital of the eountry is thus thrown into the hands in which it is moſt likely to be employed with advantage.

No law can reduce the common rate of intereſt below the loweſt ordinary market rate at the time when that law is made. Notwithſtanding the ediƈt of 1766, by which the French king attempted to reduce the rate of intereſt from five to four per cent., money continued to be lent in France at five per cent., the law being evaded in ſeveral different ways.

The ordinary market price of land, it is to be obſerved, depends every-where upon the ordinary market rate of intereſt. The perſon who has a capital from which he wiſhes to derive a revenue, without taking the trouble to employ it himſelf, deliberates whether he ſhould buy land with it, or lend it out at intereſt. The ſuperior ſecurity of land, together with ſome other advantages which almoſt every-where attend upon this ſpecies of property, will generally diſpoſe him to content himſelf with a ſmaller revenue from land, than what he might have by lending out his money at intereſt. Theſe advantages are ſufficient to compenſate a certain difference of revenue; but they will compenſate a certain difference only; and if the rent of land ſhould fall ſhort of the intereſt of money by a greater difference, nobody would buy land, which would ſoon reduce its ordinary price. On the contrary,

if

46 OF STOCK LENT AT INTEREST.

BOOK II.

if the advantages should much more than com-pensate the difference, every body would buy land, which again would soon raise its ordinary price. When interest was at ten per cent., land was commonly sold for ten and twelve years pur-chase. As interest sunk to six, five, and four per cent., the price of land rose to twenty, five and twenty, and thirty years purchase. The market rate of interest is higher in France than in England; and the common price of land is lower. In England it commonly sells at thirty; in France at twenty years purchase.

CHAP. V.

Of the different Employment of Capitals.

CHAP. V.

THOUGH all capitals are destined for the maintenance of productive labour only, yet the quantity of that labour, which equal ca-pitals are capable of putting into motion, varies extremely according to the diversity of their em-ployment; as does likewise the value which that employment adds to the annual produce of the land and labour of the country.

A capital may be employed in four different ways: either, first, in procuring the rude produce annually required for the use and consumption of the society; or, secondly, in manufacturing and preparing that rude produce for immediate use

OF THE EMPLOYMENT OF CAPITALS. 47

uſe and conſumption; or, thirdly, in tranſporting either the rude or manufactured produce from the places where they abound to thoſe where they are wanted; or, laſtly, in dividing particular portions of either into ſuch ſmall parcels as ſuit the occaſional demands of thoſe who want them. In the firſt way are employed the capitals of all thoſe who undertake the improvement or cultivation of lands, mines, or fiſheries; in the ſecond, thoſe of all maſter manufactures; in the third, thoſe of all wholeſale merchants; and in the fourth, thoſe of all retailers. It is difficult to conceive that a capital ſhould be employed in any way which may not be claſſed under ſome one or other of thoſe four.

CHAP V.

Each of thoſe four methods of employing a capital is eſſentially neceſſary either to the exiſt-ence or extenſion of the other three, or to the general conveniency of the ſociety.

Unleſs a capital was employed in furniſhing rude produce to a certain degree of abundance, neither manufactures nor trade of any kind could exiſt.

Unleſs a capital was employed in manu-facturing that part of the rude produce which requires a good deal of preparation before it can be fit for uſe and conſumption, it either would never be produced, becauſe there could be no demand for it; or if it was produced ſponta-neouſly, it would be of no value in exchange, and could add nothing to the wealth of the ſociety.

Unleſs

OF THE EMPLOYMENT OF CAPITALS.

BOOK II.

Unlefs a capital was employed in tranfporting, either the rude or manufactured produce, from the places where it abounds to thofe where it is wanted, no more of either could be produced than was neceffary for the confumption of the neighbourhood. The capital of the merchant exchanges the furplus produce of one place for that of another, and thus encourages the induftry and increafes the enjoyments of both.

Unlefs a capital was employed in breaking and dividing certain portions either of the rude or manufactured produce, into fuch fmall parcels as fuit the occafional demands of thofe who want them, every man would be obliged to purchafe a greater quantity of the goods he wanted, than his immediate occafions required. If there was no fuch trade as a butcher, for example, every man would be obliged to purchafe a whole ox or a whole fheep at a time. This would generally be inconvenient to the rich, and much more fo to the poor. If a poor workman was obliged to purchafe a month's or fix months provifions at a time, a great part of the ftock which he employs as a capital in the inftruments of his trade, or in the furniture of his fhop, and which yields him a revenue, he would be forced to place in that part of his ftock which is referved for immediate confumption, and which yields him no revenue. Nothing can be more convenient for fuch a perfon than to be able to purchafe his fubfiftence from day to day, or even from hour to hour, as he wants it. He is thereby enabled to employ almoft his whole ftock as a capital. He is thus enabled

to

OF THE EMPLOYMENT OF CAPITALS. 49

to furnifh work to a greater value, and the profit which he makes by it in this way, much more than compenfates the additional price which the profit of the retailer impofes upon the goods. The prejudices of fome political writers againft fhopkeepers and tradefmen, are altogether without foundation. So far is it from being neceffary, either to tax them, or to reftrict their numbers, that they can never be multiplied fo as to hurt the public, though they may fo as to hurt one another. The quantity of grocery goods, for example, which can be fold in a particular town, is limited by the demand of that town and its neighbourhood. The capital, therefore, which can be employed in the grocery trade, cannot exceed what is fufficient to purchafe that quantity. If this capital is divided between two different grocers, their competition will tend to make both of them fell cheaper, than if it were in the hands of one only; and if it were divided among twenty, their competition would be juft fo much the greater, and the chance of their combining together, in order to raife the price, juft fo much the lefs. Their competition might perhaps ruin fome of themfelves; but to take care of this is the bufinefs of the parties concerned, and it may fafely be trufted to their difcretion. It can never hurt either the confumer, or the producer; on the contrary, it muft tend to make the retailers both fell cheaper and buy dearer, than if the whole trade was monopolized by one or two perfons. Some of them, perhaps, may fometimes decoy a weak cuftomer to buy what

VOL. III. E he

OF THE EMPLOYMENT OF CAPITALS.

BOOK
II.

he has no occasion for. This evil, however, is of too little importance to deserve the public attention, nor would it necessarily be prevented by restricting their numbers. It is not the multitude of ale-houses, to give the most suspicious example, that occasions a general disposition to drunkenness among the common people; but that disposition arising from other causes necessarily gives employment to a multitude of ale-houses.

The persons whose capitals are employed in any of those four ways are themselves productive labourers. Their labour, when properly directed, fixes and realizes itself in the subject or vendible commodity upon which it is bestowed, and generally adds to its price the value at least of their own maintenance and consumption. The profits of the farmer, of the manufacturer, of the merchant, and retailer, are all drawn from the price of the goods which the two first produce, and the two last buy and sell. Equal capitals, however, employed in each of those four different ways, will immediately put into motion very different quantities of productive labour, and augment too in very different proportions the value of the annual produce of the land and labour of the society to which they belong.

The capital of the retailer replaces, together with its profits, that of the merchant of whom he purchases goods, and thereby enables him to continue his business. The retailer himself is the only productive labourer whom it immediately employs. In his profits, consists the whole

OF THE EMPLOYMENT OF CAPITALS. 51

whole value which its employment adds to the
annual produce of the land and labour of the
fociety.

The capital of the wholefale merchant replaces, together with their profits, the capitals of the farmers and manufacturers of whom he purchafes the rude and manufactured produce which he deals in, and thereby enables them to continue their refpective trades. It is by this fervice chiefly that he contributes indirectly to fupport the productive labour of the fociety, and to increafe the value of its annual produce. His capital employs too the failors and carriers who tranfport his goods from one place to another, and it augments the price of thofe goods by the value, not only of his profits, but of their wages. This is all the productive labour which it immediately puts into motion, and all the value which it immediately adds to the annual produce. Its operation in both thefe refpects is a good deal fuperior to that of the capital of the retailer.

Part of the capital of the mafter manufacturer is employed as a fixed capital in the inftruments of his trade, and replaces, together with its profits, that of fome other artificer of whom he purchafes them. Part of his circulating capital is employed in purchafing materials, and replaces, with their profits, the capitals of the farmers and miners of whom he purchafes them. But a great part of it is always, either annually, or in a much fhorter period, diftributed among the different workmen whom he employs. It augments the value of thofe materials by their wages, and by

E 2   their

52 **OF THE EMPLOYMENT OF CAPITALS.**

BOOK II.

their mafters profits upon the whole ftock of wages, materials, and inftruments of trade employed in the bufinefs. It puts immediately into motion, therefore, a much greater quantity of productive labour, and adds a much greater value to the annual produce of the land and labour of the fociety, than an equal capital in the hands of any wholefale merchant.

No equal capital puts into motion a greater quantity of productive labour than that of the farmer. Not only his labouring fervants, but his labouring cattle, are productive labourers. In agriculture too, nature labours along with man; and though her labour cofts no expence, its produce has its value, as well as that of the moft expenfive workmen. The moft important operations of agriculture feem intended, not fo much to increafe, though they do that too, as to direct the fertility of nature towards the production of the plants moft profitable to man. A field overgrown with briars and brambles may frequently produce as great a quantity of vegetables as the beft cultivated vineyard or corn field. Planting and tillage frequently regulate more than they animate the active fertility of nature; and after all their labour, a great part of the work always remains to be done by her. The labourers and labouring cattle, therefore, employed in agriculture, not only occafion, like the workmen in manufactures, the reproduction of a value equal to their own confumption, or to the capital which employs them, together with its owners profits; but of a much greater value. Over and above the

OF THE EMPLOYMENT OF CAPITALS. 53

the capital of the farmer and all its profits, they
regularly occafion the reproduction of the rent of
the landlord. This rent may be confidered as
the produce of thofe powers of nature, the ufe
of which the landlord lends to the farmer. It is
greater or fmaller according to the fuppofed ex‑
tent of thofe powers, or in other words, accord‑
ing to the fuppofed natural or improved fertility
of the land. It is the work of nature which re‑
mains after deducting or compenfating every
thing which can be regarded as the work of man.
It is feldom lefs than a fourth, and frequently
more than a third of the whole produce. No
equal quantity of productive labour employed in
manufactures can ever occafion fo great a repro‑
duction. In them nature does nothing; man
does all; and the reproduction muft always be in
proportion to the ftrength of the agents that oc‑
cafion it. The capital employed in agriculture,
therefore, not only puts into motion a greater
quantity of productive labour than any equal
capital employed in manufactures, but in pro‑
portion too to the quantity of productive labour
which it employs, it adds a much greater value
to the annual produce of the land and labour of
the country, to the real wealth and revenue of its
inhabitants. Of all the ways in which a capital
can be employed, it is by far the moft advan‑
tageous to the fociety.

The capitals employed in the agriculture and
in the retail trade of any fociety, muft always
refide within that fociety. Their employment is
confined almoft to a precife fpot, to the farm,

E 3   and

CHAP.
V.

OF THE EMPLOYMENT OF CAPITALS.

BOOK
II.

and to the fhop of the retailer. They muft generally too, though there are fome exceptions to this, belong to refident members of the fociety.

The capital of a wholefale merchant, on the contrary, feems to have no fixed or neceffary refidence any-where, but may wander about from place to place, according as it can either buy cheap or fell dear.

The capital of the manufacturer muft no doubt refide where the manufacture is carried on ; but where this fhall be is not always neceffarily determined. It may frequently be at a great diftance both from the place where the materials grow, and from that where the complete manufacture is confumed. Lyons is very diftant both from the places which afford the materials of its manufactures, and from thofe which confume them. The people of fafhion in Sicily are clothed in filks made in other countries, from the materials which their own produces. Part of the wool of Spain is manufactured in Great Britain, and fome part of that cloth is afterwards fent back to Spain.

Whether the merchant whofe capital exports the furplus produce of any fociety be a native or a foreigner, is of very little importance. If he is a foreigner, the number of their productive labourers is neceffarily lefs than if he had been a native by one man only ; and the value of their annual produce, by the profits of that one man. The failors or carriers whom he employs may ftill belong indifferently either to his country, or to their country, or to fome third country, in the

fame

OF THE EMPLOYMENT OF CAPITALS.

CHAP. V.

fame manner as if he had been a native. The capital of a foreigner gives a value to their furplus produce equally with that of a native, by exchanging it for fomething for which there is a demand at home. It as effectually replaces the capital of the perfon who produces that furplus, and as effectually enables him to continue his bufinefs; the fervice by which the capital of a wholefale merchant chiefly contributes to fupport the productive labour, and to augment the value of the annual produce of the fociety to which he belongs.

It is of more confequence that the capital of the manufacturer fhould refide within the country. It neceffarily puts into motion a greater quantity of productive labour, and adds a greater value to the annual produce of the land and labour of the fociety. It may, however, be very ufeful to the country, though it fhould not refide within it. The capitals of the Britifh manufacturers who work up the flax and hemp annually imported from the coafts of the Baltic, are furely very ufeful to the countries which produce them. Thofe materials are a part of the furplus produce of thofe countries which, unlefs it was annually exchanged for fomething which is in demand there, would be of no value, and would foon ceafe to be produced. The merchants who export it replace the capitals of the people who produce it, and thereby encourage them to continue the production; and the Britifh manufacturers replace the capitals of thofe merchants.

E 4

A parti-

OF THE EMPLOYMENT OF CAPITALS.

BOOK II.

A particular country, in the fame manner as a particular perfon, may frequently not have capital fufficient both to improve and cultivate all its lands, to manufacture and prepare their whole rude produce for immediate ufe and confumption, and to tranfport the furplus part either of the rude or manufactured produce to thofe diftant markets where it can be exchanged for fomething for which there is a demand at home. The inhabitants of many different parts of Great Britain have not capital fufficient to improve and cultivate all their lands. The wool of the fouthern counties of Scotland is, a great part of it, after a long land carriage through very bad roads, manufactured in Yorkfhire, for want of a capital to manufacture it at home. There are many little manufacturing towns in Great Britain, of which the inhabitants have not capital fufficient to tranfport the produce of their own induftry to thofe diftant markets where there is demand and confumption for it. If there are any merchants among them, they are properly only the agents of wealthier merchants who refide in fome of the greater commercial cities.

When the capital of any country is not fufficient for all thofe three purpofes, in proportion as a greater fhare of it is employed in agriculture, the greater will be the quantity of productive labour which it puts into motion within the country; as will likewife be the value which its employment adds to the annual produce of the land and labour of the fociety. After agriculture, the capital employed in manufactures

puts

OF THE EMPLOYMENT OF CAPITALS. 57

CHAP. V.

puts into motion the greateſt quantity of productive labour, and adds the greateſt value to the annual produce. That which is employed in the trade of exportation, has the leaſt effect of any of the three.

The country, indeed, which has not capital ſufficient for all thoſe three purpoſes, has not arrived at that degree of opulence for which it ſeems naturally deſtined. To attempt, however, prematurely and with an inſufficient capital, to do all the three, is certainly not the ſhorteſt way for a ſociety, no more than it would be for an individual, to acquire a ſufficient one. The capital of all the individuals of a nation, has its limits in the ſame manner as that of a ſingle individual, and is capable of executing only certain purpoſes. The capital of all the individuals of a nation is increaſed in the ſame manner as that of a ſingle individual, by their continually accumulating and adding to it whatever they ſave out of their revenue. It is likely to increaſe the faſteſt, therefore, when it is employed in the way that affords the greateſt revenue to all the inhabitants of the country, as they will thus be enabled to make the greateſt ſavings. But the revenue of all the inhabitants of the country is neceſſarily in proportion to the value of the annual produce of their land and labour.

It has been the principal cauſe of the rapid progreſs of our American colonies towards wealth and greatneſs, that almoſt their whole capitals have hitherto been employed in agriculture. They have no manufactures, thoſe houſhold and

coarſer

OF THE EMPLOYMENT OF CAPITALS.

BOOK
II.

coarfer manufactures excepted which neceffarily accompany the progrefs of agriculture, and which are the work of the women and children in every private family. The greater part both of the exportation and coafting trade of America, is carried on by the capitals of merchants who refide in Great Britain. Even the ftores and warehoufes from which goods are retailed in fome provinces, particularly in Virginia and Maryland, belong many of them to merchants who refide in the mother country, and afford one of the few inftances of the retail trade of a fociety being carried on by the capitals of thofe who are not refident members of it. Were the Americans, either by combination or by any other fort of violence, to ftop the importation of European manufactures, and, by thus giving a monopoly to fuch of their own countrymen as could manufacture the like goods, divert any confiderable part of their capital into this employment, they would retard inftead of accelerating the further increafe in the value of their annual produce, and would obftruct inftead of promoting the progrefs of their country towards real wealth and greatnefs. This would be ftill more the cafe, were they to attempt, in the fame manner, to monopolize to themfelves their whole exportation trade.

The courfe of human profperity, indeed, feems fcarce ever to have been of fo long continuance as to enable any great country to acquire capital fufficient for all thofe three purpofes; unlefs, perhaps, we give credit to the wonderful accounts

OF THE EMPLOYMENT OF CAPITALS. 59

counts of the wealth and cultivation of China, of thofe of ancient Egypt, and of the ancient ftate of Indoftan. Even thofe three countries, the wealthieft, according to all accounts, that ever were in the world, are chiefly renowned for their fuperiority in agriculture and manufactures. They do not appear to have been eminent for foreign trade. The ancient Egyptians had a fuperftitious antipathy to the fea; a fuperftition nearly of the fame kind prevails among the Indians; and the Chinefe have never excelled in foreign commerce. The greater part of the furplus produce of all thofe three countries feems to have been always exported by foreigners, who gave in exchange for it fomething elfe for which they found a demand there, frequently gold and filver.

It is thus that the fame capital will in any country put into motion a greater or fmaller quantity of productive labour, and add a greater or fmaller value to the annual produce of its land and labour, according to the different pro_portions in which it is employed in agriculture, manufactures, and wholefale trade. The difference too is very great, according to the different forts of wholefale trade in which any part of it is employed.

All wholefale trade, all buying in order to fell again by wholefale, may be reduced to three different forts. The home trade, the foreign trade of confumption, and the carrying trade. The home trade is employed in purchafing in one part of the fame country, and felling in another,

CHAP. V.

OF THE EMPLOYMENT OF CAPITALS.

BOOK II.

the produce of the induftry of that country. It comprehends both the inland and the coafting trade. The foreign trade of confumption is employed in purchafing foreign goods for home confumption. The carrying trade is employed in tranfacting the commerce of foreign countries, or in carrying the furplus produce of one to another.

The capital which is employed in purchafing in one part of the country in order to fell in another the produce of the induftry of that country, generally replaces by every fuch operation two diftinct capitals that had both been employed in the agriculture or manufactures of that country, and thereby enables them to continue that employment. When it fends out from the refidence of the merchant a certain value of commodities, it generally brings back in return at leaft an equal value of other commodities. When both are the produce of domeftic induftry, it neceffarily replaces by every fuch operation two diftinct capitals, which had both been employed in fupporting productive labour, and thereby enables them to continue that fupport. The capital which fends Scotch manufactures to London, and brings back Englifh corn and manufactures to Edinburgh, neceffarily replaces, by every fuch operation, two Britifh capitals which had both been employed in the agriculture or manufactures of Great Britain.

The capital employed in purchafing foreign goods for home-confumption, when this purchafe is made with the produce of domeftic induftry, replaces

OF THE EMPLOYMENT OF CAPITALS. 61

replaces too, by every fuch operation, two dif- CHAP.
tinct capitals : but one of them only is employed V.
in fupporting domeftic induftry. The capital
which fends Britifh goods to Portugal, and
brings back Portuguefe goods to Great Britain,
replaces by every fuch operation only one Britifh
capital. The other is a Portuguefe one. Though
the returns, therefore, of the foreign trade of
confumption fhould be as quick as thofe of the
home-trade, the capital employed in it will give
but one-half the encouragement to the induftry
or productive labour of the country.

But the returns of the foreign trade of confumption are very feldom fo quick as thofe of the
home-trade. The returns of the home-trade
generally come in before the end of the year,
and fometimes three or four times in the year.
The returns of the foreign trade of confumption
feldom come in before the end· of the year, and
fometimes not till after two or three years. A
capital, therefore, employed in the home-trade
will fometimes make twelve operations, or be
fent out and returned twelve times, before a capital employed in the foreign trade of confumption has made one. If the capitals are equal,
therefore, the one will give four and twenty
times more encouragement and fupport to the
induftry of the country than the other.

The foreign goods for home-confumption may
fometimes be purchafed, not with the produce of
domeftic induftry, but with fome other foreign
goods. Thefe laft, however, muft have been
purchafed either immediately with the produce
of

62 **OF THE EMPLOYMENT OF CAPITALS.**

BOOK
II.
of domeſtic induſtry, or with ſomething elſe that had been purchaſed with it; for, the caſe of war and conqueſt excepted, foreign goods can never be acquired, but in exchange for ſomething that had been produced at home either immediately, or after two or more different exchanges. The effects, therefore, of a capital employed in ſuch a round-about foreign trade of conſumption, are, in every reſpect, the ſame as thoſe of one employed in the moſt direct trade of the ſame kind, except that the final returns are likely to be ſtill more diſtant, as they muſt depend upon the returns of two or three diſtinct foreign trades. If the flax and hemp of Riga are purchaſed with the tobacco of Virginia, which had been purchaſed with Britiſh manufactures, the merchant muſt wait for the returns of two diſtinct foreign trades before he can employ the ſame capital in repurchaſing a like quantity of Britiſh manufactures. If the tobacco of Virginia had been purchaſed, not with Britiſh manufactures, but with the ſugar and rum of Jamaica which had been purchaſed with thoſe manufactures, he muſt wait for the returns of three. If thoſe two or three diſtinct foreign trades ſhould happen to be carried on by two or three diſtinct merchants, of whom the ſecond buys the goods imported by the firſt, and the third buys thoſe imported by the ſecond, in order to export them again, each merchant indeed will in this caſe receive the returns of his own capital more quickly; but the final returns of the whole capital employed in the trade will be juſt as ſlow as ever.

OF THE EMPLOYMENT OF CAPITALS. 63

ever. Whether the whole capital employed in such a round-about trade belong to one merchant or to three, can make no difference with regard to the country, though it may with regard to the particular merchants. Three times a greater capital muſt in both caſes be employed, in order to exchange a certain value of Britiſh manufactures for a certain quantity of flax and hemp, than would have been neceſſary, had the manufactures and the flax and hemp been directly exchanged for one another. The whole capital employed, therefore, in ſuch a round-about foreign trade of conſumption, will generally give leſs encouragement and ſupport to the productive labour of the country, than an equal capital employed in a more direct trade of the ſame kind.

Whatever be the foreign commodity with which the foreign goods for home-conſumption are purchaſed, it can occaſion no eſſential difference either in the nature of the trade, or in the encouragement and ſupport which it can give to the productive labour of the country from which it is carried on. If they are purchaſed with the gold of Brazil, for example, or with the ſilver of Peru, this gold and ſilver, like the tobacco of Virginia, muſt have been purchaſed with ſomething that either was the produce of the induſtry of the country, or that had been purchaſed with ſomething elſe that was ſo. So far, therefore, as the productive labour of the country is concerned, the foreign trade of conſumption which is carried on by means of gold and ſilver, has all

the

OF THE EMPLOYMENT OF CAPITALS.

BOOK II.

the advantages and all the inconveniencies of any other equally round-about foreign trade of confumption, and will replace juft as faft or juft as flow the capital which is immediately employed in fupporting that productive labour. It feems even to have one advantage over any other equally round-about foreign trade. The tranfportation of thofe metals from one place to another, on account of their fmall bulk and great value, is lefs expenfive than that of almoft any other foreign goods of equal value. Their freight is much lefs, and their infurance not greater; and no goods, befides, are lefs liable to fuffer by the carriage. An equal quantity of foreign goods, therefore, may frequently be purchafed with a fmaller quantity of the produce of domeftic induftry, by the intervention of gold and filver, than by that of any other foreign goods. The demand of the country may frequently, in this manner, be fupplied more completely and at a fmaller expence than in any other. Whether, by the continual exportation of thofe metals, a trade of this kind is likely to impoverifh the country from which it is carried on, in any other way, I fhall have occafion to examine at great length hereafter.

That part of the capital of any country which is employed in the carrying trade, is altogether withdrawn from fupporting the productive labour of that particular country, to fupport that of fome foreign countries. Though it may replace by every operation two diftinct capitals, yet neither of them belongs to that particular country.

OF THE EMPLOYMENT OF CAPITALS. 65

country. The capital of the Dutch merchant, C H A P. V. which carries the corn of Poland to Portugal, and brings back the fruits and wines of Portugal to Poland, replaces by every fuch operation two capitals, neither of which had been employed in fupporting the productive labour of Holland; but one of them in fupporting that of Poland, and the other that of Portugal. The profits only return regularly to Holland, and conftitute the whole addition which this trade neceffarily makes to the annual produce of the land and labour of that country. When, indeed, the carrying trade of any particular country is carried on with the fhips and failors of that country, that part of the capital employed in it which pays the freight, is diftributed among, and puts into motion, a certain number of productive labourers of that country. Almoft all nations that have had any confiderable fhare of the carrying trade have, in fact, carried it on in this manner. The trade itfelf has probably derived its name from it, the people of fuch countries being the carriers to other countries. It does not, however, feem effential to the nature of the trade that it fhould be fo. A Dutch merchant may, for example, employ his capital in tranfacting the commerce of Poland and Portugal, by carrying part of the furplus produce of the one to the other, not in Dutch, but in Britifh bottoms. It may be prefumed, that he actually does fo upon fome particular occafions. It is upon this account, however, that the carrying trade has been fuppofed peculiarly advantageous to fuch a country as Great

VOL. III.   F   Britain,

OF THE EMPLOYMENT OF CAPITALS.

BOOK
II.

Britain, of which the defence and security depend upon the number of its sailors and shipping: But the same capital may employ as many sailors and shipping, either in the foreign trade of consumption, or even in the home-trade, when carried on by coasting vessels, as it could in the carrying trade. The number of sailors and shipping which any particular capital can employ, does not depend upon the nature of the trade, but partly upon the bulk of the goods in proportion to their value, and partly upon the distance of the ports between which they are to be carried ; chiefly upon the former of those two circumstances. The coal-trade from Newcastle to London, for example, employs more shipping than all the carrying trade of England, though the ports are at no great distance. To force, therefore, by extraordinary encouragements, a larger share of the capital of any country into the carrying trade, than what would naturally go to it, will not always necessarily increase the shipping of that country.

The capital, therefore, employed in the home-trade of any country will generally give encouragement and support to a greater quantity of productive labour in that country, and increase the value of its annual produce more than an equal capital employed in the foreign trade of consumption : and the capital employed in this latter trade has in both these respects a still greater advantage over an equal capital employed in the carrying trade. The riches, and so far as power depends upon riches, the power of

every

OF THE EMPLOYMENT OF CAPITALS. 67

every country, muft always be in proportion to
the value of its annual produce, the fund from
which all taxes muft ultimately be paid. But
the great object of the political œconomy of
every country, is to increafe the riches and power
of that country. It ought, therefore, to give no
preference nor fuperior encouragement to the
foreign trade of confumption above the home-
trade, nor to the carrying trade above either of
the other two. It ought neither to force nor to
allure into either of thofe two channels, a greater
fhare of the capital of the country than what
would naturally flow into them of its own accord.

Each of thofe different branches of trade,
however, is not only advantageous, but neceffary and unavoidable, when the courfe of things,
without any conftraint or violence, naturally introduces it.

When the produce of any particular branch
of induftry exceeds what the demand of the
country requires, the furplus muft be fent abroad,
and exchanged for fomething for which there is
a demand at home. Without fuch exportation,
a part of the productive labour of the country
muft ceafe, and the value of its annual produce
diminifh. The land and labour of Great Britain produce generally more corn, woollens,
and hard ware, than the demand of the home-
market requires. The furplus part of them,
therefore, muft be fent abroad, and exchanged
for fomething for which there is a demand at
home. It is only by means of fuch exportation,
that this furplus can acquire a value fufficient to

F 2

com-

OF THE EMPLOYMENT OF CAPITALS.

BOOK II.

compenfate the labour and expence of producing it. The neighbourhood of the fea coaft, and the banks of all navigable rivers, are advantageous fituations for induftry, only becaufe they facilitate the exportation and exchange of fuch furplus produce for fomething elfe which is more in demand there.

When the foreign goods which are thus purchafed with the furplus produce of domeftic induftry exceed the demand of the home-market, the furplus part of them muft be fent abroad again, and exchanged for fomething more in demand at home. About ninety-fix thoufand hogfheads of tobacco are annually purchafed in Virginia and Maryland, with a part of the furplus produce of Britifh induftry. But the demand of Great Britain does not require, perhaps, more than fourteen thoufand. If the remaining eighty-two thoufand, therefore, could not be fent abroad and exchanged for fomething more in demand at home, the importation of them muft ceafe immediately, and with it the productive labour of all thofe inhabitants of Great Britain, who are at prefent employed in preparing the goods with which thefe eighty-two thoufand hogfheads are annually purchafed. Thofe goods, which are part of the produce of the land and labour of Great Britain, having no market at home, and being deprived of that which they had abroad, muft ceafe to be produced. The moft round-about foreign trade of confumption, therefore, may, upon fome occafions, be as neceffary for fupporting the productive

OF THE EMPLOYMENT OF CAPITALS. 69

tive labour of the country, and the value of its annual produce, as the moft direct.

CHAP.
V.

When the capital ftock of any country is increafed to fuch a degree, that it cannot be all employed in fupplying the confumption, and fupporting the productive labour of that particular country, the furplus part of it naturally difgorges itfelf into the carrying trade, and is employed in performing the fame offices to other countries. The carrying trade is the natural effect and fymptom of great national wealth; but it does not feem to be the natural caufe of it. Thofe ftatefmen who have been difpofed to favour it with particular eacouragements, feem to have miftaken the effect and fymptom for the caufe. Holland, in proportion to the extent of the land and the number of its inhabitants, by far the richeft country in Europe, has, accordingly, the greateft fhare of the carrying trade of Europe. England, perhaps the fecond richeft country of Europe, is likewife fuppofed to have a confiderable fhare of it; though what commonly paffes for the carrying trade of England, will frequently, perhaps, be found to be no more than a round-about foreign trade of confumption. Such are, in a great meafure, the trades which carry the goods of the Eaft and Weft Indies, and of America, to different European markets. Thofe goods are generally purchafed either immediately with the produce of Britifh induftry, or with fomething elfe which had been purchafed with that produce, and the final returns of thofe trades are generally ufed or con-

F 3

fumed

OF THE EMPLOYMENT OF CAPITALS.

BOOK
II.

fumed in Great Britain. The trade which is carried on in Britiſh bottoms between the different ports of the Mediterranean, and ſome trade of the ſame kind carried on by Britiſh merchants between the different ports of India, make, perhaps, the principal branches of what is properly the carrying trade of Great Britain.

The extent of the home-trade and of the capital which can be employed in it, is neceſſarily limited by the value of the ſurplus produce of all thoſe diſtant places within the country which have occaſion to exchange their reſpective productions with one another. That of the foreign trade of conſumption, by the value of the ſurplus produce of the whole country and of what can be purchaſed with it. That of the carrying trade, by the value of the ſurplus produce of all the different countries in the world. Its poſſible extent, therefore, is in a manner infinite in compariſon of that of the other two, and is capable of abſorbing the greateſt capitals.

The conſideration of his own private profit, is the ſole motive which determines the owner of any capital to employ it either in agriculture, in manufactures, or in ſome particular branch of the wholeſale or retail trade. The different quantities of productive labour which it may put into motion, and the different values which it may add to the annual produce of the land and labour of the ſociety, according as it is employed in one or other of thoſe different ways, never enter into his thoughts. In countries, therefore, where agriculture is the moſt profitable of all

OF THE EMPLOYMENT OF CAPITALS. 71

all employments, and farming and improving the
moft direct roads to a fplendid fortune, the capitals of individuals will naturally be employed
in the manner moft advantageous to the whole
fociety. The profits of agriculture, however,
feem to have no fuperiority over thofe of other
employments in any part of Europe. Projectors,
indeed, in every corner of it, have within thefe
few years amufed the public with moft magnificent accounts of the profits to be made by the
cultivation and improvement of land. Without
entering into any particular difcuffion of their
calculations, a very fimple obfervation may fatisfy us that the refult of them muft be falfe.
We fee every day the moft fplendid fortunes that
have been acquired in the courfe of a fingle life
by trade and manufactures, frequently from a
very fmall capital, fometimes from no capital.
A fingle inftance of fuch a fortune acquired by
agriculture in the fame time, and from fuch a
capital, has not, perhaps, occurred in Europe
during the courfe of the prefent century. In all
the great countries of Europe, however, much
good land ftill remains uncultivated, and the
greater part of what is cultivated, is far from being improved to the degree of which it is capable. Agriculture, therefore, is almoft every-
where capable of abforbing a much greater capital than has ever yet been employed in it. What
circumftances in the policy of Europe have given
the trades which are carried on in towns fo great
an advantage over that which is carried on in the

CHAP.
V.

F 4

country,

OF THE EMPLOYMENT OF CAPITALS.

BOOK II.

country, that private perfons frequently find it more for their advantage to employ their capitals in the moft diftant carrying trades of Afia and America, than in the improvement and cultivation of the moft fertile fields in their own neighbourhood, I fhall endeavour to explain at full length in the two following books.

BOOK III.

OF THE DIFFERENT PROGRESS OF OPULENCE IN DIFFERENT NATIONS.

CHAP. I.

Of the natural Progress of Opulence.

THE great commerce of every civilized fo- ciety, is that carried on between the inhabitants of the town and thofe of the country. It confifts in the exchange of rude for manufactured produce, either immediately, or by the intervention of money, or of fome fort of paper which reprefents money. The country fupplies the town with the means of fubfiftence, and the materials of manufacture. The town repays this fupply by fending back a part of the manufactured produce to the inhabitants of the country. The town, in which there neither is nor can be any reproduction of fubftances, may very properly be faid to gain its whole wealth and fubfiftence from the country. We muft not, however, upon this account, imagine that the gain of the town is the lofs of the country. The gains of both are mutual and reciprocal, and the divifion of labour is in this, as in all other cafes, advantageous to all the different perfons employed in the various occupations into which it is

fubdi-

74   OF THE PROGRESS OF OPULENCE.

BOOK III.

fubdivided. The inhabitants of the country purchafe of the town a greater quantity of manufactured goods, with the produce of a much fmaller quantity of their own labour, than they muſt have employed had they attempted to prepare them themfelves. The town affords a market for the furplus produce of the country, or what is over and above the maintenance of the cultivators, and it is there that the inhabitants of the country exchange it for fomething elfe which is in demand among them. The greater the number and revenue of the inhabitants of the town, the more extenfive is the market which it affords to thofe of the country; and the more extenfive that market, it is always the more advantageous to a great number. The corn which grows within a mile of the town, fells there for the fame price with that which comes from twenty miles diſtance. But the price of the latter muſt generally, not only pay the expence of raifing and bringing it to market, but afford too the ordinary profits of agriculture to the farmer. The proprietors and cultivators of the country, therefore, which lies in the neighbourhood of the town, over and above the ordinary profits of agriculture, gain, in the price of what they fell, the whole value of the carriage of the like produce that is brought from more diſtant parts, and they fave, befides, the whole value of this carriage in the price of what they buy. Compare the cultivation of the lands in the neighbourhood of any confiderable town, with that of thofe which lie at fome diſtance

from

OF THE PROGRESS OF OPULENCE.

from it, and you will eafily fatisfy yourfelf how C H A P. much the country is benefited by the commerce I. of the town. Among all the abfurd fpeculations that have been propagated concerning the balance of trade, it has never been pretended that either the country lofes by its commerce with the town, or the town by that with the country which maintains it.

As fubfiftence is, in the nature of things, prior to conveniency and luxury, fo the induftry which procures the former, muft neceffarily be prior to that which minifters to the latter. The cultivation and improvement of the country, therefore, which affords fubfiftence, muft, neceffarily, be prior to the increafe of the town, which furnifhes only the means of conveniency and luxury. It is the furplus produce of the country only, or what is over and above the maintenance of the cultivators, that conftitutes the fubfiftence of the town, which can therefore increafe only with the increafe of this furplus produce. The town, indeed, may not always derive its whole fubfiftence from the country in its neighbourhood, or even from the territory to which it belongs, but from very diftant countries; and this, though it forms no exception from the general rule, has occafioned confiderable variations in the progrefs of opulence in different ages and nations.

That order of things which neceffity impofes in general, though not in every particular country, is, in every particular country, promoted by the natural inclinations of man. If human infti-

tutions

OF THE PROGRESS OF OPULENCE.

BOOK III.

tutions had never thwarted thofe natural inclina- tions, the towns could no where have increafed beyond what the improvement and cultivation of the territory in which they were fituated could fupport; till fuch time at leaft, as the whole of that territory was completely cultivated and im- proved. Upon equal, or nearly equal profits, moft men will chufe to employ their capitals rather in the improvement and cultivation of land, than either in manufactures or in foreign trade. The man who employs his capital in land, has it more under his view and command, and his fortune is much lefs liable to accidents than that of the trader, who is obliged frequently to commit it, not only to the winds and the waves, but to the more uncertain elements of human folly and injuftice, by giving great credits in diftant countries to men, with whofe character and fituation he can feldom be thoroughly ac- quainted. The capital of the landlord, on the contrary, which is fixed in the improvement of his land, feems to be as well fecured as the nature of human affairs can admit of. The beauty of the country befides, the pleafures of a country life, the tranquillity of mind which it promifes, and wherever the injuftice of human laws does not difturb it, the independency which it really affords, have charms that more or lefs attract every body; and as to cultivate the ground was the original deftination of man, fo in every ftage of his exiftence he feems to retain a predilection for this primitive employment.

Without

OF THE PROGRESS OF OPULENCE.

Without the affiftance of fome artificers, indeed, the cultivation of land cannot be carried on, but with great inconveniency and continual interruption. Smiths, carpenters, wheel-wrights, and plough-wrights, mafons, and bricklayers, tanners, fhoemakers, and taylors, are people whofe fervice the farmer has frequent occafion for. Such artificers, too, ftand occafionally in need of the affiftance of one another; and as their refidence is not, like that of the farmer, neceffarily tied down to a precife fpot, they naturally fettle in the neighbourhood of one another, and thus form a fmall town or village. The butcher, the brewer, and the baker, foon join them, together with many other artificers and retailers, neceffary or ufeful for fupplying their occafional wants, and who contribute ftill further to augment the town. The inhabitants of the town and thofe of the country are mutually the fervants of one another. The town is a continual fair or market, to which the inhabitants of the country refort, in order to exchange their rude for manufactured produce. It is this commerce which fupplies the inhabitants of the town both with the materials of their work, and the means of their fubfiftence. The quantity of the finifhed work which they fell to the inhabitants of the country, neceffarily regulates the quantity of the materials and provifions which they buy. Neither their employment nor fubfiftence, therefore, can augment, but in proportion to the augmentation of the demand from the country for finifhed work ; and this demand can augment

only

OF THE PROGRESS OF OPULENCE.

BOOK III.

only in proportion to the extenfion of improvement and cultivation. Had human inftitutions, therefore, never difturbed the natural courfe of things, the progreffive wealth and increafe of the towns would, in every political fociety, be confequential, and in proportion to the improvement and cultivation of the territory or country.

In our North American colonies, where uncultivated land is still to be had upon eafy terms, no manufacturers for diftant fale have ever yet been eftablifhed in any of their towns. When an artificer has acquired a little more ftock than is neceffary for carrying on his own bufinefs in fupplying the neighbouring country, he does not, in North America, attempt to eftablifh with it a manufacture for more diftant fale, but employs it in the purchafe and improvement of uncultivated land. From artificer he becomes planter, and neither the large wages nor the eafy fubfiftence which that country affords to artificers, can bribe him rather to work for other people than for himfelf. He feels that an artificer is the fervant of his cuftomers, from whom he derives his fubfiftence; but that a planter who cultivates his own land, and derives his neceffary fubfiftence from the labour of his own family, is really a mafter, and independent of all the world.

In countries, on the contrary, where there is either no uncultivated land, or none that can be had upon eafy terms, every artificer who has acquired more ftock than he can employ in the occafional jobs of the neighbourhood, endeavours to

prepare

OF THE PROGRESS OF OPULENCE. 79

prepare work for more distant sale. The smith CHAP.
erects some sort of iron, the weaver some sort of I.
linen or woollen manufactory. Those different
manufactures come, in process of time, to be
gradually subdivided, and thereby improved and
refined in a great variety of ways, which may
easily be conceived, and which it is therefore
unneceffary to explain any further.

In seeking for employment to a capital, manufactures are, upon equal, or nearly equal profits,
naturally preferred to foreign commerce, for the
same reason that agriculture is naturally preferred to manufactures. As the capital of the
landlord or farmer is more secure than that of the
manufacturer, so the capital of the manufacturer
being at all times more within his view and command, is more secure than that of the foreign
merchant. In every period, indeed, of every society, the surplus part both of the rude and manufactured produce, or that for which there is
no demand at home, must be sent abroad, in order
to be exchanged for something for which there
is some demand at home. But whether the capital, which carries this surplus produce abroad,
be a foreign or a domestic one, is of very little
importance. If the society has not acquired
fufficient capital both to cultivate all its lands,
and to manufacture, in the completest manner,
the whole of its rude produce, there is even a
considerable advantage that that rude produce
should be exported by a foreign capital, in
order that the whole stock of the society may
be employed in more useful purposes. The
wealth

OF THE PROGRESS OF OPULENCE.

BOOK III.

wealth of ancient Egypt, that of China and Indoſtan, ſufficiently demonſtrate that a nation may attain a very high degree of opulence, though the greater part of its exportation trade be carried on by foreigners. The progreſs of our North American and Weſt Indian colonies would have been much leſs rapid, had no capital but what belonged to themſelves been employed in exporting their ſurplus produce.

According to the natural courſe of things, therefore, the greater part of the capital of every growing ſociety is, firſt, directed to agriculture, afterwards to manufactures, and laſt of all to foreign commerce. This order of things is ſo very natural, that in every ſociety that had any territory, it has always, I believe, been in ſome degree, obſerved. Some of their lands muſt have been cultivated before any conſiderable towns could be eſtabliſhed, and ſome ſort of coarſe induſtry of the manufacturing kind muſt have been carried on in thoſe towns, before they could well think of employing themſelves in foreign commerce.

But though this natural order of things muſt have taken place in ſome degree in every ſuch ſociety, it has, in all the modern ſtates of Europe, been, in many reſpects, entirely inverted. The foreign commerce of ſome of their cities has introduced all their finer manufactures, or ſuch as were fit for diſtant ſale; and manufactures and foreign commerce together, have given birth to the principal improvements of agriculture. The manners and cuſtoms which the nature of their

OF THE PROGRESS OF OPULENCE. 81

their original government introduced, and which remained after that government was greatly altered, necessarily forced them into this unnatural and retrograde order.

CHAP. I.

CHAP. II.

Of the Discouragement of Agriculture in the ancient State of Europe after the Fall of the Roman Empire.

WHEN the German and Scythian nations over-ran the western provinces of the Roman empire, the confusions which followed so great a revolution lasted for several centuries. The rapine and violence which the barbarians exercised against the ancient inhabitants, interrupted the commerce between the towns and the country. The towns were deserted, and the country was left uncultivated, and the western provinces of Europe, which had enjoyed a considerable degree of opulence under the Roman empire, sunk into the lowest state of poverty and barbarism. During the continuance of those confusions, the chiefs and principal leaders of those nations, acquired or usurped to themselves the greater part of the lands of those countries. A great part of them was uncultivated; but no part of them, whether cultivated or uncultivated, was left without a proprietor. All of them were engrossed

CHAP. II.

VOL. III.　　　　　G　　　　　grossed

OF THE DISCOURAGEMENT OF AGRICULTURE

BOOK III.

groffed, and the greater part by a few great proprietors.

This original engroffing of uncultivated lands, though a great, might have been but a tranfitory evil. They might foon have been divided again, and broke into fmall parcels either by fucceffion or by alienation. The law of primogeniture hindered them from being divided by fucceffion : the introduction of entails prevented their being broke into fmall parcels by alienation.

When land, like moveables, is confidered as the means only of fubfiftence and enjoyment, the natural law of fucceffion divides it, like them, among all the children of the family ; of all of whom the fubfiftence and enjoyment may be fuppofed equally dear to the father. This natural law of fucceffion accordingly took place among the Romans, who made no more diftinction between elder and younger, between male and female, in the inheritance of lands, than we do in the diftribution of moveables. But when land was confidered as the means, not of fubfiftence merely, but of power and protection, it was thought better that it fhould defcend undivided to one. In thofe diforderly times, every great landlord was a fort of petty prince. His tenants were his fubjects. He was their judge, and in fome refpects their legiflator in peace, and their leader in war. He made war according to his own difcretion, frequently againft his neighbours, and fometimes againft his fovereign. The fecurity of a landed eftate, therefore, the protection which

AFTER THE FALL OF THE ROMAN EMPIRE. 83

which its owner could afford to thofe who dwelt on it, depended upon its greatnefs. To divide it was to ruin it, and to expofe every part of it to be oppreffed and fwallowed up by the incurfions of its neighbours. The law of primogeniture, therefore, came to take place, not immediately, indeed, but in procefs of time, in the fucceffion of landed eftates, for the fame reafon that it has generally taken place in that of monarchies, though not always at their firft inftitution. That the power, and confequently the fecurity of the monarchy, may not be weakened by divifion, it muft defcend entire to one of the children. To which of them fo important a preference fhall be given, muft be determined by fome general rule, founded not upon the doubtful diftinctions of perfonal merit, but upon fome plain and evident difference which can admit of no difpute. Among the children of the fame family, there can be no indifputable difference but that of fex, and that of age. The male fex is univerfally preferred to the female; and when all other things are equal, the elder every-where takes place of the younger. Hence the origin of the right of primogeniture, and of what is called lineal fucceffion.

Laws frequently continue in force long after the circumftances, which firft gave occafion to them, and which could alone render them reafonable, are no more. In the prefent ftate of Europe, the proprietor of a fingle acre of land is as perfectly fecure of his poffeffion as the proprietor of a hundred thoufand. The right of primoge-

OF THE DISCOURAGEMENT OF AGRICULTURE

BOOK
III.

niture, however, ftill continues to be refpected, and as of all inftitutions it is the fitteft to fupport the pride of family diftinctions, it is ftill likely to endure for many centuries. In every other refpect, nothing can be more contrary to the real intereft of a numerous family, than a right which, in order to enrich one, beggars all the reft of the children.

Entails are the natural confequences of the law of primogeniture. They were introduced to preferve a certain lineal fucceffion, of which the law of primogeniture firft gave the idea, and to hinder any part of the original eftate from being carried out of the propofed line either by gift, or devife, or alienation; either by the folly, or by the misfortune of any of its fucceffive owners. They were altogether unknown to the Romans. Neither their fubftitutions nor fideicommiffes bear any refemblance to entails, though fome French lawyers have thought proper to drefs the modern inftitution in the language and garb of thofe antient ones.

When great landed eftates were a fort of principalities, entails might not be unreafonable. Like what are called the fundamental laws of fome monarchies, they might frequently hinder the fecurity of thoufands from being endangered by the caprice or extravagance of one man. But in the prefent ftate of Europe, when fmall as well as great eftates derive their fecurity from the laws of their country, nothing can be more completely abfurd. They are founded upon the moft abfurd of all fuppofitions, the fuppofition

that

AFTER THE FALL OF THE ROMAN EMPIRE. 85

that every fucceffive generation of men have not an equal right to the earth, and to all that it poffeffes; but that the property of the prefent generation fhould be reftrained and regulated according to the fancy of thofe who died perhaps five hundred years ago. Entails, however, are ftill refpected through the greater part of Europe, in thofe countries particularly in which noble birth is a neceffary qualification for the enjoyment either of civil or military honours. Entails are thought neceffary for maintaining this exclufive privilege of the nobility to the great offices and honours of their country; and that order having ufurped one unjuft advantage over the reft of their fellow-citizens, left their poverty fhould render it ridiculous, it is thought reafonable that they fhould have another. The common law of England, indeed, is faid to abhor perpetuities, and they are accordingly more reftricted there than in any other European monarchy; though even England is not altogether without them. In Scotland more than one-fifth, perhaps more than one-third part of the whole lands of the country, are at prefent fuppofed to be under ftrict entail.

Great tracts of uncultivated land were, in this manner, not only engroffed by particular families, but the poffibility of their being divided again was as much as poffible precluded for ever. It feldom happens, however, that a great proprietor is a great improver. In the diforderly times which gave birth to thofe barbarous inftitutions, the great proprietor was fufficiently employed

86 OF THE DISCOURAGEMENT OF AGRICULTURE

BOOK III.

ployed in defending his own territories, or in extending his jurifdiction and authority over thofe of his neighbours. He had no leifure to attend to the cultivation and improvement of land. When the eftablifhment of law and order afforded him this leifure, he often wanted the inclination, and almoft always the requifite abilities. If the expence of his houfe and perfon either equalled or exceeded his revenue, as it did very frequently, he had no ftock to employ in this manner. If he was an œconomift, he generally found it more profitable to employ his annual favings in new purchafes, than in the improvement of his old eftate. To improve land with profit, like all other commercial projects, requires an exact attention to fmall favings and fmall gains, of which a man born to a great fortune, even though naturally frugal, is very feldom capable. The fituation of fuch a perfon naturally difpofes him to attend rather to ornament which pleafes his fancy, than to profit for which he has fo little occafion. The elegance of his drefs, of his equipage, of his houfe, and houfehold furniture, are objects which from his infancy he has been accuftomed to have fome anxiety about. The turn of mind which this habit naturally forms, follows him when he comes to think of the improvement of land. He embellifhes perhaps four or five hundred acres in the neighbourhood of his houfe, at ten times the expence which the land is worth after all his improvements; and finds that if he was to improve his whole eftate in the fame manner,

and

AFTER THE FALL OF THE ROMAN EMPIRE. 87

and he has little tafte for any other, he would be
a bankrupt before he had finifhed the tenth part
of it. There ftill remain in both parts of the
United Kingdom fome great eftates which have
continued without interruption in the hands of
the fame family fince the times of feudal anarchy.
Compare the prefent condition of thofe eftates
with the poffeffions of the fmall proprietors in
their neighbourhood, and you will require no
other argument to convince you how unfavourable fuch extenfive property is to improvement.
If little improvement was to be expected from
fuch great proprietors, ftill lefs was to be hoped
for from thofe who occupied the land under
them. In the ancient ftate of Europe, the occupiers of land were all tenants at will. They
were all or almoft all flaves; but their flavery
was of a milder kind than that known among the
ancient Greeks and Romans, or even in our
Weft Indian colonies. They were fuppofed to
belong more directly to the land than to their
mafter. They could, therefore, be fold with it,
but not feparately. They could marry, provided it was with the confent of their mafter;
and he could not afterwards diffolve the marriage by felling the man and wife to different
perfons. If he maimed or murdered any of
them, he was liable to fome penalty, though
generally but to a fmall one. They were not,
however, capable of acquiring property. Whatever they acquired was acquired to their mafter,
and he could take it from them at pleafure.
Whatever cultivation and improvement could be

CHAP.
II.

G 4   carried

OF THE DISCOURAGEMENT OF AGRICULTURE

BOOK III.

carried on by means of such flaves, was properly carried on by their mafter. It was at his expence. The feed, the cattle, and the inftruments of hufbandry were all his. It was for his benefit. Such flaves could acquire nothing but their daily maintenance. It was properly the proprietor himfelf, therefore, that, in this cafe, occupied his own lands, and cultivated them by his own bondmen. This fpecies of flavery ftill fubfifts in Ruffia, Poland, Hungary, Bohemia, Moravia, and other parts of Germany. It is only in the weftern and fouth-weftern provinces of Europe, that it has gradually been abolifhed altogether.

But if great improvements are feldom to be expected from great proprietors, they are leaft of all to be expected when they employ flaves for their workmen. The experience of all ages and nations, I believe, demonftrates that the work done by flaves, though it appears to coft only their maintenance, is in the end the deareft of any. A perfon who can acquire no property, can have no other intereft but to eat as much, and to labour as little as poffible. Whatever work he does beyond what is fufficient to purchafe his own maintenance, can be fqueezed out of him by violence only, and not by any intereft of his own. In ancient Italy, how much the cultivation of corn degenerated, how unprofitable it became to the mafter when it fell under the management of flaves, is remarked by both Pliny and Columella. In the time of Ariftotle it had not been much better in ancient Greece. Speaking of the

ideal

ideal republic defcribed in the laws of Plato, to maintain five thoufand idle men (the number of warriors fuppofed neceffary for its defence), together with their women and fervants, would require, he fays, a territory of boundlefs extent and fertility, like the plains of Babylon.

The pride of man makes him love to domineer, and nothing mortifies him fo much as to be obliged to condefcend to perfuade his inferiors. Wherever the law allows it, and the nature of the work can afford it, therefore, he will generally prefer the fervice of flaves to that of freemen. The planting of fugar and tobacco can afford the expence of flave cultivation. The raifing of corn, it feems, in the prefent times, cannot. In the Englifh colonies, of which the principal produce is corn, the far greater part of the work is done by freemen. The late refolution of the Quakers in Pennfylvania to fet at liberty all their negro flaves, may fatisfy us that their number cannot be very great. Had they made any confiderable part of their property, fuch a refolution could never have been agreed to. In our fugar colonies, on the contrary, the whole work is done by flaves, and in our tobacco colonies a very great part of it. The profits of a fugar-plantation in any of our Weft Indian colonies are generally much greater than thofe of any other cultivation that is known either in Europe or America: And the profits of a tobacco plantation, though inferior to thofe of fugar, are fuperior to thofe of corn, as has already been obferved. Both can afford the expence

OF THE DISCOURAGEMENT OF AGRICULTURE

BOOK III.

pence of flave cultivation, but fugar can afford it ftill better than tobacco. The number of negroes accordingly is much greater, in proportion to that of whites, in our fugar than in our tobacco colonies.

To the flave cultivators of ancient times, gradually fucceeded a fpecies of farmers known at prefent in France by the name of Metayers. They are called in Latin, Coloni Partiarii. They have been fo long in difufe in England that at prefent I know no Englifh name for them. The proprietor furnifhed them with the feed, cattle, and inftruments of hufbandry, the whole ftock, in fhort, neceffary for cultivating the farm. The produce was divided equally between the proprietor and the farmer, after fetting afide what was judged neceffary for keeping up the ftock, which was reftored to the proprietor when the farmer either quitted, or was turned out of the farm.

Land occupied by fuch tenants is properly cultivated at the expence of the proprietor, as much as that occupied by flaves. There is, however, one very effential difference between them. Such tenants, being freemen, are capable of acquiring property, and having a certain proportion of the produce of the land, they have a plain intereft that the whole produce fhould be as great as poffible, in order that their own proportion may be fo. A flave, on the contrary, who can acquire nothing but his maintenance, confults his own eafe by making the land produce as little as poffible over and above that

main-

AFTER THE FALL OF THE ROMAN EMPIRE.

maintenance. It is probable that it was partly upon account of this advantage, and partly upon account of the encroachments which the fovereign, always jealous of the great lords, gradually encouraged their villains to make upon their authority, and which feem at laft to have been fuch as rendered this fpecies of fervitude altogether inconvenient, that tenure in villanage gradually wore out through the greater part of Europe. The time and manner, however, in which fo important a revolution was brought about, is one of the moft obfcure points in modern hiftory. The church of Rome claims great merit in it; and it is certain that fo early as the twelfth century, Alexander III. publifhed a bull for the general emancipation of flaves. It feems, however, to have been rather a pious exhortation, than a law to which exact obedience was required from the faithful. Slavery continued to take place almoft univerfally for feveral centuries afterwards, till it was gradually abolifhed by the joint operation of the two interefts above mentioned, that of the proprietor on the one hand, and that of the fovereign on the other. A villain enfranchifed, and at the fame time allowed to continue in poffeffion of the land, having no ftock of his own, could cultivate it only by means of what the landlord advanced to him, and muft, therefore, have been what the French call a Metayer.

It could never, however, be the intereft even of this laft fpecies of cultivators to lay out, in the further improvement of the land, any part of the little

OF THE DISCOURAGEMENT OF AGRICULTURE

BOOK III.

little ftock which they might fave from their own fhare of the produce, becaufe the lord, who laid out nothing, was to get one-half of whatever it produced. The tithe, which is but a tenth of the produce, is found to be a very great hindrance to improvement. A tax, therefore, which amounted to one-half, muft have been an effectual bar to it. It might be the intereft of a metayer to make the land produce as much as could be brought out of it by means of the ftock furnifhed by the proprietor; but it could never be his intereft to mix any part of his own with it. In France, where five parts out of fix of the whole kingdom are faid to be ftill occupied by this fpecies of cultivators, the proprietors com. plain that their metayers take every opportunity of employing the mafters cattle rather in carriage than in cultivation ; becaufe in the one cafe they get the whole profits to themfelves, in the other they fhare them with their landlord. This fpecies of tenants ftill fubfifts in fome parts of Scotland. They are called fteel-bow tenants. Thofe an-cient Englifh tenants, who are faid by Chief Baron Gilbert and Doctor Blackftone to have been rather bailiffs of the landlord than farmers properly fo called, were probably of the fame kind.

To this fpecies of tenancy fucceeded, though by very flow degrees, farmers properly fo called, who cultivated the land with their own ftock, paying a rent certain to the landlord. When fuch farmers have a leafe for a term of years, they may fometimes find it for their intereft to

lay

lay out part of their capital in the further improvement of the farm; becaufe they may fometimes expect to recover it, with a large profit, before the expiration of the leafe. The poffeffion even of fuch farmers, however, was long extremely precarious, and ftill is fo in many parts of Europe. They could before the expiration of their term be legally outed of their leafe, by a new purchafer; in England, even by the fictitious action of a common recovery. If they were turned out illegally by the violence of their mafter, the action by which they obtained redrefs was extremely imperfect. It did not always re-inftate them in the poffeffion of the land, but gave them damages which never amounted to the real lofs. Even in England, the country perhaps of Europe where the yeomanry has always been moft refpected, it was not till about the 14th of Henry the VIIth that the action of ejectment was invented, by which the tenant recovers, not damages only but poffeffion, and in which his claim is not neceffarily concluded by the uncertain decifion of a fingle affize. This action has been found fo effectual a remedy that, in the modern practice, when the landlord has occafion to fue for the poffeffion of the land, he feldom makes ufe of the actions which properly belong to him as landlord, the writ of right or the writ of entry, but fues in the name of his tenant, by the writ of ejectment. In England, therefore, the fecurity of the tenant is equal to that of the proprietor. In England befides a leafe for life of forty fhillings a year value is a

freehold,

94 OF THE DISCOURAGEMENT OF AGRICULTURE

BOOK freehold, and entitles the leffee to vote for a
III. member of parliament; and as a great part of
the yeomanry have freeholds of this kind, the
whole order becomes refpectable to their landlords on account of the political confideration
which this gives them. There is, I believe,
no-where in Europe, except in England, any inftance of the tenant building upon the land of
which he had no leafe, and trufting that the honour of his landlord would take no advantage of
fo important an improvement. Thofe laws and
cuftoms fo favourable to the yeomanry, have
perhaps contributed more to the prefent grandeur of England, than all their boafted regulations of commerce taken together.

The law which fecures the longeft leafes againft
fucceffors of every kind is, fo far as I know,
peculiar to Great Britain. It was introduced
into Scotland fo early as 1449, by a law of James
the IId. Its beneficial influence, however, has
been much obftructed by entails; the heirs of
entail being generally reftrained from letting
leafes for any long term of years, frequently for
more than one year. A late act of parliament
has, in this refpect, fomewhat flackened their
fetters, though they are ftill by much too ftrait.
In Scotland, befides, as no leafehold gives a vote
for a member of parliament, the yeomanry are
upon this account lefs refpectable to their landlords than in England.

In other parts of Europe, after it was found
convenient to fecure tenants both againft heirs
and purchafers, the term of their fecurity was

3 ftill

AFTER THE FALL OF THE ROMAN EMPIRE.

CHAP. II.

ftill limited to a very fhort period; in France, for example, to nine years from the commencement of the leafe. It has in that country, indeed, been lately extended to twenty feven, a period ftill too fhort to encourage the tenant to make the moft important improvements. The proprietors of land were anciently the legiflators of every part of Europe. The laws relating to land, therefore, were all calculated for what they fuppofed the intereft of the proprietor. It was for his intereft, they had imagined, that no leafe granted by any of his predeceffors fhould hinder him from enjoying, during a long term of years, the full value of his land. Avarice and injuftice are always fhort-fighted, and they did not forefee how much this regulation muft obftruct improvement, and thereby hurt in the long-run the real intereft of the landlord.

The farmers too, befides paying the rent, were anciently, it was fuppofed, bound to perform a great number of fervices to the landlord, which were feldom either fpecified in the leafe, or regulated by any precife rule, but by the ufe and wont of the manor or barony. Thefe fervices, therefore, being almoft entirely arbitrary, fubjected the tenant to many vexations. In Scotland the abolition of all fervices, not precifely ftipulated in the leafe, has in the courfe of a few years very much altered for the better the condition of the yeomanry of that country.

The public fervices to which the yeomanry were bound, were not lefs arbitrary than the private ones. To make and maintain the high roads,

OF THE DISCOURAGEMENT OF AGRICULTURE

BOOK III.

roads, a fervitude which ftill fubfifts, I believe, every-where, though with different degrees of oppreffion in different countries, was not the only one. When the king's troops, when his houfehold or his officers of any kind paffed through any part of the country, the yeomanry were bound to provide them with horfes, carriages, and provifions, at a price regulated by the purveyor. Great Britain is, I believe, the only monarchy in Europe where the oppreffion of purveyance has been entirely abolifhed. It ftill fubfifts in France and Germany.

The public taxes to which they were fubject were as irregular and oppreffive as the fervices. The ancient lords, though extremely unwilling to grant themfelves any pecuniary aid to their fovereign, eafily allowed him to tallage, as they called it, their tenants, and had not knowledge enough to forefee how much this muft in the end affect their own revenue. The taille, as it ftill fubfifts in France, may ferve as an example of thofe ancient tallages. It is a tax upon the fuppofed profits of the farmer, which they eftimate by the ftock that he has upon the farm. It is his intereft, therefore, to appear to have as little as poffible, and confequently to employ as little as poffible in its cultivation, and none in its improvement. Should any ftock happen to accumulate in the hands of a French farmer, the taille is almoft equal to a prohibition of its ever being employed upon the land. This tax befides is fuppofed to difhonour whoever is fubject to it, and to degrade him below, not only the rank of a gen-

AFTER THE FALL OF THE ROMAN EMPIRE. 97

CHAP. II.

a gentleman, but that of a burgher, and whoever rents the lands of another becomes fubject to it. No gentleman, nor even any burgher who has ftock, will fubmit to this degradation. This tax, therefore, not only hinders the ftock. which accumulates upon the land from being employed in its improvement, but drives away all other ftock from it. The ancient tenths and fifteenths, fo ufual in England in former times, feem, fo far as they affected the land, to have been taxes of the fame nature with the taille.

Under all thefe difcouragements, little improvement could be expected from the occupiers of land. That order of people, with all the liberty and fecurity which law can give, muft always improve under great difadvantages. The farmer compared with the proprietor, is as a merchant who trades with borrowed money compared with one who trades with his own. The ftock of both may improve, but that of the one, with only equal good conduct, muft always improve more flowly than that of the other, on account of the large fhare of the profits which is confumed by the intereft of the loan. The lands cultivated by the farmer muft, in the fame manner, with only equal good conduct, be improved more flowly than thofe cultivated by the proprietor; on account of the large fhare of the produce which is confumed in the rent, and which, had the farmer been proprietor, he might have employed in the further improvement of the land. The ftation of a farmer befides is, from the nature of things, inferior to that of a proprietor.

VOL. III.   H.

OF THE DISCOURAGEMENT OF AGRICULTURE

BOOK III.

prietor. Through the greater part of Europe the yeomanry are regarded as an inferior rank of people, even to the better fort of tradefmen and mechanics, and in all parts of Europe to the great merchants and mafter manufacturers. It can feldom happen, therefore, that a man of any confiderable flock fhould quit the fuperior, in order to place himfelf in an inferior flation. Even in the prefent flate of Europe, therefore, little flock is likely to go from any other profeffion to the improvement of land in the way of farming. More does perhaps in Great Britain than in any other country, though even there the great flocks which are, in fome places, employed in farming, have generally been acquired by farming, the trade, perhaps, in which of all others flock is commonly acquired moft flowly. After fmall proprietors, however, rich and great farmers are, in every country, the principal improvers. There are more fuch perhaps in England than in any other European monarchy. In the republican governments of Holland and of Berne in Switzerland, the farmers are faid to be not inferior to thofe of England.

The ancient policy of Europe was, over and above all this, unfavourable to the improvement and cultivation of land, whether carried on by the proprietor or by the farmer; firft, by the general prohibition of the exportation of corn without a fpecial licence, which feems to have been a very univerfal regulation; and fecondly, by the reftraints which were laid upon the inland commerce, not only of corn but of almoft every

other

AFTER THE FALL OF THE ROMAN EMPIRE. .99

other part of the produce of the farm, by the C H A P.
abfurd laws againft engroffers, regraters, and II.
foreftallers, and by the privileges of fairs and
markets. It has already been obferved in what
manner the prohibition of the exportation of
corn, together with fome encouragement given
to the importation of foreign corn, obftructed
the cultivation of ancient Italy, naturally the
moft fertile country in Europe, and at that time
the feat of the greateft empire in the world. To
what degree fuch reftraints upon the inland
commerce of this commodity, joined to the
general prohibition of exportation, muft have
difcouraged the cultivation of countries lefs
fertile, and lefs favourably circumftanced, it is
not perhaps very eafy to imagine.

CHAP. III.

*Of the Rife and Progrefs of Cities and Towns,
after the Fall of the Roman Empire.*

THE inhabitants of cities and towns were, C H A P.
after the fall of the Roman empire, not III.
more favoured than thofe of the country. They
confifted, indeed, of a very different order of
people from the firft inhabitants of the ancient
republics of Greece and Italy. Thefe laft were
compofed chiefly of the proprietors of lands,
among whom the public territory was originally
divided, and who found it convenient to build

H 2

their

OF THE RISE AND PROGRESS OF CITIES

BOOK III.

their houfes in the neighbourhood of one another, and to furround them with a wall, for the fake of common defence. After the fall of the Roman empire, on the contrary, the proprietors of land feem generally to have lived in fortified caftles on their own eftates, and in the midft of their own tenants and dependants. The towns were chiefly inhabited by tradefmen and mechanics, who feem in thofe days to have been of fervile, or very nearly of fervile condition. The privileges which we find granted by ancient charters to the inhabitants of fome of the principal towns in Europe, fufficiently fhew what they were before thofe grants. The people to whom it is granted as a privilege, that they might give away their own daughters in marriage without the confent of their lord, that upon their death their own children, and not their lord, fhould fucceed to their goods, and that they might difpofe of their own effects by will, muft, before thofe grants, have been either altogether, or very nearly in the fame ftate of villanage with the occupiers of land in the country.

They feem, indeed, to have been a very poor, mean fet of people, who ufed to travel about with their goods from place to place, and from fair to fair, like the hawkers and pedlars of the prefent times. In all the different countries of Europe then, in the fame manner as in feveral of the Tartar governments of Afia at prefent, taxes ufed to be levied upon the perfons and goods of travellers, when they paffed through certain manors, when they went over certain bridges, when

they

AFTER THE FALL OF THE ROMAN EMPIRE. 101

they carried about their goods from place to place in a fair, when they erected in it a booth or stall to sell them in. These different taxes were known in England by the names of passage, pontage, lastage, and stallage. Sometimes the king, sometimes a great lord, who had, it seems, upon some occasions, authority to do this, would grant to particular traders, to such particularly as lived in their own demesnes, a general exemption from such taxes. Such traders, though in other respects of servile, or very nearly of servile condition, were upon this account called Free-traders. They in return usually paid to their protector a sort of annual poll-tax. In those days protection was seldom granted without a valuable consideration, and this tax might, perhaps, be considered as compensation for what their patrons might lose by their exemption from other taxes. At first, both those poll-taxes and those exemptions seem to have been altogether personal, and to have affected only particular individuals, during either their lives, or the pleasure of their protectors. In the very imperfect accounts which have been published from Domesday-book, of several of the towns of England, mention is frequently made sometimes of the tax which particular burghers paid, each of them, either to the king, or to some other great lord, for this sort of protection; and sometimes of the general amount only of all those taxes *.

* See Brady's historical treatise of Cities and Burroughs, p. 3, &c.

H 3

But

OF THE RISE AND PROGRESS OF CITIES

BOOK
III.

But how fervile foever may have been originally the condition of the inhabitants of the towns, it appears evidently, that they arrived at liberty and independency much earlier than the occupiers of land in the country. That part of the king's revenue which arofe from fuch poll-taxes in any particular town, ufed commonly to be let in farm, during a term of years for a rent certain, fometimes to the fheriff of the county, and fometimes to other perfons. The burghers themfelves frequently got credit enough to be admitted to farm the revenues of this fort which arofe out of their own town, they becoming jointly and feverally anfwerable for the whole rent *. To let a farm in this manner was quite agreeable to the ufual œconomy of, I believe, the fovereigns of all the different countries of Europe; who ufed frequently to let whole manors to all the tenants of thofe manors, they becoming jointly and feverally anfwerable for the whole rent; but in return being allowed to collect it in their own way, and to pay it into the king's exchequer by the hands of their own bailiff, and being thus altogether freed from the infolence of the king's officers; a circumftance in thofe days regarded as of the greateft importance.

At firft, the farm of the town was probably let to the burghers, in the fame manner as it had been to other farmers, for a term of years only. In procefs of time, however, it feems to

* See Madox Firma Burgi, p. 18. alfo Hiftory of the Exchequer, chap. 10. fect. v. p. 223, firft edition.

have

AFTER THE FALL OF THE ROMAN EMPIRE. 103

have become the general practice to grant it to them in fee, that is for ever, referving a rent certain never afterwards to be augmented. The payment having thus become perpetual, the exemptions, in return, for which it was made, naturally became perpetual too. Thofe exemptions, therefore, ceafed to be perfonal, and could not afterwards be confidered as belonging to individuals as individuals, but as burghers of a particular burgh, which, upon this account, was called a Free burgh, for the fame reafon that they had been called Free-burghers or Free-traders.

Along with this grant, the important privileges above mentioned, that they might give away their own daughters in marriage, that their children fhould fucceed to them, and that they might difpofe of their own effects by will, were generally beftowed upon the burghers of the town to whom it was given. Whether fuch privileges had before been ufually granted along with the freedom of trade, to particular burghers, as individuals, I know not. I reckon it not improbable that they were, though I cannot produce any direct evidence of it. But however this may have been, the principal attributes of villanage and flavery being thus taken away from them, they now, at leaft, became really free in our prefent fenfe of the word Freedom.

Nor was this all. They were generally at the fame time erected into a commonalty or corporation, with the privilege of having magiftrates and a town council of their own, of making

CHAP.
III.

H 4   bye-

OF THE RISE AND PROGRESS OF CITIES

BOOK III.

bye-laws for their own government, of building walls for their own defence, and of reducing all their inhabitants under a fort of military difcipline, by obliging them to watch and ward; that is, as anciently underftood, to guard and defend thofe walls againft all attacks and furprifes by night as well as by day. In England they were generally exempted from fuit to the hundred and county courts; and all fuch pleas as fhould arife among them, the pleas of the crown excepted, were left to the decifion of their own magiftrates. In other countries much greater and more extenfive jurifdictions were frequently granted to them *.

It might, probably, be neceffary to grant to fuch towns as were admitted to farm their own revenues, fome fort of conpulfive jurifdiction to oblige their own citizens to make payment. In thofe diforderly times it might have been extremely inconvenient to have left them to feek this fort of juftice from any other tribunal. But it muft feem extraordinary that the fovereigns of all the different countries of Europe, fhould have exchanged in this manner for a rent certain, never more to be augmented, that branch of their revenue, which was, perhaps, of all others the moft likely to be improved by the natural courfe of things, without either expence or attention of their own: and that they fhould, be-

---

* See Madox Firma Burgi: See alfo Pfeffel in the remarkable event under Frederic II. and his fucceffors of the houfe of Suabia.

fides,

fides, have in this manner voluntarily erected a fort of independent republics in the heart of their own dominions.

In order to underftand this, it muft be remembered, that in thofe days the fovereign of perhaps no country in Europe was able to protect, through the whole extent of his dominions, the weaker part of his fubjects from the oppreffion of the great lords. Thofe whom the law could not protect, and who were not ftrong enough to defend themfelves, were obliged either to have recourfe to the protection of fome great lord, and in order to obtain it to become either his flaves or vaffals; or to enter into a league of mutual defence for the common protection of one another. The inhabitants of cities and burghs, confidered as fingle individuals, had no power to defend themfelves; but by entering into a league of mutual defence with their neighbours, they were capable of making no contemptible refiftance. The lords defpifed the burghers, whom they confidered not only as of a different order, but as a parcel of emancipated flaves, almoft of a different fpecies from themfelves. The wealth of the burghers never failed to provoke their envy and indignation, and they plundered them upon every occafion without mercy or remorfe. The burghers naturally hated and feared the lords. The king hated and feared them too; but though perhaps he might defpife, he had no reafon either to hate or fear the burghers. Mutual intereft, therefore, difpofed them to fupport the king, and the king to fupport them

OF THE RISE AND PROGRESS OF CITIES

BOOK III.

them againſt the lords. They were the enemies of his enemies, and it was his intereſt to render them as ſecure and independent of thoſe enemies as he could. By granting them magiſtrates of their own, the privilege of making bye-laws for their own government, that of building walls for their own defence, and that of reducing all their inhabitants under a ſort of military diſcipline, he gave them all the means of ſecurity and independency of the barons which it was in his power to beſtow. Without the eſtabliſhment of ſome regular government of this kind, without ſome authority to compel their inhabitants to act according to ſome certain plan or ſyſtem, no voluntary league of mutual defence could either have afforded them any permanent ſecurity, or have enabled them to give the king any conſiderable ſupport. By granting them the farm of their town in fee, he took away from thoſe whom he wiſhed to have for his friends, and if one may ſay ſo, for his allies, all ground of jealouſy and ſuſpicion that he was ever afterwards to oppreſs them, either by raiſing the farm rent of their town, or by granting it to ſome other farmer.

The princes who lived upon the worſt terms with their barons, ſeem accordingly to have been the moſt liberal in grants of this kind to their burghs. King John of England, for example, appears to have been a moſt munificent benefactor to his towns*. Philip the Firſt of France loſt all authority over his barons. Towards the

* See Madox.

end

AFTER THE FALL OF THE ROMAN EMPIRE. 107

end of his reign, his fon Lewis, known after- CHAP.
wards by the name of Lewis the Fat, confulted, III.
according to Father Daniel, with the bifhops of
the royal demefnes, concerning the moft proper
means of reftraining the violence of the great
lords. Their advice confifted of two different
propofals. One was to erect a new order of jurifdiction, by eftablifhing magiftrates and a town
council in every confiderable town of his demefnes. The other was to form a new militia, by
making the inhabitants of thofe towns, under the
command of their own magiftrates, march out
upon proper occafions to the affiftance of the
king. It is from this period, according to the
French antiquarians, that we are to date the inftitution of the magiftrates and councils of cities
in France. It was during the unprofperous
reigns of the princes of the houfe of Suabia that
the greater part of the free towns of Germany
received the firft grants of their privileges, and
that the famous Hanfeatic league firft became
formidable *.

The militia of the cities feems, in thofe times,
not to have been inferior to that of the country,
and as they could be more readily affembled
upon any fudden occafion, they frequently had
the advantage in their difputes with the neighbouring lords. In countries, fuch as Italy and
Switzerland, in which, on account either of
their diftance from the principal feat of government, of the natural ftrength of the country

* See Pfeffel.

itfelf,

108   OF THE RISE AND PROGRESS OF CITIES

B O O K itſelf, or of ſome other reaſon, the ſovereign
III.   came to loſe the whole of his authority, the
cities generally became independent republics,
and conquered all the nobility in their neighbourhood; obliging them to pull down their
caſtles in the country, and to live, like other
peaceable inhabitants, in the city. This is the
ſhort hiſtory of the republic of Berne, as well as
of ſeveral other cities in Switzerland. If you
except Venice, for of that city the hiſtory is
ſomewhat different, it is the hiſtory of all the
conſiderable Italian republics, of which ſo great
a number aroſe and periſhed, between the end of
the twelfth and the beginning of the ſixteenth
century.

In countries ſuch as France or England, where
the authority of the ſovereign, though frequently
very low, never was deſtroyed altogether, the
cities had no opportunity of becoming entirely
independent. They became, however, ſo conſiderable, that the ſovereign could impoſe no tax
upon them, beſides the ſtated farm-rent of the
town, without their own conſent. They were,
therefore, called upon to ſend deputies to the
general aſſembly of the ſtates of the kingdom,
where they might join with the clergy and the
barons in granting, upon urgent occaſions, ſome
extraordinary aid to the king. Being generally
too more favourable to his power, their deputies
ſeem, ſometimes, to have been employed by him
as a counter-balance in thoſe aſſemblies to the
authority of the great lords. Hence the origin
of

of the reprefentation of burghs in the ftates ge- CHAP.
neral of all the great monarchies in Europe. III.

Order and good government, and along with
them the liberty and fecurity of individuals,
were, in this manner, eftablifhed in cities, at a
time when the occupiers of land in the country
were expofed to every fort of violence. But men
in this defencelefs ftate naturally content themfelves with their neceffary fubfiftence; becaufe
to acquire more might only tempt the injuftice
of their oppreffors. On the contrary, when they
are fecure of enjoying the fruits of their induftry,
they naturally exert it to better their condition,
and to acquire not only the neceffaries, but the
conveniencies and elegancies of life. That induftry, therefore, which aims at fomething more
than neceffary fubfiftence, was eftablifhed in
cities long before it was commonly practifed by
the occupiers of land in the country. If in the
hands of a poor cultivator, oppreffed with the
fervitude of villanage, fome little ftock fhould
accumulate, he would naturally conceal it with
great care from his mafter, to whom it would
otherwife have belonged, and take the firft opportunity of running away to a town. The law
was at that time fo indulgent to the inhabitants
of towns, and fo defirous of diminifhing the authority of the lords over thofe of the country,
that if he could conceal himfelf there from the
purfuit of his lord for a year, he was free for
ever. Whatever ftock, therefore, accumulated
in the hands of the induftrious part of the inhabitants of the country, naturally took refuge in
cities,

OF THE RISE AND PROGRESS OF CITIES

BOOK III. cities, as the only fanctuaries in which it could be fecure to the perfon that acquired it.

The inhabitants of a city, it is true, muft always ultimately derive their fubfiftence, and the whole materials and means of their induftry, from the country. But thofe of a city fituated near either the fea-coaft or the banks of a navigable river, are not neceffarily confined to derive them from the country in their neighbourhood. They have a much wider range, and may draw them from the moft remote corners of the world, either in exchange for the manufactured produce of their own induftry, or by performing the office of carriers between diftant countries, and exchanging the produce of one for that of another. A city might in this manner grow up to great wealth and fplendor, while not only the country in its neighbourhood, but all thofe to which it traded, were in poverty and wretchednefs. Each of thofe countries, perhaps, taken fingly, could afford it but a fmall part, either of its fubfiftence, or of its employment; but all of them taken together could afford it both a great fubfiftence and a great employment. There were, however, within the narrow circle of the commerce of thofe times, fome countries that were opulent and induftrious. Such was the Greek empire as long as it fubfifted, and that of the Saracens during the reigns of the Abaffides. Such too was Egypt till it was conquered by the Turks, fome part of the coaft of Barbary, and all thofe provinces of Spain which were under the government of the Moors.

The

The cities of Italy feem to have been the firſt in Europe which were raiſed by commerce to any confiderable degree of opulence. Italy lay in the centre of what was at that time the improved and civilized part of the world. The cruſades too, though, by the great waſte of ſtock and deſtruction of inhabitants which they occaſioned, they muſt neceſſarily have retarded the progreſs of the greater part of Europe, were extremely favourable to that of ſome Italian cities. The great armies which marched from all parts to the conqueſt of the Holy Land, gave extraordinary encouragement to the ſhipping of Venice, Genoa, and Piſa, ſometimes in tranſporting them thither, and always in ſupplying them with proviſions. They were the commiſſaries, if one may ſay ſo, of thoſe armies; and the moſt deſtructive frenzy that ever befel the European nations, was a ſource of opulence to thoſe republics.

The inhabitants of trading cities, by importing the improved manufactures and expenſive luxuries of richer countries, afforded ſome food to the vanity of the great proprietors, who eagerly purchaſed them with great quantities of the rude produce of their own lands. The commerce of a great part of Europe in thoſe times, accordingly, conſiſted chiefly in the exchange of their own rude, for the manufactured produce of more civilized nations. Thus the wool of England uſed to be exchanged for the wines of France, and the fine cloths of Flanders, in the ſame manner as the corn in Poland is at this day

OF THE RISE AND PROGRESS OF CITIES.

BOOK III.

day exchanged for the wines and brandies of France, and for the filks and velvets of France and Italy.

A tafte for the finer and more improved manufactures, was in this manner introduced by foreign commerce into countries where no fuch works were carried on. But when this tafte became fo general as to occafion a confiderable demand, the merchants, in order to fave the expence of carriage, naturally endeavoured to eftablifh fome manufactures of the fame kind in their own country. Hence the origin of the firft manufactures for diftant fale that feem to have been eftablifhed in the weftern provinces of Europe, after the fall of the Roman empire.

No large country, it muft be obferved, ever did or could fubfift without fome fort of manufactures being carried on in it; and when it is faid of any fuch country that it has no manufactures, it muft always be underftood of the finer and more improved, or of fuch as are fit for diftant fale. In every large country, both the clothing and houfhold furniture of the far greater part of the people, are the produce of their own induftry. This is even more univerfally the cafe in thofe poor countries which are commonly faid to have no manufactures, than in thofe rich ones that are faid to abound in them. In the latter, you will generally find, both in the clothes and houfhold furniture of the loweft rank of people, a much greater proportion of foreign productions than in the former.

3

Thofe

AFTER THE FALL OF THE ROMAN EMPIRE. 113

CHAP. III.

Those manufactures which are fit for distant sale, seem to have been introduced into different countries in two different ways.

Sometimes they have been introduced, in the manner above mentioned, by the violent operation, if one may say so, of the stocks of particular merchants and undertakers, who established them in imitation of some foreign manufactures of the same kind. Such manufactures, therefore, are the offspring of foreign commerce, and such seem to have been the ancient manufactures of silks, velvets, and brocades, which flourished in Lucca, during the thirteenth century. They were banished from thence by the tyranny of one of Machiavel's heroes, Castruccio Castracani. In 1310, nine hundred families were driven out of Lucca, of whom thirty-one retired to Venice, and offered to introduce there the silk manufacture*. Their offer was accepted; many privileges were conferred upon them, and they began the manufacture with three hundred workmen. Such too seem to have been the manufactures of fine cloths that anciently flourished in Flanders, and which were introduced into England in the beginning of the reign of Elizabeth; and such are the present silk manufactures of Lyons and Spital-fields. Manufactures introduced in this manner are generally employed upon foreign materials, being imitations of foreign manufactures. When the Venetian manu-

* See Sandi Istoria Civile de Vinezia, Part 2. vol. i. page 247, and 256.

VOL. III.   I   facture

OF THE RISE AND PROGRESS OF CITIES

BOOK III.

facture was firſt eſtabliſhed, the materials were all brought from Sicily and the Levant. The more ancient manufacture of Lucca was likewiſe carried on with foreign materials. The cultivation of mulberry trees, and the breeding of ſilk-worms, ſeem not to have been common in the northern parts of Italy before the ſixteenth century. Thoſe arts were not introduced into France till the reign of Charles IX. The manufactures of Flanders were carried on chiefly with Spaniſh and Engliſh wool. Spaniſh wool was the material, not of the firſt woollen manufacture of England, but of the firſt that was fit for diſtant ſale. More than one half the materials of the Lyons manufacture is at this day foreign ſilk; when it was firſt eſtabliſhed, the whole or very nearly the whole was ſo. No part of the materials of the Spital-fields manufacture is ever likely to be the produce of England. The feat of ſuch manufactures, as they are generally introduced by the ſcheme and project of a few individuals, is ſometimes eſtabliſhed in a maritime city, and ſometimes in an inland town, according as their intereſt, judgment or caprice happen to determine.

At other times manufactures for diſtant ſale grow up naturally, and as it were of their own accord, by the gradual refinement of thoſe houſhold and coarſer manufactures which muſt at all times be carried on even in the pooreſt and rudeſt countries. Such manufactures are generally employed upon the materials which the country produces, and they ſeem frequently to have

AFTER THE FALL OF THE ROMAN EMPIRE. 115

have been firſt refined and improved in ſuch inland countries as were, not indeed at a very
great, but at a conſiderable diſtance from the ſea
coaſt, and ſometimes even from all water carriage. An inland country naturally fertile and
eaſily cultivated, produces a great ſurplus of proviſions beyond what is neceſſary for maintaining
the cultivators, and on account of the expence of
land carriage, and inconveniency of river navigation, it may frequently be difficult to ſend this
ſurplus abroad. Abundance, therefore, renders proviſions cheap, and encourages a great
number of workmen to ſettle in the neighbourhood, who find that their induſtry can there procure them more of the neceſſaries and conveniences of life than in other places. They work
up the materials of manufacture which the land
produces, and exchange their finiſhed work,
or what is the ſame thing the price of it, for
more materials and proviſions. They give a
new value to the ſurplus part of the rude produce,
by ſaving the expence of carrying it to the water
ſide, or to ſome diſtant market; and they furniſh
the cultivators with ſomething in exchange for
it that is either uſeful or agreeable to them, upon eaſier terms than they could have obtained
it before. The cultivators get a better price for
their ſurplus produce, and can purchaſe cheaper
other conveniences which they have occaſion
for. They are thus both encouraged and enabled to increaſe this ſurplus produce by a further
improvement and better cultivation of the land;
and as the fertility of the land had given birth

OF THE RISE AND PROGRESS OF CITIES

BOOK
III.

to the manufacture, fo the progrefs of the manufacture re-acts upon the land, and increafes ftill further its fertility. The manufactures firft fupply the neighbourhood, and afterwards, as their work improves and refines, more diftant markets. For though neither the rude produce, nor even the coarfe manufacture, could, without the greateft difficulty, fupport the expence of a confiderable land carriage, the refined and improved manufacture eafily may. In a fmall bulk it frequently contains the price of a great quantity of rude produce. A piece of fine cloth, for example, which weighs only eighty pounds, contains in it, the price, not only of eighty pounds weight of wool, but fometimes of feveral thoufand weight of corn, the maintenance of the different working people, and of their immediate employers. The corn, which could with difficulty have been carried abroad in its own fhape, is in this manner virtually exported in that of the complete manufacture, and may eafily be fent to the remoteft corners of the world. In this manner have grown up naturally, and as it were of their own accord, the manufactures of Leeds, Halifax, Sheffield, Birmingham, and Wolverhampton. Such manufactures are the offspring of agriculture. In the modern hiftory of Europe, their extenfion and improvement have generally been pofterior to thofe which were the offspring of foreign commerce. England was noted for the manufacture of fine cloths made of Spanifh wool, more than a century before any of thofe which now flourifh in the places above

mentioned

-mentioned were fit for foreign fale. The extenfion and improvement of thefe laft could not take
place but in confequence of the extenfion and improvement of agriculture, the laft and greateft
effect of foreign commerce, and of the manufactures immediately introduced by it, and which
I fhall now proceed to explain.

CHAP. IV.

How the Commerce of the Towns contributed to the Improvement of the Country.

THE increafe and riches of commercial and
manufacturing towns, contributed to the
improvement and cultivation of the countries to
which they belonged, in three different ways.

Firft, by affording a great and ready market
for the rude produce of the country, they gave
encouragement to its cultivation and further improvement. This benefit was not even confined
to the countries in which they were fituated, but
extended more or lefs to all thofe with which
they had any dealings. To all of them they
afforded a market for fome part either of their
rude or manufactured produce, and confequently
gave fome encouragement to the induftry and
improvement of all. Their own country, however, on account of its neighbourhood, neceffarily derived the greateft benefit from this market.

118   HOW THE COMMERCE OF TOWNS

BOOK Its rude produce being charged with lefs car-
III. riage, the traders could pay the growers a better
price for it, and yet afford it as cheap to the confumers as that of more diftant countries.

Secondly, the wealth acquired by the inhabitants of cities was frequently employed in purchafing fuch lands as were to be fold, of which a
great part would frequently be uncultivated.
Merchants are commonly ambitious of becoming
country gentlemen, and when they do, they are
generally the beft of all improvers. A merchant
is accuftomed to employ his money chiefly in
profitable projects; whereas a mere country gentleman is accuftomed to employ it chiefly in
expence. The one often fees his money go from
him and return to him again with a profit: the
other, when once he parts with it, very feldom
expects to fee any more of it. Thofe different
habits naturally affect their temper and difpofition in every fort of bufinefs. A merchant is
commonly a bold; a country gentleman, a timid
undertaker. The one is not afraid to lay out at
once a large capital upon the improvement of
his land, when he has a probable profpect of
raifing the value of it in proportion to the expence. The other, if he has any capital, which
is not always the cafe, feldom ventures to employ it in this manner. If he improves at all, it
is commonly not with a capital, but with what
he can fave out of his annual revenue. Whoever has had the fortune to live in a mercantile
town fituated in an unimproved country, muft
have frequently obferved how much more fpirited
the

IMPROVED THE COUNTRY.

the operations of merchants were in this way, C H A P.
than thofe of mere country gentlemen. The IV.
habits, befides, of order, œconomy and attention, to which mercantile bufinefs naturally
forms a merchant, render him much fitter to
execute, with profit and fucceſs, any project of
improvement.

Thirdly, and laſtly, commerce and manufactures gradually introduced order and good government, and with them, the liberty and fecurity of individuals, among the inhabitants of the
country, who had before lived almoſt in a continual ſtate of war with their neighbours, and of
fervile dependency upon their fuperiors. This,
though it has been the leaſt obferved, is by far
the moſt important of all their effects. Mr.
Hume is the only writer who, fo far as I know,
has hitherto taken notice of it.

In a country which has neither foreign commerce, nor any of the finer manufactures, a great
proprietor, having nothing for which he can exchange the greater part of the produce of his
lands which is over and above the maintenance
of the cultivators, confumes the whole in ruſtic
hofpitality at home. If this furplus produce is
fufficient to maintain a hundred or a thoufand
men, he can make ufe of it in no other way than
by maintaining a hundred or a thoufand men.
He is at all times, therefore, furrounded with a
multitude of retainers and dependants, who having no equivalent to give in return for their maintenance, but being fed entirely by his bounty,
muſt obey him, for the fame reafon that fol-

I 4   diers

HOW THE COMMERCE OF TOWNS

BOOK III.

diers muft obey the prince who pays them. Before the extenfion of commerce and manufactures in Europe, the hofpitality of the rich and the great, from the fovereign down to the fmalleft baron, exceeded every thing which in the prefent times we can eafily form a notion of. Weftminfter hall was the dining-room of William Rufus, and might frequently, perhaps, not be too large for his company. It was reckoned a piece of magnificence in Thomas Becket, that he ftrowed the floor of his hall with clean hay or rufhes in the feafon, in order that the knights and fquires, who could not get feats, might not fpoil their fine clothes when they fat down on the floor to eat their dinner. The great Earl of Warwick is faid to have entertained every day at his different manors, thirty thoufand people; and though the number here may have been exaggerated, it muft, however, have been very great to admit of fuch exaggeration. A hofpitality nearly of the fame kind was exercifed not many years ago in many different parts of the Highlands of Scotland. It feems to be common in all nations to whom commerce and manufactures are little known. I have feen, fays Doctor Pocock, an Arabian chief dine in the ftreets of a town where he had come to fell his cattle, and invite all paffengers, even common beggars, to fit down with him and partake of his banquet.

The occupiers of land were in every refpect as dependent upon the great proprietor as his retainers. Even fuch of them as were not in a ftate of villanage, were tenants at will, who paid

a rent

a rent in no refpect equivalent to the fubfiftence which the land afforded them. A crown, half a crown, a fheep, a lamb, was fome years ago in the Highlands of Scotland a common rent for lands which maintained a family. In fome places it is fo at this day; nor will money at prefent purchafe a greater quantity of commodities there than in other places. In a country where the furplus produce of a large eftate muft be con⸗ fumed upon the eftate itfelf, it will frequently be more convenient for the proprietor, that part of it be confumed at a diftance from his own houfe, provided they who confume it are as dependent upon him as either his retainers or his menial fervants. He is thereby faved from the embar⸗ raffment of either too large a company or too large a family. A tenant at will, who poffeffes land fufficient to maintain his family for little more than a quit-rent, is as dependent upon the proprietor as any fervant or retainer whatever, and muft obey him with as little referve. Such a proprietor, as he feeds his fervants and retain⸗ ers at his own houfe, fo he feeds his tenants at their houfes. The fubfiftence of both is derived from his bounty, and its continuance depends upon his good pleafure.

Upon the authority which the great proprie⸗ tors neceffarily had in fuch a ftate of things over their tenants and retainers, was founded the power of the ancient barons. They neceffarily became the judges in peace, and the leaders in war, of all who dwelt upon their eftates. They could maintain order and execute the law within their refpective

HOW THE COMMERCE OF TOWNS

BOOK III.

refpective demefnes, becaufe each of them could there turn the whole force of all the inhabitants againft the injuftice of any one. No other perfon had fufficient authority to do this. The king in particular had not. In thofe ancient times he was little more than the greateft proprietor in his dominions, to whom, for the fake of common defence againft their common enemies, the other great proprietors paid certain refpects. To have enforced payment of a fmall debt within the lands of a great proprietor, where all the inhabitants were armed and accuftomed to ftand by one another, would have coft the king, had he attempted it by his own authority, almoft the fame effort as to extinguifh a civil war. He was, therefore, obliged to abandon the adminiftration of juftice through the greater part of the country, to thofe who were capable of adminiftering it; and for the fame reafon to leave the command of the country militia to thofe whom that militia would obey.

It is a miftake to imagine that thofe territorial jurifdictions took their origin from the feudal law. Not only the higheft jurifdictions both civil and criminal, but the power of levying troops, of coining money, and even that of making byelaws for the government of their own people, were all rights poffeffed allodially by the great proprietors of land feveral centuries before even the name of the feudal law was known in Europe. The authority and jurifdiction of the Saxon lords in England, appear to have been as great before the conqueft, as that of any of the Norman lords

IMPROVED THE COUNTRY.

lords after it. But the feudal law is not fuppofed to have become the common law of England till after the conqueft. That the moft extenfive authority and jurifdictions were poffeffed by the great lords in France allodially, long before the feudal law was introduced into that country, is a matter of fact that admits of no doubt. That authority and thofe jurifdictions all neceffarily flowed from the ftate of property and manners juft now defcribed. Without remounting to the remote antiquities of either the French or Englifh monarchies, we may find in much later times many proofs that fuch effects muft always flow from fuch caufes. It is not thirty years ago fince Mr. Cameron of Lochiel, a gentleman of Lochabar in Scotland, without any legal warrant whatever, not being what was then called a lord of regality, nor even a tenant in chief, but a vaffal of the Duke of Argyle, and without being fo much as a juftice of peace, ufed, notwithftanding, to exercife the higheft criminal jurifdiction over his own people. He is faid to have done fo with great equity, though without any of the formalities of juftice; and it is not improbable that the ftate of that part of the country at that time made it neceffary for him to affume this authority in order to maintain the public peace. That gentleman, whofe rent never exceeded five hundred pounds a year, carried, in 1745, eight hundred of his own people into the rebellion with him,

The

HOW THE COMMERCE OF TOWNS

BOOK III.

The introduction of the feudal law, fo far from extending, may be regarded as an attempt to moderate the authority of the great allodial lords. It eftablifhed a regular fubordination, accompanied with a long train of fervices and duties, from the king down to the fmalleft proprietor. During the minority of the proprietor, the rent, together with the management of his lands, fell into the hands of his immediate fuperior, and, confequently, thofe of all great proprietors into the hands of the king, who was charged with the maintenance and education of the pupil, and who, from his authority as guardian, was fuppofed to have a right of difpofing of him in marriage, provided it was in a manner not unfuitable to his rank. But though this inftitution neceffarily tended to ftrengthen the authority of the king, and to weaken that of the great proprietors, it could not do either fufficiently for eftablifhing order and good government among the inhabitants of the country; becaufe it could not alter fufficiently that ftate of property and manners from which the diforders arofe. The authority of government ftill continued to be, as before, too weak in the head and too ftrong in the inferior members, and the exceffive ftrength of the inferior members was the caufe of the weaknefs of the head. After the inftitution of feudal fubordination, the king was as incapable of reftraining the violence of the great lords as before. They ftill continued to make war according to their own difcretion, almoft

IMPROVED THE COUNTRY.

almoft continually upon one another, and very C H A P. IV.
frequently upon the king; and the open country
ftill continued to be a fcene of violence, rapine,
and diforder.

But what all the violence of the feudal inftitutions could never have effected, the filent and
infenfible operation of foreign commerce and manufactures gradually brought about. Thefe gradually furnifhed the great proprietors with fomething for which they could exchange the whole
furplus produce of their lands, and which they
could confume themfelves without fharing it
either with tenants or retainers. All for ourfelves, and nothing for other people, feems, in
every age of the world, to have been the vile
maxim of the mafters of mankind. As foon,
therefore, as they could find a method of con-
fuming the whole value of their rents themfelves,
they had no difpofition to fhare them with any
other perfons. For a pair of dimond buckles
perhaps, or for fomething as frivolous and ufelefs, they exchanged the maintenance, or what
is the fame thing, the price of the maintenance
of a thoufand men for a year, and with it the
whole weight and authority which it could give
them. The buckles, however, were to be all
their own, and no other human creature was to
have any fhare of them; whereas in the more
ancient method of expence they muft have fhared
with at leaft a thoufand people. With the judges
that were to determine the preference, this difference was perfectly decifive; and thus, for the
gratification of the moft childifh, the meaneft and

4   the

HOW THE COMMERCE OF TOWNS

BOOK
III.

the moft fordid of all vanities, they gradually bartered their whole power and authority.

In a country where there is no foreign commerce, nor any of the finer manufactures, a man of ten thoufand a year cannot well employ his revenue in any other way than in maintaining, perhaps, a thoufand families, who are all of them neceffarily at his command. In the prefent ftate of Europe, a man of ten thoufand a year can fpend his whole revenue, and he generally does fo, without directly maintaining twenty people, or being able to command more than ten footmen not worth the commanding. Indirectly, perhaps, he maintains as great or even a greater number of people than he could have done by the ancient method of expence. For though the quantity of precious productions for which he exchanges his whole revenue be very fmall, the number of workmen employed in collecting and preparing it, muft neceffarily have been very great. Its great price generally arifes from the wages of their labour, and the profits of all their immediate employers. By paying that price he indirectly pays all thofe wages and profits, and thus indirectly contributes to the maintenance of all the workmen and their employers. He generally contributes, however, but a very fmall proportion to that of each, to very few perhaps a tenth, to many not a hundredth, and to fome not a thoufandth, nor even a ten thoufandth part of their whole annual maintenance. Though he contributes, therefore, to the maintenance of them all, they are all more or lefs independent of

IMPROVED THE COUNTRY.

127

CHAP.
IV.

of him, becaufe generally they can all be maintained without him.

When the great proprietors of land fpend their rents in maintaining their tenants and retainers, each of them maintains entirely all his own tenants and all his own retainers. But when they fpend them in maintaining tradefmen and artificers, they may, all of them, taken together, perhaps, maintain as great, or, on account of the wafte which attends ruftic hofpitality, a greater number of people than before. Each of them, however, taken fingly, contributes often but a very fmall fhare to the maintenance of any individual of this greater number. Each tradefman or artificer derives his fubfiftence from the employment, not of one, but of a hundred or a thoufand different cuftomers. Though in fome meafure obliged to them all, therefore, he is not abfolutely dependent upon any one of them.

The perfonal expence of the great proprietors having in this manner gradually increafed, it was impoffible that the number of their retainers fhould not as gradually diminifh, till they were at laft difmiffed altogether. The fame caufe gradually led them to difmifs the unneceffary part of their tenants. Farms were enlarged, and the occupiers of land, notwithftanding the complaints of depopulation, reduced to the number neceffary for cultivating it, according to the imperfect ftate of cultivation and improvement in thofe times. By the removal of the unneceffary mouths, and by exacting from the farmer the full value of the farm, a greater furplus, or what

is

BOOK III. is the fame thing, the price of a greater furplus, was obtained for the proprietor, which the merchants and manufacturers foon furnifhed him with a method of fpending upon his own perfon in the fame manner as he had done the reft. The fame caufe continuing to operate, he was defirous to raife his rents above what his lands, in the actual ftate of their improvement, could afford. His tenants could agree to this upon one condition only, that they fhould be fecured in their poffeffion, for fuch a term of years as might give them time to recover with profit whatever they fhould lay out in the further improvement of the land. The expenfive vanity of the landlord made him willing to accept of this condition; and hence the origin of long leafes.

Even a tenant at will, who pays the full value of the land, is not altogether dependent upon the landlord. The pecuniary advantages which they receive from one another, are mutual and equal, and fuch a tenant will expofe neither his life nor his fortune in the fervice of the proprietor. But if he has a leafe for a long term of years, he is altogether independent; and his landlord muft not expect from him even the moft trifling fervice beyond what is either exprefsly ftipulated in the leafe, or impofed upon him by the common and known law of the country.

The tenants having in this manner become independent, and the retainers being difmiffed, the great proprietors were no longer capable of interrupting the regular execution of juftice, or

of

IMPROVED THE COUNTRY.

CHAP. IV.

of difturbing the peace of the country. Having fold their birth-right, not like Efau for a mefs of pottage in time of hunger and neceffity, but in the wantonnefs of plenty, for trinkets and baubles, fitter to be the play-things of children than the ferious purfuits of men, they became as infignificant as any fubftantial burgher or tradef-man in a city. A regular government was efta-blifhed in the country as well as in the city, nobody having fufficient power to difturb its operations in the one, any more than in the other.

It does not, perhaps, relate to the prefent fubject, but I cannot help remarking it, that very old families, fuch as have poffeffed fome confiderable eftate from father to fon for many fucceffive generations, are very rare in commer-cial countries. In countries which have little commerce, on the contrary, fuch as Wales or the Highlands of Scotland, they are very com-mon. The Arabian hiftories feem to be all full of genealogies, and there is a hiftory written by a Tartar Khan, which has been tranflated into feveral European languages, and which contains fcarce any thing elfe; a proof that ancient fami-lies are very common among thofe nations. In countries where a rich man can fpend his revenue in no other way than by maintaining as many people as it can maintain, he is not apt to run out, and his benevolence it feems is feldom fo violent as to attempt to maintain more than he can afford. But where he can fpend the greateft revenue upon his own perfon, he frequently has

VOL. III.   K   no

HOW THE COMMERCE OF TOWNS

BOOK III.

no bounds to his expence, becaufe he frequently has no bounds to his vanity, or to his affection for his own perfon. In commercial countries, therefore, riches, in fpite of the moft violent regulations of law to prevent their diffipation, very feldom remain long in the fame family. Among fimple nations, on the contrary, they frequently do without any regulations of law: for among nations of fhepherds, fuch as the Tartars and Arabs, the confumable nature of their property neceffarily renders all fuch regulations impoffible.

A revolution of the greateft importance to the public happinefs, was in this manner brought about by two different orders of people, who had not the leaft intention to ferve the public. To gratify the moft childifh vanity was the fole motive of the great proprietors. The merchants and artificers, much lefs ridiculous, acted merely from a view to their own intereft, and in purfuit of their own pedlar principle of turning a penny wherever a penny was to be got. Neither of them had either knowledge or forefight of that great revolution which the folly of the one, and the induftry of the other, was gradually bringing about.

It is thus that through the greater part of Europe the commerce and manufactures of cities, inftead of being the effect, have been the caufe and occafion of the improvement and cultivation of the country.

This order, however, being contrary to the natural courfe of things, is neceffarily both flow and uncertain. Compare the flow progrefs of

3   thofe

thofe European countries of which the wealth CHAP.
depends very much upon their commerce and IV.
manufactures, with the rapid advances of our
North American colonies, of which the wealth
is founded altogether in agriculture. Through
the greater part of Europe, the number of inhabitants is not fuppofed to double in lefs than five
hundred years. In feveral of our North American colonies, it is found to double in twenty or
five-and-twenty years. In Europe, the law of
primogeniture, and perpetuities of different
kinds, prevent the divifion of great eftates, and
thereby hinder the multiplication of fmall proprietors. A fmall proprietor, however, who knows
every part of his little territory, views it with all
the affection which property, efpecially fmall property, naturally infpires, and who upon that account takes pleafure not only in cultivating but
in adorning it, is generally of all improvers the
moft induftrious, the moft intelligent, and the
moft fuccefsful. The fame regulations, befides,
keep fo much land out of the market, that there
are always more capitals to buy than there is
land to fell, fo that what is fold always fells at a
monopoly price. The rent never pays the intereft of the purchafe-money, and is befides burdened with repairs and other occafiònal charges,
to which the intereft of money is not liable.
To purchafe land is every-where in Europe a
moft unprofitable employment of a fmall capital.
For the fake of the fuperior fecurity, indeed, a
man of moderate circumftances, when he retires
from bufinefs, will fometimes chufe to lay out

K 2 his

his little capital in land. A man of profeffion too, whofe revenue is derived from another fource, often loves to fecure his favings in the fame way. But a young man, who, inftead of applying to trade or to fome profeffion, fhould employ a capital of two or three thoufand pounds in the purchafe and cultivation of a fmall piece of land, might indeed expect to live very happily, and very independently, but muft bid adieu, for ever, to all hope of either great fortune or great illuftration, which by a different employment of his ftock he might have had the fame chance of acquiring with other people. Such a perfon too, though he cannot afpire at being a proprietor, will often difdain to be a farmer. The fmall quantity of land, therefore, which is brought to market, and the high price of what is brought thither, prevents a great number of capitals from being employed in its cultivation and improvement which would otherwife have taken that direction. In North America, on the contrary, fifty or fixty pounds is often found a fufficient ftock to begin a plantation with. The purchafe and improvement of uncultivated land, is there the moft profitable employment of the fmalleft as well as of the greateft capitals, and the moft direct road to all the fortune and illuftration which can be acquired in that country. Such land, indeed, is in North America to be had almoft for nothing, or at a price much below the value of the natural produce; a thing impoffible in Europe, or, indeed, in any country where all lands have long been

private

private property. If landed eftates, however, were divided equally among all the children, upon the death of any proprietor who left a numerous family, the eftate would generally be fold. So much land would come to market, that it could no longer fell at a monopoly price. The free rent of the land would go nearer to pay the intereft of the purchafe-money, and a fmall capital might be employed in purchafing land as profitably as in any other way.

England, on account of the natural fertility of the foil, of the great extent of the fea-coaft in proportion to that of the whole country, and of the many navigable rivers which run through it, and afford the conveniency of water carriage to fome of the moft inland parts of it, is perhaps as well fitted by nature as any large country in Europe, to be the feat of foreign commerce, of manufactures for diftant fale, and of all the improvements which thefe can occafion. From the beginning of the reign of Elizabeth too, the Englifh legiflature has been peculiarly attentive to the interefts of commerce and manufactures, and in reality there is no country in Europe, Holland itfelf not excepted, of which the law is, upon the whole, more favourable to this fort of induftry. Commerce and manufactures have accordingly been continually advancing during all this period. The cultivation and improvement of the country has, no doubt, been gradually advancing too: But it feems to have followed flowly, and at a diftance, the more rapid progrefs of commerce and manufactures. The greater part

HOW THE COMMERCE OF TOWNS

BOOK III. part of the country muft probably have been cultivated before the reign of Elizabeth; and a very great part of it ftill remains uncultivated, and the cultivation of the far greater part, much inferior to what it might be. The law of England, however, favours agriculture not only indirectly by the protection of commerce, but by feveral direct encouragements. Except in times of fcarcity, the exportation of corn is not only free, but encouraged by a bounty. In times of moderate plenty, the importation of foreign corn is loaded with duties that amount to a prohibition. The importation of live cattle, except from Ireland, is prohibited at all times, and it is but of late that it was permitted from thence. Thofe who cultivate the land, therefore, have a monopoly againft their countrymen for the two greateft and moft important articles of land produce, bread and butcher's-meat. Thefe encouragements, though at bottom, perhaps, as I fhall endeavour to fhow hereafter, altogether illufory, fufficiently demonftrate at leaft the good intention of the legiflature to favour agriculture. But what is of much more importance than all of them, the yeomanry of England are rendered as fecure, as independent, and as refpectable as law can make them. No country, therefore, in which the right of primogeniture takes place, which pays tithes, and where perpetuities, though contrary to the fpirit of the law, are admitted in fome cafes, can give more encouragement to agriculture than England. Such, however, notwithftanding, is the ftate of its cultivation.

What

IMPROVED THE COUNTRY.

CHAP. IV.

What would it have been, had the law given no direct encouragement to agriculture befides what arifes indirectly from the progrefs of commerce, and had left the yeomanry in the fame condition as in moft other countries of Europe? It is now more than two hundred years fince the beginning of the reign of Elizabeth, a period as long as the courfe of human profperity ufually endures.

France feems to have had a confiderable fhare of foreign commerce near a century before England was diftinguifhed as a commercial country. The marine of France was confiderable, according to the notions of the times, before the expedition of Charles the VIIIth to Naples. The cultivation and improvement of France, however, is upon the whole, inferior to that of England. The law of the country has never given the fame direct encouragement to agriculture.

The foreign commerce of Spain and Portugal to the other parts of Europe, though chiefly carried on in foreign fhips, is very confiderable. That to their colonies is carried on in their own, and is much greater, on account of the great riches and extent of thofe colonies. But it has never introduced any confiderable manufactures for diftant fale into either of thofe countries, and the greater part of both ftill remains uncultivated. The foreign commerce of Portugal is of older ftanding that that of any great country in Europe, except Italy.

Italy is the only great country of Europe which feems to have been cultivated and improved

K 4   proved

HOW THE COMMERCE OF TOWNS

BOOK III.

proved in every part, by means of foreign commerce and manufactures for diftant fale. Before the invafion of Charles the VIIIth, Italy, according to Guicciardin, was cultivated not lefs in the moft mountainous and barren parts of the country, than in the plaineft and moft fertile. The advantageous fituation of the country, and the great number of independent ftates which at that time fubfifted in it, probably contributed not a little to this general cultivation. It is not impoffible too, notwithftanding this general expreffion of one of the moft judicious and referved of modern hiftorians, that Italy was not at that time better cultivated than England is at prefent.

The capital, however, that is acquired to any country by commerce and manufactures, is all a very precarious and uncertain poffeffion, till fome part of it has been fecured and realized in the cultivation and improvement of its lands. A merchant, it has been faid very properly, is not neceffarily the citizen of any particular country. It is in a great meafure indifferent to him from what place he carries on his trade; and a very trifling difguft will make him remove his capital, and together with it all the induftry which it fupports, from one country to another. No part of it can be faid to belong to any particular country, till it has been fpread as it were over the face of that country, either in buildings, or in the lafting improvement of lands. No veftige now remains of the great wealth, faid to have been poffeffed by the greater part of the Hans towns,

except

IMPROVED THE COUNTRY. 137

except in the obfcure hiftories of the thirteenth C H A P.
and fourteenth centuries. It is even uncertain IV.
where fome of them were fituated, or to what
towns in Europe the Latin names given to fome
of them belong. But though the misfortunes of
Italy in the end of the fifteenth and beginning
of the fixteenth centuries greatly diminifhed the
commerce and manufactures of the cities of
Lombardy and Tufcany, thofe countries ftill
continue to be among the moft populous and
beft cultivated in Europe. The civil wars of
Flanders, and the Spanifh government which
fucceeded them, chafed away the great commerce of Antwerp, Ghent, and Bruges. But
Flanders ftill continues to be one of the richeft,
beft cultivated, and moft populous provinces of
Europe. The ordinary revolutions of war and
government eafily dry up the fources of that
wealth which arifes from commerce only. That
which arifes from the more folid improvements
of agriculture, is much more durable, and cannot
be deftroyed but by thofe more violent con-
vulfions, occafioned by the depredations of
hoftile and barbarous nations, continued for a
century or two together; fuch as thofe that
happened for fome time before and after the
fall of the Roman empire in the weftern provinces of Europe.

(138)

BOOK IV.

OF SYSTEMS OF POLITICAL ŒCONOMY.

INTRODUCTION.

BOOK IV.

Introduct.

POLITICAL œconomy, confidered as a branch of the fcience of a ftatefman or legiflator, propofes two diftinct objects : firft, to provide a plentiful revenue or fubfiftence for the people, or, more properly, to enable them to provide fuch a revenue or fubfiftence for themfelves; and fecondly, to fupply the ftate or commonwealth with a revenue fufficient for the public fervices. It propofes to enrich both the people and the fovereign.

The different progrefs of opulence in different ages and nations, has given occafion to two different fyftems of political œconomy, with regard to enriching the people. The one may be called the fyftem of commerce, the other that of agriculture. I fhall endeavour to explain both as fully and diftinctly as I can, and fhall begin with the fyftem of commerce. It is the modern fyftem, and is beft underftood in our own country and in our own times.

CHAP. I.

Of the Principle of the commercial, or mercantile System.

THAT wealth confifts in money, or in gold and filver, is a popular notion which naturally arifes from the double function of money, as the inftrument of commerce, and as the meafure of value. In confequence of its being the inftrument of commerce, when we have money we can more readily obtain whatever elfe we have cccafion for, than by means of any other commodity. The great affair, we always find, is to get money. When that is obtained, there is no difficulty in making any fubfequent purchafe. In confequence of its being the meafure of value, we eftimate that of all other commodities by the quantity of money which they will exchange for. We fay of a rich man that he is worth a great deal, and of a poor man that he is worth very little money. A frugal man, or a man eager to be rich, is faid to love money; and a carelefs, a generous, or a profufe man, is faid to be indifferent about it. To grow rich is to get money; and wealth and money, in fhort, are, in common language, confidered as in every refpect fynonymous.

A rich country, in the fame manner as a rich man, is fuppofed to be a country abounding in money; and to heap up gold and filver in any

country

OF THE PRINCIPLE OF

BOOK
IV.

country is fuppofed to be the readieft way to enrich it. For fome time after the difcovery of America, the firft enquiry of the Spaniards, when they arrived upon any unknown coaft, ufed to be, if there was any gold or filver to be found in the neighbourhood ? By the information which they received, they judged whether it was worth while to make a fettlement there, or if the country was worth the conquering. Plano Carpino, a monk, fent ambaffador from the King of France to one of the fons of the famous Gengis Khan, fays that the Tartars ufed frequently to afk him, if there was plenty of fheep and oxen in the kingdom of France ? Their enquiry had the fame object with that of the Spaniards. They wanted to know if the country was rich enough to be worth the conquering. Among the Tartars, as among all other nations of fhepherds, who are generally ignorant of the ufe of money, cattle are the inftruments of commerce and the meafures of value. Wealth, therefore, according to them, confifted in cattle, as according to the Spaniards it confifted in gold and filver. Of the two, the Tartar notion, perhaps, was the neareft to the truth.

Mr. Locke remarks a diftinction between money and other moveable goods. All other moveable goods, he fays, are of fo confumable a nature, that the wealth which confifts in them cannot be much depended on, and a nation which abounds in them one year may, without any exportation, but merely by their own wafte and extravagance, be in great want of them the next.

THE MERCANTILE SYSTEM. 141

next. Money, on the contrary, is a steady friend, C H A P. which, though it may travel about from hand to I. hand, yet if it can be kept from going out of the country, is not very liable to be wasted and confumed. Gold and filver, therefore, are, according to him, the most folid and fubstantial part of the moveable wealth of a nation, and to multiply those metals ought, he thinks, upon that account, to be the great object of its political œconomy.

Others admit, that if a nation could be feparated from all the world, it would be of no confequence how much, or how little money circulated in it. The confumable goods which were circulated by means of this money, would only be exchanged for a greater or a fmaller number of pieces; but the real wealth or poverty of the country, they allow, would depend altogether upon the abundance or fcarcity of those confumable goods. But it is otherwife, they think, with countries which have connections with foreign nations, and which are obliged to carry on foreign wars, and to maintain fleets and armies in diftant countries. This, they fay, cannot be done, but by fending abroad money to pay them with; and a nation cannot fend much money abroad, unlefs it has a good deal at home. Every fuch nation, therefore, must endeavour in time of peace to accumulate gold and filver, that, when occafion requires, it may have wherewithal to carry on foreign wars.

In confeqhence of thefe popular notions, all the different nations of Europe have ftudied, though to little purpofe, every poffible means of

2 ac-

OF THE PRINCIPLE OF

BOOK IV.

accumulating gold and filver in their refpective countries. Spain and Portugal, the proprietors of the principal mines which fupply Europe with thofe metals, have either prohibited their exportation under the fevereft penalties, or fubjected it to a confiderable duty. The like prohibition feems anciently to have made a part of the policy of moft other European nations. It is even to be found, where we fhould leaft of all expect to find it, in fome old Scotch acts of parliament, which forbid, under heavy penalties, the carrying gold or filver *forth of the kingdom.* The like policy anciently took place both in France and England.

When thofe countries became commercial, the merchants found this prohibition, upon many occafions, extremely inconvenient. They could frequently buy more advantageoufly with gold and filver than with any other commodity, the foreign goods which they wanted, either to import into their own, or to carry to fome other foreign country. They remonftrated, therefore, againft this prohibition as hurtful to trade.

They reprefented, firft, that the exportation of gold and filver in order to purchafe foreign goods, did not always diminifh the quantity of thofe metals in the kingdom. That, on the contrary, it might frequently increafe that quantity; becaufe, if the confumption of foreign goods was not thereby increafed in the country, thofe goods might be re-exported to foreign countries, and, being there fold for a large profit, might bring back much more treafure

than

THE MERCANTILE SYSTEM. 143

than was originally fent out to purchafe them. Mr. Mun compares this operation of foreign trade to the feed-time and harveft of agriculture. " If we only behold," fays he, " the actions of " the hufbandman in the feed time, when he " cafteth away much good corn into the ground, " we fhall account him rather a madman than a " hufbandman. But when we confider his " labours in the harveft, which is the end of his " endeavours, we fhall find the worth and plenti- " ful increafe of his actions."

They reprefented, fecondly, that this prohibition could not hinder the exportation of gold and filver, which, on account of the fmallnefs of their bulk in proportion to their value, could eafily be fmuggled abroad. That this exportation could only be prevented by a proper attention to, what they called, the balance of trade. That when the country exported to a greater value than it imported, a balance became due to it from foreign nations, which was neceffarily paid to it in gold and filver, and thereby increafed the quantity of thofe metals in the kingdom. But that when it imported to a greater value than it exported, a contrary balance became due to foreign nations, which was neceffarily paid to them in the fame manner, and thereby diminifhed that quantity. That in this cafe, to prohibit the exportation of thofe metals could not prevent it, but only by making it more dangerous, render it more expenfive. That the exchange was thereby turned more againft the country which owed the balance, than it

otherwife

144   OF THE PRINCIPLE OF

BOOK otherwife might have been; the merchant who
IV. purchafed a bill upon the foreign country being
obliged to pay the banker who fold it, not only
for the natural rifk, trouble, and expence of
fending the money thither, but for the extraordinary rifk arifing from the prohibition. But that
the more the exchange was againft any country,
the more the balance of trade became neceffarily
againft it; the money of that country becoming
neceffarily of fo much lefs value, in comparifon
with that of the country to which the balance
was due. That if the exchange between England and Holland, for example, was five per cent.
againft England, it would require a hundred and
five ounces of filver in England to purchafe a
bill for a hundred ounces of filver in Holland:
that a hundred and five ounces of filver in England, therefore, would be worth only a hundred
ounces of filver in Holland, and would purchafe
only a proportionable quantity of Dutch goods;
but that a hundred ounces of filver in Holland,
on the contrary, would be worth a hundred
and five ounces in England, and would purchafe a proportionable quantity of Englifh
goods: that the Englifh goods which were
fold to Holland would be fold fo much cheaper;
and the Dutch goods which were fold to England, fo much dearer, by the difference of the
exchange; that the one would draw fo much
lefs Dutch money to England, and the other
fo much more Englifh money to Holland,
as this difference amounted to: and that the
balance of trade, therefore, would neceffarily be

                                                fo

THE MERCANTILE SYSTEM.

CHAP.
I.

so much more against England, and would require a greater balance of gold and silver to be exported to Holland.

Those arguments were partly solid and partly sophistical. They were solid so far as they asserted that the exportation of gold and silver in trade might frequently be advantageous to the country. They were solid too, in asserting that no prohibition could prevent their exportation, when private people found any advantage in exporting them. But they were sophistical in supposing, that either to preserve or to augment the quantity of those metals required more the attention of government, than to preserve or to augment the quantity of any other useful commodities, which the freedom of trade, without any such attention, never fails to supply in the proper quantity. They were sophistical too, perhaps, in asserting that the high price of exchange necessarily increased, what they called, the unfavourable balance of trade, or occasioned the exportation of a greater quantity of gold and silver. That high price, indeed, was extremely disadvantageous to the merchants who had any money to pay in foreign countries. They paid so much dearer for the bills which their bankers granted them upon those countries. But though the risk arising from the prohibition might occasion some extraordinary expence to the bankers, it would not necessarily carry any more money out of the country. This expence would generally be all laid out in the country, in smuggling the money out of it, and could seldom occasion

VOL. III.   L   the

146 · OF THE PRINCIPLE OF.

BOOK the exportation of a fingle fix-pence beyond the
IV. precife fum drawn for. The high price of
exchange too would naturally difpofe the
merchants to endeavour to make their exports
nearly balance their imports, in order that
they might have this high exchange to pay upon
as fmall a fum as poffible. The high price
of exchange, befides, muft neceffarily have
operated as a tax, in raifing the price of foreign
goods, and thereby diminifhing their confumption. It would tend, therefore, not to increafe,
but to diminifh, what they called, the unfavourable balance of trade, and confequently the
exportation of gold and filver.

Such as they were, however, thofe arguments
convinced the people to whom they were
addreffed. They were addreffed by merchants
to parliaments, and to the councils of princes, to
nobles, and to country gentlemen; by thofe who
were fuppofed to underftand trade, to thofe who
were confcious to themfelves that they knew
nothing about the matter. That foreign trade
enriched the country, experience demonftrated
to the nobles and country gentlemen, as well as
to the merchants; but how, or in what manner,
none of them well knew. The merchants knew
perfectly in what manner it enriched themfelves.
It was their bufinefs to know it. But to know
in what manner it enriched the country, was no
part of their bufinefs. This fubject never came
into their confideration, but when they had occafion to apply to their country for fome change in
the laws relating to foreign trade. In then
became

THE MERCANTILE SYSTEM.

became neceffary to fay fomething about the beneficial effects of foreign trade, and the manner in which thofe effects were obftructed by the laws as they then ftood. To the judges who were to decide the bufinefs, it appeared a moft fatisfactory account of the matter, when they were told that foreign trade brought money into the country, but that the laws in queftion hindered it from bringing fo much as it otherwife would do. Thofe arguments therefore produced the wifhed-for effect. The prohibition of exporting gold and filver was in France and England confined to the coin of thofe refpective countries. The exportation of foreign coin and of bullion was made free. In Holland, and in fome other places, this liberty was extended even to the coin of the country. The attention of government was turned away from guarding againft the exportation of gold and filver, to watch over the balance of trade, as the only caufe which could occafion any augmentation or diminution of thofe metals. From one fruitlefs care it was turned away to another care much more intricate, much more embarraffing, and juft equally fruitlefs. The title of Mun's book, England's Treafure in Foreign Trade, became a fundamental maxim in the political œconomy, not of England only, but of all other commercial countries. The inland or home trade, the moft important of all, the trade in which an equal capital affords the greateft revenue, and creates the greateft employment to the people of the country, was confidered as fubfidiary only to foreign trade. It

CHAP.
I.

neither

BOOK
IV.
neither brought money into the country, it was said, nor carried any out of it. The country therefore could never become either richer or poorer by means of it, except so far as its profperity or decay might indirectly influence the ftate of foreign trade.

A country that has no mines of its own muft undoubtedly draw its gold and filver from foreign countries, in the fame manner as one that has no vineyards of its own muft draw its wines. It does not feem neceffary, however, that the attention of government fhould be more turned towards the one than towards the other object. A country that has wherewithal to buy wine, will always get the wine which it has occafion for; and a country that has wherewithal to buy gold and filver, will never be in want of thofe metals. They are to be bought for a certain price like all other commodities, and as they are the price of all other commodities, fo all other commodities are the price of thofe metals. We truft with perfect fecurity that the freedom of trade, without any attention of government, will always fupply us with the wine which we have occafion for: and we may truft with equal fecurity that it will always fupply us with all the gold and filver which we can afford to purchafe or to employ, either in circulating our commodities, or in other ufes.

The quantity of every commodity which human induftry can either purchafe or produce, naturally regulates itfelf in every country according to the effectual demand, or according to the
demand

THE MERCANTILE SYSTEM, 149

demand of thofe who are willing to pay the whole C H A P.
rent, labour and profits which muft be paid in L.
order to prepare and bring it to market. But no
commodities regulate themfelves more eafily or
more exactly according to this effectual demand
than gold and filver; becaufe, on account of the
fmall bulk and great value of thofe metals, no
commodities can be more eafily tranfported from
one place to another, from the places where they
are cheap, to thofe where they are dear, from the
places where they exceed, to thofe where they
fall fhort of this effectual demand. If there were
in England, for example, an effectual demand
for an additional quantity of gold, a packet-boat
could bring from Lifhon, or from wherever elfe
it was to be had, fifty tuns of gold, which could
be coined into more than five millions of guineas.
But if there were an effectual demand for grain
to the fame value, to import it would require, at
five guineas a tun, a million of tuns of fhipping,
or a thoufand fhips of a thoufand tuns each.
The navy of England would not be fufficient.

When the quantity of gold and filver imported
into any country exceeds the effectual demand,
no vigilance of government can prevent their
exportation. All the fanguinary laws of Spain
and Portugal are not able to keep their gold and
filver at home. The continual importations
from Peru and Brazil exceed the effectual demand
of thofe countries, and fink the price of thofe
metals there below that in the neighbouring
countries. If, on the contrary, in any particular
country their quantity fell fhort of the effectual

L 3 demand,

OF THE PRINCIPLE OF

BOOK IV.

demand, fo as to raife their price above that of the neighbouring countries, the government would have no occafion to take any pains to import them. If it were even to take pains to prevent their importation, it would not be able to effectuate it. Thofe metals, when the Spartans had got wherewithal to purchafe them, broke through all the barriers which the laws of Lycurgus oppofed to their entrance into Lacedemon. All the fanguinary laws of the cuftoms are not able to prevent the importation of the teas of the Dutch and Gottenburgh Eaft India companies; becaufe fomewhat cheaper than thofe of the Britifh company. A pound of tea, however, is about a hundred times the bulk of one of the higheft prices, fixteen fhillings, that is commonly paid for it in filver, and more than two thoufand times the bulk of the fame price in gold, and confequently juft fo many times more difficult to fmuggle.

It is partly owing to the eafy tranfportation of gold and filver from the places where they abound to thofe where they are wanted, that the price of thofe metals does not fluctuate continually like that of the greater part of other commodities, which are hindered by their bulk from fhifting their fituation, when the market happens to be either over or under ftocked with them. The price of thofe metals, indeed, is not altogether exempted from variation, but the changes to which it is liable are generally flow, gradual, and uniform. In Europe, for example, it is fuppofed, without much foundation, perhaps, that,

THE MERCANTILE SYSTEM. 151

that, during the courfe of the prefent and pre- CHAP.
ceding century, they have been conftantly, but I.
gradually, finking in their value, on account of
the continual importations from the Spanifh
Weft Indies. But to make any fudden change
in the price of gold and filver, fo as to raife or
lower at once, fenfibly and remarkably, the
money price of all other commodities, requires
fuch a revolution in commerce as that occafioned
by the difcovery of America.

If, notwithftanding all this, gold and filver
fhould at any time fall fhort in a country which
has wherewithal to purchafe them, there are
more expedients for fupplying their place, than
that of almoft any other commodity. If the
materials of manufacture are wanted, induftry
muft ftop. If provifions are wanted, the people
muft ftarve. But if money is wanted, barter
will fupply its place, though with a good deal of
inconveniency. Buying and felling upon credit,
and the different dealers compenfating their
credits with one another, once a month or once
a year, will fupply it with lefs inconveniency.
A well-regulated paper money will fupply it,
not only without any inconveniency, but, in
fome cafes, with fome advantages. Upon every
account, therefore, the attention of government
never was fo unneceffarily employed, as when
directed to watch over the prefervation or increafe
of the quantity of money in any country.

No complaint, however, is more common than
that of a fcarcity of money. Money, like wine,
muft always be fcarce with thofe who have

L 4 neither

BOOK IV.

neither wherewithal to buy it, nor credit to borrow it. Thofe who have either, will feldom be in want either of the money, or of the wine which they have occafion for. This complaint, however, of the fcarcity of money, is not always confined to improvident fpendthrifts. It is fometimes general through a whole mercantile town, and the country in its neighbourhood. Over-trading is the common caufe of it. Sober men, whofe projects have been difproportioned to their capitals, are as likely to have neither where-withal to buy money, nor credit to borrow it, as prodigals whofe expence has been difpropor-tioned to their revenue. Before their projects can be brought to bear, their ftock is gone, and their credit with it. They run about every-where to borrow money, and every body tells them that they have none to lend. Even fuch general complaints of the fcarcity of money do not always prove that the ufual number of gold and filver pieces are not circulating in the coun-try, but that many people want thofe pieces who have nothing to give for them. When the pro-fits of trade happen to be greater than ordinary, over-trading becomes a general error both among great and fmall dealers. They do not always fend more money abroad than ufual, but they buy upon credit both at home and abroad, an unufual quantity of goods, which they fend to fome diftant market, in hopes that the returns will come in before the demand for payment. The demand comes before the returns, and they have nothing at hand, with which they can either purchafe

THE MERCANTILE SYSTEM.

153

purchase money, or give folid fecurity for borrowing. It is not any fcarcity of gold and filver, but the difficulty which fuch people find in borrowing, and which their creditors find in getting payment, that occafions the general complaint of the fcarcity of money.

It would be too ridiculous to go about ferioufly to prove, that wealth does not confift in money, or in gold and filver; but in what money purchafes, and is valuable only for purchafing. Money, no doubt, makes always a part of the national capital; but it has already been fhown that it generally makes but a fmall part, and always the moft unprofitable part of it.

It is not becaufe wealth confifts more effentially in money than in goods, that the merchant finds it generally more eafy to buy goods with money, than to buy money with goods; but becaufe money is the known and eftablifhed inftrument of commerce, for which every thing is readily given in exchange, but which is not always with equal readinefs to be got in exchange for every thing. The greater part of goods befides are more perifhable than money, and he may frequently fuftain a much greater lofs by keeping them. When his goods are upon hand too, he is more liable to fuch demands for money as he may not be able to anfwer, than when he has got their price in his coffers. Over and above all this, his profit arifes more directly from felling than from buying, and he is upon all thefe accounts generally much more anxious to exchange his goods for money, than his

money

CHAP.
I.

BOOK IV. money for goods. But though a particular merchant, with abundance of goods in his warehouse, may fometimes be ruined by not being able to fell them in time, a nation or country is not liable to the fame accident. The whole capital of a merchant frequently confifts in perifhable goods deftined for purchafing money. But it is but a very fmall part of the annual produce of the land and labour of a country which can ever be deftined for purchafing gold and filver from their neighbours. The far greater part is circulated and confumed among themfelves; and even of the furplus which is fent abroad, the greater part is generally deftined for the purchafe of other foreign goods. Though gold and filver, therefore, could not be had in exchange for the goods deftined to purchafe them, the nation would not be ruined. It might, indeed, fuffer fome lofs and inconveniency, and be forced upon fome of thofe expedients which are neceffary for fupplying the place of money. The annual produce of its land and labour, however, would be the fame, or very nearly the fame, as ufual, becaufe the fame, or very nearly the fame confumable capital would be employed in maintaining it. And though goods do not always draw money fo readily as money draws goods, in the long-run they draw it more neceffarily than even it draws them. Goods can ferve many other purpofes befides purchafing money, but money can ferve no other purpofe befides purchafing goods. Money, therefore, neceffarily runs after goods, but goods do not always or neceffarily run after money.

money. The man who buys, does not always C H A P.
mean to fell again, but frequently to ufe or to I.
confume; whereas he who fells, always means
to buy again. The one may frequently have
done the whole, but the other can never have
done more than the one-half of his bufinefs. It
is not for its own fake that men defire money,
but for the fake of what they can purchafe with it.

Confumable commodities, it is faid, are foon
deftroyed; whereas gold and filver are of a more
durable nature, and, were it not for this continual exportation, might be accumulated for
ages together, to the incredible augmentation
of the real wealth of the country. Nothing,
therefore, it is pretended, can be more difadvantageous to any country, than the trade which
confifts in the exchange of fuch lafting for fuch
perifhable commodities. We do not, however,
reckon that trade difadvantageous which confifts in the exchange of the hard-ware of England
for the wines of France; and yet hard-ware is a
very durable commodity, and were it not for this
continual exportation, might too be accumulated
for ages together, to the incredible augmentation
of the pots and pans of the country. But it
readily occurs that the number of fuch utenfils
is in every country neceffarily limited by the ufe
which there is for them; that it would be abfurd
to have more pots and pans than were neceffary
for cooking the victuals ufually confumed there;
and that if the quantity of victuals were to increafe, the number of pots and pans would
readily increafe along with it, a part of the increafed

156 OF THE PRINCIPLE OF

BOOK IV.

creafed quantity of victuals being employed in purchafing them, or in maintaining an additional number of workmen whofe bufinefs it was to make them. It fhould as readily occur that the quantity of gold and filver is in every country limited by the ufe which there is for thofe metals; that their ufe confifts in circulating commodities as coin, and in affording a fpecies of houfhold furniture as plate; that the quantity of coin in every country is regulated by the value of the commodities which are to be circalated by it: increafe that value, and immediately a part of it will be fent abroad to purchafe, wherever it is to be had, the additional quantity of coin requifite for circulating them : that the quantity of plate is regulated by the number and wealth of thofe private families who chufe to indulge themfelves in that fort of magnificence : increafe the number and wealth of fuch families, and a part of this increafed wealth will moft probably be employed in purchafing, wherever it is to be found, an additional quantity of plate : that to attempt to increafe the wealth of any country, either by introducing or by detaining in it an unneceffary quantity of gold and filver, is as abfurd as it would be to attempt to increafe the good cheer of private families, by obliging them to keep an unneceffary number of kitchen utenfils. As the expence of purchafing thofe unneceffary utenfils would diminifh inftead of increafing either the quantity or goodnefs of the family provifions; fo the expence of purchafing an unneceffary quantity of gold and filver muft, in every country, as

necef-

THE MERCANTILE SYSTEM. 157

neceffarily diminifh the wealth which feeds, CHAP.
clothes, and lodges, which maintains and em- I.
ploys the people. Gold and filver, whether in
the fhape of coin or of plate, are utenfils, it muft
be remembered, as much as the furniture of the
kitchen. Increafe the ufe for them, increafe the
confumable commodities which are to be circulated, managed, and prepared by means of
them, and you will infallibly increafe the quantity; but if you attempt, by extraordinary means,
to increafe the quantity, you will as infallibly
diminifh the ufe and even the quantity too, which
in thofe metals can never be greater than what
the ufe requires. Were they ever to be accumulated beyond this quantity, their tranfportation is fo eafy, and the lofs which attends their
lying idle and unemployed fo great, that no law
could prevent their being immediately fent out
of the country.

It is not always neceffary to accumulate gold
and filver, in order to enable a country to carry
on foreign wars, and to maintain fleets and
armies in diftant countries. Fleets and armies
are maintained, not with gold and filver, but
with confumable goods. The nation which, from
the annual produce of its domeftic induftry,
from the annual revenue arifing out of its
lands, labour, and confumable ftock, has wherewithal to purchafe thofe confumable goods in
diftant countries, can maintain foreign wars
there.

A nation may purchafe the pay and provifions
of an army in a diftant country three different
ways; by fending abroad either, firft, fome part
of

OF THE PRINCIPLE OF

BOOK IV.

of its accumulated gold and filver; or fecondly, fome part of the annual produce of its manufactures; or laft of all, fome part of its annual rude produce.

The gold and filver which can properly be confidered as accumulated or ftored up in any country, may be diftinguifhed into three parts; firft, the circulating money; fecondly, the plate of private families; and laft of all, the money which may have been collected by many years parfimony, and laid up in the treafury of the prince.

It can feldom happen that much can be fpared from the circulating money of the country; becaufe in that there can feldom be much redundancy. The value of goods annually bought and fold in any country requires a certain quantity of money to circulate and diftribute them to their proper confumers, and can give employment to no more. The channel of circulation neceffarily draws to itfelf a fum fufficient to fill it, and never admits any more. Something, however, is generally withdrawn from this channel in the cafe of foreign war. By the great number of people who are maintained abroad, fewer are maintained at home. Fewer goods are circulated there, and lefs money becomes neceffary to circulate them. An extraordinary quantity of paper money, of fome fort or other too, fuch as exchequer notes, navy bills, and bank bills in England, is generally iffued upon fuch occafions, and by fupplying the place of circulating gold and filver, gives an opportunity of fending a greater quantity of it abroad. All this,

THE MERCANTILE SYSTEM. 159

this, however, could afford but a poor refource CHAP. for maintaining a foreign war, of great expence and feveral years duration.

The melting down the plate of private families, has upon every occafion been found a ftill more infignificant one. The French, in the beginning of the laft war, did not derive fo much advantage from this expedient as to compenfate the lofs of the fafhion.

The accumulated treafures of the prince have, in former times, afforded a much greater and more lafting refource. In the prefent times, if you except the King of Pruffia, to accumulate treafure feems to be no part of the policy of European princes.

The funds which maintained the foreign wars of the prefent century, the moft expenfive perhaps which hiftory records, feem to have had little dependency upon the exportation either of the circulating money, or of the plate of private families, or of the treafure of the prince. The laft French war coft Great Britain upwards of ninety millions, including not only the feventy-five millions of new debt that was contracted, but the additional two fhillings in the pound land tax, and what was annually borrowed of the finking fund. More than two-thirds of this expence were laid out in diftant countries; in Germany, Portugal, America, in the ports of the Mediterranean, in the Eaft and Weft Indies. The Kings of England had no accumulated treafure. We never heard of any extraordinary quantity of plate being melted down. The circulating

culating gold and silver of the country, had not been supposed to exceed eighteen millions. Since the late recoinage of the gold, however, it is believed to have been a good deal under-rated. Let us suppose, therefore, according to the most exaggerated computation which I remember to have either seen or heard of, that gold and silver together, it amounted to thirty millions. Had the war been carried on, by means of our money, the whole of it must, even according to this computation, have been sent out and returned again at least twice, in a period of between six and seven years. Should this be supposed, it would afford the most decisive argument to demonstrate how necessary it is for government to watch over the preservation of money, since upon this supposition the whole money of the country must have gone from it and returned to it again, two different times in so short a period, without any body's knowing any thing of the matter. The channel of circulation, however, never appeared more empty than usual during any part of this period. Few people wanted money who had wherewithal to pay for it. The profits of foreign trade, indeed, were greater than usual during the whole war; but especially towards the end of it. This occasioned, what it always occasions, a general over-trading in all the parts of Great Britain; and this again occasioned the usual complaint of the scarcity of money, which always follows over-trading. Many people wanted it, who had neither wherewithal to buy it, nor credit to borrow it; and because the debtors found

THE MERCANTILE SYSTEM. 161

found it difficult to borrow, the creditors found it difficult to get payment. Gold and silver, however, were generally to be had for their value, by those who had that value to give for them.

The enormous expence of the late war, therefore, must have been chiefly defrayed, not by the exportation of gold and silver, but by that of British commodities of some kind or other. When the government, or those who acted under them, contracted with a merchant for a remittance to some foreign country, he would naturally endeavour to pay his foreign correspondent, upon whom he had granted a bill, by sending abroad rather commodities than gold and silver. If the commodities of Great Britain were not in demand in that country, he would endeavour to send them to some other country, in which he could purchase a bill upon that country. The transportation of commodities, when properly suited to the market, is always attended with a considerable profit; whereas that of gold and silver is scarce ever attended with any. When those metals are sent abroad in order to purchase foreign commodities, the merchant's profit arises, not from the purchase, but from the sale of the returns. But when they are sent abroad merely to pay a debt, he gets no returns, and consequently no profit. He naturally, therefore, exerts his invention to find out a way of paying his foreign debts, rather by the exportation of commodities than by that of gold and silver. The great quantity of British goods exported

CHAP. L.

VOL. III. M during

162 OF THE PRINCIPLE OF

BOOK during the courfe of the late war, without bring-
IV. ing back any returns, is accordingly remarked
by the author of " The prefent State of the
Nation."

Befides the three forts of gold and filver above
mentioned, there is in all great commercial
countries a good deal of bullion alternately imported and exported for the purpofes of foreign
trade. This bullion, as it circulates among
different commercial countries in the fame manner as the national coin circulates in every particular country, may be confidered as the money
of the great mercantile republic. The national
coin receives its movement and direction from
the commodities circulated within the precincts
of each particular country: the money of the
mercantile republic, from thofe circulated between different countries. Both are employed
in facilitating exchanges, the one between different individuals of the fame, the other between
thofe of different nations. Part of this money
of the great mercantile republic may have been,
and probably was, employed in carrying on the
late war. In time of a general war, it is natural
to fuppofe that a movement and direction fhould
be impreffed upon it, different from what it
ufually follows in profound peace ; that it fhould
circulate more about the feat of war, and be
more employed in purchafing there, and in the
neighbouring countries, the pay and provifions
of the different armies. But whatever part of
this money of the mercantile republic, Great
Britain may have annually employed in this

2 manner,

manner, it muft have been annually purchafed, either with Britifh commodities, or with fomething elfe that had been purchafed with them; which ftill brings us back to commodities, to the annual produce of the land and labour of the country, as the ultimate refources which enabled us to carry on the war. It is natural indeed to fuppofe, that fo great an annual expence muft have been defrayed from a great annual produce. The expence of 1761, for example, amounted to more than nineteen millions. No accumulation could have fupported fo great an annual profufion. There is no annual produce even of gold and filver which could have fupported it. The whole gold and filver annually imported into both Spain and Portugal, according to the beft accounts, does not commonly much exceed fix millions fterling, which, in fome years, would fcarce have paid four months expence of the late war.

The commodities moft proper for being tranfported to diftant countries, in order to purchafe there, either the pay and provifions of an army, or fome part of the money of the mercantile republic to be employed in purchafing them, feem to be the finer and more improved manufactures; fuch as contain a great value in a fmall bulk, and can, therefore, be exported to a great diftance at little expence. A country whofe induftry produces a great annual furplus of fuch manufactures, which are ufually exported to foreign countries, may carry on for many years a very expenfive foreign war, without either exporting

BOOK IV.

exporting any confiderable quantity of gold and filver, or even having any fuch quantity to export. A confiderable part of the annual furplus of its manufactures muft, indeed, in this cafe be exported, without bringing back any returns to the country, though it does to the merchant; the government purchafing of the merchant his bills upon foreign countries, in order to purchafe there the pay and provifions of an army. Some part of this furplus, however, may ftill continue to bring back a return. The manufacturers, during the war, will have a double demand upon them, and be called upon, firft, to work up goods to be fent abroad, for paying the bills drawn upon foreign countries for the pay and provifions of the army; and, fecondly, to work up fuch as are neceffary for purchafing the common returns that had ufually been confumed in the country. In the midft of the moft deftructive foreign war, therefore, the greater part of manufactures may frequently flourifh greatly; and, on the contrary, they may decline on the return of the peace. They may flourifh amidft the ruin of their country, and begin to decay upon the return of its profperity. The different ftate of many different branches of the Britifh manufactures during the late war, and for fome time after the peace, may ferve as an illuftration of what has been juft now faid.

No foreign war of great expence or duration could conveniently be carried on by the exportation of the rude produce of the foil. The expence of fending fuch a qnantity of it to a

foreign

foreign country as might purchafe the pay and provifions of an army, would be too great. Few countries too produce much more rude produce than what is fufficient for the fubfiftence of their own inhabitants. To fend abroad any great quantity of it, therefore, would be to fend abroad a part of the neceffary fubfiftence of the people. It is otherwife with the exportation of manufactures. The maintenance of the people employed in them is kept at home, and only the furplus part of their work is exported. Mr. Hume frequently takes notice of the inability of the ancient kings of England to carry on, without interruption, any foreign war of long duration. The Englifh, in thofe days, had nothing wherewithal to purchafe the pay and provifions of their armies in foreign countries, but either the rude produce of the foil, of which no confiderable part could be fpared from the home confumption, or a few manufactures of the coarfeft kind, of which, as well as of the rude produce, the tranfportation was too expenfive. This inability did not arife from the want of money, but of the finer and more improved manufactures. Buying and felling was tranfacted by means of money in England then, as well as now. The quantity of circulating money muft have borne the fame proportion to the number and value of purchafes and fales ufually tranfacted at that time, which it does to thofe tranfacted at prefent; or rather it muft have borne a greater proportion becaufe there was then no paper, which now occupies a great part of the employment of gold and

166   OF THE PRINCIPLE OF

BOOK and filver. Among nations to whom commerce
 IV.   and manufactures are little known, the fovereign,
upon extraordinary occafions, can feldom draw
any confiderable aid from his fubjects, for reafons
which fhall be explained hereafter. It is in fuch
countries, therefore, that he generally endeavours
to accumulate a treafure, as the only refource
againft fuch emergencies. Independent of this
neceffity, he is in fuch a fituation naturally difpofed to the parfimony requifite for accumulation. In that fimple ftate, the expence even of
a fovereign is not directed by the vanity which
delights in the gaudy finery of a court, but is
employed in bounty to his tenants, and hofpitality to his retainers. But bounty and hofpitality very feldom lead to extravagance ; though
vanity almoft always does. Every Tartar chief,
accordingly, has a treafure. The treafures of
Mazepa, chief of the Coffacs in the Ukraine,
the famous ally of Charles the XIIth, are faid to
have been very great. The French kings of the
Merovingian race had all treafures. When they
divided their kingdom among their different
children, they divided their treafure too. The
Saxon princes, and the firft kings after the conqueft, feem likewife to have accumulated treafures. The firft exploit of every new reign was
commonly to feize the treafure of the preceding
king, as the moft effential meafure for fecuring
the fucceffion. The fovereigns of improved and
commercial countries are not under the fame
neceffity of accumulating treafures, becaufe they
can generally draw from their fubjects extraordi-
                                        nary

THE MERCANTILE SYSTEM. 167

nary aids upon extraordinary occafions. They
are likewife lefs difpofed to do fo. They naturally, perhaps neceffarily, follow the mode of the
times, and their expence comes to be regulated
by the fame extravagant vanity which directs
that of all the other great proprietors in their
dominions. The infignificant pageantry of their
court becomes every day more brilliant, and the
expence of it not only prevents accumulation,
but frequently encroaches upon the funds deftined for more neceffary expences. What Der-
cyllidas faid of the court of Perfia, may be ap-
plied to that of feveral European princes, that
he faw there much fplendor but little ftrength,
and many fervants but few foldiers.

The importation of gold and filver is not the
principal, much lefs the fole benefit which a
nation derives from its foreign trade. Between
whatever places foreign trade is carried on, they
all of them derive two diftinct benefits from it.
It carries out that furplus part of the produce
of their land and labour for which there is no
demand among them, and brings back in return
for it fomething elfe for which there is a demand.
It gives a value to their fuperfluities, by exchanging them for fomething elfe, which may
fatisfy a part of their wants, and increafe their
enjoyments. By means of it, the narrownefs of
the home market does not hinder the divifion of
labour in any particular branch of art or manufacture from being carried to the higheft per-
fection. By opening a more extenfive market
for whatever part of the produce of their labour

M 4   may

168   OF THE PRINCIPLE OF

B O O K may exceed the home confumption, it encourages
   IV.   them to improve its productive powers, and to
augment its annual produce to the utmoft, and
thereby to increafe the real revenue and wealth
of the fociety. Thefe great and important fervices
foreign trade is continually occupied in performing, to all the different countries between which
it is carried on. They all derive great benefit
from it, though that in which the merchant refides generally derives the greateft, as he is generally more employed in fupplying the wants,
and carrying out the fuperfluities of his own,
than of any other particular country. To import
the gold and filver which may be wanted, into
the countries which have no mines, is, no doubt,
a part of the bufinefs of foreign commerce. It
is, however, a moft infignificant part of it. A
country which carried on foreign trade merely
upon this account, could fcarce have occafion
to freight a fhip in a century.

It is not by the importation of gold and filver,
that the difcovery of America has enriched
Europe. By the abundance of the American
mines, thofe metals have become cheaper. A
fervice of plate can now be purchafed for about
a third part of the corn, or a third part of the
labour, which it would have coft in the fifteenth
century. With the fame annual expence of
labour and commodities, Europe can annually
purchafe about three times the quantity of plate
which it could have purchafed at that time.
But when a commodity comes to be fold for a
third part of what had been its ufual price, not
                                          only

THE MERCANTILE SYSTEM.

169

only thofe who purchafe it before can purchafe three times their former quantity, but it is brought down to the level of a much greater number of purchafers, perhaps to more than ten, perhaps to more than twenty times the former number. So that there may be in Europe at prefent not only more than three times, but more than twenty or thirty times the quantity of plate which would have been in it, even in its prefent ftate of improvement, had the difcovery of the American mines never been made. So far Europe has, no doubt, gained a real conveniency, though furely a very trifling one. The cheapnefs of gold and filver render thofe metals rather lefs fit for the purpofes of money than they were before. In order to make the fame purchafes, we muft load ourfelves with a greater quantity of them, and carry about a fhilling in our pocket where a groat would have done before. It is difficult to fay which is moft trifling, this inconveniency, or the oppofite conveniency. Neither the one nor the other could have made any very effential change in the ftate of Europe. The difcovery of America, however, certainly made a moft effential one. By opening a new and inexhauftible market to all the commodities of Europe, it gave occafion to new divifions of labour and improvements of art, which, in the narrow circle of the ancient commerce, could never have taken place for want of a market to take off the greater part of their produce. The productive powers of labour were improved, and its produce increafed in all the different countries

CHAP. I.

170   OF THE PRINCIPLE OF

BOOK tries of Europe, and together with it the real
 IV.   revenue and wealth of the inhabitants. The
commodities of Europe were almoft all new to
America, and many of thofe of America were
new to Europe. A new fet of exchanges, therefore, began to take place which had never been
thought of before, and which fhould naturally
have proved as advantageous to the new, as it
certainly did to the old continent. The favage
injuftice of the Europeans rendered an event,
which ought to have been beneficial to all, ruinous and deftructive to feveral of thofe unfortunate countries.

The difcovery of a paffage to the Eaft Indies,
by the Cape of Good Hope, which happened
much about the fame time, opened, perhaps, a
ftill more extenfive range to foreign commerce
than even that of America, notwithftanding the
greater diftance. There were but two nations
in America, in any refpect fuperior to favages,
and thefe were deftroyed almoft as foon as difcovered. The reft were mere favages. But the
empires of China, Indoftan, Japan, as well as
feveral others in the Eaft Indies, without having
richer mines of gold or filver, were in every
other refpect much richer, better cultivated, and
more advanced in all arts and manufactures than
either Mexico or Peru, even though we fhould
credit, what plainly deferves no credit, the exaggerated accounts of the Spanifh writers, concerning the ancient ftate of thofe empires. But
rich and civilized nations can always exchange
to a much greater value with one another, than
                                        with

THE MERCANTILE SYSTEM. 171

with favages and barbarians. Europe, however, C H A P. has hitherto derived much lefs advantage from its commerce with the Eaft Indies, than from that with America. The Portuguefe monopolized the Eaft India trade to themfelves for about a century, and it was only indirectly and through them, that the other nations of Europe could either fend out or receive any goods from that country. When the Dutch, in the beginning of the laft century, began to encroach upon them, they vefted their whole Eaft India commerce in an exclufive company. The Englifh, French, Swedes, and Danes, have all followed their example, fo that no great nation in Europe has ever yet had the benefit of a free commerce to the Eaft Indies. No other reafon need be affigned why it has never been fo advantageous as the trade to America, which, between almoft every nation of Europe and its own colonies, is free to all its fubjects. The exclufive privileges of thofe Eaft India companies, their great riches, the great favour and protection which thefe have procured them from their refpective governments, have excited much envy againft them. This envy has frequently reprefented their trade as altogether pernicious, on account of the great quantities of filver, which it every year exports from the countries from which it is carried on. The parties concerned have replied, that their trade, by this continual exportation of filver, might, indeed, tend to impoverifh Europe in general, but not the particular country from which it was carried on; becaufe, by the exportation

172 OF THE PRINCIPLE OF

BOOK ation a part of the returns to other European
IV. countries, it annually brought home a much
greater quantity of that metal than it carried
out. Both the objection and the reply are
founded in the popular notion which I have been
juft now examining. It is, therefore, unneceffary
to fay any thing further about either. By the
annual exportation of filver to the Eaft Indies,
plate is probably fomewhat dearer in Europe than
it otherwife might have been; and coined filver
probably purchafes a larger quantity both of
labour and commodities. The former of thefe
two effects is a very fmall lofs, the latter a very
fmall advantage; both too infignificant to deferve any part of the public attention. The
trade to the Eaft Indies, by opening a market
to the commodities of Europe, or, what comes
nearly to the fame thing, to the gold and filver
which is purchafed with thofe commodities, muft
neceffarily tend to increafe the annual production
of European commodities, and confequently the
real wealth and revenue of Europe. That it
has hitherto increafed them fo little, is probably
owing to the reftraints which it every-where
labours under.

I thought it neceffary, though at the hazard
of being tedious, to examine at full length this
popular notion that wealth confifts in money, or
in gold and filver. Money in common language, as I have already obferved, frequently
fignifies wealth; and this ambiguity of expreffion
has rendered this popular notion fo familiar to
us, that even they, who are convinced of its abfurdity,

THE MERCANTILE SYSTEM. 173

furdity, are very apt to forget their own principles, and in the courfe of their reafonings to
take it for granted as a certain and undeniable
truth. Some of the beft Englifh writers upon
commerce fet out with obferving, that the wealth
of a country confifts, not in its gold and filver
only, but in its lands, houfes, and confumable
goods of all different kinds. In the courfe of
their reafonings, however, the lands, houfes,
and confumable goods feem to flip out of their
memory, and the ftrain of their argument frequently fuppofes that all wealth confifts in gold
and filver, and that to multiply thofe metals is
the great objeɛt of national induftry and commerce.

The two principles being eftablifhed, however, that wealth confifted in gold and filver,
and that thofe metals could be brought into a
country which had no mines only by the balance
of trade, or by exporting to a greater value than
it imported, it neceffarily became the great objeɛt of political œconomy to diminifh as much
as poffible the importation of foreign goods for
home confumption, and to increafe as much as
poffible the exportation of the produce of
domeftic induftry. Its two great engines for
enriching the country, therefore, were reftraints
upon importation, and encouragements to exportation.

The reftraints upon importation were of two
kinds.

Firft, Reftraints upon the importation of
fuch foreign goods for home confumption as

CHAP. L.

could

3

OF THE PRINCIPLE OF

BOOK IV.

could be produced at home, from whatever country they were imported.

Secondly, Reftraints upon the importation of goods of almoft all kinds from thofe particular countries with which the balance of trade was fuppofed to be difadvantageous.

Thofe different reftraints confifted fometimes in high duties, and fometimes in abfolute prohibitions.

Exportation was encouraged fometimes by drawbacks, fometimes by bounties, fometimes by advantageous treaties of commerce with foreign ftates, and fometimes by the eftablifhment of colonies in diftant countries.

Drawbacks were given upon two different occafions. When the home-manufactures were fubject to any duty or excife, either the whole or a part of it was frequently drawn back upon their exportation; and when foreign goods liable to a duty were imported in order to be exported again, either the whole or a part of this duty was fometimes given back upon fuch exportation.

Bounties were given for the encouragement either of fome beginning manufactures, or of fuch forts of induftry of other kinds as were fuppofed to deferve particular favour.

By advantageous treaties of commerce, particular privileges were procured in fome foreign ftate for the goods and merchants of the country, beyond what were granted to thofe of other countries.

By the eftablifhment of colonies in diftant countries, not only particular privileges, but a

monopoly

THE MERCANTILE SYSTEM. 175

monopoly was frequently procured for the goods and merchants of the country which eſtabliſhed them.

The two ſorts of reſtraihts upon importation above-mentioned, together with theſe four encouragements to exportation, conſtitute the ſix principal means by which the commercial ſyſtem propoſes to increaſe the quantity of gold and ſilver in any country by turning the balance of trade in its favour. I ſhall conſider each of them in a particular chapter, and without taking much further notice of their ſuppoſed tendency to bring money into the country, I ſhall examine chiefly what are likely to be the effects of each of them upon the annual produce of its induſtry. According as they tend either to increaſe or diminiſh the value of this annual produce, they muſt evidently tend either to increaſe or diminiſh the real wealth and revenue of the country.

CHAP.

BOOK
IV.

CHAP. II.

*Of Reſtraints upon the Importation from foreign
Countries of ſuch Goods as can be produced at
Home.*

BY reſtraining, either by high duties, or by
absolute prohibitions, the importation of
ſuch goods from foreign countries as can be produced at home, the monopoly of the home-
market is more or leſs ſecured to the domeſtic
induſtry employed in producing them. Thus
the prohibition of importing either live cattle or
ſalt proviſions from foreign countries ſecures to
the graziers of Great Britain the monopoly of
the home-market for butcher's-meat. The high
duties upon the importation of corn, which in
times of moderate plenty amount to a prohibition, give a like advantage to the growers of that
commodity. The prohibition of the importation of foreign woollens is equally favourable
the woollen manufactures. The ſilk manufacture, though altogether employed upon foreign
materials, has lately obtained the ſame advantage.
The linen manufacture has not yet obtained it,
but is making great ſtrides towards it. Many
other ſorts of manufactures have, in the ſame
manner, obtained in Great Britain, either altogether, or very nearly a monopoly againſt their
countrymen. The variety of goods of which the
importation into Great Britain is prohibited,

either

OF RESTRAINTS UPON IMPORTATION. 177

either abfolutely, or under certain circumftances, C H A P. greatly exceeds what can eafily be fufpected by II. thofe who are not well acquainted with the laws of the cuftoms.

That this monopoly of the home-market frequently gives great encouragement to that particular fpecies of induftry which enjoys it, and frequently turns towards that employment a greater fhare of both the labour and ftock of the fociety than would otherwife have gone to it, cannot be doubted. But whether it tends either to increafe the general induftry of the fociety, or to give it the moft advantageous direction, is not, perhaps, altogether fo evident.

The general induftry of the fociety never can exceed what the capital of the fociety can employ. As the number of workmen that can be kept in employment by any particular perfon muft bear a certain proportion to his capital, fo the number of thofe that can be continually employed by all the members of a great fociety, muft bear a certain proportion to the whole capital of that fociety, and never can exceed that proportion. No regulation of commerce can increafe the quantity of induftry in any fociety beyond what its capital can maintain. It can only divert a part of it into a direction into which it might not otherwife have gone; and it is by no means certain that this artificial direction is likely to be more advantageous to the fociety than that into which it would have gone of its own accord.

Every individual is continually exerting himfelf to find out the moft advantageous employ-

VOL. III. N ment

OF RESTRAINTS UPON IMPORTATION.

BOOK IV.

ment for whatever capital he can command. It is his own advantage, indeed, and not that of the fociety, which he has in view. But the ftudy of his own advantage naturally, or rather neceffarily leads him to prefer that employment which is moft advantageous to the fociety.

Firft, every individual endeavours to employ his capital as near home as he can, and confequently as much as he can in the fupport of domeftic induftry; provided always that he can thereby obtain the ordinary, or not a great deal lefs than the ordinary profits of ftock.

Thus, upon equal or nearly equal profits, every wholefale merchant naturally prefers the home-trade to the foreign trade of confumption, and the foreign trade of confumption to the carrying trade. In the home-trade his capital is never fo long out of his fight as it frequently is in the foreign trade of confumption. He can know better the character and fituation of the perfons whom he trufts, and if he fhould happen to be deceived, he knows better the laws of the country from which he muft feek redrefs. In the carrying trade, the capital of the merchant is, as it were, divided between two foreign countries, and no part of it is ever neceffarily brought home, or placed under his own immediate view and command. The capital which an Amfterdam merchant employs in carrying corn from Konnigfberg to Lifbon, and fruit and wine from Lifbon to Konnigfberg, muft generally be the one-half of it at Konnigfberg and the other half at Lifbon. No part of it need ever come

OF RESTRAINTS UPON IMPORTATION. 179

come to Amfterdam. The natural refidence of fuch a merchant fhould either be at Konnigfberg or Lifbon, and it can only be fome very particular circumftances which can make him prefer the refidence of Amfterdam. The uneafinefs, however, which he feels at being feparated fo far from his capital, generally determines him to bring part both of the Konnigfberg goods which he deftines for the market of Lifbon, and of the Lifbon goods which he deftines for that of Konnigfberg, to Amfterdam: and though this neceffarily fubjects him to a double charge of loading and unloading, as well as to the payment of fome duties and cuftoms, yet for the fake of having fome part of his capital always under his own view and command, he willingly fubmits to this extraordinary charge; and it is in this manner that every country which has any confiderable fhare of the carrying trade, becomes always the emporium, or general market, for the goods of all the different countries whofe trade it carries on. The merchant, in order to fave a fecond loading and unloading, endeavours always to fell in the home-market as much of the goods of all thofe different countries as he can, and thus, fo far as he can, to convert his carrying trade into a foreign trade of confumption. A merchant, in the fame manner, who is engaged in the foreign trade of confumption, when he collects goods for foreign markets, will always be glad, upon equal or nearly equal profits, to fell as great a part of them at home as he can. He faves himfelf the rifk and trouble of exportation, when,

OF RESTRAINTS UPON IMPORTATION.

BOOK IV.

when, fo far as he can, he thus converts his foreign trade of confumption into a home-trade. Home is in this manner the center, if I may fay fo, round which the capitals of the inhabitants of every country are continually circulating, and towards which they are always tending, though by particular caufes they may fometimes be driven off and repelled from it towards more diftant employments. But a capital employed in the home-trade, it has already been fhown, neceffarily puts into motion a greater quantity of domeftic induftry, and gives revenue and employment to a greater number of the inhabitants of the country, than an equal capital employed in the foreign trade of confumption : and one employed in the foreign trade of confumption has the fame advantage over an equal capital employed in the carrying trade. Upon equal, or only nearly equal' profits, therefore, every individual naturally inclines to employ his capital in the manner in which it is likely to afford the greateft fupport to domeftic induftry, and to give revenue and employment to the greateft number of people of his own country.

Secondly, every individual who employs his capital in the fupport of domeftic induftry, neceffarily endeavours fo to direct that induftry, that its produce may be of the greateft poffible value.

The produce of induftry is what it adds to the fubject or materials upon which it is employed. In proportion as the value of this produce is great or fmall, fo will likewife be the profits of the employer. But it is only for the fake of profit that

3

OF RESTRAINTS UPON IMPORTATION.

CHAP. II.

that any man employs a capital in the fupport of induftry; and he will always, therefore, endeavour to employ it in the fupport of that induftry of which the produce is likely to be of the greateft value, or to exchange for the greateft quantity either of money or of other goods.

But the annual revenue of every fociety is always precifely equal to the exchangeable value of the whole annual produce of its induftry, or rather is precifely the fame thing with that exchangeable value. As every individual, therefore, endeavours as much as he can both to employ his capital in the fupport of domeftic induftry, and fo to direct that induftry that its produce may be of the greateft value; every individual neceffarily labours to render the annual revenue of the fociety as great as he can. He generally, indeed, neither intends to promote the public intereft, nor knows how much he is promoting it. By preferring the fupport of domeftic to that of foreign induftry, he intends only his own fecurity; and by directing that induftry in fuch a manner as its produce may be of the greateft value, he intends only his own gain, and he is in this, as in many other cafes, led by an invifible hand to promote an end which was no part of his intention. Nor is it always the worfe for the fociety that it was no part of it. By purfuing his own intereft he frequently promotes that of the fociety more effectually than when he really intends to promote it. I have never known much good done by thofe who affected to trade for the public good. It is an

affectation,

OF RESTRAINTS UPON IMPORTATION.

BOOK IV.

affectation, indeed, not very common among merchants, and very few words need be employed in diffuading them from it.

What is the fpecies of domeftic induftry which his capital can employ, and of which the produce is likely to be of the greateft value, every individual, it is evident, can, in his local fituation, judge much better than any ftatefman or lawgiver can do for him. The ftatefman, who fhould attempt to direct private people in what manner they ought to employ their capitals, would not only load himfelf with a moft unneceffary attention, but affume an authority which could fafely be trufted, not only to no fingle perfon, but to no council or fenate whatever, and which would no-where be fo dangerous as in the hands of a man who had folly and prefumption enough to fancy himfelf fit to exercife it.

To give the monopoly of the home-market to the produce of domeftic induftry, in any particular art or manufacture, is in fome meafure to direct private people in what manner they ought to employ their capitals, and muft, in almoft all cafes, be either a ufelefs or a hurtful regulation. If the produce of domeftic can be brought there as cheap as that of foreign induftry, the regulation is evidently ufelefs. If it cannot, it muft generally be hurtful. It is the maxim of every prudent mafter of a family, never to attempt to make at home what it will coft him more to make than to buy. The taylor does not attempt to make his own fhoes, but buys them of the fhoemaker. The fhoemaker does not attempt to

make

OF RESTRAINTS UPON IMPORTATION.

make his own clothes, but employs a taylor. CHAP. II.
The farmer attempts to make neither the one
nor the other, but employs thofe different artificers. All of them find it for their intereft to
employ their whole induftry in a way in which
they have fome advantage over their neighbours,
and to purchafe with a part of its produce, or
what is the fame thing, with the price of a part
of it, whatever elfe they have occafion for.

What is prudence in the conduct of every
private family, can fcarce be folly in that of a
great kingdom. If a foreign country can fupply
us with a commodity cheaper than we ourfelves
can make it, better buy it of them with fome
part of the produce of our own induftry, employed in a way in which we have fome advantage. The general induftry of the country, being
always in proportion to the capital which employs it, will not thereby be diminifhed, no more
than that of the above-mentioned artificers; but
only left to find out the way in which it can be
employed with the greateft advantage. It is certainly not employed to the greateft advantage,
when it is thus directed towards an object which
it can buy cheaper than it can make. The value
of its annual produce is certainly more or lefs
diminifhed, when it is thus turned away from
producing commodities evidently of more value
than the commodity which it is directed to produce. According to the fuppofition, that commodity could be purchafed from foreign countries
cheaper than it can be made at home. It could,
therefore, have been purchafed with a part only

of

OF RESTRAINTS UPON IMPORTATION.

BOOK IV.

of the commodities, or, what is the fame thing, with a part only of the price of the commodities, which the induftry employed by an equal capital would have produced at home, had it been left to follow its natural courfe. The induftry of the country, therefore, is thus turned away from a more, to a lefs advantageous employment, and the exchangeable value of its annual produce, inftead of being increafed, according to the intention of the law-giver, muft neceffarily be diminifhed by every fuch regulation.

By means of fuch regulations, indeed, a particular manufacture may fometimes be acquired fooner than it could have been otherwife, and after a certain time may be made at home as cheap or cheaper than in the foreign country. But though the induftry of the fociety may be thus carried with advantage into a particular channel fooner than it could have been otherwife, it will by no means follow that the fum total, either of its induftry, or of its revenue, can ever be augmented by any fuch regulation. The induftry of the fociety can augment only in proportion as its capital augments, and its capital can augment only in proportion to what can be gradually faved out of its revenue. But the immediate effect of every fuch regulation is to diminifh its revenue, and what diminifhes its revenue is certainly not very likely to augment its capital fafter than it would have augmented of its own accord, had both capital and induftry been left to find out their natural employments.

Though

OF RESTRAINTS UPON IMPORTATION.

185

CHAP.
II.

Though for want of such regulations the society should never acquire the proposed manufacture, it would not, upon that account, necessarily be the poorer in any one period of its duration. In every period of its duration its whole capital and industry might still have been employed, though upon different objects, in the manner that was most advantageous at the time. In every period its revenue might have been the greatest which its capital could afford, and both capital and revenue might have been augmented with the greatest possible rapidity.

The natural advantages which one country has over another in producing particular commodities are sometimes so great, that it is acknowledged by all the world to be in vain to struggle with them. By means of glasses, hotbeds, and hot-walls, very good grapes can be raised in Scotland, and very good wine too can be made of them at about thirty times the expence for which at least equally good can be brought from foreign countries. Would it be a reasonable law to prohibit the importation of all foreign wines, merely to encourage the making of claret and burgundy in Scotland? But if there would be a manifest absurdity in turning towards any employment, thirty times more of the capital and industry of the country, than would be necessary to purchase from foreign countries an equal quantity of the commodities wanted, there must be an absurdity, though not altogether so glaring, yet exactly of the same kind, in turning

towards

186 OF RESTRAINTS UPON IMPORTATION.

BOOK IV.

towards any fuch employment a thirtieth, or even a three hundredth part more of either. Whether the advantages which one country has over another, be natural or acquired, is in this refpect of no confequence. As long as the one country has thofe advantages, and the other wants them, it will always be more advantageous for the latter, rather to buy of the former than to make. It is an acquired advantage only, which one artificer has over his neighbour, who exercifes another trade; and yet they both find it more advantageous to buy of one another, than to make what does not belong to their particular trades.

Merchants and manufacturers are the people who derive the greateft advantage from this monopoly of the home-market. The prohibition of the importation of foreign cattle, and of falt provifions, together with the high duties upon foreign corn, which in times of moderate plenty amount to a prohibition, are not near fo advantageous to the graziers and farmers of Great Britain, as other regulations of the fame kind are to its merchants and manufacturers. Manufactures, thofe of the finer kind efpecially, are more eafily tranfported from one country to another than corn or cattle. It is in the fetching and carrying manufactures, accordingly, that foreign trade is chiefly employed. In manufactures, a very fmall advantage will enable foreigners to underfell our own workmen, even in the home-market. It will require a very great one to enable them to do fo in the rude produce

of

OF RESTRAINTS UPON IMPORTATION. 187

CHAP. II.

of the foil. If the free importation of foreign manufactures were permited, feveral of the home manufactures would probably fuffer, and fome of them, perhaps, go to ruin altogether, and a confiderable part of the ftock and induftry at prefent employed in them, would be forced to find out fome other employment. But the freeft importation of the rude produce of the foil could have no fuch effect upon the agriculture of the country.

If the importation of foreign cattle, for example, were made ever fo free, fo few could be imported, that the grazing trade of Great Britain could be little affected by it. Live cattle are, perhaps, the only commodity of which the tranfportation is more expenfive by fea than by land. By land they carry themfelves to market. By fea, not only the cattle, but their food and their water too, muft be carried at no fmall expence and inconveniency. The fhort fea between Ireland and Great Britain, indeed, renders the importation of Irifh cattle more eafy. But though the free importation of them, which was lately permitted only for a limited time, were rendered perpetual, it could have no confiderable effect upon the intereft of the graziers of Great Britain. Thofe parts of Great Britain which border upon the Irifh fea are all grazing countries. Irifh cattle could never be imported for their ufe, but muft be drove through thofe very extenfive countries, at no fmall expence and inconveniency, before they could arrive at their proper market. Fat cattle could not be drove

fo

188   OF RESTRAINTS UPON IMPORTATION.

BOOK
IV.

fo far. Lean cattle, therefore, only could be imported, and fuch importation could interfere, not with the intereft of the feeding or fattening countries, to which, by reducing the price of lean cattle, it would rather be advantageous, but with that of the breeding countries only. The fmall number of Irifh cattle imported fince their importation was permitted, together with the good price at which lean cattle ftill continue to fell, feem to demonftrate that even the breeding countries of Great Britain are never likely to be much affected by the free importation of Irifh cattle. The common people of Ireland, indeed, are faid to have fometimes oppofed with violence the exportation of their cattle. But if the exporters had found any great advantage in continuing the trade, they could eafily, when the law was on their fide, have conquered this mobbifh oppofition.

Feeding and fattening countries, befides, muft always be highly improved, whereas breeding countries are generally uncultivated. The high price of lean cattle, by augmenting the value of uncultivated land, is like a bounty againft improvement. To any country which was highly improved throughout, it would be more advantageous to import its lean cattle than to breed them. The province of Holland, accordingly, is faid to follow this maxim at prefent. The mountains of Scotland, Wales and Northumberland, indeed, are countries not capable of much improvement, and feem deftined by nature to be the breeding countries of Great Britain.

The

OF RESTRAINTS UPON IMPORTATION.

The freeſt importation of foreign cattle could have no other effect than to hinder thofe breeding countries from taking advantage of the increafing population and improvement of the reſt of the kingdom, from raifing their price to an exorbitant height, and from laying a real tax upon all the more improved and cultivated parts of the country.

The freeſt importation of falt provifions, in the fame manner, could have as little effect upon the intereft of the graziers of Great Britain as that of live cattle. Salt provifions are not only a very bulky commodity, but when compared with frefh meat, they are a commodity both of worfe quality, and as they coſt more labour and expence, of higher price. They could never, therefore, come into competition with the frefh meat, though they might with the falt provifions of the country. They might be ufed for victualling fhips for diſtant voyages, and fuch like ufes, but could never make any confiderable part of the food of the people. The fmall quantity of falt proviſſons imported from Ireland fince their importation was rendered free, is an experimental proof that our graziers have nothing to apprehend from it. It does not appear that the price of butcher's-meat has ever been fenfibly affected by it.

Even the free importation of foreign corn could very little affect the intereft of the farmers of Great Britain. Corn is a much more bulky commodity than butcher's-meat. A pound of wheat at a penny is as dear as a pound of butcher's

190   OF RESTRAINTS UPON IMPORTATION.

BOOK
IV.

cher's-meat at fourpence. The fmall quantity of foreign corn imported even in times of the greateft fcarcity, may fatisfy our farmers that they can have nothing to fear from the freeft importation. The average quantity imported one year with another, amounts only, according to the very well informed author of the tracts upon the corn trade, to twenty-three thoufand feven hundred and twenty-eight quarters of all forts of grain, and does not exceed the five hundredth and feventy-one part of the annual confumption. But as the bounty upon corn occafions a greater exportation in years of plenty, fo it muft of confequence occafion a greater importation in years of fcarcity, than in the actual ftate of tillage would otherwife take place. By means of it, the plenty of one year does not compenfate the fcarcity of another, and as the average quantity exported is neceffarily augmented by it, fo muft likewife, in the actual ftate of tillage, the average quantity imported. If there were no bounty, as lefs corn would be exported, fo it is probable that, one year with another, lefs would be imported than at prefent. The corn merchants, the fetchers and carriers of corn between Great Britain and foreign countries, would have much lefs employment, and might fuffer confiderably; but the country gentlemen and farmers could fuffer very little. It is in the corn merchants accordingly, rather than in the country gentlemen and farmers, that I have obferved the greateft anxiety for the renewal and continuation of the bounty.

Country

OF RESTRAINTS UPON IMPORTATION. 191

Country gentlemen and farmers are, to their great honour, of all people, the leaft fubject to the wretched fpirit of monopoly. The undertaker of a great manufactory is fometimes alarmed if another work of the fame kind is eftablifhed within twenty miles of him. The Dutch undertaker of the woollen manufacture at Abbeville ftipulated, that no work of the fame kind fhould be eftablifhed within thirty leagues of that city. Farmers and country gentlemen, on the contrary, are generally difpofed rather to promote than to obftruct the cultivation and improvement of their neighbours farms and eftates. They have no fecrets, fuch as thofe of the greater part of manufacturers, but are generally rather fond of communicating to their neighbours, and of extending as far as poffible any new practice which they have found to be advantageous. *Pius Queftus*, fays old Cato, *ftabiliffimufque, minimeque invidiofus; minimeque male cogitantes funt, qui in eo ftudio occupati funt.* Country gentlemen and farmers, difperfed in different parts of the country, cannot fo eafily combine as merchants and manufacturers, who being collected into towns, and accuftomed to that exclufive corporation fpirit which prevails in them, naturally endeavour to obtain againft all their countrymen, the fame exclufive privilege which they generally poffefs againft the inhabitants of their refpective towns. They accordingly feem to have been the original inventors of thofe reftraints upon the importation of foreign goods, which fecure to them the monopoly of the home-market. It

was

OF RESTRAINTS UPON IMPORTATION.

BOOK IV.

was probably in imitation of them, and to put themfelves upon a level with thofe who, they found, were difpofed to opprefs them, that the country gentlemen and farmers of Great Britain fo far forgot the generofity which is natural to their ftation, as to demand the exclufive privilege of fupplying their countrymen with corn and butcher's-meat. They did not perhaps take time to confider, how much lefs their intereft could be affected by the freedom of trade, than that of the people whofe example they followed.

To prohibit by a perpetual law the importation of foreign corn and cattle, is in reality to enact, that the population and induftry of the country fhall at no time exceed what the rude produce of its own foil can maintain.

There feem, however, to be two cafes in which it will generally be advantageous to lay fome burden upon foreign, for the encouragement of domeftic induftry.

The firft is, when fome particular fort of induftry is neceffary for the defence of the country. The defence of Great Britain, for example, depends very much upon the number of its failors and fhipping. The act of navigation, therefore, very properly endeavours to give the failors and fhipping of Great Britain the monopoly of the trade of their own country, in fome cafes, by abfolute prohibitions, and in others by heavy burdens upon the fhipping of foreign countries. The following are the principal difpofitions of this act.

Firft,

OF RESTRAINTS UPON IMPORTATION. 193

First, all ſhips, of which the owners, maſters, CHAP.
and three-fourths of the mariners are not Britiſh II.
ſubjects, are prohibited, upon pain of forfeiting
ſhip and cargo, from trading to the Britiſh ſettlements and plantations, or from being employed
in the coaſting trade of Great Britain.

Secondly, a great variety of the moſt bulky
articles of importation can be brought into Great
Britain only, either in ſuch ſhips as are above
deſcribed, or in ſhips of the country where thoſe
goods are produced, and of which the owners,
maſters, and three-fourths of the mariners, are
of that particular country ; and when imported
even in ſhips of this latter kind, they are ſubject
to double aliens duty. If imported in ſhips of
any other country, the penalty is forfeiture of
ſhip and goods. When this act was made, the
Dutch were, what they ſtill are, the great carriers of Europe, and by this regulation they were
entirely excluded from being the carriers to
Great Britain, or from importing to us the goods
of any other European country.

Thirdly, a great variety of the moſt bulky
articles of importation are prohibited from being
imported, even in Britiſh ſhips, from any country
but that in which they are produced ; under pain
of forfeiting ſhip and cargo. This regulation too
was probably intended againſt the Dutch. Holland was then, as now, the great emporium for
all European goods, and by this regulation, Britiſh
ſhips were hindered from loading in Holland the
goods of any other European country.

VOL. III.   O   Fourthly,

OF RESTRAINTS UPON IMPORTATION.

BOOK IV.

Fourthly, falt fifh of all kinds, whale-fins, whale-bone, oil, and blubber, not caught by and cured on board Britifh veffels, when imported into Great Britain, are fubjected to double aliens duty. The Dutch, as they are ftill the principal, were then the only fifhers in Europe that attempted to fupply foreign nations with fifh. By this regulation, a very heavy burden was laid upon their fupplying Great Britain.

When the act of navigation was made, though England and Holland were not actually at war, the moft violent animofity fubfifted between the two nations. It had begun during the government of the Long parliament, which firft framed this act, and it broke out foon after in the Dutch wars during that of the Protector and of Charles the Second. It is not impoffible, therefore, that fome of the regulations of this famous act, may have proceeded from national animofity. They are as wife, however, as if they had all been dictated by the moft deliberate wifdom. National animofity at that particular time aimed at the very fame object which the moft deliberate wifdom would have recommended, the diminution of the naval power of Holland, the only naval power which could endanger the fecurity of England.

The act of navigation is not favourable to foreign commerce, or to the growth of that opulence which can arife from it. The intereft of a nation in its commercial relations to foreign nations is, like that of a merchant, with regard to the different people with whom he deals, to buy

OF RESTRAINTS UPON IMPORTATION. 195

as cheap and to fell as dear as poffible. But it will be moft likely to buy cheap, when by the moft perfect freedom of trade it encourages all nations to bring to it the goods which it has occafion to purchafe; and, for the fame reafon, it will be moft likely to fell dear, when its markets are thus filled with the greateft number of buyers. The act of navigation, it is true, lays no burden upon foreign fhips that come to export the produce of Britifh induftry. Even the ancient aliens duty, which ufed to be paid upon all goods exported as well as imported, has, by feveral fubfequent acts, been taken off from the greater part of the articles of exportation. But if foreigners, either by prohibitions or high duties, are hindered from coming to fell, they cannot always afford to come to buy; becaufe coming without a cargo, they muft lofe the freight from their own country to Great Britain. By diminifhing the number of fellers, therefore, we neceffarily diminifh that of buyers, and are thus likely not only to buy foreign goods dearer, but to fell our own cheaper, than if there was a more perfect freedom of trade. As defence, however, is of much more importance than opulence, the act of navigation is, perhaps, the wifeft of all the commercial regulations of England.

The fecond cafe, in which it will generally be advantageous to lay fome burden upon foreign for the encouragement of domeftic induftry, is, when fome tax is impofed at home upon the produce of the latter. In this cafe, it feems reafon-

O 2   able

OF RESTRAINTS UPON IMPORTATION.

BOOK IV.

able that an equal tax fhould be impofed upon the like produce of the former. This would not give the monopoly of the home market to domeftic induftry, nor turn towards a particular employment a greater fhare of the ftock and labour of the country, than what would naturally go to it. It would only hinder any part of what would naturally go to it from being turned away by the tax, into a lefs natural direction, and would leave the competition between foreign and domeftic induftry, after the tax, as nearly as poffible upon the fame footing as before it. In Great Britain, when any fuch tax is laid upon the produce of domeftic induftry, it is ufual at the fame time, in order to ftop the clamorous complaints of our merchants and manufacturers, that they will be underfold at home, to lay a much heavier duty upon the importation of all foreign goods of the fame kind.

This fecond limitation of the freedom of trade according to fome people fhould, upon fome occafions, be extended much farther than to the precife foreign commodities which could come into competition with thofe which had been taxed at home. When the neceffaries of life have been taxed in any country, it becomes proper, they pretend, to tax not only the like neceffaries of life imported from other countries, but all forts of foreign goods which can come into competition with any thing that is the produce of domeftic induftry. Subfiftence, they fay, becomes neceffarily dearer in confequence

of

OF RESTRAINTS UPON IMPORTATION. 197

CHAP.
II.

of fuch taxes; and the price of labour muft always rife with the price of the labourers' fubfiftence. Every commodity, therefore, which is the produce of 'domeftic induftry, though not immediately taxed itfelf, becomes dearer in confequence of fuch taxes, becaufe the labour which produces it becomes fo. Such taxes, therefore, are really equivalent, they fay, to a tax upon every particular commodity produced at home. In order to put domeftic upon the fame footing with foreign induftry, therefore, it becomes neceffary, they think, to lay fome duty upon every foreign commodity, equal to this enhancement of the price of the home commodities with which it can come into competition.

Whether taxes upon the neceffaries of life, fuch as thofe in Great Britain upon foap, falt, leather, candles, &c. neceffarily raife the price of labour, and confequently that of all other commodities, I fhall confider hereafter, when I come to treat of taxes. Suppofing, however, in the mean time, that they have this effect, and they have it undoubtedly, this general enhancement of the price of all commodities, in confequence of that of labour, is a cafe which differs in the two following refpects from that of a particular commodity, of which the price was enhanced by a particular tax immediately impofed upon it,

Firft, it might always be known with great exactnefs how far the price of fuch a commodity could be enhanced by fuch a tax: but how far the general enhancement of the price of labour might

O 3

OF RESTRAINTS UPON IMPORTATION.

BOOK IV. might affect that of every different commodity about which labour was employed, could never be known with any tolerable exactnefs. It would be impoffible, therefore, to proportion with any tolerable exactnefs the tax upon every foreign, to this enhancement of the price of every home commodity.

Secondly, taxes upon the neceffaries of life have nearly the fame effect upon the circumftances of the people as a poor foil and a bad climate. Provifions are thereby rendered dearer in the fame manner as if it required extraordinary labour and expence to raife them. As in the natural fcarcity arifing from foil and climate, it would be abfurd to direct the people in what manner they ought to employ their capitals and induftry, fo is it likewife in the artificial fcarcity arifing from fuch taxes. To be left to accommodate, as well as they could, their induftry to their fituation, and to find out thofe employments in which, notwithftanding their unfavourable circumftances, they might have fome advantage either in the home or in the foreign market, is what in both cafes would evidently be moft for their advantage. To lay a new tax upon them, becaufe they are already overburdened with taxes, and becaufe they already pay too dear for the neceffaries of life, to make them likewife pay too dear for the greater part of other commodities, is certainly a moft abfurd way of making amends.

Such taxes, when they have grown up to a certain height, are a curfe equal to the barrennefs

OF RESTRAINTS UPON IMPORTATION. 199

CHAP.
II.

nefs of the earth and the inclemency of the heavens; and yet it is in the richeft and moft induftrious countries that they have been moft generally impofed. No other countries could fupport fo great a diforder. As the ftrongeft bodies only can live and enjoy health, under an unwholefome regimen; fo the nations only, that in every fort of induftry have the greateft natural and acquired advantages, can fubfift and profper under fuch taxes. Holland is the country in Europe in which they abound moft, and which from peculiar circumftances continues to profper, not by means of them, as has been moft abfurdly fuppofed, but in fpite of them.

As there are two cafes in which it will generally be advantageous to lay fome burden upon foreign, for the encouragement of domeftic induftry; fo there are two others in which it may fometimes be a matter of deliberation; in the one, how far it is proper to continue the free importation of certain foreign goods; and in the other, how far, or in what manner, it may be proper to reftore that free importation after it has been for fome time interrupted.

The cafe in which it may fometimes be a matter of deliberation how far it is proper to continue the free importation of certain foreign goods, is, when fome foreign nation reftrains by high duties or prohibitions the importation of fome of our manufactures into their country. Revenge in this cafe naturally dictates retaliation, and that we fhould impofe the like duties and prohibitions upon the importation of fome

o 4
or

OF RESTRAINTS UPON IMPORTATION.

BOOK IV.

or all of their manufactures into ours. Nations accordingly feldom fail to retaliate in this manner. The French have been particularly forward to favour their own manufactures by reftraining the importation of fuch foreign goods as could come into competition with them. In this confifted a great part of the policy of Mr. Colbert, who, notwithftanding his great abilities, feems in this cafe to have been impofed upon by the fophiftry of merchants and manufacturers, who are always demanding a monopoly againft their countrymen. It is at prefent the opinion of the moft intelligent men in France that his operations of this kind have not been beneficial to his country. That minifter, by the tarif of 1667, impofed very high duties upon a great number of foreign manufactures. Upon his refufing to moderate them in favour of the Dutch, they in 1671 prohibited the importation of the wines, brandies, and manufactures of France. The war of 1672 feems to have been in part occafioned by this commercial difpute. The peace of Nimeguen put an end to it in 1678, by moderating fome of thofe duties in favour of the Dutch, who in confequence took off their prohibition. It was about the fame time that the French and Englifh began mutually to opprefs each other's induftry, by the like duties and prohibitions, of which the French, however, feem to have fet the firft example. The fpirit of hoftility which has fubfifted between the two nations ever fince, has hitherto hindered them from being moderated on either fide.

OF RESTRAINTS UPON IMPORTATION. 201

fide. In 1697 the Englifh prohibited the importation of bonelace, the manufacture of Flanders. The government of that country, at that time under the dominion of Spain, prohibited in return the importation of Englifh woollens. In 1700, the prohibition of importing bonelace into England, was taken off upon condition that the importation of Englifh woollens into Flanders fhould be put on the fame footing as before.

There may be good policy in retaliations of this kind, when there is a probability that they will procure the repeal of the high duties or prohibitions complained of. The recovery of a great foreign market will generally more than compenfate the tranfitory inconveniency of paying dearer during a fhort time for fome forts of goods. To judge whether fuch retaliations are likely to produce fuch an effect, does not, perhaps, belong fo much to the fcience of a legif-lator, whofe deliberations ought to be governed by general principles which are always the fame, as to the fkill of that infidious and crafty animal, vulgarly called a ftatefman or politician, whofe councils are directed by the momentary fluctuations of affairs. When there is no probability that any fuch repeal can be procured, it feems a bad method of compenfating the injury done to certain claffes of our people, to do another injury ourfelves, not only to thofe claffes, but to almoft all the other claffes of them. When our neighbours prohibit fome manufacture of ours, we generally prohibit, not only the fame, for that alone would feldom affect them confiderably,

but

OF RESTRAINTS UPON IMPORTATION.

BOOK IV.

but fome other other manufacture of theirs. This may no doubt give encouragement to fome particular clafs of workmen among ourfelves, and by excluding fome of their rivals, may enable them to raife their price in the home-market. Thofe workmen, however, who fuffered by our neighbours' prohibition will not be bene-fitted by ours. On the contrary, they and almoft all the other claffes of our citizens will thereby be obliged to pay dearer than before for certain goods. Every fuch law, therefore, impofes a real tax upon the whole country, not in favour of that particular clafs of workmen who were injured by our neighbours' prohibition, but of fome other clafs.

The cafe in which it may fometimes be a matter of deliberation, how far, or in what man-ner, it is proper to reftore the free importation of foreign goods, after it has been for fome time interrupted, is, when particular manufactures, by means of high duties or prohibitions upon all foreign goods which can come into competition with them, have been fo far extended as to employ a great multitude of hands. Humanity may in this cafe require that the freedom of trade fhould be reftored only by flow gradations, and with a good deal of referve and circum-fpection. Were thofe high duties and prohi-bitions taken away all at once, cheaper foreign goods of the fame kind might be poured fo faft into the home market, as to deprive all at once many thoufands of our people of their ordinary employment and means of fubfiftence. The diforder

OF RESTRAINTS UPON IMPORTATION. 203

diforder which this would occafion might no CHAP.
doubt be very confiderable. It would in all II.
probability, however, be much lefs than is commonly imagined, for the two following reafons:

Firft, all thofe manufactures, of which any part is commonly exported to other European countries without a bounty, could be very little affected by the freeft importation of foreign goods. Such manufactures muft be fold as cheap abroad as any other foreign goods of the fame quality and kind, and confequently muft be fold cheaper at home. They would ftill, therefore, keep poffeffion of the home market, and though a capricious man of fafhion might fometimes prefer foreign wares, merely becaufe they were foreign, to cheaper and better goods of the fame kind that were made at home, this folly could, from the nature of things, extend to fo few, that it could make no fenfible impreffion upon the general employment of the people. But a great part of all the different branches of our woollen manufacture, of our tanned leather, and of our hard-ware, are annually exported to other European countries without any bounty, and thefe are the manufactures which employ the greateft number of hands. The filk, perhaps, is the manufacture which would fuffer the moft by this freedom of trade, and after it the linen, though the latter much lefs than the former.

Secondly, though a great number of people fhould, by thus reftoring the freedom of trade, be thrown all at once out of their ordinary employment and common method of fubfiftence,

it

OF RESTRAINTS UPON IMPORTATION.

BOOK IV.

it would by no means follow that they would thereby be deprived either of employment or fubfiftence. By the reduction of the army and navy at the end of the late war, more than a hundred thoufand foldiers and feamen, a number equal to what is employed in the greateft manufactures, were all at once thrown out of their ordinary employment; but, though they no doubt fuffered fome inconveniency, they were not thereby deprived of all employment and fubfiftence. The greater part of the feamen, it is probable, gradually betook themfelves to the merchant-fervice as they could find occafion, and in the mean time both they and the foldiers were abforbed in the great mafs of the people, and employed in a great variety of occupations. Not only no great convulfion, but no fenfible difor-der arofe from fo great a change in the fituation of more than a hundred thoufand men, all accuftomed to the ufe of arms, and many of them to rapine and plunder. The number of vagrants was fcarce any-where fenfibly increafed by it, even the wages of labour were not reduced by it in any occupation, fo far as I have been able to learn, except in that of feamen in the merchant-fervice. But if we compare together the habits of a foldier and of any fort of manufacturer, we fhall find that thofe of the latter do not tend fo much to difqualify him from being employed in a new trade, as thofe of the former from being employed in any. The manufacturer has always been accuftomed to look for his fubfiftence from his labour only: the foldier to expect it from his pay.

OF RESTRAINTS UPON IMPORTATION.

pay. Application and induſtry have been familiar
to the one ; idleneſs and diſſipation to the other.
But it is ſurely much eaſier to change the direction of induſtry from one ſort of labour to
another, than to turn idleneſs and diſſipation
to any. To the greater part of manufactures
beſides, it has already been obſerved, there are
other collateral manufactures of ſo ſimilar a
nature, that a workman can eaſily transfer his
induſtry from one of them to another. The
greater part of ſuch workmen too are occaſionally
employed in country labour. The ſtock which
employed them in a particular manufacture
before, will ſtill remain in the country to employ
an equal number of people in ſome other way.
The capital of the country remaining the ſame,
the demand for labour will likewiſe be the ſame,
or very nearly the ſame, though it may be
exerted in different places and for different occupations. Soldiers and ſeamen, indeed, when
diſcharged from the King's ſervice, are at liberty
to exerciſe any trade, within any town or place
of Great Britain or Ireland. Let the ſame
natural liberty of exerciſing what ſpecies of induſtry they pleaſe, be reſtored to all His Majeſty's
ſubjects, in the ſame manner as to ſoldiers and
ſeamen ; that is, break down the excluſive
privileges of corporations, and repeal the ſtatute
of apprenticeſhip, both which are real encroachments upon natural liberty, and add to theſe the
repeal of the law of ſettlements, ſo that a poor
workman, when thrown out of employment either
in one trade, or in one place, may ſeek for it in
another

C H A P.
II.

OF RESTRAINTS UPON IMPORTATION.

BOOK IV.

another trade or in another place, without the fear either of a profecution or of a removal, and neither the public nor the individuals will fuffer much more from the occafional difbanding fome particular claffes of manufacturers, than from that of foldiers. Our manufacturers have no doubt great merit with their country, but they cannot have more than thofe who defend it with their blood, nor deferve to be treated with more delicacy.

To expect, indeed, that the freedom of trade fhould ever be entirely reftored in Great Britain, is as abfurd as to expect that an Oceana or Utopia fhould ever be eftablifhed in it. Not only the prejudices of the public, but what is much more unconquerable, the private interefts of many individuals, irrefiftibly oppofe it. Were the officers of the army to oppofe with the fame zeal and unanimity any reduction in the number of forces, with which mafter manufacturers fet themfelves againft every law that is likely to increafe the number of their rivals in the home market; were the former to animate the foldiers, in the fame manner as the latter enflame their workmen, to attack with violence and outrage the propofers of any fuch regulation; to attempt to reduce the army would be as dangerous as it has now become to attempt to diminifh in any refpect the monopoly which our manufacturers have obtained againft us. This monopoly has fo much increafed the number of fome particular tribes of them, that, like an over-grown ftanding army, they have become formidable to the

govern-

OF RESTRAINTS UPON IMPORTATION.

CHAP. II.

government, and upon many occafions inti-
midate the legiflature. The member of parliament who fupports every propofal for ftrength-
ening this monopoly, is fure to acquire not
only the reputation of underftanding trade, but
great popularity and influence with an order
of men whofe numbers and wealth render them
of great importance. If he oppofes them, on
the contrary, and ftill more if he has authority
enough to be able to thwart them, neither the
moft acknowledged probity, nor the higheft
rank, nor the greateft public fervices, can protect
him from the moft infamous abufe and detraction,
from perfonal infults, nor fometimes from real
danger, arifing from the infolent outrage of
furious and difappointed monopolifts.

The undertaker of a great manufacture, who,
by the home markets being fuddenly laid open
to the competition of foreigners, fhould be
obliged to abandon his trade, would no doubt
fuffer very confiderably. That part of his capital
which had ufually been employed in purchafing
materials and in paying his workmen, might,
without much difficulty, perhaps, find another
employment. But that part of it which was
fixed in workhoufes, and in the inftruments of
trade, could fcarce be difpofed of without confiderable lofs. The equitable regard, therefore,
to his intereft requires that changes of this kind
fhould never be introduced fuddenly, but flowly,
gradually, and after a very long warning. The
legiflature, were it poffible that its deliberations
could be always directed, not by the clamorous
importunity

208 OF RESTRAINTS UPON IMPORTATION.

BOOK IV. importunity of partial interefts, but by an extenfive view of the general good, ought upon this very account, perhaps, to be particularly careful neither to eftablifh any new monopolies of this kind, nor to extend further thofe which are already eftablifhed. Every fuch regulation introduces fome degree of real diforder into the conftitution of the ftate, which it will be difficult afterwards to cure without occafioning another diforder.

How far it may be proper to impofe taxes upon the importation of foreign goods, in order, not to prevent their importation, but to raife a revenue for government, I fhall confider hereafter when I come to treat of taxes. Taxes impofed with a view to prevent, or even to diminifh importation, are evidently as deftructive of the revenue of the cuftoms as of the freedom of trade.

CHAP. III.

Of the extraordinary Reſtraints upon the Importation of Goods of almoſt all Kinds, from thoſe Countries with which the Balance is ſuppoſed to be diſadvantageous.

PART I.

Of the Unreaſonableneſs of thoſe Reſtraints, even upon the Principles of the Commercial Syſtem.

TO lay extraordinary reſtraints upon the importation of goods of almoſt all kinds, from thoſe particular countries with which the balance of trade is ſuppoſed to be diſadvantageous, is the ſecond expedient by which the commercial ſyſtem propoſes to increaſe the quantity of gold and ſilver. Thus in Great Britain, Sileſia lawns may be imported for home conſumption, upon paying certain duties. But French cambrics and lawns are prohibited to be imported, except into the port of London, there to be warehouſed for exportation. Higher duties are impoſed upon the wines of France than upon thoſe of Portugal, or indeed of any other country. By what is called the impoſt 1692, a duty of five and twenty per cent., of the rate or value, was laid upon all French goods ; while the goods of other nations were, the greater part of them, ſubjected to much lighter duties, ſeldom exceeding

BOOK IV. ing five per cent. The wine, brandy, salt and vinegar of France were indeed excepted; these commodities being subjected to other heavy duties, either by other laws, or by particular clauses of the same law. In 1696, a second duty of twenty-five per cent., the first not having been thought a sufficient discouragement, was imposed upon all French goods, except brandy; together with a new duty of five and twenty pounds upon the ton of French wine, and another of fifteen pounds upon the ton of French vinegar. French goods have never been omitted in any of those general subsidies, or duties of five per cent., which have been imposed upon all, or the greater part of the goods enumerated in the book of rates. If we count the one third and two third subsidies as making a complete subsidy between them, there have been five of these general subsidies; so that before the commencement of the present war seventy-five per cent. may be considered as the lowest duty, to which the greater part of the goods of the growth, produce, or manufacture of France were liable. But upon the greater part of goods, those duties are equivalent to a prohibition. The French in their turn have, I believe, treated our goods and manufactures just as hardly; though I am not so well acquainted with the particular hardships which they have imposed upon them. Those mutual restraints have put an end to almost all fair commerce between the two nations, and smugglers are now the principal importers, either of British goods into France, or of French goods

into

into Great Britain. The principles which I have been examining in the foregoing chapter took their origin from private interest and the spirit of monopoly; those which I am going to examine in this, from national prejudice and animosity. They are, accordingly, as might well be expected, still more unreasonable. They are so, even upon the principles of the commercial system.

First, though it were certain that in the case of a free trade between France and England, for example, the balance would be in favour of France, it would by no means follow that such a trade would be disadvantageous to England, or that the general balance of its whole trade would thereby be turned more against it. If the wines of France are better and cheaper than those of Portugal, or its linens than those of Germany, it would be more advantageous for Great Britain to purchase both the wine and the foreign linen which it had occasion for of France, than of Portugal and Germany. Though the value of the annual importations from France would thereby be greatly augmented, the value of the whole annual importations would be diminished, in proportion as the French goods of the same quality were cheaper than those of the other two countries. This would be the case, even upon the supposition that the whole French goods imported were to be consumed in Great Britain.

But, secondly, a great part of them might be re-exported to other countries, where, being sold with profit, they might bring back a return equal

BOOK IV. in value, perhaps, to the prime coft of the whole French goods imported. What has frequently been faid of the Eaft India trade might poffibly be true of the French; that though the greater part of Eaft India goods were bought with gold and filver, the re-exportation of a part of them to other countries, brought back more gold and filver to that which carried on the trade than the prime coft of the whole amounted to. One of the moft important branches of the Dutch trade, at prefent, confifts in the carriage of French goods to other European countries. Some part even of the French wine drank in Great Britain is clandeftinely imported from Holland and Zealand. If there was either a free trade between France and England, or if French goods could be imported upon paying only the fame duties as thofe of other European nations, to be drawn back upon exportation, England might have fome fhare of a trade which is found fo advantageous to Holland.

Thirdly, and laftly, there is no certain criterion by which we can determine on which fide what is called the balance between any two countries lies, or which of them exports to the greateft value. National prejudice and animofity, prompted always by the private intereft of particular traders, are the principles which generally direct our judgment upon all queftions concerning it. There are two criterions, however, which have frequently been appealed to upon fuch occafions, the cuftom-houfe books and the courfe of exchange. The cuftom-houfe books, I think,

OF RESTRAINTS UPON IMPORTATION. 213

I think, it is now generally acknowledged, are a very uncertain criterion, on account of the inaccuracy of the valuation at which the greater part of goods are rated in them. The courfe of exchange is, perhaps, almoft equally fo.

When the exchange between two places, fuch as London and Paris, is at par, it is faid to be a fign that the debts due from London to Paris are compenfated by thofe due from Paris to London. On the contrary, when a premium is paid at London for a bill upon Paris, it is faid to be a fign that the debts due from London to Paris are not compenfated by thofe due from Paris to London, but that a balance in money muft be fent out from the latter place; for the rifk, trouble, and expence of exporting which, the premium is both demanded and given. But the ordinary ftate of debt and credit between thofe two cities muft neceffarily be regulated, it is faid, by the ordinary courfe of their dealings with one another. When neither of them imports from the other to a greater amount than it exports to that other, the debts and credits of each may compenfate one another. But when one of them imports from the other to a greater value than it exports to that other, the former neceffarily becomes indebted to the latter in a greater fum than the latter becomes indebted to it: the debts and credits of each do not compenfate one another, and money muft be fent out from that place of which the debts over-balance the credits. The ordinary courfe of exchange, therefore, being an indication of the ordinary

CHAP.
III.

ftate

BOOK IV.

ftate of debt and credit between two places, muft likewife be an indication of the ordinary courfe of their exports and imports, as thefe neceffarily regulate that ftate.

But though the ordinary courfe of exchange fhould be allowed to be a fufficient indication of the ordinary ftate of debt and credit between any two places, it would not from thence follow, that the balance of trade was in favour of that place which had the ordinary ftate of debt and credit in its favour. The ordinary ftate of debt and credit between any two places is not always entirely regulated by the ordinary courfe of their dealings with one another; but is often influenced by that of the dealings of either with many other places. If it is ufual, for example, for the merchants of England to pay for the goods which they buy of Hamburgh, Dantzic, Riga, &c. by bills upon Holland, the ordinary ftate of debt and credit between England and Holland will not be regulated entirely by the ordinary courfe of the dealings of thofe two countries with one another, but will be influenced by that of the dealings of England with thofe other places. England may be obliged to fend out every year money to Holland, though its annual exports to that country may exceed very much the annual value of its imports from thence; and though what is called the balance of trade may be very much in favour of England.

In the way, befides, in which the par of exchange has hitherto been computed, the ordinary courfe of exchange can afford no fufficient indi-

cation

OF RESTRAINTS UPON IMPORTATION. 215

CHAP.
III.

cation that the ordinary ftate of debt and credit is in favour of that country which feems to have, or which is fuppofed to have, the ordinary courfe of exchange in its favour: or, in other words, the real exchange may be, and, in fact, often is fo very different from the computed one, that from the courfe of the latter, no certain conclu- fion can, upon many occafions, be drawn con- cerning that of the former.

When for a fum of money paid in England, containing, according to the ftandard of the Englifh mint, a certain number of ounces of pure filver, you receive a bill for a fum of money to be paid in France, containing, according to the ftandard of the French mint, an equal num- ber of ounces of pure filver, exchange is faid to be at par between England and France. When you pay more, you are fuppofed to give a pre- mium, and exchange is faid to be againft Eng- land, and in favour of France. When you pay lefs, you are fuppofed to get a premium, and exchange is faid to be againft France, and in favour of England.

But, firft, we cannot always judge of the value of the current money of different countries by the ftandard of their refpective mints. In fome it is more, in others it is lefs worn, clipt, and otherwife degenerated from that ftandard. But the value of the current coin of every country, compared with that of any other country, is in proportion, not to the quantity of pure filver which it ought to contain, but to that which it actually does contain. Before the reformation of

P 4

the

216 OF RESTRAINTS UPON IMPORTATION.

BOOK IV.

the filver coin in King William's time, exchange between England and Holland, computed, in the ufual manner, according to the ftandard of their refpective mints, was five and twenty per cent. againft England. But the value of the current coin of England, as we learn from Mr. Lowndes, was at that time rather more than five and twenty per cent. below its ftandard value. The real exchange, therefore, may even at that time have been in favour of England, notwithftanding the computed exchange was fo much againft it; a fmaller number of ounces of pure filver, actually paid in England, may have purchafed a bill for a greater number of ounces of pure filver to be paid in Holland, and the man who was fuppofed to give, may in reality have got the premium. The French coin was, before the late reformation of the Englifh gold coin, much lefs worn than the Englifh, and was, perhaps, two or three per cent. nearer its ftandard. If the computed exchange with France, therefore, was not more than two or three per cent. againft England, the real exchange might have been in its favour. Since the reformation of the gold coin, the exchange has been conftantly in favour of England, and againft France.

Secondly, in fome countries, the expence of coinage is defrayed by the government; in others, it is defrayed by the private people, who carry their bullion to the mint, and the government even derives fome revenue from the coinage. In England it is defrayed by the government, and if you carry a pound weight of ftandard filver to

the

OF RESTRAINTS UPON IMPORTATION. 217

CHAP.
III.

the mint, you get back fixty-two fhillings, containing a pound weight of the like ftandard filver. In France, a duty of eight per cent. is deducted for the coinage, which not only defrays the expence of it, but affords a fmall revenue to the government. In England, as the coinage cofts nothing, the current coin can never be much more valuable than the quantity of bullion which it actually contains. In France, the workmanfhip, as you pay for it, adds to the value, in the fame manner as to that of wrought plate. A fum of French money, therefore, containing a certain weight of pure filver, is more valuable than a fum of Englifh money containing an equal weight of pure filver, and muft require more bullion, or other commodities, to purchafe it. Though the current coin of the two countries, therefore, were equally near the ftandards of their refpective mints, a fum of Englifh money could not well purchafe a fum of French money, containing an equal number of ounces of pure filver, nor confequently a bill upon France for fuch a fum. If for fuch a bill no more additional money was paid than what was fufficient to compenfate the expence of the French coinage, the real exchange might be at par between the two countries, their debts and credits might mutually compenfate one another, while the computed exchange was confiderably in favour of France. If lefs than this was paid, the real exchange might be in favour of England, while the computed was in favour of France,

Thirdly,

BOOK IV. Thirdly, and laftly, in fome places, as at Amfterdam, Hamburgh, Venice, &c. foreign bills of exchange are paid in what they call bank money; while in others, as at London, Lifbon, Antwerp, Leghorn, &c. they are paid in the common currency of the country. What is called bank money is always of more value than the fame nominal fum of common currency. A thoufand guilders in the bank of Amfterdam, for example, are of more value than a thoufand guilders of Amfterdam currency. The difference between them is called the agio of the bank, which, at Amfterdam, is generally about five per cent. Suppofing the current money of the two countries equally near to the ftandard of their refpective mints, and that the one pays foreign bills in this common currency, while the other pays them in bank money, it is evident that the computed exchange may be in favour of that which pays in bank money, though the real exchange fhould be in favour of that which pays in current money; for the fame reafon that the computed exchange may be in favour of that which pays in better money, or in money nearer to its own ftandard, though the real exchange fhould be in favour of that which pays in worfe. The computed exchange, before the late reformation of the gold coin, was generally againft London with Amfterdam, Hamburgh, Venice, and, I believe, with all other places which pay in what is called bank money. It will by no means follow, however, that the real exchange was againft it. Since the reformation of the gold coin,

OF RESTRAINTS UPON IMPORTATION. 219

coin, it has been in favour of London even with CHAP. thofe places. The computed exchange has ge- III. nerally been in favour of London with Lifbon, Antwerp, Leghorn, and, if you except France, I believe, with moft other parts of Europe that pay in common currency; and it is not impro- bable that the real exchange was fo too.

Digreffion concerning Banks of Depofit, particularly concerning that of Amfterdam.

THE currency of a great ftate, fuch as France or England, generally confifts al- moft entirely of its own coin. Should this cur- rency, therefore, be at any time worn, clipt, or otherwife degraded below its ftandard value, the ftate by a reformation of its coin can effectually re-eftablifh its currency. But the currency of a fmall ftate, fuch as Genoa or Hamburgh, can feldom confift altogether in its own coin, but muft be made up, in a great meafure, of the coins of all the neighbouring ftates with which its inhabitants have a continual intercourfe. Such a ftate, therefore, by reforming its coin, will not always be able to reform its currency. If foreign bills of exchange are paid in this cur- rency, the uncertain value of any fum, of what is in its own nature fo uncertain, muft render the exchange always very much againft fuch a ftate, its currency being, in all foreign ftates, neceffa- rily valued even below what it is worth.

In

OF RESTRAINTS UPON IMPORTATION.

BOOK IV.

In order to remedy the inconvenience to which this difadvantageous exchange muft have fubjected their merchants, fuch fmall states, when they began to attend to the intereft of trade, have frequently enacted, that foreign bills of exchange of a certain value fhould be paid, not in common currency, but by an order upon, or by a transfer in the books of a certain bank, eftablifhed upon the credit, and under the protection of the ftate; this bank being always obliged to pay, in good and true money, exactly according to the ftandard of the ftate. The banks of Venice, Genoa, Amfterdam, Hamburgh, and Nuremberg, feem to have been all originally eftablifhed with this view, though fome of them may have afterwards been made fubfervient to other purpofes. The money of fuch banks being better than the common currency of the country, neceffarily bore an agio, which was greater or fmaller, according as the currency was fuppofed to be more or lefs degraded below the ftandard of the ftate. The agio of the bank of Hamburgh, for example, which is faid to be commonly about fourteen per cent. is the fuppofed difference between the good ftandard money of the ftate, and the clipt, worn, and diminifhed currency poured into it from all the neighbouring ftates.

Before 1609 the great quantity of clipt and worn foreign coin, which the extenfive trade of Amfterdam brought from all parts of Europe, reduced the value of its currency about nine per cent. below that of good money frefh from

the

OF RESTRAINTS UPON IMPORTATION.

the mint. Such money no fooner appeared than it was melted down or carried away, as it always is in fuch circumftances. The merchants, with plenty of currency, could not always find a fufficient quantity of good money to pay their bills of exchange; and the value of thofe bills, in fpite of feveral regulations which were made to prevent it, became in a great meafure uncertain.

In order to remedy thefe inconveniencies, a bank was eftablifhed in 1609 under the guarantee of the city. This bank received both foreign coin, and the light and worn coin of the country at its real intrinfic value in the good ftandard money of the country, deducting only fo much as was neceffary for defraying the expence of coinage, and the other neceffary expence of management. For the value which remained, after this fmall deduction was made, it gave a credit in its books. This credit was called bank money, which, as it reprefented money exactly according to the ftandard of the mint, was always of the fame real value, and intrinfically worth more than current money. It was at the fame time enacted, that all bills drawn upon or negotiated at Amfterdam of the value of fix hundred guilders and upwards fhould be paid in bank money, which at once took away all uncertainty in the value of thofe bills. Every merchant, in confequence of this regulation, was obliged to keep an account with the bank in order to pay his foreign bills of exchange, which neceffarily occafioned a certain demand for bank money.

Bank

OF RESTRAINTS UPON IMPORTATION.

BOOK IV.

Bank money, over and above both its intrinfic fuperiority to currency, and the additional value which this demand neceffarily gives it, has likewife fome other advantages. It is fecure from fire, robbery, and other accidents; the city of Amfterdam is bound for it; it can be paid away by a fimple transfer, without the trouble of counting, or the rifk of tranfporting it from one place to another. In confequence of thofe different advantages, it feems from the beginning to have borne an agio, and it is generally believed that all the money originally depofited in the bank was allowed to remain there, nobody caring to demand payment of a debt which he could fell for a premium in the market. By demanding payment of the bank, the owner of a bank credit would lofe this premium. As a fhilling frefh from the mint will buy no more goods in the market than one of our common worn fhillings, fo the good and true money which might be brought from the coffers of the bank into thofe of a private perfon, being mixed and confounded with the common currency of the country, would be of no more value than that currency, from which it could no longer be readily diftinguifhed. While it remained in the coffers of the bank, its fuperiority was known and afcertained. When it had come into thofe of a private perfon, its fuperiority could not well be afcertained without more trouble than perhaps the difference was worth. By being brought from the coffers of the bank, befides, it loft all the other advantages of bank money; its fecurity,

OF RESTRAINTS UPON IMPORTATION. 223

rity, its eafy and fafe transferability, its ufe in paying foreign bills of exchange. Over and above all this, it could not be brought from thofe coffers, as it will appear by and by, without previoufly paying for the keeping.

Thofe depofits of coin, or thofe depofits which the bank was bound to reftore in coin, conftituted the original capital of the bank, or the whole value of what was reprefented by what is called bank money. At prefent they are fuppofed to conftitute but a very fmall part of it. In order to facilitate the trade in bullion, the bank has been for thefe many years in the practice of giving credit in its books upon depofits of gold and filver bullion. This credit is generally about five per cent. below the mint price of fuch bullion. The bank grants at the fame time what is called a recipice or receipt, intitling the perfon who makes the depofit, or the bearer, to take out the bullion again at any time within fix months, upon retransferring to the bank a quantity of bank money equal to that for which credit had been given in its books when the depofit was made, and upon paying one-fourth per cent. for the keeping, if the depofit was in filver ; and one-half per cent. if it was in gold ; but at the fame time declaring, that in default of fuch payment, and upon the expiration of this term, the depofit fhould belong to the bank at the price at which it had been received, or for which credit had been given in the transfer books. What is thus paid for the keeping of the depofit may be confidered as a fort of warehoufe

224 OF RESTRAINTS UPON IMPORTATION.

BOOK IV.

houfe rent; and why this warehoufe rent fhould be fo much dearer for gold than for filver, feveral different reafons have been affigned. The finenefs of gold, it has been faid, is more difficult to be afcertained than that of filver. Frauds are more eafily practifed, and occafion a greater lofs in the more precious metal. Silver, befides, being the ftandard metal, the ftate, it has been faid, wifhes to encourage more the making of depofits of filver than thofe of gold.

Depofits of bullion are moft commonly made when the price is fomewhat lower than ordinary; and they are taken out again when it happens to rife. In Holland the market price of bullion is generally above the mint price, for the fame reafon that it was fo in England before the late reformation of the gold coin. The difference is faid to be commonly from about fix to fixteen ftivers upon the mark, or eight ounces of filver of eleven parts fine, and one part alloy. The bank price, or the credit which the bank gives for depofits of fuch filver (when made in foreign coin, of which the finenefs is well known and afcertained, fuch as Mexico dollars), is twenty-two guilders the mark; the mint price is about twenty-three guilders, and the market price is from twenty-three guilders fix, to twenty-three guilders fixteen ftivers, or from two to three per cent. above the mint price *. The proportions

---

* The following are the prices at which the bank of Amftery dam at prefent (September, 1775) receives bullion and coin of different kinds:

SIL-

OF RESTRAINTS UPON IMPORTATION. 225

tions between the bank price, the mint price, and the market price of gold bullion, are nearly the fame. A perfon can generally fell his receipt for the difference between the mint price of bullion and the market price. A receipt for bullion is almoft always worth fomething, and it very feldom happens, therefore, that any body fuffers his receipt to expire, or allows his bullion to fall to the bank at the price at which it had been received, either by not taking it out before the end of the fix months, or by neglecting to pay the one-fourth or one-half per cent. in order to obtain a new receipt for another fix months. This, however, though it happens feldom, is faid to happen fometimes, and more frequently

CHAP.
III.

SILVER.

Mexico dollars	Guilders.
French crowns	} B—22 per mark.
Englifh filver coin	
Mexico dollars new coin	• 21 10
Ducatoons • - - •	3
Rix dollars • - • - •	2 8

Bar filver containing $\frac{11}{12}$ fine filver 21 per mark, and in this proportion down to $\frac{1}{4}$ fine, on which 5 guilders are given.
Fine bars, 23 per mark.

GOLD.

Portugal coin	
Guineas	} B—310 per mark.
Louis d'ors new	
Ditto old • - - -	• 300
New ducats - - - - -	4 19 8 per ducat.

Bar or ingot gold is received in proportion to its finenefs compared with the above foreign gold coin. Upon fine bars the bank gives 340 per mark. In general, however, fomething more is given upon coin of a known finenefs, than upon gold and filver bars, of which the finenefs cannot be afcertained but by a procefs of melting and affaying.

VOL. III.   Q   with

OF RESTRAINTS UPON IMPORTATION.

BOOK IV.

with regard to gold, than with regard to filver, on account of the higher warehoufe-rent which is paid for the keeping of the more precious metal.

The perfon who by making a depofit of bullion obtains both a bank credit and a receipt, pays his bills of exchange as they become due with his bank credit; and either fells or keeps his receipt according as he judges that the price of bullion is likely to rife or to fall. The receipt and the bank credit feldom keep long together, and there is no occafion that they fhould. The perfon who has a receipt, and who wants to take out bullion, finds always plenty of bank credits, or bank money to buy at the ordinary price; and the perfon who has bank money, and wants to take out bullion, finds receipts always in equal abundance.

The owners of bank credits, and the holders of receipts, conftitute two different forts of creditors againft the bank. The holder of a receipt cannot draw out the bullion for which it is granted, without re-affigning to the bank a fum of bank money equal to the price at which the bullion had been received. If he has no bank money of his own, he muft purchafe it of thofe who have it. The owner of bank money cannot draw out bullion without producing to the bank receipts for the quantity which he wants. If he has none of his own, he muft buy them of thofe who have them. The holder of a receipt, when he purchafes bank money, purchafes the power

of

OF RESTRAINTS UPON IMPORTATION. 227

of taking out a quantity of bullion, of which the CHAP.
mint price is five per cent. above the bank price. III.
The agio of five per cent. therefore, which he
commonly pays for it, is paid, not for an imaginary, but for a real value. The owner of bank
money, when he purchafes a receipt, purchafes
the power of taking out a quantity of bullion of
which the market price is commonly from two to
three per cent. above the mint price. The price
which he pays for it, therefore, is paid likewife
for a real value. The price of the receipt, and
the price of the bank money, compound or make
up between them the full value or price of the
bullion.

Upon depofits of the coin current in the country, the bank grants receipts likewife as well as
bank credits; but thofe receipts are frequently
of no value, and will bring no price in the market. Upon ducatoons, for example, which in
the currency pafs for three guilders three ftivers
each, the bank gives a credit of three guilders
only, or five per cent. below their current value.
It grants a receipt likewife intitling the bearer
to take out the number of ducatoons depofited
at any time within fix months, upon paying one-
fourth per cent. for the keeping. This receipt
will frequently bring no price in the market.
Three guilders bank money generally fell in the
market for three guilders three ftivers, the full
value of the ducatoons, if they were taken out of
the bank; and before they can be taken out,
one-fourth per cent. muft be paid for the keep-

Q 2 ing

OF RESTRAINTS UPON IMPORTATION.

BOOK IV.

ing, which would be mere loſs to the holder of the receipt. If the agio of the bank, however, ſhould at any time fall to three per cent. ſuch receipts might bring ſome price in the market, and might ſell for one and three-fourths per cent. But the agio of the bank being now generally about five per cent. ſuch receipts are frequently allowed to expire, or, as they expreſs it, to fall to the bank. The receipts which are given for depoſits of gold ducats fall to it yet more frequently, becauſe a higher warehouſe-rent, or one-half per-cent. muſt be paid for the keeping of them before they can be taken out again. The five per cent. which the bank gains, when depoſits either of coin or bullion are allowed to fall to it, may be confidered as the warehouſe-rent for the perpetual keeping of ſuch depoſits.

The ſum of bank money for which the receipts are expired muſt be very confiderable. It muſt comprehend the whole original capital of the bank, which, it is generally ſuppoſed, has been allowed to remain there from the time it was firſt depoſited, nobody caring either to renew his receipt or to take out his depoſit, as, for the reaſons already aſſigned, neither the one nor the other could be done without loſs. But whatever may be the amount of this ſum, the proportion which it bears to the whole maſs of bank money is ſuppoſed to be very ſmall. The bank of Amſterdam has for theſe many years paſt been the great warehouſe of Europe for bullion,

OF RESTRAINTS UPON IMPORTATION.

CHAP. III.

tion, for which the receipts are very feldom allowed to expire, or, as they exprefs it, to fall to the bank. The far greater part of the bank money, or of the credits upon the books of the bank, is fuppofed to have been created, for thefe many years paft, by fuch depofits which the dealers in bullion are continually both making and withdrawing.

No demand can be made upon the bank but by means of a recipice or receipt. The fmaller mafs of bank money, for which the receipts are expired, is mixed and confounded with the much greater mafs for which they are ftill in force; fo that, though there may be a confiderable fum of bank money, for which there are no receipts, there is no fpecific fum or portion of it, which may not at any time be demanded by one. The bank cannot be debtor to two perfons for the fame thing; and the owner of bank money who has no receipt, cannot demand payment of the bank till he buys one. In ordinary and quiet times, he can find no difficulty in getting one to buy at the market price, which generally correfponds with the price at which he can fell the coin or bullion it intitles him to take out of the bank.

It might be otherwife during a public calamity; an invafion, for example, fuch as that of the French in 1672. The owners of bank money being then all eager to draw it out of the bank, in order to have it in their own keeping, the demand for receipts might raife their price to an exorbitant height. The holders of them might

OF RESTRAINTS UPON IMPORTATION.

BOOK IV.

might form extravagant expectations, and, inſtead of two or three per cent. demand half the bank money for which credit had been given upon the depoſits that the receipts had reſpectively been granted for. The enemy, informed of the conſtitution of the bank, might even buy them up, in order to prevent the carrying away of the treaſure. In ſuch emergencies, the bank, it is ſuppoſed, would break through its ordinary rule of making payment only to the holders of receipts. The holders of receipts, who had no bank money, muſt have received within two or three per cent. of the value of the depoſit for which their reſpective receipts had been granted. The bank, therefore, it is ſaid, would in this caſe make no ſcruple of paying, either with money or bullion, the full value of what the owners of bank money who could get no receipts were credited for in its books; paying at the ſame time two or three per cent. to ſuch holders of receipts as had no bank money, that being the whole value which in this ſtate of things could juſtly be ſuppoſed due to them.

Even in ordinary and quiet times it is the intereſt of the holders of receipts to depreſs the agio, in order either to buy bank money (and conſequently the bullion, which their receipts would then enable them to take out of the bank) ſo much cheaper, or to ſell their receipts to thoſe who have bank money, and who want to take out bullion, ſo much dearer; the price of a receipt being generally equal to the difference between the market price of bank money, and

that

OF RESTRAINTS UPON IMPORTATION. 231

that of the coin or bullion for which the receipt
had been granted. It is the intereft of the owners of bank money, on the contrary, to raife
the agio, in order either to fell their bank money fo much dearer, or to buy a receipt fo much
cheaper. To prevent the ftock-jobbing tricks
which thofe oppofite interefts might fometimes
occafion, the bank has of late years come to the
refolution to fell at all times bank money for
currency, at five per cent. agio, and to buy it
in again at four per cent. agio. In confequence
of this refolution, the agio can never either rife
above five, or fink below four per cent. and the
proportion between the market price of bank
and that of current money, is kept at all times
very near to the proportion between their intrinfic values. Before this refolution was taken,
the market price of bank money ufed fometimes
to rife fo high as nine per cent. agio, and fometimes to fink fo low as par, according as oppofite
interefts happened to influence the market.

. The bank of Amfterdam profeffes to lend out
no part of what is depofited with it, but, for
every guilder for which it gives credit in its
books, to keep in its repofitories the value of a
guilder either in money or bullion. That it keeps
in its repofitories all the money or bullion for
which there are receipts in force, for which it is
at all times liable to be called upon, and which,
in reality, is continually going from it and returning to it again, cannot well be doubted.
But whether it does fo likewife with regard to
that part of its capital, for which the receipts

CHAP.
III.

Q 4   are

BOOK IV.

are long ago expired, for which in ordinary and quiet times it cannot be called upon, and which in reality is very likely to remain with it for ever, or as long as the States of the United Provinces subfift, may perhaps appear more uncertain. At Amfterdam, however, no point of faith is better eftablifhed than that for every guilder, circulated as bank money, there is a correfpondent guilder in gold or filver to be found in the treafure of the bank. The city is guarantee that it fhould be fo. The bank is under the direction of the four reigning burgomafters, who are changed every year. Each new fet of burgomafters vifits the treafure, compares it with the books, receives it upon oath, and delivers it over, with the fame awful folemnity, to the fet which fucceeds; and in that fober and religious country oaths are not yet difregarded. A rotation of this kind feems alone a fufficient fecurity againft any practices which cannot be avowed. Amidft all the revolutions which faction has ever occafioned in the government of Amfterdam, the prevailing party has at no time accufed their predeceffors of infidelity in the adminiftration of the bank. No accufation could have affected more deeply the reputation and fortune of the difgraced party, and if fuch an accufation could have been fupported, we may be affured that it would have been brought. In 1672, when the French King was at Utrecht, the bank of Amfterdam paid fo readily as left no doubt of the fidelity with which it had obferved its engagements. Some of the pieces which were then

brought

brought from its repofitories appeared to have been fcorched with the fire which happened in the town-houfe foon after the bank was eftablifhed. Thofe pieces, therefore, muft have lain there from that time.

What may be the amount of the treafure in the bank, is a queftion which has long employed the fpeculations of the curious. Nothing but conjecture can be offered concerning it. It is generally reckoned that there are about two thoufand people who keep accounts with the bank, and allowing them to have, one with another, the value of fifteen hundred pounds fterling lying upon their refpective accounts (a very large allowance), the whole quantity of bank money, and confequently of treafure in the bank, will amount to about three millions fterling, or at eleven guilders the pound fterling, thirty-three millions of guilders; a great fum, and fufficient to carry on a very extenfive circulation; but vaftly below the extravagant ideas which fome people have formed of this treafure.

The city of Amfterdam derives a confiderable revenue from the bank. Befides what may be called the warehoufe-rent above mentioned, each perfon, upon firft opening an account with the bank, pays a fee of ten guilders; and for every new account three guilders three ftivers; for every transfer two ftivers; and if the transfer is for lefs than three hundred guilders, fix ftivers, in order to difcourage the multiplicity of fmall tranfactions. The perfon who neglects to balance his account twice in the year forfeits twenty-

234   OF RESTRAINTS UPON IMPORTATION.

BOOK
IV.

twenty-five guilders. The perfon who orders a transfer for more than is upon his account, is obliged to pay three per cent. for the fum overdrawn, and his order is fet afide into the bargain. The bank is fuppofed too to make a confiderable profit by the fale of the foreign coin or bullion which fometimes falls to it by the expiring of receipts, and which is always kept till it can be fold with advantage. It makes a profit likewife by felling bank money at five per cent. agio, and buying it in at four. Thefe different emoluments amount to a good deal more than what is neceffary for paying the falaries of officers, and defraying the expence of management. What is paid for the keeping of bullion upon receipts, is alone fuppofed to amount to a neat annual revenue of between one hundred and fifty thoufand and two hundred thoufand guilders. Public utility, however, and not revenue, was the original object of this inftitution. Its object was to relieve the merchants from the inconvenience of a difadvantageous exchange. The revenue which has arifen from it was unforefeen, and may be confidered as accidental. But it is now time to return from this long digreffion, into which I have been infenfibly led in endeavouring to explain the reafons why the exchange between the countries which pay in what is called bank money, and thofe which pay in common currency, fhould generally appear to be in favour of the former, and againft the latter. The former pay in a fpecies of money of which the intrinfic value is always the fame, and exactly

agreeable

OF RESTRAINTS UPON IMPORTATION. 235

agreeable to the ſtandard of their reſpective C H A P.
mints; the latter is a ſpecies of money of which III.
the intrinſic value is continually varying, and is
almoſt always more or leſs below that ſtandard.

PART II.

Of the Unreaſonableneſs of thoſe extraordinary Reſtraints upon
other Principles.

IN the foregoing Part of this Chapter I have
endeavoured to ſhew, even upon the principles of the commercial ſyſtem, how unneceſſary
it is to lay extraordinary reſtraints upon the
importation of goods from thoſe countries with
which the balance of trade is ſuppoſed to be
diſadvantageous.

Nothing, however, can be more abſurd than
this whole doctrine of the balance of trade, upon
which, not only theſe reſtraints, but almoſt all
the other regulations of commerce are founded.
When two places trade with one another, this
doctrine ſuppoſes that, if the balance be even,
neither of them either loſes or gains; but if it
leans in any degree to one ſide, that one of them
loſes, and the other gains in proportion to its
declenſion from the exact equilibrium. Both
ſuppoſitions are falſe. A trade which is forced
by means of bounties and monopolies, may be,
and commonly is diſadvantageous to the country
in whoſe favour it is meant to be eſtabliſhed, as
I ſhall endeavour to ſhew hereafter. But that

trade

236   OF RESTRAINTS UPON IMPORTATION.

BOOK IV.

trade, which, without force or conftraint, is naturally and regularly carried on between any two places, is always advantageous, though not always equally fo, to both.

By advantage or gain, I underftand, not the increafe of the quantity of gold and filver, but that of the exchangeable value of the annual produce of the land and labour of the country, or the increafe of the annual revenue of its inhabitants.

If the balance be even, and if the trade between the two places confift altogether in the exchange of their native commodities, they will, upon moft occafions, not only both gain, but they will gain equally, or very near equally: each will in this cafe afford a market for a part of the furplus produce of the other: each will replace a capital which had been employed in raifing and preparing for the market this part of the furplus produce of the other, and which had been diftributed among, and given revenue and maintenance to a certain number of its inhabitants. Some part of the inhabitants of each, therefore, will indirectly derive their revenue and maintenance from the other. As the commodities exchanged too are fuppofed to be of equal value, fo the two capitals employed in the trade will, upon moft occafions, be equal, or very nearly equal; and both being employed in raifing the native commodities of the two countries, the revenue and maintenance which their diftribution will afford to the inhabitants of each will be equal, or very nearly equal. This revenue and

OF RESTRAINTS UPON IMPORTATION. 237

and maintenance, thus mutually afforded, will be greater or fmaller in proportion to the extent of their dealings. If thefe fhould annually amount to an hundred thoufand pounds, for example, or to a million on each fide, each of them would afford an annual revenue in the one cafe of an hundred thoufand pounds, in the other, of a million, to the inhabitants of the other.

If their trade fhould be of fuch a nature that one of them exported to the other nothing but native commodities, while the returns of that other confifted altogether in foreign goods; the balance in this cafe, would ftill be fuppofed even, commodities being paid for with commodities. They would, in this cafe too, both gain, but they would not gain equally; and the inhabitants of the country which exported nothing but native commodities would derive the greateft revenue from the trade. If England, for example, fhould import from France nothing but the native commodities of that country, and, not having fuch commodities of its own as were in demand there, fhould annually repay them by fending thither a large quantity of foreign goods, tobacco, we fhall fuppofe, and Eaft India goods; this trade, though it would give fome revenue to the inhabitants of both countries, would give more to thofe of France than to thofe of England. The whole French capital annually employed in it would annually be diftributed among the people of France. But that part of the Englifh capital only which was employed in producing the Englifh commodities with which thofe

foreign

CHAP. III.

238 OF RESTRAINTS UPON IMPORTATION.

BOOK
IV.

foreign goods were purchafed, would be annually diftributed among the people of England. The greater part of it would replace the capitals which had been employed in Virginia, Indoftan, and China, and which had given revenue and maintenance to the inhabitants of thofe diftant countries. If the capitals were equal, or nearly equal, therefore, this employment of the French capital would augment much more the revenue of the people of France, than that of the Englifh capital would the revenue of the people of England. France would in this cafe carry on a direct foreign trade of confumption with England; whereas England would carry on a round-about trade of the fame kind with France. The different effects of a capital employed in the direct, and of one employed in the round-about foreign trade of confumption, have already been fully explained.

There is not, probably, between any two countries, a trade which confifts altogether in the exchange either of native commodities on both fides, or of native commodities on one fide and of foreign goods on the other. Almoft all countries exchange with one another partly native and partly foreign goods. That country, however, in whofe cargoes there is the greateft proportion of native, and the leaft of foreign goods, will always be the principal gainer.

If it was not with tobacco and Eaft India goods, but with gold and filver, that England paid for the commodities annually imported from France, the balance, in this cafe, would be fuppofed

OF RESTRAINTS UPON IMPORTATION. 239

poſed uneven, commodities not being paid for with commodities, but with gold and ſilver. The trade, however, would, in this caſe, as in the foregoing, give ſome revenue to the inhabitants of both countries, but more to thoſe of France than to thoſe of England. It would give ſome revenue to thoſe of England. The capital which had been employed in producing the Engliſh goods that purchaſed this gold and ſilver, the capital which had been diſtributed among, and given revenue to, certain inhabitants of England, would thereby be replaced, and enabled to continue that employment. The whole capital of England would no more be diminiſhed by this exportation of gold and ſilver, than by the exportation of an equal value of any other goods. On the contrary, it would, in moſt caſes, be augmented. No goods are ſent abroad but thoſe for which the demand is ſuppoſed to be greater abroad than at home, and of which the returns conſequently, it is expected, will be of more value at home than the commodities exported. If the tobacco which, in England, is worth only a hundred thouſand pounds, when ſent to France will purchaſe wine which is, in England, worth a hundred and ten thouſand pounds, the exchange will augment the capital of England by ten thouſand pounds. If a hundred thouſand pounds of Engliſh gold, in the ſame manner, purchaſe French wine, which, in England, is worth a hundred and ten thouſand, this exchange will equally augment the capital of England by ten thouſand pounds. As a merchant who has

CHAP.
III.

a hundred

OF RESTRAINTS UPON IMPORTATION.

BOOK
IV.

a hundred and ten thoufand pounds worth of wine in his cellar, is a richer man than he who has only a hundred thoufand pounds worth of tobacco in his warehoufe, fo is he likewife a richer man than he who has only a hundred thoufand pounds worth of gold in his coffers. He can put into motion a greater quantity of induftry, and give revenue, maintenance, and employment, to a greater number of people than either of the other two. But the capital of the country is equal to the capitals of all its different inhabitants, and the quantity of induftry which can be annually maintained in it, is equal to what all thofe different capitals can maintain. Both the capital of the country, therefore, and the quantity of induftry which can be annually maintained in it, muft generally be augmented by this exchange. It would, indeed, be more advantageous for England that it could purchafe the wines of France with its own hard-ware and broad-cloth, than with either the tobacco of Virginia, or the gold and filver of Brazil and Peru. A direct foreign trade of confumption is always more advantageous than a round-about one. But a round-about foreign trade of confumption, which is carried on with gold and filver, does not feem to be lefs advantageous than any other equally round-about one. Neither is a country which has no mines, more likely to be exhaufted of gold and filver by this annual exportation of thofe metals, than one which does not grow tobacco by the like annual exportation of that plant. As a country which has wherewithal

withal to buy tobacco will never be long in want of it, fo neither will one be long in want of gold and filver which has wherewithal to purchafe thofe metals.

It is a lofing trade, it is faid, which a workman carries on with the alehoufe; and the trade which a manufacturing nation would naturally carry on with a wine country, may be confidered as a trade of the fame nature. I anfwer, that the trade with the alehoufe is not neceffarily a lofing trade. In its own nature it is juft as advantageous as any other, though, perhaps, fomewhat more liable to be abufed. The employment of a brewer, and even that of a retailer of fermented liquors, are as neceffary divifions of labour as any other. It will generally be more advantageous for a workman to buy of the brewer the quantity he has occafion for, than to brew it himfelf, and if he is a poor workman, it will generally be more advantageous for him to buy it, by little and little, of the retailer, than a large quantity of the brewer. He may no doubt buy too much of either, as he may of any other dealers in his neighbourhood, of the butcher, if he is a glutton, or of the draper, if he affects to be a beau among his companions. It is advantageous to the great body of workmen, notwithftanding, that all thefe trades fhould be free, though this freedom may be abufed in all of them, and is more likely to be fo, perhaps, in fome than in others. Though individuals, befides, may fometimes ruin their fortunes by an exceffive confumption of fermented liquors, there

VOL. III.   R   feems

OF RESTRAINTS UPON IMPORTATION.

BOOK IV.

seems to be no risk that a nation should do so. Though in every country there are many people who spend upon such liquors more than they can afford, there are always many more who spend less. It deserves to be remarked too, that, if we consult experience, the cheapness of wine seems to be a cause, not of drunkenness, but of sobriety. The inhabitants of the wine countries are in general the soberest people in Europe; witness the Spaniards, the Italians, and the inhabitants of the southern provinces of France. People are seldom guilty of excess in what is their daily fare. Nobody affects the character of liberality and good fellowship, by being profuse of a liquor which is as cheap as small beer. On the contrary, in the countries which, either from excessive heat or cold, produce no grapes, and where wine consequently is dear and a rarity, drunkenness is a common vice, as among the northern nations, and all those who live between the tropics, the negroes, for example, on the coast of Guinea. When a French regiment comes from some of the northern provinces of France, where wine is somewhat dear, to be quartered in the southern, where it is very cheap, the soldiers, I have frequently heard it observed, are at first debauched by the cheapness and novelty of good wine; but after a few months residence, the greater part of them become as sober as the rest of the inhabitants. Were the duties upon foreign wines, and the excises upon malt, beer, and ale, to be taken away all at once, it might, in the same manner, occasion in Great

Britain

OF RESTRAINTS UPON IMPORTATION.

Britain a pretty general and temporary drunkenness among the middling and inferior ranks of people; which would probably be soon followed by a permanent and almost universal sobriety. At present drunkenness is by no means the vice of people of fashion, or of those who can easily afford the most expensive liquors. A gentleman drunk with ale, has scarce ever been seen among us. The restraints upon the wine trade in Great Britain, besides, do not so much seem calculated to hinder the people from going, if I may say so, to the alehouse, as from going where they can buy the best and cheapest liquor. They favour the wine trade of Portugal, and discourage that of France. The Portuguese, it is said, indeed, are better customers for our manufactures than the French, and should therefore be encouraged in preference to them. As they give us their custom, it is pretended, we should give them ours. The sneaking arts of underling tradesmen are thus erected into political maxims, for the conduct of a great empire; for it is the most underling tradesmen only who make it a rule to employ chiefly their own customers. A great trader purchases his goods always where they are cheapest and best, without regard to any little interest of this kind.

By such maxims as these, however, nations have been taught that their interest consisted in beggaring all their neighbours. Each nation has been made to look with an invidious eye upon the prosperity of all the nations with which it trades, and to consider their gain as its own lofs.

OF RESTRAINTS UPON IMPORTATION.

BOOK IV.

loſs. Commerce, which ought naturally to be, among nations, as among individuals, a bond of union and friendſhip, has become the moſt fertile ſource of diſcord and animoſity. The capricious ambition of kings and miniſters has not, during the preſent and the preceding century, been more fatal to the repoſe of Europe, than the impertinent jealouſy of merchants and manufacturers. The violence and injuſtice of the rulers of mankind is an ancient evil, for which, I am afraid, the nature of human affairs can ſcarce admit of a remedy. But the mean rapacity, the monopolizing ſpirit of merchants and manufacturers, who neither are, nor ought to be, the rulers of mankind, though it cannot perhaps be corrected, may very eaſily be prevented from diſturbing the tranquillity of any body but themſelves.

That it was the ſpirit of monopoly which originally both invented and propagated this doctrine, cannot be doubted; and they who firſt taught it were by no means ſuch fools as they who believed it. In every country it always is and muſt be the intereſt of the great body of the people to buy whatever they want of thoſe who ſell it cheapeſt. The propoſition is ſo very manifeſt, that it ſeems ridiculous to take any pains to prove it; nor could it ever have been called in queſtion, had not the intereſted ſophiſtry of merchants and manufacturers confounded the common ſenſe of mankind. Their intereſt is, in this reſpect, directly oppoſite to that of the great body of the people. As it is the intereſt of the freemen

of

OF RESTRAINTS UPON IMPORTATION. 245

CHAP.
III.

of a corporation to hinder the reft of the inhabitants from employing any workmen but themfelves, fo it is the intereft of the merchants and manufacturers of every country to fecure to themfelves the monopoly of the home market. Hence in Great Britain, and in moft other European countries, the extraordinary duties upon almoft all goods imported by alien merchants. Hence the high duties and prohibitions upon all thofe foreign manufactures which can come into competition with our own. Hence too the extraordinary reftraints upon the importation of almoft all forts of goods from thofe countries with which the balance of trade is fuppofed to be difadvantageous; that is, from thofe againft whom national animofity happens to be moft violently inflamed.

The wealth of a neighbouring nation, however, though dangerous in war and politics, is certainly advantageous in trade. In a ftate of hoftility it may enable our enemies to maintain fleets and armies fuperior to our own; but in a ftate of peace and commerce it muft likewife enable them to exchange with us to a greater value, and to afford a better market, either for the immediate produce of our own induftry, or for whatever is purchafed with that produce. As a rich man is likely to be a better cuftomer to the induftrious people in his neighbourhood, than a poor, fo is likewife a rich nation. A rich man, indeed, who is himfelf a manufacturer, is a very dangerous neighbour to all thofe who deal in the fame way. All the reft of the neighbourhood,

R 3

246 OF RESTRAINTS UPON IMPORTATION.

BOOK IV. bourhood, however, by far the greateſt number, profit by the good market which his expence affords them. They even profit by his underſelling the poorer workmen who deal in the ſame way with him. The manufacturers of a rich nation, in the ſame manner, may no doubt be very dangerous rivals to thoſe of their neighbours. This very competition, however, is advantageous to the great body of the people, who profit greatly beſides by the good market which the great expence of ſuch a nation affords them in every other way. Private people who want to make a fortune, never think of retiring to the remote and poor provinces of the country, but reſort either to the capital, or to ſome of the great commercial towns. They know, that, where little wealth circulates, there is little to be got, but that where a great deal is in motion, ſome ſhare of it may fall to them. The ſame maxims which would in this manner direct the common ſenſe of one, or ten, or twenty individuals, ſhould regulate the judgment of one, or ten, or twenty millions, and ſhould make a whole nation regard the riches of its neighbours, as a probable cauſe and occaſion for itſelf to acquire riches. A nation that would enrich itſelf by foreign trade, is certainly moſt likely to do ſo when its neighbours are all rich, induſtrious, and commercial nations. A great nation ſurrounded on all ſides by wandering ſavages and poor barbarians might, no doubt, acquire riches by the cultivation of its own lands, and by its own interior commerce, but not by foreign trade. It ſeems to have been

in

OF RESTRAINTS UPON IMPORTATION. 247

CHAP.
III.

in this manner that the ancient Egyptians and the modern Chinese acquired their great wealth. The ancient Egyptians, it is said, neglected foreign commerce, and the modern Chinese, it is known, hold it in the utmost contempt, and scarce deign to afford it the decent protection of the laws. The modern maxims of foreign commerce, by aiming at the impoverishment of all our neighbours, so far as they are capable of producing their intended effect, tend to render that very commerce insignificant and contemptible.

It is in consequence of these maxims that the commerce between France and England has in both countries been subjected to so many discouragements and restraints. If those two countries, however, were to consider their real interest, without either mercantile jealousy or national animosity, the commerce of France might be more advantageous to Great Britain than that of any other country, and for the same reason that of Great Britain to France. France is the nearest neighbour to Great Britain. In the trade between the southern coast of England and the northern and north-western coasts of France, the returns might be expected, in the same manner as in the inland trade, four, five, or six times in the year. The capital, therefore, employed in this trade, could in each of the two countries keep in motion four, five, or six times the quantity of industry, and afford employment and subsistence to four, five, or six times the number of

R 4

people,

OF RESTRAINTS UPON IMPORTATION.

BOOK IV.

people, which an equal capital could do in the greater part of the other branches of foreign trade. Between the parts of France and Great Britain moſt remote from one another, the returns might be expected, at leaſt, once in the year, and even this trade would ſo far be at leaſt equally advantageous as the greater part of the other branches of our foreign European trade. It would be, at leaſt, three times more advantageous, than the boaſted trade with our North American colonies, in which the returns were ſeldom made in leſs than three years, frequently not in leſs than four or five years. France, beſides, is ſuppoſed to contain twenty-four millions of inhabitants. Our North American colonies were never ſuppoſed to contain more than three millions : And France is a much richer country than North America; though, on account of the more unequal diſtribution of riches, there is much more poverty and beggary in the one country, than in the other. France therefore could afford a market at leaſt eight times more extenſive, and, on account of the ſuperior frequency of the returns, four and twenty times more advantageous, than that which our North American colonies ever afforded. The trade of Great Britain would be juſt as advantageous to France, and, in proportion to the wealth, population and proximity of the reſpective countries, would have the ſame ſuperiority over that which France carries on with her own colonies. Such is the very great difference between that trade

which

OF RESTRAINTS UPON IMPORTATION. 249

CHAP.
III.

which the wisdom of both nations has thought proper to discourage, and that which it has favoured the most.

But the very same circumstances which would have rendered an open and free commerce between the two countries so advantageous to both, have occasioned the principal obstructions to that commerce. Being neighbours, they are necessarily enemies, and the wealth and power of each becomes, upon that account, more formidable to the other; and what would increase the advantage of national friendship, serves only to inflame the violence of national animosity. They are both rich and industrious nations; and the merchants and manufacturers of each, dread the competition of the skill and activity of those of the other. Mercantile jealousy is excited, and both inflames, and is itself inflamed, by the violence of national animosity: And the traders of both countries have announced, with all the passionate confidence of interested falsehood, the certain ruin of each, in consequence of that unfavourable balance of trade, which, they pretend, would be the infallible effect of an unrestrained commerce with the other.

There is no commercial country in Europe of which the approaching ruin has not frequently been foretold by the pretended doctors of this system, from an unfavourable balance of trade. After all the anxiety, however, which they have excited about this, after all the vain attempts of almost all trading nations to turn that balance in their own favour and against their neighbours,

it

OF RESTRAINTS UPON IMPORTATION.

BOOK IV.

it does not appear that any one nation in Europe has been in any respect impoverished by this cause. Every town and country, on the contrary, in proportion as they have opened their ports to all nations, instead of being ruined by this free trade, as the principles of the commercial system would lead us to expect, have been enriched by it. Though there are in Europe, indeed, a few towns which in some respects deserve the name of free ports, there is no country which does so. Holland, perhaps, approaches the nearest to this character of any, though still very remote from it ; and Holland, it is acknowledged, not only derives its whole wealth, but a great part of its necessary subsistence, from foreign trade.

There is another balance, indeed, which has already been explained, very different from the balance of trade, and which, according as it happens to be either favourable or unfavourable, necessarily occasions the prosperity or decay of every nation. This is the balance of the annual produce and consumption. If the exchangeable value of the annual produce, it has already been observed, exceeds that of the annual consumption, the capital of the society must annually increase in proportion to this excess. The society in this case lives within its revenue, and what is annually saved out of its revenue, is naturally added to its capital, and employed so as to increase still further the annual produce. If the exchangeable value of the annual produce, on the contrary, fall short of the annual

OF RESTRAINTS UPON IMPORTATION. 251

consumption, the capital of the society must annually decay in proportion to this deficiency. The expence of the society in this case exceeds its revenue, and necessarily encroaches upon its capital. Its capital, therefore, must necessarily decay, and, together with it, the exchangeable value of the annual produce of its industry.

This balance of produce and confumption is entirely different from, what is called, the balance of trade. It might take place in a nation which had no foreign trade, but which was entirely feparated from all the world. It may take place in the whole globe of the earth, of which the wealth, population, and improvement, may be either gradually increafing or gradually decaying.

The balance of produce and confumption may be conftantly in favour of a nation, though what is called the balance of trade be generally againft it. A nation may import to a greater value than it exports for half a century, perhaps, together; the gold and filver which comes into it during all this time may be all immediately fent out of it; its circulating coin may gradually decay, different forts of paper money being fubftituted in its place, and even the debts too which it contracts in the principal nations with whom it deals, may be gradually increafing; and yet its real wealth, the exchangeable value of the annual produce of its lands and labour, may, during the fame period, have been increafing in a much greater proportion. The ftate of our North American colonies, and of the trade which

252 OF DRAWBACKS.

BOOK
IV.

which they carried on with Great Britain, before the commencement of the prefent difturbances *, may ferve as a proof that this is by no means an impoffible fuppofition.

CHAP. IV.
Of Drawbacks.

CHAP.
IV.

MERCHANTS and manufactures are not contented with the monopoly of the home market, but defire likewife the moft extenfive foreign fale for their goods. Their country has no jurifdiction in foreign nations, and therefore can feldom procure them any monopoly there. They are generally obliged, therefore, to content themfelves with petitioning for certain encouragements to exportation.

Of thefe encouragements what are called Drawbacks feem to be the moft reafonable. To allow the merchant to draw back upon exportation, either the whole or a part of whatever excife or inland duty is impofed upon domeftic induftry, can never occafion the exportation of a greater quantity of goods than what would have been exported had no duty been impofed. Such encouragements do not tend to turn towards any particular employment a greater fhare of the capital of the country, than what would go to that employment of its own accord, but only to hinder the duty from driving away any part of

* This paragraph was written in the year 1775.

that

OF DRAWBACKS.

that fhare to other employments. They tend not to overturn that balance which naturally eftablifhes itfelf among all the various employ- ments of the fociety ; but to hinder it from being overturned by the duty. They tend not to de- ftroy, but to preferve, what it is in moft cafes ad- vantageous to preferve, the natural divifion and diftribution of labour in the fociety.

The fame thing may be faid of the drawbacks upon the re-exportation of foreign goods im- ported; which in Great Britain generally amount to by much the largeft part of the duty upon importation. By the fecond of the rules annexed to the act of parliament, which impofed, what is now called, the old fubfidy, every mer- chant, whether Englifh or alien, was allowed to draw back half that duty upon exportation ; the Englifh merchant, provided the exportation took place within twelve months ; the alien, provided it took place within nine months. Wines, cur- rants, and wrought filks were the only goods which did not fall within this rule, having other and more advantageous allowances. The duties impofed by this act of parliament were, at that time, the only duties upon the importation of foreign goods. The term within which this, and all other drawbacks, could be claimed, was after- wards (by 7 Geo. I. chap. 21. fect. 10.) extended to three years.

The duties which have been impofed fince the old fubfidy, are, the greater part of them, wholly drawn back upon exportation. This ge- neral rule, however, is liable to a great number

of

OF DRAWBACKS.

BOOK IV.

of exceptions, and the doctrine of drawbacks has become a much lefs fimple matter, than it was at their firft inftitution.

Upon the exportation of fome foreign goods, of which it was expected that the importation would greatly exceed what was neceffary for the home confumption, the whole duties are drawn back, without retaining even half the old fubfidy. Before the revolt of our North American colonies, we had the monopoly of the tobacco of Maryland and Virginia. We imported about ninety-fix thoufand hogfheads, and the home confumption was not fuppofed to exceed fourteen thoufand. To facilitate the great exportation which was neceffary, in order to rid us of the reft, the whole duties were drawn back, provided the exportation took place within three years.

We ftill have, though not altogether, yet very nearly, the monopoly of the fugars of our Weft Indian iflands. If fugars are exported within a year, therefore, all the duties upon importation are drawn back, and if exported within three years, all the duties, except half the old fubfidy, which ftill continues to be retained upon the exportation of the greater part of goods. Though the importation of fugar exceeds, a good deal, what is neceffary for the home confumption, the excefs is inconfiderable, in comparifon of what it ufed to be in tobacco.

Some goods, the particular objects of the jealoufy of our own manufacturers, are prohibited to be imported for home confumption. They may,

OF DRAWBACKS. 255

CHAP.
IV.

may, however, upon paying certain duties, be imported and warehoufed for exportation. But upon fuch exportation, no part of thefe duties are drawn back. Our manufacturers are unwilling, it feems, that even this reftricted importation fhould be encouraged, and are afraid left fome part of thefe goods fhould be ftolen out of the warehoufe, and thus come into competition with their own. It is under thefe regulations only that we can import wrought filks, French cambrics and lawns, callicoes painted, printed, ftained, or dyed, &c.

We are unwilling even to be the carriers of French goods, and choofe rather to forego a profit to ourfelves, than to fuffer thofe whom we confider as our enemies, to make any profit by our means. Not only half the old fubfidy, but the fecond twenty-five per cent. is retained upon the exportation of all French goods.

By the fourth of the rules annexed to the old fubfidy, the drawback allowed upon the exportation of all wines amounted to a great deal more than half the duties which were, at that time, paid upon their importation; and it feems, at that time, to have been the object of the legiflature to give fomewhat more than ordinary encouragement to the carrying trade in wine. Several of the other duties too, which were impofed, either at the fame time, or fubfequent to the old fubfidy; what is called the additional duty, the new fubfidy, the one-third and two-thirds fubfidies, the impoft 1692, the coinage on wine, were allowed to be wholly drawn back

upon

256   OF DRAWBACKS.

BOOK IV. upon exportation. All thofe duties, however, except the additional duty and impoft 1691, being paid down in ready money, upon importation, the intereft of fo large a fum occafioned an expence, which made it unreafonable to expect any profitable carrying trade in this article. Only a part, therefore, of the duty called the impoft on wine, and no part of the twenty-five pounds the ton upon French wines, or of the duties impofed in 1745, in 1763, and in 1778, were allowed to be drawn back upon exportation. The two impofts of five per cent., impofed in 1779 and 1781, upon all the former duties of cuftoms, being allowed to be wholly drawn back upon the exportation of all other goods, were likewife allowed to be drawn back upon that of wine. The laft duty that has been particularly impofed upon wine, that of 1780, is allowed to be wholly drawn back, an indulgence, which, when fo many heavy duties are retained, moft probably could never occafion the exportation of a fingle ton of wine. Thefe rules take place with regard to all places of lawful exportation, except the Britifh colonies in America.

The 15th Charles II. chap. 7., called an act for the encouragement of trade, had given Great Britain the monopoly of fupplying the colonies with all the commodities of the growth or manufacture of Europe; and confequently with wines. In a country of fo extenfive a coaft as our North American and Weft Indian colonies, where our authority was always fo very

4   flender,

flender, and where the inhabitants were allowed CHAP. to carry out, in their own fhips, their non- IV. enumerated commodities, at firft, to all parts of Europe, and afterwards, to all parts of Europe South of Cape Finifterre, it is not very probable that this monopoly could ever be much refpected; and they probably, at all times, found means of bringing back fome cargo from the countries to which they were allowed to carry out one. They feem however, to have found fome difficulty in importing European wines from the places of their growth, and they could not well import them from Great Britain, where they were loaded with many heavy duties, of which a confiderable part was not drawn back upon exportation. Madeira wine, not being a European commodity, could be imported directly into America and the Weft Indies, countries which, in all their non-enumerated commodities, enjoyed a free trade to the ifland of Madeira. Thefe circumftances had probably introduced that general tafte for Madeira wine, which our officers found eftablifhed in all our colonies at the commencement of the war which began in 1755, and which they brought back with them to the mother-country, where that wine had not been much in fafhion before. Upon the conclufion of that war, in 1763 (by the 4th Geo. III. Chap. 15. Sect. 12.), all the duties, except 3*l.* 10*s.*, were allowed to be drawn back, upon the exportation to the colonies of all wines, except French wines, to the commerce and confumption of which, national prejudice would allow

OF DRAWBACKS.

BOOK IV.

allow no fort of encouragement. The period between the granting of this indulgence and the revolt of our North American colonies was probably too fhort to admit of any confiderable change in the cuftoms of thofe countries.

The fame act, which, in the drawback upon all wines, except French wines, thus favoured the colonies fo much more than other countries; in thofe, upon the greater part of other commodities, favoured them much lefs. Upon the exportation of the greater part of commodities to other countries, half the old fubfidy was drawn back. But this law enacted, that no part of that duty fhould be drawn back upon the exportation to the colonies of any commodities, of the growth or manufacture either of Europe or the Eaft Indies, except wines, white callicoes and muflins.

Drawbacks were, perhaps, originally granted for the encouragement of the carrying trade, which, as the freight of the fhips is frequently paid by foreigners in money, was fuppofed to be peculiarly fitted for bringing gold and filver into the country. But though the carrying trade certainly deferves no peculiar encouragement, though the motive of the inftitution was, perhaps, abundantly foolifh, the inftitution itfelf feems reafonable enough. Such drawbacks cannot force into this trade a greater fhare of the capital of the country than what would have gone to it of its own accord, had there been no duties upon importation. They only prevent its being excluded altogether by thofe duties.

The

OF DRAWBACKS. 259

The carrying trade, though it deſerves no pre- C H A P.
ference, ought not to be precluded, but to be IV.
left free like all other trades. It is a neceſſary
reſource for thoſe capitals which cannot find
employment either in the agriculture or in the
manufactures of the country, either in its home
trade or in its foreign trade of conſumption.

The revenue of the cuſtoms, inſtead of ſuffer-
ing, profits from ſuch drawbacks, by that part of
the duty which is retained. If the whole duties
had been retained, the foreign goods upon which
they are paid, could ſeldom have been exported,
nor conſequently imported, for want of a market.
The duties, therefore, of which a part is retained, would never have been paid.

Theſe reaſons ſeem ſufficiently to juſtify drawbacks, and would juſtify them, though the whole
duties, whether upon the produce of domeſtic
induſtry, or upon foreign goods, were always
drawn back upon exportation. The revenue of
exciſe would in this caſe, indeed, ſuffer a little,
and that of the cuſtoms a good deal more ; but
the natural balance of induſtry, the natural
diviſion and diſtribution of labour, which is
always more or leſs diſturbed by ſuch duties,
would be more nearly re-eſtabliſhed by ſuch
a regulation.

Theſe reaſons, however, will juſtify drawbacks
only upon exporting goods to thoſe countries
which are altogether foreign and independent,
not to thoſe in which our merchants and manufacturers enjoy a monopoly. A drawback, for example, upon the exportation of European goods

s 2 to

260   OF DRAWBACKS.

BOOK to our American colonies, will not always occa-
IV.   sion a greater exportation than what would have
taken place without it.   By means of the monopoly which our merchants and manufacturers
enjoy there, the same quantity might frequently,
perhaps, be sent thither, though the whole
duties were retained.   The drawback, therefore, may frequently be pure loss to the revenue
of excise and customs, without altering the state
of the trade, or rendering it in any respect more
extensive.   How far such drawbacks can be
justified, as a proper encouragement to the industry of our colonies, or how far it is advantageous to the mother-country, that they should
be exempted from taxes which are paid by all
the rest of their fellow-subjects, will appear hereafter when I come to treat of colonies.

Drawbacks, however, it must always be understood, are useful only in those cases in which the
goods for the exportation of which they are
given, are really exported to some foreign country ; and not clandestinely re-imported into our
own.   That some drawbacks, particularly those
upon tobacco, have frequently been abused in
this manner, and have given occasion to many
frauds equally hurtful both to the revenue and
to the fair trader, is well known.

CHAP. V.

Of Bounties.

BOUNTIES upon exportation are, in Great Britain, frequently petitioned for, and fometimes granted to the produce of particular branches of domeftic induftry. By means of them our merchants and manufacturers, it is pretended, will be enabled to fell their goods as cheap or cheaper than their rivals in the foreign market. A greater quantity, it is faid, will thus be exported, and the balance of trade confequently turned more in favour of our own country. We cannot give our workmen a monopoly in the foreign, as we have done in the home market. We cannot force foreigners to buy their goods, as we have done our own countrymen. The next beft expedient, it has been thought, therefore, is to pay them for buying. It is in this manner that the mercantile fyftem propofes to enrich the whole country, and to put money into all our pockets by means of the balance of trade.

Bounties, it is allowed, ought to be given to thofe branches of trade only which cannot be carried on without them. But every branch of trade in which the merchant can fell his goods for a price which replaces to him, with the ordinary profits of ftock, the whole capital employed in preparing and fending them to market, can be

BOOK IV. carried on without a bounty. Every such branch is evidently upon a level with all the other branches of trade which are carried on without bounties, and cannot therefore require one more than they. Those trades only require bounties in which the merchant is obliged to sell his goods for a price which does not replace to him his capital, together with the ordinary profit; or in which he is obliged to sell them for less than it really costs him to send them to market. The bounty is given in order to make up this loss, and to encourage him to continue, or perhaps to begin, a trade of which the expence is supposed to be greater than the returns, of which every operation eats up a part of the capital employed in it, and which is of such a nature, that, if all other trades resembled it, there would soon be no capital left in the country.

The trades, it is to be observed, which are carried on by means of bounties, are the only ones which can be carried on between two nations for any considerable time together, in such a manner as that one of them shall always and regularly lose, or sell its goods for less than it really costs to send them to market. But if the bounty did not repay to the merchant what he would otherwise lose upon the price of his goods, his own interest would soon oblige him to employ his stock in another way, or to find out a trade in which the price of the goods would replace to him, with the ordinary profit, the capital employed in sending them to market. The effect of bounties, like that of all the other

expedients

expedients of the mercantile fyftem, can only be C H A P.
to force the trade of a country into a channel
much lefs advantageous than that in which it
would naturally run of its own accord.

The ingenious and well-informed author of
the tracts upon the corn-trade has fhown very
clearly, that fince the bounty upon the exportation of corn was firft eftablifhed, the price of the
corn exported, valued moderately enough, has
exceeded that of the corn imported, valued very
high, by a much greater fum than the amount of
the whole bounties which have been paid during
that period. This, he imagines, upon the true
principles of the mercantile fyftem, is a clear
proof that this forced corn trade is beneficial to
the nation; the value of the exportation exceeding that of the importation by a much greater
fum than the whole extraordinary expence which
the public has been at in order to get it exported.
He does not confider that this extraordinary
expence, or the bounty, is the fmalleft part
of the expence which the exportation of corn
really cofts the fociety. The capital which the
farmer employed in raifing it, muft likewife be
taken into the account. Unlefs the price of the
corn when fold in the foreign markets replaces,
not only the bounty, but this capital, together
with the ordinary profits of ftock, the fociety is
a lofer by the difference, or the national ftock
is fo much diminifhed. But the very reafon for
which it has been thought neceffary to grant a
bounty, is the fuppofed infufficiency of the price
to do this.

s 4

The

BOOK IV.

The average price of corn, it has been said, has fallen confiderably fince the eftablifhment of the bounty. That the average price of corn began to fall fomewhat towards the end of the laft century, and has continued to do fo during the courfe of the fixty-four firft years of the prefent, I have already endeavoured to fhow. But this event, fuppofing it to be as real as I believe it to be, muft have happened in fpite of the bounty, and cannot poffibly have happened in confequence of it. It has happened in France, as well as in England, though in France there was, not only no bounty, but, till 1764, the exportation of corn was fubjected to a general prohibition. This gradual fall in the average price of grain, it is probable, therefore, is ultimately owing neither to the one regulation nor to the other, but to that gradual and infenfible rife in the real value of filver, which, in the firft book of this difcourfe, I have endeavoured to fhow has taken place in the general market of Europe, during the courfe of the prefent century. It feems to be altogether impoffible that the bounty could ever contribute to lower the price of grain.

In years of plenty, it has already been obferved, the bounty, by occafioning an extraordinary exportation, neceffarily keeps up the price of corn in the home market above what it would naturally fall to. To do fo was the avowed purpofe of the inftitution. In years of fcarcity, though the bounty is frequently fufpended, yet the great exportation which it occafions in years

of

OF BOUNTIES.

of plenty, muft frequently hinder more or lefs the plenty of one year from relieving the fcarcity of another. Both in years of plenty, and in years of fcarcity, therefore, the bounty necef-farily tends to raife the money price of corn fomewhat higher than it otherwife would be in the home market.

That, in the actual ftate of tillage, the bounty muft neceffarily have this tendency, will not, I apprehend, be difputed by any reafonable perfon. But it has been thought by many people that it tends to encourage tillage, and that in two different ways; firft, by opening a more exten-five foreign market to the corn of the farmer, it tends, they imagine, to increafe the demand for, and confequently the production of that com-modity; and fecondly, by fecuring to him a better price than he could otherwife expect in the actual ftate of tillage, it tends, they fuppofe, to encourage tillage. This double encouragement muft, they imagine, in a long period of years, occafion fuch an increafe in the production of corn, as may lower its price in the home market, much more than the bounty can raife it, in the actual ftate which tillage may, at the end of that period, happen to be in.

I anfwer, that whatever extenfion of the foreign market can be occafioned by the bounty, muft, in every particular year, be altogether at the expence of the home market; as every bufhel of corn which is exported by means of the bounty, and which would not have been exported without the bounty, would have remained in the

home

OF BOUNTIES.

BOOK IV.

home market to increafe the confumption, and to lower the price of that commodity. The corn bounty, it is to be obferved, as well as every other bounty upon exportation, impofes two different taxes upon the people; firft, the tax which they are obliged to contribute, in order to pay the bounty; and fecondly, the tax which arifes from the advanced price of the commodity in the home market, and which, as the whole body of the people are purchafers of corn, muft, in this particular commodity, be paid by the whole body of the people. In this particular commodity, therefore, this fecond tax is by much the heavieft of the two. Let us fuppofe that, taking one year with another, the bounty of five fhillings upon the exportation of the quarter of wheat, raifes the price of that commodity in the home market only fixpence the bufhel, or four fhillings the quarter, higher than it otherways would have been in the actual ftate of the crop. Even upon this very moderate fuppofition, the great body of the people, over and above contributing the tax which pays the bounty of five fhillings upon every quarter of wheat exported, muft pay another of four fhillings upon every quarter which they themfelves confume. But, according to the very well informed author of the tracts upon the corntrade, the average proportion of the corn exported to that confumed at home, is not more than that of one to thirty-one. For every five fhillings, therefore, which they contribute to the payment of the firft tax, they muft contribute fix

pounds

pounds four shillings to the payment of the second. So very heavy a tax upon the first neceffary of life, must either reduce the subsistence of the labouring poor, or it must occasion some augmentation in their pecuniary wages, proportionable to that in the pecuniary price of their subsistence. So far as it operates in the one way, it must reduce the ability of the labouring poor to educate and bring up their children, and must, so far, tend to restrain the population of the country. So far as it operates in the other, it must reduce the ability of the employers of the poor, to employ so great a number as they otherwise might do, and must, so far, tend to restrain the industry of the country. The extraordinary exportation of corn, therefore, occasioned by the bounty, not only, in every particular year, diminishes the home, just as much as it extends the foreign market and confumption, but, by restraining the population and industry of the country, its final tendency is to stunt and restrain the gradual extension of the home market; and thereby, in the long run, rather to diminish, than to augment, the whole market and confumption of corn.

This enhancement of the money price of corn, however, it has been thought, by rendering that commodity more profitable to the farmer, must neceffarily encourage its production.

I answer, that this might be the case if the effect of the bounty was to raife the real price of corn, or to enable the farmer, with an equal quantity of it, to maintain a greater number

of

268   OF BOUNTIES.

BOOK
IV.

of labourers in the fame manner, whether liberal, moderate, or fcanty, that other labourers are commonly maintained in his neighbourhood. But neither the bounty, it is evident, nor any other human inftitution, can have any fuch effect. It is not the real, but the nominal price of corn, which can in any confiderable degree be effected by the bounty. And though the tax which that inftitution impofes upon the whole body of the people, may be very burdenfome to thofe who pay it, it is of very little advantage to thofe who receive it.

The real effect of the bounty is not fo much to raife the real value of corn, as to degrade the real value of filver; or to make an equal quantity of it exchange for a fmaller quantity, not only of corn, but of all other home-made commodities: for the money price of corn regulates that of all other home-made commodities.

It regulates the money price of labour, which muft always be fuch as to enable the labourer to purchafe a quantity of corn fufficient to maintain him and his family either in the liberal, moderate, or fcanty manner in which the advancing, ftationary or declining circumftances of the fociety oblige his employers to maintain him.

It regulates the money price of all the other parts of the rude produce of land, which, in every period of improvement, muft bear a certain proportion to that of corn, though this proportion is different in different periods. It regulates, for example, the money price of grafs and hay, of butcher's meat, of horfes, and the

main-

OF BOUNTIES. 269

maintenance of horſes, of land carriage conſe- C H A P.
quently, or of the greater part of the inland com- V.
merce of the country.

By regulating the money price of all the other
parts of the rude produce of land, it regulates
that of the materials of almoſt all manufactures.
By regulating the money price of labour, it regulates that of manufacturing art and induſtry.
And by regulating both, it regulates that of the
complete manufacture. The money price of
labour, and of every thing that is the produce
either of land or labour, muſt neceſſarily either riſe
or fall in proportion to the money price of corn.

Though in conſequence of the bounty, therefore, the farmer ſhould be enabled to ſell his corn
for four ſhillings a buſhel inſtead of three and
ſixpence, and to pay his landlord a money rent
proportionable to this riſe in the money price of
his produce; yet if, in conſequence of this riſe
in the price of corn, four ſhillings will purchaſe
no more home-made goods of any other kind
than three and ſixpence would have done before,
neither the circumſtances of the farmer, nor thoſe
of the landlord, will be much mended by this
change. The farmer will not be able to cultivate much better: the landlord will not be able
to live much better. In the purchaſe of foreign
commodities this enhancement in the price of
corn may give them ſome little advantage. In
that of home-made commodities it can give them
none at all. And almoſt the whole expence of
the farmer, and the far greater part even of that
of the landlord, is in home-made commodities,

That

270

OF BOUNTIES.

BOOK IV.

That degradation in the value of filver which is the effect of the fertility of the mines, and which operates equally, or very near equally, through the greater part of the commercial world, is a matter of very little confequence to any particular country. The confequent rife of all money prices, though it does not make thofe who receive them really richer, does not make them really poorer. A fervice of plate becomes really cheaper, and every thing elfe remains precifely of the fame real value as before..

But that degradation in the value of filver which, being the effect either of the peculiar fituation, or of the political inftitutions of a particular country, takes place only in that country, is a matter of very great confequence, which, far from tending to make any body really richer, tends to make every body really poorer. The rife in the money price of all commodities, which is in this cafe peculiar to that country, tends to difcourage more or lefs every fort of induftry which is carried on within it, and to enable foreign nations, by furnifhing almoft all forts of goods for a fmaller quantity of filver than its own workmen can afford to do, to underfell them, not only in the foreign, but even in the home market.

It is the peculiar fituation of Spain and Portugal as proprietors of the mines, to be the diftributors of gold and filver to all the other countries of Europe. Thofe metals ought naturally, therefore, to be fomewhat cheaper in Spain and Portugal than in any other part of

Europe.

OF BOUNTIES.

Europe. The difference, however, fhould be no more than the amount of the freight and infurance; and, on account of the great value and fmall bulk of thofe metals, their freight is no great matter, and their infurance is the fame as that of any other goods of equal value. Spain and Portugal, therefore, could fuffer very little from their peculiar fituation, if they did not aggravate its difadvantages by their political inftitutions.

Spain by taxing, and Portugal by prohibiting the exportation of gold and filver, load that exportation with the expence of fmuggling, and raife the value of thofe metals in other countries fo much more above what it is in their own, by the whole amount of this expence. When you dam up a ftream of water, as foon as the dam is full, as much water muft run over the damhead as if there was no dam at all. The prohibition of exportation cannot detain a greater quantity of gold and filver in Spain and Portugal than what they can afford to employ, than what the annual produce of their land and labour will allow them to employ, in coin, plate, gilding, and other ornaments of gold and filver. When they have got this quantity the dam is full, and the whole ftream which flows in afterwards muft run over. The annual exportation of gold and filver from Spain and Portugal accordingly is, by all accounts, notwithftanding thefe reftraints, very near equal to the whole annual importation. As the water, however,

BOOK IV.

however, muſt always be deeper behind the dam-head than before it, ſo the quantity of gold and ſilver which theſe reſtraints detain in Spain and Portugal muſt, in proportion to the annual produce of their land and labour, be greater than what is to be found in other countries. The higher and ſtronger the dam-head, the greater muſt be the difference in the depth of water behind and before it. The higher the tax, the higher the penalties with which the prohibition is guarded, the more vigilant and ſevere the police which looks after the execution of the law, the greater muſt be the difference in the proportion of gold and ſilver to the annual produce of the land and labour of Spain and Portugal, and to that of other countries. It is ſaid accordingly to be very conſiderable, and that you frequently find there a profuſion of plate in houſes, where there is nothing elſe which would, in other countries, be thought ſuitable or correſpondent to this ſort of magnificence. The cheapneſs of gold and ſilver, or what is the ſame thing, the dearneſs of all commodities, which is the neceſſary effect of this redundancy of the precious metals, diſcourages both the agriculture and manufactures of Spain and Portugal, and enables foreign nations to ſupply them with many ſorts of rude, and with almoſt all ſorts of manufactured produce, for a ſmaller quantity of gold and ſilver than what they themſelves can either raiſe or make them for at home. The tax and prohibition operate in two different ways. They

not

OF BOUNTIES. 273

not only lower very much the value of the CHAP. precious metals in Spain and Portugal, but by V. detaining there a certain quantity of thofe metals which would otherwife flow over other countries, they keep up their value in thofe other countries fomewhat above what it otherwife would be, and thereby give thofe countries a double advantage in their commerce with Spain and Portugal. Open the flood-gates, and there will prefently be lefs water above, and more below, the dam-head, and it will foon come to a level in both places. Remove the tax and the prohibition, and as the quantity of gold and filver will diminifh confiderably in Spain and Portugal, fo it will increafe fomewhat in other countries, and the value of thofe metals, their proportion to the annual produce of land and labour, will foon come to a level, or very near to a level, in all. The lofs which Spain and Portugal could fuftain by this exportation of their gold and filver would be altogether nominal and imaginary. The nominal value of their goods, and of the annual produce of their land and labour, would fall, and would be exprefled or reprefented by a fmaller quantity of filver than before : but their real value would be the fame as before, and would be fufficient to maintain, command, and employ, the fame quantity of labour· As the nominal value of their goods would fall, the real value of what remained of their gold and filver would rife, and a fmaller quantity of thofe metals would anfwer all the fame purpofes of commerce and circulation which had employed a

VOL III. T greater

274   OF BOUNTIES.

BOOK greater quantity before. The gold and filver
 IV. which would go abroad would not go abroad for
nothing, but would bring back an equal value
of goods of fome kind or another. Thofe goods
too would not be all matters of mere luxury and
expence, to be confumed by idle people who
produce nothing in return for their confumption.
As the real wealth and revenue of idle people
would not be augmented by this extraordinary
exportation of gold and filver, fo neither would
their confumption be much augmented by it.
Thofe goods would, probably, the greater part
of them, and certainly fome part of them, confift in materials, tools, and provifions, for the
employment and maintenance of induftrious people, who would reproduce, with a profit, the
full value of their confumption. A part of the
dead ftock of the fociety would thus be turned
into active ftock, and would put into motion a
greater quantity of induftry than had been employed before. The annual produce of their
land and labour would immediately be augmented a little, and in a few years would, probably, be augmented a great deal; their induftry
being thus relieved from one of the moft oppreffive burdens which it at prefent labours
under.

The bounty upon the exportation of corn
neceffarily operates exactly in the fame way as
this abfurd policy of Spain and Portugal.
Whatever be the actual ftate of tillage, it renders
our corn fomewhat dearer in the home market
than it otherwife would be in that ftate, and

2   fomewhat

OF BOUNTIES.

fomewhat cheaper in the foreign; and as the average money price of corn regulates more or lefs that of all other commodities, it lowers the value of filver confiderably in the one, and tends to raife it a little in the other. It enables foreigners, the Dutch in particular, not only to eat our corn cheaper than they otherwife could do, but fometimes to eat it cheaper than even our own people can do upon the fame occafions; as we are affured by an excellent authority, that of Sir Matthew Decker. It hinders our own workmen from furnifhing their goods for fo fmall a quantity of filver as they otherwife might do; and enables the Dutch to furnifh their's for a fmaller. It tends to render our manufactures fomewhat dearer in every market, and their's fomewhat cheaper than they otherwife would be, and confequently to give their induftry a double advantage over our own.

The bounty, as it raifes in the home market, not fo much the real, as the nominal price of our corn, as it augments, not the quantity of labour which a certain quantity of corn can maintain and employ, but only the quantity of filver which it will exchange for, it difcourages our manufactures, without rendering any confiderable fervice either to our farmers or country gentlemen. It puts, indeed, a little more money into the pockets of both, and it will perhaps be fomewhat difficult to perfuade the greater part of them that this is not rendering them a very confiderable fervice. But if this money finks in its value, in the quantity of labour, provifions,

and

BOOK and home-made commodities of all different
IV. kinds which it is capable of purchasing, as much
as it rises in its quantity, the service will be little
more than nominal and imaginary.

There is, perhaps, but one set of men in the
whole commonwealth to whom the bounty either
was or could be essentially serviceable. These
were the corn merchants, the exporters and importers of corn. In years of plenty the bounty
necessarily occasioned a greater exportation than
would otherwise have taken place; and by hindering the plenty of one year from relieving the
scarcity of another, it occasioned in years of
scarcity a greater importation than would otherwise have been necessary. It increased the business of the corn merchant in both; and in years
of scarcity, it not only enabled him to import a
greater quantity, but to sell it for a better price,
and consequently with a greater profit than he
could otherwise have made, if the plenty of one
year had not been more or less hindered from
relieving the scarcity of another. It is in this
set of men, accordingly, that I have observed
the greatest zeal for the continuance or renewal
of the bounty.

Our country gentlemen, when they imposed
the high duties upon the importation of foreign
corn, which in times of moderate plenty amount
to a prohibition, and when they established the
bounty, seem to have imitated the conduct of
our manufacturers. By the one institution, they
secured to themselves the monopoly of the home
market, and by the other they endeavoured
to

to prevent that market from ever being over-stocked with their commodity. By both they endeavoured to raise its real value, in the same manner as our manufacturers had, by the like inftitutions, raifed the real value of many different forts of manufactured goods. They did not perhaps attend to the great and effential difference which nature has eftablifhed between corn and almoft every other fort of goods. When, either by the monopoly of the home market, or by a bounty upon exportation, you enable our woollen or linen manufacturers to fell their goods for fomewhat a better price than they otherwife could get for them, you raife, not only the nominal, but the real price of thofe goods. You render them equivalent to a greater quantity of labour and fubfiftence, you encreafe not only the nominal, but the real profit, the real wealth and revenue of thofe manufacturers, and you enable them either to live better themfelves, or to employ a greater quantity of labour in thofe particular manufactures. You really encourage thofe manufactures, and direct towards them a greater quantity of the induftry of the country, than what would probably go to them of its own accord. But when by the like inftitutions you raife the nominal or money-price of corn, you do not raife its real value. You do not increafe the real wealth, the real revenue either of our farmers or country gentlemen. You do not encourage the growth of corn, becaufe you do not enable them to maintain and employ more labourers in raifing it. The nature of

278   OF BOUNTIES.

BOOK of things has ftamped upon corn a real value
IV. which cannot be altered by merely altering its
money price. No bounty upon exportation, no
monopoly of the home market, can raife that
value. The freeft competition cannot lower it.
Through the world in general that value is equal
to the quantity of labour which it can maintain,
and in every particular place it is equal to the
quantity of labour which it can maintain in the
way, whether liberal, moderate, or fcanty, in
which labour is commonly maintained in that
place. Woollen or linen cloth are not the regulating commodities by which the real value of
all other commodities muft be finally meafured
and determined; corn is. The real value of
every other commodity is finally meafured and
determined by the proportion which its average
money price bears to the average money price of
corn. The real value of corn does not vary
with thofe variations in its average money price,
which fometimes occur from one century to
another. It is the real value of filver which
varies with them.

Bounties upon the exportation of any home-
made commodity are liable, firft, to that general
objection which may be made to all the different
expedients of the mercantile fyftem; the objection of forcing fome part of the induftry of the
country into a channel lefs advantageous than
that in which it would run of its own accord:
and, fecondly, to the particular objection of
forcing it, not only into a channel that is lefs
advantageous, but into one that is actually dif-
advan-

BOUNTIES. 279

advantageous; the trade which cannot be carried
on but by means of a bounty being neceffarily a
lofing trade. The bounty upon the exportation
of corn is liable to this further objection, that it
can in no refpect promote the raifing of that
particular commodity of which it was meant to
encourage the production. When our country
gentlemen, therefore, demanded the eftablifhment of the bounty, though they acted in imitation of our merchants and manufacturers, they
did not act with that complete comprehenfion of
their own intereft which commonly directs the
conduct of thofe two other orders of people.
They loaded the public revenue with a very
confiderable expence; they impofed a very heavy
tax upon the whole body of the people; but they
did not, in any fenfible degree, increafe the real
value of their own commodity; and by lowering
fomewhat the real value of filver, they difcouraged, in fome degree, the general induftry
of the country, and, inftead of advancing, retarded more or lefs the improvement of their
own lands, which neceffarily depends upon the
general induftry of the country.

To encourage the production of any commodity, a bounty upon production, one fhould
imagine, would have a more direct operation,
than one upon exportation. It would, befides,
impofe only one tax upon the people, that which
they muft contribute in order to pay the bounty.
Inftead of raifing, it would tend to lower the
price of the commodity in the home market;
and thereby, inftead of impofing a fecond tax

upon

280   OF BOUNTIES.

BOOK upon the people, it might, at leaft in part, re-
IV.   pay them for what they had contributed to the
      firft. Bounties upon production, however, have
      been very rarely granted. The prejudices efta-
      blifhed by the commercial fyftem have taught
      us to believe, that national wealth arifes more
      immediately from exportation than from pro-
      duction. It has been more favoured accord-
      ingly, as the more immediate means of bringing
      money into the country. Bounties upon pro-
      duction, it has been faid too, have been found
      by experience more liable to frauds than thofe
      upon exportation. How far this is true, I know
      not. That bounties upon exportation have been
      abufed to many fraudulent purpofes, is very
      well known. But it is not the intereft of mer-
      chants and manufacturers, the great inventors
      of all thefe expedients, that the home market
      fhould be overftocked with their goods, an event
      which a bounty upon production might fome-
      times occafion. A bounty upon exportation, by
      enabling them to fend abroad the furplus part,
      and to keep up the price of what remains in the
      home market, effectually prevents this. Of all
      the expedients of the mercantile fyftem, accord-
      ingly, it is the one of which they are the fondeft.
      I have known the different undertakers of fome
      particular works agree privately among them-
      felves to give a bounty out of their own pockets
      upon the exportation of a certain proportion of
      the goods which they dealt in. This expedient
      fucceeded fo well, that it more than doubled the
      price of their goods in the home market, not-
                              withftanding

OF BOUNTIES. 281

withftanding a very confiderable increafe in the produce. The operation of the bounty upon corn muft have been wonderfully different, if it has lowered the money price of that commodity.

Something like a bounty upon production, however, has been granted upon fome particular occafions. The tonnage bounties given to the white-herring and whale-fifheries may, perhaps, be confidered as fomewhat of this nature. They tend directly, it may be fuppofed, to render the goods cheaper in the home market than they otherwife would be. In other refpects their effects, it muft be acknowledged, are the fame as thofe of bounties upon exportation. By means of them a part of the capital of the country is employed in bringing goods to market, of which the price does not repay the coft, together with the ordinary profits of ftock.

But though the tonnage bounties to thofe fifheries do not contribute to the opulence of the nation, it may perhaps be thought that they contribute to its defence, by augmenting the number of its failors and fhipping. This, it may be alleged, may fometimes be done by means of fuch bounties at a much fmaller expence, than by keeping up a great ftanding navy, if I may ufe fuch an expreffion, in the fame way as a ftanding army.

Notwithftanding thefe favourable allegations, however, the following confiderations difpofe me to believe, that in granting at leaft one of thefe bounties, the legiflature has been very grofsly impofed upon.

Firft,

OF BOUNTIES.

BOOK IV.

Firſt, the herring buſs bounty ſeems too large. From the commencement of the winter fiſhing 1771 to the end of the winter fiſhing 1781, the tonnage bounty upon the herring buſs fiſhery has been at thirty ſhillings the ton. During theſe eleven years the whole number of barrels caught by the herring buſs fiſhery of Scotland amounted to 378,347. The herrings caught and cured at ſea, are called ſea ſticks. In order to render them what are called merchantable herrings, it is neceſſary to repack them with an additional quantity of ſalt; and in this caſe, it is reckoned, that three barrels of ſea ſticks, are uſually repacked into two barrels of merchantable herrings. The number of barrels of merchantable herrings, therefore, caught during theſe eleven years, will amount only, according to this account, to 252,231$\frac{1}{3}$. During theſe eleven years the tonnage bounties paid amounted to 155,463*l.* 11*s.* or to 8*s.* 2$\frac{1}{4}$*d.* upon every barrel of ſea ſticks, and to 12*s.* 3$\frac{1}{4}$*d.* upon every barrel of merchantable herrings.

The ſalt with which theſe herrings are cured, is ſometimes Scotch, and ſometimes foreign ſalt; both which are delivered free of all exciſe duty to the fiſh-curers. The exciſe duty upon Scotch ſalt is at preſent 1*s.* 6*d.* that upon foreign ſalt 10*s.* the buſhel. A barrel of herrings is ſuppoſed to require about one buſhel and one-fourth of a buſhel foreign ſalt. Two buſhels are the ſuppoſed average of Scotch ſalt. If the herrings are entered for exportation, no part of this duty is paid up; if entered for home conſumption, whether

OF BOUNTIES.

whether the herrings were cured with foreign or with Scotch falt, only one fhilling the barrel is paid up. It was the whole Scotch duty upon a bufhel of falt, the quantity which, at a low eftimation, had been fuppofed neceffary for curing a barrel of herrings. In Scotland, foreign falt is very little ufed for any other purpofe but the curing of fifh. But from the 5th April 1771, to the 5th April 1782, the quantity of foreign falt imported amounted to 936,974 bufhels, at eighty-four pounds the bufhel: the quantity of Scotch falt delivered from the works to the fifh-curers, to no more than 168,226, at fifty-fix pounds the bufhel only. It would appear, therefore, that it is principally foreign falt that is ufed in the fifheries. Upon every barrel of herrings exported there is, befides, a bounty of 2s. 8d. and more than two-thirds of the bufs caught herrings are exported. Put all thefe things together, and you will find that, during thefe eleven years, every barrel of bufs caught herrings, cured with Scotch falt when exported, has coft government 17s. 11¼d.; and when entered for home confumption 14s. 3¾d.: and that every barrel cured with foreign falt, when exported, has coft government 1l. 7s. 5¾d.; and when entered for home confumption 1l. 3s. 9¼d. The price of a barrel of good merchantable herrings runs from feventeen and eighteen to four and five and twenty fhillings; about a guinea at an average*.

---

* See the accounts at the end of the volume.

Secondly,

OF BOUNTIES.

BOOK
IV.

Secondly, the bounty to the white herring fifhery is a tonnage bounty; and is proportioned to the burden of the fhip, not to her diligence or fuccefs in the fifhery; and it has, I am afraid, been too common for veffels to fit out for the fole purpofe of catching, not the fifh, but the bounty. In the year 1759, when the bounty was at fifty fhillings the ton, the whole bufs fifhery of Scotland brought in only four barrels of fea fticks. In that year each barrel of fea fticks coft government in bounties alone 113*l.* 15*s.*; each barrel of merchantable herrings 159*l.* 7*s.* 6*d.*

Thirdly, the mode of fifhing for which this tonnage bounty in the white herring fifhery has been given (by buffes or decked veffels from twenty to eighty tons burthen), feems not fo well adapted to the fituation of Scotland as to that of Holland; from the practice of which country it appears to have been borrowed. Holland lies at a great diftance from the feas to which herrings are known principally to refort; and can, therefore, carry on that fifhery only in decked veffels, which can carry water and provifions fufficient for a voyage to a diftant fea. But the Hebrides or weftern iflands, the iflands of Shetland, and the northern and north-weftern coafts of Scotland, the countries in whofe neighbourhood the herring fifhery is principally carried on, are every where interfected by arms of the fea, which run up a confiderable way into the land, and, which, in the language of the country, are called fea-lochs. It is to thefe fea-lochs that the herrings principally refort during the feafons

OF BOUNTIES. 285

fons in which they vifit thofe feas; for the vifits of this, and, I am affured, of many other forts of fifh, are not quite regular and conftant. A boat fifhery, therefore, feems to be the mode of fifhing beft adapted to the peculiar fituation of Scotland : the fifhers carrying the herrings on fhore, as faft as they are taken, to be either cured or confumed frefh. But the great encouragement which a bounty of thirty fhillings the ton gives to the bufs fifhery, is neceffarily a difcouragement to the boat fifhery; which, having no fuch bounty, cannot bring its cured fifh to market upon the fame terms as the bufs fifhery. The boat fifhery, accordingly, which, before the eftablifhment of the bufs bounty, was very confiderable, and is faid to have employed a number of feamen, not inferior to what the bufs fifhery employs at prefent, is now gone almoft entirely to decay. Of the former extent, however, of this now ruined and abandoned fifhery, I muft acknowledge, that I cannot pretend to fpeak with much precifion. As no bounty was paid upon the outfit of the boat-fifhery, no account was taken of it by the officers of the cuftoms or falt duties.

Fourthly, in many parts of Scotland, during certain feafons of the year, herrings make no inconfiderable part of the food of the common people. A bounty, which tended to lower their price in the home market, might contribute a good deal to the relief of a great number of our fellow-fubjeċts, whofe circumftances are by no means affluent. But the herring bufs bounty contributes to no fuch good purpofe. It has ruined the boat fifhery, which is, by far, the

beft

286   OF BOUNTIES.

BOOK beft adapted for the fupply of the home market,
IV.   and the additional bounty of 2*s*. 8*d*. the barrel
upon exportation, carries the greater part, more
than two thirds, of the produce of the bufs
fifhery abroad. Between thirty and forty years
ago, before the eftablifhment of the bufs bounty,
fixteen fhillings the barrel, I have been affured,
was the common price of white herrings. Between ten and fifteen years ago, before the boat
fifhery was entirely ruined, the price is faid to
have run from feventeen to twenty fhillings the
barrel. For thefe laft five years, it has, at an
average, been at twenty-five fhillings the barrel.
This high price, however, may have been owing
to the real fcarcity of the herrings upon the
coaft of Scotland. I muft obferve too, that the
cafk or barrel, which is ufually fold with the
herrings, and of which the price is included in
all the foregoing prices, has, fince the commencement of the American war, rifen to about
double its former price, or from about three
fhillings to about fix fhillings. I muft likewife
obferve, that the accounts I have received of
the prices of former times, have been by no
means quite uniform and confiftent ; and an old
man of great accuracy and experience has affured
me, that more than fifty years ago, a guinea was
the ufual price of a barrel of good merchantable
herrings ; and this, I imagine, may ftill be
looked upon as the average price. All accounts,
however, I think, agree, that the price has not
been lowered in the home market, in confequence of the bufs bonnty.

When

OF BOUNTIES. 287

When the undertakers of fifheries, after fuch liberal bounties have been beftowed upon them, continue to fell their commodity at the fame, or even at a higher price than they were accuftomed to do before, it might be expected that their profits fhould be very great; and it is not improbable that thofe of fome individuals may have been fo. In general, however, I have every reafon to believe, they have been quite otherwife. The ufual effect of fuch bounties is to encourage rafh undertakers to adventure in a bufinefs which they do not underftand, and what they lofe by their own negligence and ignorance, more than compenfates all that they can gain by the utmoft liberality of government. In 1750, by the fame act which firft gave the bounty of thirty fhillings the ton for the encouragement of the white herring fifhery (the 23 Geo. II. chap. 24.), a joint ftock company was erected, with a capital of five hundred thoufand pounds, to which the fubfcribers (over and above all other encouragements, the tonnage bounty juft now mentioned, the exportation bounty of two fhillings and eight pence the barrel, the delivery of both Britifh and foreign falt duty free,) were, during the fpace of fourteen years, for every hundred pounds which they fubfcribed and paid into the ftock of the fociety, entitled to three pounds a year, to be paid by the receiver-general of the cuftoms in equal half-yearly payments. Befides this great company, the refidence of whofe governor and directors was to be in London, it was declared

lawful

C H A P.
V.

OF BOUNTIES.

BOOK IV.

lawful to erect different fishing-chambers in all the different out-ports of the kingdom, provided a sum not less than ten thousand pounds was subscribed into the capital of each, to be managed at its own risk, and for its own profit and loss. The same annuity, and the same encouragements of all kinds, were given to the trade of those inferior chambers, as to that of the great company. The subscription of the great company was soon filled up, and several different fishing-chambers were erected in the different out-ports of the kingdom. In spite of all these encouragements, almost all those different companies, both great and small, lost either the whole, or the greater part of their capitals; scarce a vestige now remains of any of them, and the white herring fishery is now entirely, or almost entirely, carried on by private adventurers.

If any particular manufacture was necessary, indeed, for the defence of the society, it might not always be prudent to depend upon our neighbours for the supply; and if such manufacture could not otherwise be supported at home, it might not be unreasonable that all the other branches of industry should be taxed in order to support it. The bounties upon the exportation of British-made sail-cloth, and British-made gun-powder, may, perhaps, both be vindicated upon this principle.

But though it can very seldom be reasonable to tax the industry of the great body of the people, in order to support that of some particular

OF BOUNTIES. 289

ticular clafs of manufacturers; yet in the wantonnefs of great profperity, when the public enjoys a greater revenue than it knows well what to do with, to give fuch bounties to favourite manufactures, may, perhaps, be as natural, as to incur any other idle expence. In public, as well as in private expences, great wealth may, perhaps, frequently be admitted as an apology for great folly. But there muft furely be fomething more than ordinary abfurdity, in continuing fuch profufion in times of general difficulty and diftrefs.

What is called a bounty is fometimes no more than a drawback, and confequently is not liable to the fame objections as what is properly a bounty. The bounty, for example, upon refined fugar exported, may be confidered as a drawback of the duties upon the brown and mufcovado fugars, from which it is made. The bounty upon wrought filk exported, a drawback of the duties upon raw and thrown filk imported. The bounty upon gunpowder exported, a drawback of the duties upon brimftone and faltpetre imported. In the language of the cuftoms thofe allowances only are called drawbacks, which are given upon goods exported in the fame form in which they are imported. When that form has been fo altered by manufacture of any kind, as to come under a new denomination, they are called bounties.

Premiums given by the public to artifts and manufacturers who excel in their particular occupations, are not liable to the fame objections

VOL. III.　　　U　　　as

290 OF THE CORN TRADE AND CORN LAWS.

BOOK
IV.

as bounties. By encouraging extraordinary dexterity and ingenuity, they ferve to keep up the emulation of the workmen actually employed in thofe refpective occupations, and are not confiderable enough to turn towards any one of them a greater fhare of the capital of the country than what would go to it of its own accord. Their tendency is not to overturn the natural balance of employments, but to render the work which is done in each as perfect and complete as poffible. The expence of premiums, befides, is very trifling; that of bounties very great. The bounty upon corn alone has fometimes coft the public in one year more than three hundred thoufand pounds.

Bounties are fometimes called premiums, as drawbacks are fometimes called bounties. But we muft in all cafes attend to the nature of the thing, without paying any regard to the word.

Digreffion concerning the Corn Trade and Corn Laws.

I CANNOT conclude this chapter concerning bounties, without obferving that the praifes which have been beftowed upon the law which eftablifhes the bounty upon the exportation of corn, and upon that fyftem of regulations which is connected with it, are altogether unmerited. A particular examination of the nature of the corn trade, and of the principal Britifh laws which relate to it, will fufficiently demonftrate

the

OF THE CORN TRADE AND CORN LAWS. 291

the truth of this affertion. The great importance of this fubject muft juftify the length of the digreffion.

The trade of the corn merchant is compofed of four different branches, which, though they may fometimes be all carried on by the famo perfon, are in their own nature four feparate and diftinct trades. Thefe are, firft, the trade of the inland dealer; fecondly, that of the merchant importer for home confumption; thirdly, that of the merchant exporter of home produce for foreign confumption; and, fourthly, that of the merchant carrier, or of the importer of corn in order to export it again.

I. The intereft of the inland dealer, and that of the great body of the people, how oppofite foever they may at firft fight appear, are, even in years of the greateft fcarcity, exactly the fame. It is his intereft to raife the price of his corn as high as the real fcarcity of the feafon requires, and it can never be his intereft to raife it higher. By raifing the price he difcourages the confumption, and puts every body, more or lefs, but particularly the inferior ranks of people, upon thrift and good management. If, by raifing it too high, he difcourages the confumption fo much, that the fupply of the feafon is likely to go beyond the confumption of the feafon, and to laft for fome time after the next crop begins to come in, he runs the hazard, not only of lofing a confiderable part of his corn by natural caufes, but of being obliged to fell what remains of it for much lefs than what he might have had

for

292 OF THE CORN TRADE AND CORN LAWS.

BOOK
IV.

for it feveral months before. If by not raifing the price high enough he difcourages the confumption fo little, that the fupply of the feafon is likely to fall fhort of the confumption of the feafon, he not only lofes a part of the profit which he might otherwife have made, but he expofes the people to fuffer before the end of the feafon, inftead of the hardfhips of a dearth, the dreadful horrors of a famine. It is the intereft of the people, that their daily, weekly, and monthly confumption, fhould be proportioned as exactly as poffible to the fupply of the feafon. The intereft of the inland corn dealer is the fame. By fupplying them, as nearly as he can judge, in this proportion, he is likely to fell all his corn for the higheft price, and with the greateft profit ; and his knowledge of the ftate of the crop, and of his daily, weekly, and monthly fales, enable him to judge, with more or lefs accuracy, how far they really are fupplied in this manner. Without intending the intereft of the people, he is neceffarily led, by a regard to his own intereft, to treat them, even in years of fcarcity, pretty much in the fame manner as the prudent mafter of a veffel is fometimes obliged to treat his crew. When he forefees that provifions are likely to run fhort, he puts them upon fhort allowance. Though from excefs of caution he fhould fometimes do this without any real neceffity, yet all the inconveniencies which his crew can thereby fuffer are inconfiderable, in comparifon of the danger, mifery, and ruin, to which they might fometimes be expofed by a lefs

provident

OF THE CORN TRADE AND CORN LAWS. 293

provident conduct. Though from excefs of avarice, in the fame manner, the inland corn merchant fhould fometimes raife the price of his corn fomewhat higher than the fcarcity of the feafon requires, yet all the inconveniencies which the people can fuffer from this conduct, which effectually fecures them from a famine in the end of the feafon, are inconfiderable, in comparifon of what they might have been expofed to by a more liberal way of dealing in the beginning of it. The corn merchant himfelf is likely to fuffer the moft by this excefs of avarice; not only from the indignation which it generally excites againft him, but, though he fhould efcape the effects of this indignation, from the quantity of corn which it neceffarily leaves upon his hands in the end of the feafon, and which, if the next feafon happens to prove favourable, he muft always fell for a much lower price than he might otherwife have had.

Were it poffible, indeed, for one great company of merchants to poffefs themfelves of the whole crop of an extenfive country, it might, perhaps, be their intereft to deal with it as the Dutch are faid to do with the fpiceries of the Moluccas, to deftroy or throw away a confiderable part of it, in order to keep up the price of the reft. But it is fcarce poffible, even by the violence of law, to eftablifh fuch an extenfive monopoly with regard to corn; and, wherever the law leaves the trade free, it is of all commodities the leaft liable to be engroffed or monopolized by the force of a few large capitals,

CHAP.
V.

U 3   which

OF THE CORN TRADE AND CORN LAWS.

BOOK IV.

which buy up the greater part of it. Not only its value far exceeds what the capitals of a few private men are capable of purchafing, but fuppofing they were capable of purchafing it, the manner in which it is produced renders this purchafe altogether impracticable. As in every civilized country it is the commodity of which the annual confumption is the greateft, fo a greater quantity of induftry is annually employed in producing corn than in producing any other commodity. When it firft comes from the ground too, it is neceffarily divided among a greater number of owners than any other commodity; and thefe owners can never be collected into one place like a number of independent manufacturers, but are neceffarily fcattered through all the different corners of the country. Thefe firft owners either immediately fupply the confumers in their own neighbourhood, or they fupply other inland dealers, who fupply thofe confumers. The inland dealers in corn, therefore, including both the farmer and the baker, are neceffarily more numerous than the dealers in any other commodity, and their difperfed fituation renders it altogether impoffible for them to enter into any general combination. If in a year of fcarcity, therefore, any of them fhould find that he had a good deal more corn upon hand than, at the current price, he could hope to difpofe of before the end of the feafon, he would never think of keeping up this price to his own lofs, and to the fole benefit of his rivals and competitors, but would immediately lower it,

OF THE CORN TRADE AND CORN LAWS. 295

CHAP. V.

it, in order to get rid of his corn before the new crop began to come in. The fame motives, the fame interefts, which would thus regulate the conduct of any one dealer, would regulate that of every other, and oblige them all in general to fell their corn at the price which, according to the beft of their judgment, was moft fuitable to the fcarcity or plenty of the feafon.

Whoever examines, with attention, the hiftory of the dearths and famines which have afflicted any part of Europe, during either the courfe of the prefent, or that of the two preceding centuries, of feveral of which we have pretty exact accounts, will find, I believe, that a dearth never has arifen from any combination among the inland dealers in corn, nor from any other caufe but a real fcarcity, occafioned fometimes, perhaps, and in fome particular places, by the wafte of war, but in by far the greateft number of cafes, by the fault of the feafons; and that a famine has never arifen from any other caufe but the violence of government attempting, by improper means, to remedy the inconveniencies of a dearth.

In an extenfive corn country, between all the different parts of which there is a free commerce and communication, the fcarcity occafioned by the moft unfavourable feafons can never be fo great as to produce a famine; and the fcantieft crop, if managed with frugality and œconomy, will maintain, through the year, the fame number of people that are commonly fed in a more affluent manner by one of moderate plenty.

U 4

The

OF THE CORN TRADE AND CORN LAWS.

BOOK IV.

The feafons moft unfavourable to the crop are thofe of exceffive drought or exceffive rain. But, as corn grows equally upon high and low lands, upon grounds that are difpofed to be too wet, and upon thofe that are difpofed to be too dry, either the drought or the rain which is hurtful to one part of the country is favourable to another; and though both in the wet and in the dry feafon the crop is a good deal lefs than in one more properly tempered, yet in both what is loft in one part of the country is in fome meafure compenfated by what is gained in the other. In rice countries, where the crop not only requires a very moift foil, but where, in a certain period of its growing, it muft be laid under water, the effects of a drought are much more difmal. Even in fuch countries, however, the drought is, perhaps, fcarce ever fo univerfal, as neceffarily to occafion a famine, if the government would allow a free trade. The drought in Bengal, a few years ago, might probably have occafioned a very great dearth. Some improper regulations, fome injudicious reftraints, impofed by the fervants of the Eaft India Company upon the rice trade, contributed, perhaps, to turn that dearth into a famine.

When the government, in order to remedy the inconveniencies of a dearth, orders all the dealers to fell their corn at what it fuppofes a reafonable price, it either hinders them from bringing it to market, which may fometimes produce a famine, even in the beginning of the feafon; or if they bring it thither, it enables the

OF THE CORN TRADE AND CORN LAWS. 297

the people, and thereby encourages them to confume it fo faft, as muft neceffarily produce a
famine before the end of the feafon. The unlimited, unreftrained freedom of the corn trade,
as it is the only effectual preventative of the mi-
feries of a famine, fo it is the beft palliative of
the inconveniencies of a dearth; for the inconveniencies of a real fcarcity cannot be remedied;
they can only be palliated. No trade deferves
more the full protection of the law, and no trade
requires it fo much; becaufe no trade is fo much
expofed to popular odium.

In years of fcarcity the inferior ranks of people impute their diftrefs to the avarice of the corn
merchant, who becomes the object of their
hatred and indignation. Inftead of making profit upon fuch occafions, therefore, he is often
in danger of being utterly ruined, and of having
his magazines plundered and deftroyed by their
violence. It is in years of fcarcity, however,
when prices are high, that the corn merchant
expects to make his principal profit. He is generally in contract with fome farmers to furnifh
him for a certain number of years with a certain
quantity of corn at a certain price. This contract price is fettled according to what is fuppofed to be the moderate and reafonable, that is,
the ordinary or average price, which, before the
late years of fcarcity, was commonly about eight-
and-twenty-fhillings for the quarter of wheat,
and for that of other grain in proportion. In
years of fcarcity, therefore, the corn merchant
buys a great part of his corn for the ordinary
price,

BOOK IV.

price, and fells it for a much higher. That this extraordinary profit, however, is no more than fufficient to put his trade upon a fair level with other trades, and to compenfate the many loffes which he fuftains upon other occafions, both from the perifhable nature of the commodity itfelf, and from the frequent and unforefeen fluctuations of its price, feems evident enough, from this fingle circumftance, that great fortunes are as feldom made in this as in any other trade. The popular odium, however, which attends it in years of fcarcity, the only years in which it can be very profitable, renders people of character and fortune averfe to enter into it. It is abandoned to an inferior fet of dealers ; and millers, bakers, mealmen, and meal factors, together with a number of wretched huckfters, are almoft the only middle people that, in the home market, come between the grower and the confumer.

The ancient policy of Europe, inftead of dif-countenancing this popular odium againft a trade fo beneficial to the public, feems, on the contrary, to have authorifed and encouraged it.

By the 5th and 6th of Edward VI. cap. 14. it was enacted, That whoever fhould buy any corn or grain with intent to fell it again, fhould be reputed an unlawful engroffer, and fhould, for the firft fault, fuffer two months imprifonment, and forfeit the value of the corn ; for the fecond, fuffer fix months imprifonment, and forfeit double the value ; and for the third, be fet in the pillory, fuffer imprifonment during the king's pleafure,

pleafure, and forfeit all his goods and chattels. C H A P.
The ancient policy of moft other parts of Europe V.
was no better than that of England.

Our anceftors feem to have imagined that the
people would buy their corn cheaper of the farmer than of the corn merchant, who, they were
afraid, would require, over and above the price
which he paid to the farmer, an exorbitant profit to himfelf. They endeavoured, therefore, to
annihilate his trade altogether. They even endeavoured to hinder as much as poffible any
middle man of any kind from coming in between the grower and the confumer; and this
was the meaning of the many reftraints which
they impofed upon the trade of thofe whom they
called kidders or carriers of corn, a trade which
nobody was allowed to exercife without a licence
afcertaining his qualifications as a man of probity and fair dealing. The authority of three
juftices of the peace was, by the ftatute of
Edward VI. neceffary, in order to grant this
licence. But even this reftraint was afterwards
thought infufficient, and by a ftatute of Elizabeth, the privilege of granting it was confined to
the quarter-feffions.

The ancient policy of Europe endeavoured in
this manner to regulate agriculture, the great
trade of the country, by maxims quite different
from thofe which it eftablifhed with regard to
manufactures, the great trade of the towns. By
leaving the farmer no other cuftomers but either
the confumers or their immediate factors, the
kidders and carriers of corn, it endeavoured to

4 force

OF THE CORN TRADE AND CORN LAWS.

BOOK IV.

force him to exercife the trade, not only of a farmer, but of a corn merchant or corn retailer. On the contrary, it in many cafes prohibited the manufacturer from exercifing the trade of a fhopkeeper, or from felling his own goods by retail. It meant by the one law to promote the general intereft of the country, or to render corn cheap, without, perhaps, its being well underftood how this was to be done. By the other it meant to promote that of a particular order of men, the fhopkeepers, who would be fo much underfold by the manufacturer, it was fuppofed, that their trade would be ruined if he was allowed to retail at all.

The manufacturer, however, though he had been allowed to keep a fhop, and to fell his own goods by retail, could not have underfold the common fhopkeeper. Whatever part of his capital he might have placed in his fhop, he muft have withdrawn it from his manufacture. In order to carry on his bufinefs on a level with that of other people, as he muft have had the profit of a manufacturer on the one part, fo he muft have had that of a fhopkeeper upon the other. Let us fuppofe, for example, that in the particular town where he lived, ten per cent. was the ordinary profit both of manufacturing and fhopkeeping ftock; he muft in this cafe have charged upon every piece of his own goods which he fold in his fhop, a profit of twenty per cent. When he carried them from his workhoufe to his fhop, he muft have valued them at the price for which he could have fold them to a

dealer

OF THE CORN TRADE AND CORN LAWS. 301

CHAP. V.

dealer or shopkeeper, who would have bought them by wholesale. If he valued them lower, he lost a part of the profit of his manufacturing capital. When again he sold them from his shop, unless he got the same price at which a shopkeeper would have sold them, he lost a part of the profit of his shopkeeping capital. Though he might appear, therefore, to make a double profit upon the same piece of goods, yet as these goods made successively a part of two distinct capitals, he made but a single profit upon the whole capital employed about them; and if he made less than his profit, he was a loser, or did not employ his whole capital with the same advantage as the greater part of his neighbours.

What the manufacturer was prohibited to do, the farmer was in some measure enjoined to do; to divide his capital between two different employments; to keep one part of it in his granaries and stack yard, for supplying the occasional demands of the market; and to employ the other in the cultivation of his land. But as he could not afford to employ the latter for less than the ordinary profits of farming stock, so he could as little afford to employ the former for less than the ordinary profits of mercantile stock. Whether the stock which really carried on the business of the corn merchant belonged to the person who was called a farmer, or to the person who was called a corn merchant, an equal profit was in both cases requisite, in order to indemnify its owner for employing it in this manner; in order to put his business upon a level with other trades,

OF THE CORN TRADE AND CORN LAWS.

BOOK IV.

trades, and in order to hinder him from having an intereſt to change it as ſoon as poſſible for ſome other. The farmer, therefore, who was thus forced to exerciſe the trade of a corn merchant, could not afford to ſell his corn cheaper than any other corn merchant would have been obliged to do in the caſe of a free competition.

The dealer who can employ his whole ſtock in one ſingle branch of buſineſs, has an advantage of the ſame kind with the workman who can employ his whole labour in one ſingle operation. As the latter acquires a dexterity which enables him, with the ſame two hands, to perform a much greater quantity of work ; ſo the former acquires ſo eaſy and ready a method of tranſacting his buſineſs, of buying and diſpoſing of his goods, that with the ſame capital he can tranſact a much greater quantity of buſineſs. As the one can commonly afford his work a good deal cheaper, ſo the other can commonly afford his goods ſomewhat cheaper than if his ſtock and attention were both employed about a greater variety of objects. The greater part of manufacturers could not afford to retail their own goods ſo cheap as a vigilant and active ſhopkeeper, whoſe ſole buſineſs it was to buy them by wholeſale, and to retail them again. The greater part of farmers could ſtill leſs afford to retail their own corn, to ſupply the inhabitants of a town, at perhaps four or five miles diftance from the greater part of them, ſo cheap as a vigilant and active corn merchant, whoſe

ſole

OF THE CORN TRADE AND CORN LAWS. 303

fole bufinefs it was to purchafe corn by wholefale, to collect it into a great magazine, and to
retail it again.

CHAP.
V.

The law which prohibited the manufacturer
from exercifing the trade of a fhopkeeper, endeavoured to force this divifion in the employment
of ftock to go on fafter than it might otherwife
have done. The law which obliged the farmer
to exercife the trade of a corn merchant, endeavoured to hinder it from going on fo faft. Both
laws were evident violations of natural liberty,
and therefore unjuft; and they were both too as
impolitic as they were unjuft. It is the intereft
of every fociety, that things of this kind fhould
never either be forced or obftructed. The man
who employs either his labour or his ftock in a
greater variety of ways than his fituation renders
neceffary, can never hurt his neighbour by un-
derfelling him. He may hurt himfelf, and he
generally does fo. Jack of all trades will never
be rich, fays the proverb. But the law ought
always to truft people with the care of their own
intereft, as in their local fituations they muft generally be able to judge better of it than the
legiflator can do. The law, however, which
obliged the farmer to exercife the trade of a
corn merchant, was by far the moft pernicious of
the two.

It obftructed not only that divifion in the
employment of ftock which is fo advantageous
to every fociety, but it obftructed likewife the
improvement and cultivation of the land. By
obliging the farmer to carry on two trades inftead

304 OF THE CORN TRADE AND CORN LAWS.

BOOK IV.

ftead of one, it forced him to divide his capital into two parts, of which one only could be employed in cultivation. But if he had been at liberty to fell his whole crop to a corn merchant as faft as he could threfh it out, his whole capital might have returned immediately to the land, and have been employed in buying more cattle, and hiring more fervants, in order to improve and cultivate it better. But by being obliged to fell his corn by retail, he was obliged to keep a great part of his capital in his granaries and ftack yard through the year, and could not, therefore, cultivate fo well as with the fame capital he might otherwife have done. This law, therefore, neceffarily obftructed the improvement of the land, and, inftead of tending to render corn cheaper, muft have tended to render it fcarcer, and therefore dearer, than it would otherwife have been.

After the bufinefs of the farmer, that of the corn merchant is in reality the trade which, if properly protected and encouraged, would contribute the moft to the raifing of corn. It would fupport the trade of the farmer, in the fame manner as the trade of the wholefale dealer fupports that of the manufacturer.

The wholefale dealer, by affording a ready market to the manufacturer, by taking his goods off his hand as faft as he can make them, and by fometimes even advancing their price to him before he has made them, enables him to keep his whole capital, and fometimes even more than his whole capital, conftantly employed in manu-

facturing,

OF THE CORN TRADE AND CORN LAWS. 305

facturing, and consequently to manufacture a much greater quantity of goods than if he was obliged to difpofe of them himfelf to the immediate confumers, or even to the retailers. As the capital of the wholefale merchant too is generally fufficient to replace that of many manufacturers, this intercourfe between him and them interefts the owner of a large capital to fupport the owners of a great number of fmall ones, and to affift them in thofe loffes and misfortunes which might otherwife prove ruinous to them.

An intercourfe of the fame kind univerfally eftablifhed between the farmers and the corn merchants, would be attended with effects equally beneficial to the farmers. They would be enabled to keep their whole capitals, and even more than their whole capitals, conftantly employed in cultivation. In cafe of any of thofe accidents, to which no trade is more liable than theirs, they would find in their ordinary cuftomer, the wealthy corn merchant, a perfon who had both an intereft to fupport them, and the ability to do it, and they would not, as at prefent, be entirely dependent upon the forbearance of their landlord, or the mercy of his fteward. Were it poffible, as perhaps it is not, to eftablifh this intercourfe univerfally, and all at once, were it poffible to turn all at once the whole farming ftock of the kingdom to its proper bufinefs, the cultivation of land, withdrawing it from every other employment into which any part of it may be at prefent diverted, and were it poffible, in order to fupport and affift upon occafion the

VOL. III. x operations

OF THE CORN TRADE AND CORN LAWS.

BOOK IV.

operations of this great flock, to provide all at once another flock almoſt equally great, it is not perhaps very eaſy to imagine how great, how extenſive, and how ſudden would be the improvement which this change of circumſtances would alone produce upon the whole face of the country.

The ſtatute of Edward VI., therefore, by prohibiting as much as poſſible any middle man from coming in between the grower and the conſumer, ·endeavoured to annihilate a trade, of which the free exerciſe is not only the beſt palliative of the inconveniencies of a dearth, but the beſt preventative of that calamity : after the trade of the farmer, no trade contributing ſo much to the growing of corn as that of the corn merchant.

The rigour of this law was afterwards ſoftened by ſeveral ſubſequent ſtatutes, which ſucceſſively permitted the engroſſing of corn when the price of wheat ſhould not exceed twenty, twenty-four, thirty-two, and forty ſhillings the quarter. At laſt, by the 15th of Charles II. c. 7. the engroſſing or buying of corn in order to ſell it again, as long as the price of wheat did not exceed forty-eight ſhillings the quarter, and that of other grain in proportion, was declared lawful to all perſons not being foreſtallers, that is, not ſelling again in the ſame market within three months. All the freedom which the trade of the inland corn dealer has ever yet enjoyed, was beſtowed upon it by this ſtatute. The ſtatute of the twelfth of the preſent King, which repeals almoſt

, all

OF THE CORN TRADE AND CORN LAWS. 307

all the other ancient laws against engroffers and foreftallers, does not repeal the reftrictions of this particular ftatute, which therefore ftill continue in force.

CHAP.
V.

This ftatute, however, authorifes in fome meafure two very abfurd popular prejudices.

Firft, it fuppofes that when the price of wheat has rifen fo high as forty-eight fhillings the quarter, and that of other grain in proportion, corn is likely to be fo engroffed as to hurt the people. But from what has been already faid, it feems evident enough that corn can at no price be fo engroffed by the inland dealers as to hurt the people: and forty-eight fhillings the quarter befides, though it may be confidered as a very high price, yet in years of fcarcity it is a price which frequently takes place immediately after harveft, when fcarce any part of the new crop can be fold off, and when it is impoffible even for ignorance to fuppofe that any part of it can be fo engroffed as to hurt the people.

Secondly, it fuppofes that there is a certain price at which corn is likely to be foreftalled, that is, bought up in order to be fold again foon after in the fame market, fo as to hurt the people. But if a merchant ever buys up corn, either going to a particular market or in a particular market, in order to fell it again foon after in the fame market, it muft be becaufe he judges that the market cannot be fo liberally fupplied through the whole feafon as upon that particular occafion, and that the price, therefore, muft foon rife. If he judges wrong in this, and if the

X 2

price

OF THE CORN TRADE AND CORN LAWS.

BOOK IV.

price does not rife, he not only lofes the whole profit of the ftock which he employs in this manner, but a part of the ftock itfelf; by the expence and lofs which neceffarily attend the ftoring and keeping of corn. He hurts himfelf, therefore, much more effentially than he can hurt even the particular people whom he may hinder from fupplying themfelves upon that particular market day, becaufe they may afterwards fupply themfelves juft as cheap upon any other market day. If he judges right, inftead of hurting the great body of the people, he renders them a moft important fervice. By making them feel the inconveniencies of a dearth fomewhat earlier than they otherwife might do, he prevents their feeling them afterwards fo feverely as they certainly would do, if the cheapnefs of price encouraged them to confume fafter than fuited the real fcarcity of the feafon. When the fcarcity is real, the beft thing that can be done for the people is to divide the inconveniencies of it as equally as poffible through all the different months, and weeks, and days of the year. The intereft of the corn merchant makes him ftudy to do this as exactly as he can; and as no other perfon can have either the fame intereft, or the fame knowledge, or the fame abilities to do it fo exactly as he, this moft important operation of commerce ought to be trufted entirely to him; or, in other words, the corn trade, fo far at leaft as concerns the fupply of the home market, ought to be left perfectly free.

The

The popular fear of engroffing and fore ftalling may be compared to the popular terrors and fufpicions of witchcraft. The unfortunate wretches accufed of this latter crime were not more innocent of the misfortunes imputed to them, than thofe who have been accufed of the former. The law which put an end to all profecutions againft witchcraft, which put it out of any man's power to gratify his own malice by accufing his neighbour of that imaginary crime, feems effectually to have put an end to thofe fears and fufpicions, by taking away the great caufe which encouraged and fupported them. The law which fhould reftore entire freedom to the inland trade of corn, would probably prove as effectual to put an end to the popular fears of engroffing and foreftalling.

The 15th of Charles II. c. 7. however, with all its imperfections, has perhaps contributed more both to the plentiful fupply of the home market, and to the increafe of tillage, than any other law in the ftatute book. It is from this law that the inland corn trade has derived all the liberty and protection which it has ever yet enjoyed; and both the fupply of the home market, and the intereft of tillage, are much more effectually promoted by the inland, than either by the importation or exportation trade.

The proportion of the average quantity of all forts of grain imported into Great Britain to that of all forts of grain confumed, it has been computed by the author of the tracts upon the corn trade, does not exceed that of one to five

X 3   hundred

310   OF THE CORN TRADE AND CORN LAWS.

BOOK hundred and feventy.   For fupplying the home
IV.   market, therefore, the importance of the inland
trade muft be to that of the importation trade
as five hundred and feventy to one.

The average quantity of all forts of grain
exported from Great Britain does not, according
to the fame author, exceed the one-and-thirtieth
part of the annual produce.   For the encouragement of tillage, therefore, by providing a market
for the home produce, the importance of the
inland trade muft be to that of the exportation
trade as thirty to one.

I have no great faith in political arithmetic,
and I mean not to warrant the exactnefs of
either of thefe computations.   I mention them
only in order to fhow of how much lefs confequence, in the opinion of the moft judicious and
experienced perfons, the foreign trade of corn is
than the home trade.   The great cheapnefs of
corn in the years immediately preceding the
eftablifhment of the bounty, may perhaps, with
reafon, be afcribed in fome meafure to the
operation of this ftatute of Charles II., which
had been enacted about five-and-twenty years
before, and which had therefore full time to
produce its effect.

A very few words will fufficiently explain all
that I have to fay concerning the other three
branches of the corn trade.

II. The trade of the merchant importer of
foreign corn for home confumption, evidently
contributes to the immediate fupply of the home
market, and muft fo far be immediately beneficial

OF THE CORN TRADE AND CORN LAWS.   311

ficial to the great body of the people. It tends, CHAP.
indeed, to lower fomewhat the average money   V.
price of corn, but not to diminifh its real value,
or the quantity of labour which it is capable of
maintaining. If importation was at all times
free, our farmers and country gentlemen would,
probably, one year with another, get lefs money
for their corn than they do at prefent, when
importation is at moft times in effeft prohibited;
but the money which they got would be of more
value, would buy more goods of all other kinds,
and would employ more labour. Their real
wealth, their real revenue, therefore, would be
the fame as at prefent, though it might be expreffed by a fmaller quantity of filver; and they
would neither be difabled nor difcouraged from
cultivating corn as much as they do at prefent.
On the contrary, as the rife in the real value of
filver, in confequence of lowering the money
price of corn, lowers fomewhat the money price
of all other commodities, it gives the induftry
of the country, where it takes place, fome advantage in all foreign markets, and thereby tends
to encourage and increafe that induftry. But
the extent of the home market for corn muft be
in proportion to the general induftry of the
country where it grows, or to the number of
thofe who produce fomething elfe, and therefore have fomething elfe, or what comes to the
fame thing, the price of fomething elfe, to give
in exchange for corn. But in every country the
home market, as it is the neareft and moft convenient, fo is it likewife the greateft and moft

X 4   important

312 OF THE CORN TRADE AND CORN LAWS.

B O O K important market for corn. That rife in the
IV. real value of filver, therefore, which is the effect
of lowering the, average money price of corn,
tends to enlarge the greateft and moft important
market for corn, and thereby to encourage,
inftead of difcouraging, its growth.

By the 22d of Charles II. c. 13, the importation of wheat, whenever the price in the home
market did not exceed fifty-three fhillings and
four pence the quarter, was fubjected to a duty
of fixteen fhillings the quarter; and to a duty of
eight fhillings whenever the price did not exceed
four pounds. The former of thefe two prices
has, for more than a century paft, taken place
only in times of very great fcarcity; and the
latter has, fo far as I know, not taken place at
all. Yet, till wheat had rifen above this latter
price, it was by this ftatute fubjected to a very
high duty; and, till it had rifen above the former, to a duty which amounted to a prohibition.
The importation of other forts of grain was
reftrained at rates, and by duties, in proportion to
the value of the grain, almoft equally high [*].

[*] Before the 13th of the prefent King, the following were the duties
payable upon the importation of the different forts of grain:

Grain.	Duties.		Duties.	Duties.
Beans to 28s. per qr.	19s. 10d: after till	40s.	16s. 8d. then	12d.
Barley to 28s.	19s. 10d.	32s.	16s.	12d.
Malt is prohibited by the annual Malt-tax Bill.				
Oats to 16s.	5s. 10d. after			9½d.
Peafe to 40s.	16s, 0d, after			9½d.
Rye to 36s.	19s. 10d.	till	40s. - 16s. 8d. then 12d.	
Wheat to 44s.	21s. 9d.	till	53s. 4d. 17s. then 8s.	
till 4l. and after that about 1s. 4d.				
Buck wheat to 32s. per qr. to pay 16s.				

Thefe different duties were impofed, partly by the 22d of Charles II.
in place of the Old Subfidy, partly by the New Subfidy, by the One-
third and Two-thirds Subfidy, and by the Subfidy 1747.

Subfe-

OF THE CORN TRADE AND CORN LAWS.   .   313

Subfequent laws ftill further increafed thofe C H A P.
duties.
                                                V.

The diftrefs which, in years of fcarcity, the
ftrict execution of thofe laws might have brought
upon the people, would probably have been very
great.   But, upon fuch occafions, its execution
was generally fufpended by temporary ftatutes,
which permitted, for a limited time, the importation of foreign corn.   The neceffity of thefe
temporary ftatutes fufficiently demonftrates the
impropriety of this general one.

These reftraints upon importation, though
prior to the eftablifhment of the bounty, were
dictated by the fame fpirit, by the fame principles, which afterwards enacted that regulation.
How hurtful foever in themfelves, thefe or fome
other reftraints upon importation became neceffary in confequence of that regulation.   If, when
wheat was either below forty-eight fhillings the
quarter, or not much above it, foreign corn
could have been imported either duty free, or
upon paying only a fmall duty, it might have
been exported again, with the benefit of the
bounty, to the great lofs of the public revenue,
and to the entire perverfion of the inftitution,
of which the object was to extend the market
for the home growth, not that for the growth of
foreign countries.

III. The trade of the merchant exporter of
corn for foreign confumption, certainly does not
contribute directly to the plentiful fupply of the
home market.   It does fo, however, indirectly.
From whatever fource this fupply may be ufually
                                        drawn,

314 OF THE CORN TRADE AND CORN LAWS.

BOOK IV.

drawn, whether from home growth or from foreign importation, unlefs more corn is either ufually grown, or ufually imported into the country, than what is ufually confumed in it, the fupply of the home market can never be very plentiful. But unlefs the furplus can, in all ordinary cafes, be exported, the growers will be careful never to grow more, and the importers never to import more, than what the bare confumption of the home market requires. That market will very feldom be overftocked; but it will generally be underftocked, the people, whofe bufinefs it is to fupply it, being generally afraid left their goods fhould be left upon their hands. The prohibition of exportation limits the improvement and cultivation of the country to what the fupply of its own inhabitants requires. The freedom of exportation enables it to extend cultivation for the fupply of foreign nations.

By the 12th of Charles II. c. 4. the exportation of corn was permitted whenever the price of wheat did not exceed forty fhillings the quarter, and that of other grain in proportion. By the 15th of the fame prince, this liberty was extended till the price of wheat exceeded forty-eight fhillings the quarter; and by the 22d, to all higher prices. A poundage, indeed, was to be paid to the king upon fuch exportation. But all grain was rated fo low in the book of rates, that this poundage amounted only upon wheat to a fhilling, upon oats to four pence, and upon all other grain to fix pence the quarter. By the 1ft of William and Mary, the act which eftablifhed

OF THE CORN TRADE AND CORN LAWS. 315

blifhed the bounty, this fmall duty was virtually
taken off whenever the price of wheat did not
exceed forty-eight fhillings the quarter; and by
the 11th and 12th of William III. c. 20. it was
exprefsly taken off at all higher prices.

The trade of the merchant exporter was, in
this manner, not only encouraged by a bounty,
but rendered much more free than that of the
inland dealer. By the laft of thefe ftatutes, corn
could be engroffed at any price for exportation;
but it could not be engroffed for inland fale,
except when the price did not exceed forty-eight
fhillings the quarter. The intereft of the inland dealer, however, it has already been fhown,
can never be oppofite to that of the great body
of the people. That of the merchant exporter
may, and in fact fometimes is. If, while his
own country labours under a dearth, a neighbouring country fhould be afflicted with a famine, it
might be his intereft to carry corn to the latter
country in fuch quantities as might very much
aggravate the calamities of the dearth. The
plentiful fupply of the home market was not the
direct object of thofe ftatutes; but, under the
pretence of encouraging agriculture, to raife
the money price of corn as high as poffible,
and thereby to occafion, as much as poffible, a
conftant dearth in the home market. By the
difcouragement of importation, the fupply of
that market, even in times of great fcarcity,
was confined to the home growth; and by the
encouragement of exportation, when the price
was fo high as forty-eight fhillings the quarter,
that

CHAP.
V.

OF THE CORN TRADE AND CORN LAWS.

BOOK IV.

that market was not, even in times of considerable scarcity, allowed to enjoy the whole of that growth. The temporary laws, prohibiting for a limited time the exportation of corn, and taking off for a limited time the duties upon its importation, expedients to which Great Britain has been obliged so frequently to have recourse, sufficiently demonstrate the impropriety of her general system. Had that system been good, she would not so frequently have been reduced to the necessity of departing from it.

Were all nations to follow the liberal system of free exportation and free importation, the different states into which a great continent was divided would so far resemble the different provinces of a great empire. As among the different provinces of a great empire the freedom of the inland trade appears, both from reason and experience, not only the best palliative of a dearth, but the most effectual preventative of a famine; so would the freedom of the exportation and importation trade be among the different states into which a great continent was divided. The larger the continent, the easier the communication through all the different parts of it, both by land and by water, the less would any one particular part of it ever be exposed to either of these calamities, the scarcity of any one country being more likely to be relieved by the plenty of some other. But very few countries have entirely adopted this liberal system. The freedom of the corn trade is almost every where more or less restrained, and,

in

OF THE CORN TRADE AND CORN LAWS. 317

in many countries, is confined by such absurd **C H A P.**
regulations, as frequently aggravate the un- **V.**
avoidable misfortune of a dearth, into the
dreadful calamity of a famine. The demand of
such countries for corn may frequently become
so great and so urgent, that a small state in their
neighbourhood, which happened at the same
time to be labouring under some degree of
dearth, could not venture to supply them without exposing itself to the like dreadful calamity.
The very bad policy of one country may thus
render it in some measure dangerous and impru-
dent to establish what would otherwise be the
best policy in another. The unlimited freedom
of exportation, however, would be much less
dangerous in great states, in which the growth
being much greater, the supply could seldom be
much affected by any quantity of corn that was
likely to be exported. In a Swiss canton, or
in some of the little states of Italy, it may,
perhaps, sometimes be necessary to restrain the
exportation of corn. In such great countries as
France or England it scarce ever can. To
hinder, besides, the farmer from sending his goods
at all times to the best market, is evidently to
sacrifice the ordinary laws of justice to an idea of
public utility, to a sort of reasons of state ; an act
of legislative authority which ought to be exercised only, which can be pardoned only in
cases of the most urgent necessity. The price
at which the exportation of corn is prohibited,
if it is ever to be prohibited, ought always to be
a very high price.

The

OF THE CORN TRADE AND CORN LAWS.

BOOK IV.

The laws concerning corn may every where be compared to the laws concerning religion. The people feel themselves fo much interefted in what relates either to their fubfiftence in this life, or to their happinefs in a life to come, that government muft yield to their prejudices, and, in order to preferve the public tranquillity, eftablifh that fyftem which they approve of. It is upon this account, perhaps, that we fo feldom find a reafonable fyftem eftablifhed with regard to either of thofe two capital objects.

IV. The trade of the merchant carrier, or of the importer of foreign corn in order to export it again, contributes to the plentiful fupply of the home market. It is not indeed the direct purpofe of his trade to fell his corn there. But he will generally be willing to do fo, and even for a good deal lefs money than he might expect in a foreign market; becaufe he faves in this manner the expence of loading and unloading, of freight and infurance. The inhabitants of the country, which, by means of the carrying trade, becomes the magazine and ftorehoufe for the fupply of other countries, can very feldom be in want themfelves. Though the carrying trade might thus contribute to reduce the average money price of corn in the home market, it would not thereby lower its real value. It would only raife fomewhat the real value of filver.

The carrying trade was in effect prohibited in Great Britain, upon all ordinary occafions, by the high duties upon the importation of foreign corn,

OF THE CORN TRADE AND CORN LAWS.   319

corn, of the greater part of which there was no
drawback; and upon extraordinary occasions,
when a scarcity made it necessary to suspend
those duties by temporary statutes, exportation
was always prohibited. By this system of laws,
therefore, the carrying trade was in effect prohibited upon all occasions.

That system of laws, therefore, which is connected with the establishment of the bounty,
seems to deserve no part of the praise which has
been bestowed upon it. The improvement and
prosperity of Great Britain, which has been so
often ascribed to those laws, may very easily be
accounted for by other causes. That security
which the laws in Great Britain give to every
man that he shall enjoy the fruits of his own
labour, is alone sufficient to make any country
flourish, notwithstanding these and twenty other
absurd regulations of commerce; and this security was perfected by the revolution, much about
the same time that the bounty was established.
The natural effort of every individual to better
his own condition, when suffered to exert itself
with freedom and security, is so powerful a principle, that it is alone, and without any assistance,
not only capable of carrying on the society to
wealth and prosperity, but of surmounting a
hundred impertinent obstructions with which the
folly of human laws too often incumbers its operations; though the effect of these obstructions
is always more or less either to encroach upon its
freedom, or to diminish its security. In Great
Britain industry is perfectly secure; and though

it

320 OF THE CORN TRADE AND CORN LAWS.

BOOK IV.

it is far from being perfectly free, it is as free or freer than in any other part of Europe.

Though the period of the greatest prosperity and improvement of Great Britain, has been posterior to that system of laws which is connected with the bounty, we must not upon that account impute it to those laws. It has been posterior likewise to the national debt. But the national debt has most assuredly not been the cause of it.

Though the system of laws which is connected with the bounty, has exactly the same tendency with the police of Spain and Portugal; to lower somewhat the value of the precious metals in the country where it takes place; yet Great Britain is certainly one of the richest countries in Europe, while Spain and Portugal are perhaps among the most beggarly. This difference of situation, however, may easily be accounted for from two different causes. First, the tax in Spain, the prohibition in Portugal of exporting gold and silver, and the vigilant police which watches over the execution of those laws, must, in two very poor countries, which between them import annually upwards of six millions sterling, operate, not only more directly, but much more forcibly in reducing the value of those metals there, than the corn laws can do in Great Britain. And, secondly, this bad policy is not in those countries counter-balanced by the general liberty and security of the people. Industry is there neither free nor secure, and the civil and ecclesiastical governments of both Spain

2   and

OF THE CORN TRADE AND CORN LAWS. 321

CHAP. V.

and Portugal, are fuch as would alone be fuffi-cient to perpetuate their prefent ftate of poverty, even though their regulations of commerce were as wife as the greater part of them are abfurd and foolifh.

The 13th of the prefent King, c. 43. feems to have eftablifhed a new fyftem with regard to the corn laws, in many refpe&ts better than the ancient one, but in one or two refpe&ts perhaps not quite fo good.

By this ftatute the high duties upon importa-tion for home confumption are taken off fo foon as the price of middling wheat rifes to forty-eight fhillings the quarter; that of middling rye, peafe or beans, to thirty-two fhillings; that of barley to twenty-four fhillings; and that of oats to fixteen fhillings; and inftead of them a fmall duty is impofed of only fix-pence upon the quar-ter of wheat, and upon that of other grain in proportion. With regard to all thefe different forts of grain, but particularly with regard to wheat, the home market is thus opened to fo-reign fupplies at prices confiderably lower than before.

By the fame ftatute the whole bounty of five fhillings upon the exportation of wheat ceafes fo foon as the price rifes to forty-four fhillings the quarter, inftead of forty-eight, the price at which it ceafed before; that of two fhillings and fix-pence upon the exportation of barley ceafes fo foon as the price rifes to twenty-two fhillings, inftead of twenty-four, the price at which it

VOL. III.   Y   ceafed

OF THE CORN TRADE AND CORN LAWS.

BOOK
IV.

ceafed before; that of two fhillings and fix-pence upon the exportation of oatmeal ceafes fo foon as the price rifes to fourteen fhillings, inftead of fifteen, the price at which it ceafed before. The bounty upon rye is reduced from three fhillings and fixpence to three fhillings, and it ceafes fo foon as the price rifes to twenty-eight fhillings, inftead of thirty-two, the price at which it ceafed before. If bounties are as improper as I have endeavoured to prove them to be, the fooner they ceafe, and the lower they are, fo much the better.

The fame ftatute permits, at the loweft prices, the importation of corn, in order to be exported again, duty free, provided it is in the mean time lodged in a warehoufe under the joint locks of the King and the importer. This liberty, indeed, extends to no more than twenty-five of the different ports of Great Britain. They are, however, the principal ones, and there may not, perhaps, be warehoufes proper for this purpofe in the greater part of the others.

So far this law feems evidently an improvement upon the ancient fyftem.

But by the fame law a bounty of two fhillings the quarter is given for the exportation of oats whenever the price does not exceed fourteen fhillings. No bounty had ever been given before for the exportation of this grain, no more than for that of peafe or beans.

By the fame law too, the exportation of wheat is prohibited fo foon as the price rifes to forty-
four

OF TREATIES OF COMMERCE. 323

four fhillings the quarter; that of rye fo foon as
it rifes to twenty-eight fhillings; that of barley
fo foon as it rifes to twenty-two fhillings; and
that of oats fo foon as they rife to fourteen fhillings. Thofe feveral prices feem all of them a
good deal too low, and there feems to be an
impropriety, befides, in prohibiting exportation
altogether at thofe precife prices at which that
bounty, which was given in order to force it,
is withdrawn. The bounty ought certainly either
to have been withdrawn at a much lower price,
or exportation ought to have been allowed at a
much higher.

So far, therefore, this law feems to be inferior
to the ancient fyftem. With all its imperfections,
however, we may perhaps fay of it what was faid
of the laws of Solon, that, though not the beft
in itfelf, it is the beft which the interefts, prejudices, and temper of the times would admit of.
It may perhaps in due time prepare the way for
a better.

CHAP. VI.

Of Treaties of Commerce.

WHEN a nation binds itfelf by treaty either
to permit the entry of certain goods
from one foreign country which it prohibits from
all others, or to exempt the goods of one country
from duties to which it fubjects thofe of all others,

the

OF TREATIES OF COMMERCE.

BOOK IV.

the country, or at leaſt the merchants and manufacturers of the country, whoſe commerce is ſo favoured, muſt neceſſarily derive great advantage from the treaty. Thoſe merchants and manufacturers enjoy a ſort of monopoly in the country which is ſo indulgent to them. That country becomes a market both more extenſive and more advantageous for their goods: more extenſive, becauſe the goods of other nations being either excluded or ſubjected to heavier duties, it takes off a greater quantity of theirs: more advantageous, becauſe the merchants of the favoured country, enjoying a ſort of monopoly there, will often ſell their goods for a better price than if expoſed to the free competition of all other nations.

Such treaties, however, though they may be advantageous to the merchants and manufacturers of the favoured, are neceſſarily diſadvantageous to thoſe of the favouring country. A monopoly is thus granted againſt them to a foreign nation; and they muſt frequently buy the foreign goods they have occaſion for, dearer than if the free competition of other nations was admitted. That part of its own produce with which ſuch a nation purchaſes foreign goods, muſt conſequently be ſold cheaper, becauſe when two things are exchanged for one another, the cheapneſs of the one is a neceſſary conſequence, or rather is the ſame thing with the dearneſs of the other. The exchangeable value of its annual produce, therefore, is likely to be diminiſhed by every ſuch treaty. This diminution, however,

can

OF TREATIES OF COMMERCE.

can scarce amount to any positive loss, but only to a lessening of the gain which it might otherwise make. Though it sells its goods cheaper than it otherwise might do, it will not probably sell them for less than they cost; nor, as in the case of bounties, for a price which will not replace the capital employed in bringing them to market, together with the ordinary profits of stock. The trade could not go on long if it did. Even the favouring country, therefore, may still gain by the trade, though less than if there was a free competition.

Some treaties of commerce, however, have been supposed advantageous upon principles very different from these; and a commercial country has sometimes granted a monopoly of this kind against itself to certain goods of a foreign nation, because it expected that in the whole commerce between them, it would annually sell more than it would buy, and that a balance in gold and silver would be annually returned to it. It is upon this principle that the treaty of commerce between England and Portugal, concluded in 1703, by Mr. Methuen, has been so much commended. The following is a literal translation of that treaty, which consists of three articles only :—

ART. I.

His Sacred Royal Majesty of Portugal promises, both in his own name, and that of his successors, to admit, for ever hereafter, into

Portugal,

326 OF TREATIES OF COMMERCE.

BOOK IV.

Portugal, the woollen cloths, and the reft of the woollen manufactures of the Britifh, as was accuftomed, till they were prohibited by the law; neverthelefs upon this condition:

ART. II.

That is to fay, that Her Sacred Royal Majefty of Great Britain fhall, in her own name, and that of her fucceffors, be obliged, for ever hereafter, to admit the wines of the growth of Portugal into Britain: fo that at no time, whether there fhall be peace or war between the kingdoms of Britain and France, any thing more fhall be demanded for thefe wines by the name of cuftom or duty, or by whatfoever other title, directly or indirectly, whether they fhall be imported into Great Britain in pipes or hogfheads, or other cafks, than what fhall be demanded for the like quantity or meafure of French wine, deducting or abating a third part of the cuftom or duty. But if at any time this deduction or abatement of cuftoms, which is to be made as aforefaid, fhall in any manner be attempted and prejudiced, it fhall be juft and lawful for His Sacred Royal Majefty of Portugal, again to prohibit the woollen cloths, and the reft of the Britifh woollen manufactures.

ART. III.

The Moft Excellent Lords the Plenipotentiaries promife and take upon themfelves, that their above-named mafters fhall ratify this treaty; and

OF TREATIES OF COMMERCE.

and within the fpace of two months the ratifications fhall be exchanged.

By this treaty the crown of Portugal becomes bound to admit the Englifh woollens upon the fame footing as before the prohibition; that is, not to raife the duties which had been paid before that time. But it does not become bound to admit them upon any better terms than thofe of any other nation, of France or Holland for example. The crown of Great Britain, on the contrary, becomes bound to admit the wines of Portugal, upon paying only two thirds of the duty, which is paid for thofe of France, the wines moft likely to come into competition with them. So far this treaty, therefore, is evidently advantageous to Portugal, and difadvantageous to Great Britain.

It has been celebrated, however, as a mafter-piece of the commercial policy of England. Portugal receives annually from the Brazils a greater quantity of gold than can be employed in its domeftic commerce, whether in the fhape of coin or of plate. The furplus is too valuable to be allowed to lie idle and locked up in coffers, and as it can find no advantageous market at home, it muft, notwithftanding any prohibition, be fent abroad, and exchanged for fomething for which there is a more advantageous market at home. A large fhare of it comes annually to England, in return either for Englifh goods, or for thofe of other European nations that receive their returns through England. Mr. Baretti was

328 OF TREATIES OF COMMERCE.

BOOK IV.

was informed that the weekly packet-boat from Lisbon brings, one week with another, more than fifty thousand pounds in gold to England. The sum had probably been exaggerated. It would amount to more than two millions six hundred thousand pounds a year, which is more than the Brazils are supposed to afford.

Our merchants were some years ago out of humour with the crown of Portugal. Some privileges which had been granted them, not by treaty, but by the free grace of that crown, at the solicitation, indeed, it is probable, and in return for much greater favours, defence and protection, from the crown of Great Britain, had been either infringed or revoked. The people, therefore, usually most interested in celebrating the Portugal trade, were then rather disposed to represent it as less advantageous than it had commonly been imagined. The far greater part, almost the whole, they pretended, of this annual importation of gold, was not on account of Great Britain, but of other European nations; the fruits and wines of Portugal annually imported into Great Britain nearly compensating the value of the British goods sent thither.

Let us suppose, however, that the whole was on account of Great Britain, and that it amounted to a still greater sum than Mr. Baretti seems to imagine: this trade would not, upon that account, be more advantageous than any other in which, for the same value sent out, we received an equal value of consumable goods in return.

It

OF TREATIES OF COMMERCE. 329

·It is but a very fmall part of this importation
which, it can be fuppofed, is employed as an
annual addition either to the plate or to the coin
of the kingdom. The reft muft all be fent
abroad and exchanged for confumable goods
of fome kind or other. But if thofe confumable
goods were purchafed directly with the produce
of Englifh induftry, it would be more for the
advantage of England, than firft to purchafe with
that produce the gold of Portugal, and afterwards to purchafe with that gold thofe confumable goods. A direct foreign trade of confumption is always more advantageous than a
round-about one; and to bring the fame value
of foreign goods to the home market, requires
a much fmaller capital in the one way than in
the other. If a fmaller fhare of its induftry,
therefore, had been employed in producing goods
fit for the Portugal market, and a greater in producing thofe fit for the other markets, where
thofe confumable goods for which there is a
demand in Great Britain are to be had, it would
have been more for the advantage of England.
To procure both the gold, which it wants for
its own ufe, and the confumable goods, would,
in this way, employ a much fmaller capital than
at prefent. There would be a fpare capital,
therefore, to be employed for other purpofes,
in exciting an additional quantity of induftry,
and in raifing a greater annual produce.

Though Britain were entirely excluded from
the Portugal trade, it could find very little difficulty in procuring all the annual fupplies of gold
which

OF TREATIES OF COMMERCE.

BOOK IV.

which it wants, either for the purpofes of plate, or of coin, or of foreign trade. Gold, like every other commodity, is always fomewhere or another to be got for its value by thofe who have that value to give for it. The annual furplus of gold in Portugal, befides, would ftill be fent abroad, and though not carried away by Great Britain, would be carried away by fome other nation, which would be glad to fell it again for its price, in the fame manner as Great Britain does at prefent. In buying gold of Portugal, indeed, we buy it at the firft hand; whereas, in buying it of any other nation, except Spain, we fhould buy it at the fecond, and might pay fomewhat dearer. This difference, however, would furely be too infignificant to deferve the public attention.

Almoft all our gold, it is faid, comes from Portugal. With other nations the balance of trade is either againft us, or not much in our favour. But we fhould remember, that the more gold we import from one country, the lefs we muft neceffarily import from all others. The effectual demand for gold, like that for every other commodity, is in every country limited to a certain quantity. If nine-tenths of this quantity are imported from one country, there remains a tenth only to be imported from all others. The more gold befides that is annually imported from fome particular countries, over and above what is requifite for plate and for coin, the more muft neceffarily be exported to fome others; and the more that moft infignificant

OF TREATIES OF COMMERCE. 331

CHAP.
VI.

cant object of modern policy, the balance of trade, appears to be in our favour with some particular countries, the more it must necessarily appear to be against us with many others.

It was upon this silly notion, however, that England could not subsist without the Portugal trade, that, towards the end of the late war, France and Spain, without pretending either offence or provocation, required the King of Portugal to exclude all British ships from his ports, and for the security of this exclusion, to receive into them French or Spanish garrisons. Had the King of Portugal submitted to those ignominious terms which his brother-in-law the King of Spain proposed to him, Britain would have been freed from a much greater inconveniency than the loss of the Portugal trade, the burden of supporting a very weak ally, so unprovided of every thing for his own defence, that the whole power of England, had it been directed to that single purpose, could scarce perhaps have defended him for another campaign. The loss of the Portugal trade would, no doubt, have occasioned a considerable embarrassment to the merchants at that time engaged in it, who might not, perhaps, have found out, for a year or two, any other equally advantageous method of employing their capitals; and in this would probably have consisted all the inconveniency which England could have suffered from this notable piece of commercial policy.

The great annual importation of gold and silver is neither for the purpose of plate nor of coin,

OF TREATIES OF COMMERCE.

BOOK IV.

coin, but of foreign trade. A round-about foreign trade of confumption can be carried on more advantageoufly by means of thefe metals than of almoft any other goods. As they are the univerfal inftruments of commerce, they are more readily received in return for all commodities than any other goods; and on account of their fmall bulk and great value, it cofts lefs to tranfport them backward and forward from one place to another than almoft any other fort of merchandize, and they lofe lefs of their value by being fo tranfported. Of all the commodities, therefore, which are bought in one foreign country, for no other purpofe but to be fold or exchanged again for fome other goods in another, there are none fo convenient as gold and filver.

In facilitating all the different round-about foreign trades of confumption which are carried on in Great Britain, confifts the principal advantage of the Portugal trade; and though it is not a capital advantage, it is, no doubt, a confiderable one.

That any annual addition which, it can reafonably be fuppofed, is made either to the plate or to the coin of the kingdom, could require but a very fmall annual importation of gold and filver, feems evident enough; and though we had no direct trade with Portugal, this fmall quantity could always, fomewhere or another, be very eafily got.

Though the goldfmiths trade be very confiderable in Great Britain, the far greater part of the new plate which they annually fell, is

made

OF TREATIES OF COMMERCE.

333

CHAP.
VI.

made from other old plate melted down; fo that the addition annually made to the whole plate of the kingdom cannot be very great, and could require but a very fmall annual importation.

It is the fame cafe with the coin. Nobody imagines, I believe, that even the greater part of the annual coinage, amounting, for ten years together, before the late reformation of the gold coin, to upwards of eight hundred thoufand pounds a year in gold, was an annual addition to the money before current in the kingdom. In a country where the expence of the coinage is defrayed by the government, the value of the coin, even when it contains its full ftandard weight of gold and filver, can never be much greater than that of an equal quantity of thofe metals uncoined; becaufe it requires only the trouble of going to the mint, and the delay perhaps of a few weeks, to procure for any quantity of uncoined gold and filver an equal quantity of thofe metals in coin. But, in every country, the greater part of the current coin is almoft always more or lefs worn, or otherwife degenerated from its ftandard. In Great Britain it was, before the late reformation, a good deal fo, the gold being more than two per cent. and the filver more than eight per cent. below its ftandard weight. But if forty-four guineas and a half, containing their full ftandard weight, a pound weight of gold, could purchafe very little more than a pound weight of uncoined gold, forty-four guineas and a half wanting a part of their weight could not purchafe a pound weight,

and

334   OF TREATIES OF COMMERCE.

BOOK and fomething was to be added in order to make
  IV. up the deficiency. The current price of gold
bullion at market, therefore, inftead of being
the fame with the mint price, or 46*l.* 14*s.* 6*d.*
was then about 47*l.* 14*s.* and fometimes about
forty-eight pounds. When the greater part of
the coin, however, was in this degenerate condition, forty-four guineas and a half, frefh from
the mint, would purchafe no more goods in the
market than any other ordinary guineas, becaufe
when they came into the coffers of the merchant,
being confounded with other money, they could
not afterwards be diftinguifhed without more
trouble than the difference was worth. Like
other guineas they were worth no more than
46*l.* 14*s.* 6*d.* If thrown into the melting pot,
however, they produced, without any fenfible
lofs, a pound weight of ftandard gold, which
could be fold at any time for between 47*l.* 14*s.*
and 48*l.* either in gold or filver, as fit for all
the purpofes of coin as that which had been
melted down. There was an evident profit,
therefore, in melting down new coined money,
and it was done fo inftantaneoufly, that no pre-
caution of government could prevent it. The
operations of the mint were, upon this account,
fomewhat like the web of Penelope; the work
that was done in the day was undone in the night.
The mint was employed, not fo much in making
daily additions to the coin, as in replacing the
very beft part of it which was daily melted down.

Were the private people, who carry their
gold and filver to the mint, to pay themfelves

2   for

OF TREATIES OF COMMERCE.

335

**C H A P.
VI.**

for the coinage, it would add to the value of thofe metals in the fame manner as the fafhion does to that of plate. Coined gold and filver would be more valuable than uncoined. The feignorage, if it was not exorbitant, would add to the bullion the whole value of the duty ; becaufe, the government having every where the exclufive privilege of coining, no coin can come to market cheaper than they think proper to afford it. If the duty was exorbitant indeed, that is, if it was very much above the real value of the labour and expence requifite for coinage, falfe coiners, both at home and abroad, might be encouraged, by the great difference between the value of bullion and that of coin, to pour in fo great a quantity of counterfeit money as might reduce the value of the government money. In France, however, though the feignorage is eight per cent. no fenfible inconveniency of this kind is found to arife from it. The dangers to which a falfe coiner is every where expofed, if he lives in the country of which he counterfeits the coin, and to which his agents or correfpondents are expofed if he lives in a foreign country, are by far too great to be incurred for the fake of a profit of fix or feven per cent.

The feignorage in France raifes the value of the coin higher than in proportion to the quantity of pure gold which it contains. Thus by the edict of January 1726, the * mint price

* See Dictionaire des Monnoies, tom. ii. article Seigneurage, p. 489. par M. Abot de Bazinghen, Confeiller-Comiffaire en la Cour des Monnoies à Paris.

of

OF TREATIES OF COMMERCE.

BOOK IV.

of fine gold of twenty-four carats was fixed at feven hundred and forty livres nine fous and one denier one-eleventh, the mark of eight Paris ounces. The gold coin of France, making an allowance for the remedy of the mint, contains twenty-one carats and three-fourths of fine gold, and two carats one-fourth of alloy. The mark of ftandard gold, therefore, is worth no more than about fix hundred and feventy-one livres ten deniers. But in France this mark of ftandard gold is coined into thirty Louis-d'ors of twenty-four livres each, or into feven hundred and twenty livres. The coinage, therefore, increafes the value of a mark of ftandard gold bullion, by the difference between fix hundred and feventy-one livres ten deniers, and feven hundred and twenty livres ; or by forty-eight livres nineteen fous and two deniers.

A feignorage will, in many cafes, take away altogether, and will, in all cafes, diminifh the profit of melting down the new coin. This profit always arifes from the difference between the quantity of bullion which the common currency ought to contain, and that which it actually does contain. If this difference is lefs than the feignorage, there will be lofs inftead of profit. If it is equal to the feignorage, there will neither be profit nor lefs. If it is greater than the feignorage, there will indeed be fome profit, but lefs than if there was no feignorage. If, before the late reformation of the gold coin, for example, there had been a feignorage of five per cent. upon the coinage, there would have been

OF TREATIES OF COMMERCE.

337

been a lofs of three per cent. upon the melting
down of the gold coin. If the feignorage had
been two per cent. there would have been neither
profit nor lofs. If the feignorage had been one
per cent. there would have been a profit, but
of one per cent. only inftead of two per cent.
Wherever money is received by tale, therefore,
and not by weight, a feignorage is the moft
effectual preventative of the melting down of the
coin, and, for the fame reafon, of its exportation. It is the beft and heavieft pieces that are
commonly either melted down or exported; becaufe it is upon fuch that the largeft profits are
made.

The law for the encouragement of the coinage, by rendering it duty-free, was firft enacted,
during the reign of Charles II., for a limited
time; and afterwards continued, by different
prolongations, till 1769, when it was rendered
perpetual. The bank of England, in order to
replenifh their coffers with money, are frequently
obliged to carry bullion to the mint; and it was
more for their intereft, they probably imagined,
that the coinage fhould be at the expence of the
government, than at their own. It was, probably, out of complaifance to this great company that the government agreed to render this
law perpetual. Should the cuftom of weighing
gold, however, come to be difufed, as it is very
likely to be on account of its inconveniency;
fhould the gold coin of England come to be received by tale, as it was before the late re-
coinage, this great company may, perhaps, find

VOL. III.   z   that

CHAP.
VI.

OF TREATIES OF COMMERCE.

BOOK IV. that they have upon this, as upon fome other occafions, miftaken their own intereft not a little.

Before the late recoinage, when the gold currency of England was two per cent. below its ftandard weight, as there was no feignorage, it was two per cent. below the value of that quantity of ftandard gold bullion which it ought to have contained. When this great company, therefore, bought gold bullion in order to have it coined, they were obliged to pay for it two per cent. more than it was worth after the coinage. But if there had been a feignorage of two per cent. upon the coinage, the common gold currency, though two per cent. below its ftandard weight, would notwithftanding have been equal in value to the quantity of ftandard gold which it ought to have contained; the value of the fafhion compenfating in this cafe the diminution of the weight. They would indeed have had the feignorage to pay, which being two per cent. their lofs upon the whole tranfaction would have been two per cent. exactly the fame, but no greater than it actually was.

If the feignorage had been five per cent. and the gold currency only two per cent. below its ftandard weight, the bank would in this cafe have gained three per cent. upon the price of the bullion; but as they would have had a feignorage of five per cent. to pay upon the coinage, their lofs upon the whole tranfaction would, in the fame manner, have been exactly two per cent.

If

OF TREATIES OF COMMERCE. 339

CHAP. VI.

If the feignorage had been only one per cent. and the gold currency two per cent. below its ftandard weight, the bank would in this cafe have loft only one per cent. upon the price of the bullion; but as they would likewife have had a feignorage of one per cent. to pay, their lofs upon the whole tranfaction would have been exactly two per cent. in the fame manner as in all other cafes.

If there was a reafonable feignorage, while at the fame time the coin contained its full ftandard weight, as it has done very nearly fince the late re-coinage, whatever the bank might lofe by the feignorage, they would gain upon the price of the bullion; and whatever they might gain upon the price of the bullion, they would lofe by the feignorage. They would neither lofe nor gain, therefore, upon the whole tranfaction, and they would in this, as in all the foregoing cafes, be exactly in the fame fituation as if there was no feignorage.

When the tax upon a commodity is fo moderate as not to encourage fmuggling, the merchant who deals in it, though he advances, does not properly pay the tax, as he gets it back in the price of the commodity. The tax is finally paid by the laft purchafer or confumer. But money is a commodity with regard to which every man is a merchant. Nobody buys it but in order to fell it again; and with regard to it there is in ordinary cafes no laft purchafer or confumer. When the tax upon coinage, therefore, is fo moderate as not to encourage falfe coining,

OF TREATIES OF COMMERCE.

BOOK IV.

coining, though every body advances the tax, nobody finally pays it; becaufe every body gets it back in the advanced value of the coin.

A moderate feignorage therefore would not in any cafe augment the expence of the bank, or of any other private perfons who carry their bullion to the mint in order to be coined, and the want of a moderate feignorage does not in any cafe diminifh it. Whether there is or is not a feignorage, if the currency contains its full ftandard weight, the coinage cofts nothing to any body, and if it is fhort of that weight, the coinage muft always coft the difference between the quantity of bullion which ought to be contained in it, and that which actually is contained in it.

The government, therefore, when it defrays the expence of coinage, not only incurs fome fmall expence, but lofes fome fmall revenue which it might get by a proper duty; and neither the bank nor any other private perfons are in the fmalleft degree benefited by this ufelefs piece of public generofity.

The directors of the bank, however, would probably be unwilling to agree to the impofition of a feignorage upon the authority of a fpeculation which promifes them no gain, but only pretends to infure them from any lofs. In the prefent ftate of the gold coin, and as long as it continues to be received by weight, they certainly would gain nothing by fuch a change. But if the cuftom of weighing the gold coin fhould ever go into difufe, as it is very likely to do, and if the gold coin fhould ever fall into the fame ftate of

degradation

OF TREATIES OF COMMERCE. 341

degradation in which it was before the late re-coinage, the gain, or more properly the favings of the bank, in confequence of the impofition of a feignorage, would probably be very confiderable. The bank of England is the only company which fends any confiderable quantity of bullion to the mint, and the burden of the annual coinage falls entirely, or almoft entirely, upon it. If this annual coinage had nothing to do but to repair the unavoidable loffes and neceffary wear and tear of the coin, it could feldom exceed fifty thoufand or at moft a hundred thoufand pounds. But when the coin is degraded below its ftandard weight, the annual coinage muft, befides this, fill up the large vacuities which exportation and the melting pot are continually making in the current coin. It was upon this account that during the ten or twelve years immediately preceding the late reformation of the gold coin, the annual coinage amounted at an average to more than eight hundred and fifty thoufand pounds. But if there had been a feignorage of four or five per cent. upon the gold coin, it would probably, even in the ftate in which things then were, have put an effectual ftop to the bufinefs both of exportation and of the melting pot. The bank, inftead of lofing every year about two and a half per cent. upon the bullion which was to be coined into more than eight hundred and fifty thoufand pounds, or incurring an annual lofs of more than twenty-one thoufand two hundred and fifty

z 3   pounds,

CHAP.
VI.

OF TREATIES OF COMMERCE.

BOOK IV.

pounds, would not probably have incurred the tenth part of that lofs.

The revenue allotted by parliament for defraying the expence of the coinage is but fourteen thoufand pounds a year, and the real expence which it cofts the government, or the fees of the officers of the mint, do not upon ordinary occafions, I am affured, exceed the half of that fum. The faving of fo very fmall a fum, or even the gaining of another which could not well be much larger, are objects too inconfiderable, it may be thought, to deferve the ferious attention of government. But the faving of eighteen or twenty thoufand pounds a year in cafe of an event which is not improbable, which has frequently happened before, and which is very likely to happen again, is furely an object which well deferves the ferious attention even of fo great a company as the bank of England.

Some of the foregoing reafonings and obfervations might perhaps have been more properly placed in thofe chapters of the firft book which treat of the origin and ufe of money, and of the difference between the real and the nominal price of commodities. But as the law for the encouragement of coinage derives its origin from thofe vulgar prejudices which have been introduced by the mercantile fyftem; I judged it more proper to referve them for this chapter. Nothing could be more agreeable to the fpirit of that fyftem than a fort of bounty upon the production of money, the very thing which, it fuppofes,

OF COLONIES. 343

poſes, conſtitutes the wealth of every nation. It C H A P.
is one of its many admirable expedients for VI.
enriching the country.

CHAP. VII.

Of Colonies.

PART FIRST.

Of the Motives for eſtabliſhing new Colonies.

THE intereſt which occaſioned the firſt ſet- C H A P.
tlement of the different European colonies VII.
in America and the Weſt Indies, was not altogether ſo plain and diſtinct as that which directed the eſtabliſhment of thoſe of ancient
Greece and Rome.

All the different ſtates of ancient Greece
poſſeſſed, each of them, but a very ſmall territory, and when the people in any one of them
multiplied beyond what that territory could
eaſily maintain, a part of them were ſent in queſt
of a new habitation in ſome remote and diſtant
part of the world ; the warlike neighbours who
ſurrounded them on all ſides, rendering it difficult for any of them to enlarge very much its
territory at home. The colonies of the Dorians
reſorted chiefly to Italy and Sicily, which, in the
times preceding the foundation of Rome, were
inhabited by barbarous and uncivilized nations :

z 4 thoſe

OF COLONIES.

BOOK IV.

thofe of the Ionians and Eolians, the two other great tribes of the Greeks, to Afia Minor and the iflands of the Egean Sea, of which the inhabitants feem at that time to have been pretty much in the fame ftate as thofe of Sicily and Italy. The mother city, though fhe confidered the colony as a child, at all times entitled to great favour and affiftance, and owing in return much gratitude and refpect, yet confidered it as an emancipated child, over whom fhe pretended to claim no direct authority or jurifdiction. The colony fettled its own form of government, enacted its own laws, elected its own magiftrates, and made peace or war with its neighbours as an independent ftate, which had no occafion to wait for the approbation or confent of the mother city. Nothing can be more plain and diftinct than the intereft which directed every fuch eftablifhment.

Rome, like moft of the other ancient republics, was originally founded upon an Agrarian law, which divided the public territory in a certain proportion among the different citizens who compofed the ftate. The courfe of human affairs, by marriage, by fucceffion, and by alienation, neceffarily deranged this original divifion, and frequently threw the lands, which had been allotted for the maintenance of many different families into the poffeffion of a fingle perfon. To remedy this diforder, for fuch it was fuppofed to be, a law was made, reftricting the quantity of land which any citizen could poffefs to five hundred jugers, about three hundred and

fifty

OF COLONIES.

fifty Englifh acres. This law, however, though we read of its having been executed upon one or two occafions, was either neglected or evaded, and the inequality of fortunes went on continually increafing. The greater part of the citizens had no land, and without it the manners and cuftoms of thofe times rendered it difficult for a freeman to maintain his independency. In the prefent times, though a poor man has no land of his own, if he has a little ftock, he may either farm the lands of another, or he may carry on fome little retail trade; and if he has no ftock, he may find employment either as a country labourer, or as an artificer. But, among the ancient Romans, the lands of the rich were all cultivated by flaves, who wrought under an overfeer, who was likewife a flave; fo that a poor freeman had little chance of being employed either as a farmer or as a labourer. All trades and manufactures too, even the retail trade, were carried on by the flaves of the rich for the benefit of their mafters, whofe wealth, authority, and protection made it difficult for a poor freeman to maintain the competition againft them. The citizens, therefore, who had no land, had fcarce any other means of fubfiftence but the bounties of the candidates at the annual elections. The tribunes, when they had a mind to animate the people againft the rich and the great, put them in mind of the ancient divifion of lands, and reprefented that law which reftricted this fort of private property as the fundamental law of the republic. The people became

CHAP. VII.

346 OF COLONIES.

BOOK IV.

came clamorous to get land, and the rich and the great, we may believe, were perfectly determined not to give them any part of theirs. To satisfy them in some measure, therefore, they frequently proposed to send out a new colony. But conquering Rome was, even upon such occasions, under no necessity of turning out her citizens to seek their fortune, if one may say so, through the wide world, without knowing where they were to settle. She assigned them lands generally in the conquered provinces of Italy, where, being within the dominions of the republic, they could never form any independent state; but were at best but a sort of corporation, which, though it had the power of enacting bye-laws for its own government, was at all times subject to the correction, jurisdiction, and legislative authority of the mother city. The sending out a colony of this kind, not only gave some satisfaction to the people, but often established a sort of garrison too in a newly conquered province, of which the obedience might otherwise have been doubtful. A Roman colony, therefore, whether we consider the nature of the establishment itself, or the motives for making it, was altogether different from a Greek one. The words accordingly, which in the original languages denote those different establishments, have very different meanings. The Latin word (*Colonia*) signifies simply a plantation. The Greek word (ἀποικία), on the contrary, signifies a separation of dwelling, a departure from home, a going out of the house. But, though the

Roman

OF COLONIES. 347

Roman colonies were in many refpects different CHAP. VII. from the Greek ones, the intereft which prompted to eftablifh them was equally plain and diftinct. Both inftitutions derived their origin either from irrefiftible neceffity, or from clear and evident utility.

The eftablifhment of the European colonies in America and the Weft Indies arofe from no neeeffity: and though the utility which has refulted from them has been very great, it is not altogether fo clear and evident. It was not underftood at their firft eftablifhment, and was not the motive either of that eftablifhment or of the difcoveries which gave occafion to it ; and the nature, extent, and limits of that utility are not, perhaps, well underftood at this day.

The Venetians, during the fourteenth and fifteenth centuries, carried on a very advantageous commerce in fpiceries, and other Eaft India goods, which they diftributed among the other nations of Europe. They purchafed them chiefly in Egypt, at that time under the dominion of the Mammeluks, the enemies of the Turks, of whom the Venetians were the enemies ; and this union of intereft, affifted by the money of Venice, formed fuch a connection as gave the Venetians almoft a monopoly of the trade.

The great profits of the Venetians tempted the avidity of the Portuguefe. They had been endeavouring, during the courfe of the fifteenth century, to find out by fea a way to the countries from which the Moors brought them ivory and gold duft acrofs the Defart. They difcovered

the

348　　　　　　　　　　OF COLONIES.

BOOK IV.

the Madeiras, the Canaries, the Azores, the Cape de Verd iſlands, the coaſt of Guinea, that of Loango, Congo, Angola, and Benguela, and, finally, the Cape of Good Hope. They had long wiſhed to ſhare in the profitable traffic of the Venetians, and this laſt diſcovery opened to them a probable proſpect of doing ſo. In 1497, Vaſco de Gama failed from. the port of Liſbon with a fleet of four ſhips, and, after a navigation of eleven months, arrived upon the coaſt of Indoſtan, and thus completed a courſe of diſcoveries which had been purſued with great ſteadineſs, and with very little interruption, for near a century together.

Some years before this, while the expectations of Europe were in ſuſpenſe about the projects of the Portugueſe, of which the ſucceſs appeared yet to be doubtful, a Genoeſe pilot formed the yet more daring project of ſailing to the Eaſt Indies by the Weſt. The ſituation of thoſe countries was at that time very imperfectly known in Europe. The few European travellers who had been there had magnified the diſtance; perhaps through ſimplicity and ignorance, what was really very great, appearing almoſt infinite to thoſe who could not meaſure it; or, perhaps, in order to increaſe ſomewhat more the marvellous of their own adventures in viſiting regions ſo immenſely remote from Europe. The longer the way was by the Eaſt, Columbus very juſtly concluded, the ſhorter it would be by the Weſt. He propoſed, therefore, to take that way, as both the ſhorteſt and the ſureſt, and he had the good fortune to

convince

OF COLONIES. 349

convince Ifabella of Caftile of the probability of his project. He failed from the port of Palos in Auguft 1492, near five years before the expedition of Vafco de Gama fet out from Portugal, and, after a voyage of between two and three months, difcovered firft fome of the fmall Bahama or Lucayan iflands, and afterwards the great ifland of St. Domingo.

CHAP. VII.

But the countries which Columbus difcovered, either in this or in any of his fubfequent voyages, had no refemblance to thofe which he had gone in queft of. Inftead of the wealth, cultivation and populoufnefs of China and Indoftan, he found, in St. Domingo, and in all the other parts of the new world which he ever vifited, nothing but a country quite covered with wood, uncultivated, and inhabited only by fome tribes of naked and miferable favages. He was not very willing, however, to believe that they were not the fame with fome of the countries defcribed by Marco Polo, the firft European who had vifited, or at leaft had left behind him any defcription of China or the Eaft Indies; and a very flight refemblance, fuch as that which he found between the name of Cibao, a mountain in St. Domingo, and that of Cipango, mentioned by Marco Polo, was frequently fufficient to make him return to his favourite prepoffeffion, though contrary to the cleareft evidence. In his letters to Ferdinand and Ifabella he called the countries which he had difcovered, the Indies. He entertained no doubt but that they were the extremity of thofe which had been

defcribed

350 OF COLONIES.

BOOK IV.

defcribed by Marco Polo, and that they were not very diftant from the Ganges, or from the countries which had been conquered by Alexander. Even when at laft convinced that they were different, he ftill flattered himfelf that thofe rich countries were at no great diftance, and in a fubfequent voyage, accordingly, went in queft of them along the coaft of Terra Firma, and towards the ifthmus of Darien.

In confequence of this miftake of Columbus, the name of the Indies has ftuck to thofe unfortunate countries ever fince; and when it was at laft clearly difcovered that the new were altogether different from the old Indies, the former were called the Weft, in contradiftinction to the latter, which were called the Eaft Indies.

It was of importance to Columbus, however, that the countries which he had difcovered, whatever they were, fhould be reprefented to the court of Spain as of very great confequence; and, in what conftitutes the real riches of every country, the animal and vegetable productions of the foil, there was at that time nothing which could well juftify fuch a reprefentation of them.

The Cori, fomething between a rat and a rabbit, and fuppofed by Mr. Buffon to be the fame with the Aperea of Brazil, was the largeft viviparous quadruped in St. Domingo. This fpecies feems never to have been very numerous, and the dogs and cats of the Spaniards are faid to have long ago almoft entirely extirpated it, as well as fome other tribes of a ftill fmaller fize. Thefe, however, together with a pretty large lizard, called

OF COLONIES. 351

called the Ivano or Iguana, conftituted the C H A P. VII.
principal part of the animal food which the land
afforded.

The vegetable food of the inhabitants, though from their want of induftry not very abundant, was not altogether fo fcanty. It confifted in Indian corn, yams, potatoes, bananes, &c. plants which were then altogether unknown in Europe, and which have never fince been very much efteemed in it, or fuppofed to yield a fuftenance equal to what is drawn from the common forts of grain and pulfe, which have been cultivated in this part of the world time out of mind.

The cotton plant indeed afforded the material of a very important manufacture, and was at that time to Europeans undoubtedly the moft valuable of all the vegetable productions of thofe iflands. But though in the end of the fifteenth century the muflins and other cotton goods of the Eaft Indies were much efteemed in every part of Europe, the cotton manufacture itfelf was not cultivated in any part of it. Even this production, therefore, could not at that time appear in the eyes of Europeans to be of very great confequence.

Finding nothing either in the animals or vegetables of the newly difcovered countries, which could juftify a very advantageous reprefentation of them, Columbus turned his view towards their minerals; and in the richnefs of the productions of this third kingdom, he flattered himfelf, he had found a full compenfation for the infignificancy of thofe of the other two. The little

OF COLONIES.

BOOK IV.

little bits of gold with which the inhabitants ornamented their drefs, and which, he was informed, they frequently found in the rivulets and torrents that fell from the mountains, were fufficient to fatisfy him that thofe mountains abounded with the richeft gold mines. St. Domingo, therefore, was reprefented as a country abounding with gold, and, upon that account (according to the prejudices not only of the prefent times, but of thofe times), an inexhauftible fource of real wealth to the crown and kingdom of Spain. When Columbus, upon his return from his firft voyage, was introduced with a fort of triumphal honours to the fovereigns of Caftile and Arragon, the principal productions of the countries which he had difcovered were carried in folemn proceffion before him. The only valuable part of them confifted in fome little fillets, bracelets, and other ornaments of gold, and in fome bales of cotton. The reft were mere objects of vulgar wonder and curiofity; fome reeds of an extraordinary fize, fome birds of a very beautiful plumage, and fome ftuffed fkins of the huge alligator and manati; all of which were preceded by fix or feven of the wretched natives, whofe fingular colour and appearance added greatly to the novelty of the fhew.

In confequence of the reprefentations of Columbus, the council of Caftile determined to take poffeffion of countries of which the inhabitants were plainly incapable of defending themfelves. The pious purpofe of converting them to Chriftianity fanctified the injuftice of the project. But the

OF COLONIES. 353

the hope of finding treasures of gold there, was CHAP. VII.
the sole motive which prompted to undertake it;
and to give this motive the greater weight, it
was proposed by Columbus that the half of all
the gold and silver that should be found there
should belong to the crown. This proposal was
approved of by the council.

As long as the whole or the far greater part of
the gold, which the first adventurers imported
into Europe, was got by so very easy a method
as the plundering of the defenceless natives, it
was not perhaps very difficult to pay even this
heavy tax. But when the natives were once
fairly stript of all that they had, which, in St.
Domingo, and in all the other countries discovered by Columbus, was done completely in six
or eight years, and when in order to find more
it had become necessary to dig for it in the
mines, there was no longer any possibility of
paying this tax. The rigorous exaction of it,
accordingly, first occasioned, it is said, the total
abandoning of the mines of St. Domingo, which
have never been wrought since. It was soon
reduced, therefore, to a third; then to a fifth;
afterwards to a tenth; and at last to a twentieth
part of the gross produce of the gold mines.
The tax upon silver continued for a long time
to be a fifth of the gross produce. It was reduced to a tenth only in the course of the present century. But the first adventurers do not
appear to have been much interested about silver.
Nothing less precious than gold seemed worthy
of their attention.

VOL. III.   A A   All

OF COLONIES.

BOOK IV.

All the other enterprifes of the Spaniards in the New World, fubfequent to thofe of Columbus, feem to have been prompted by the fame motive. It was the facred thirft of gold that carried Oieda, Nicueffa, and Vafco Nugnes de Balboa, to the ifthmus of Darien, that carried Cortez to Mexico, and Almagro and Pizzarro to Chili and Peru. When thofe adventurers arrived upon any unknown coaft, their firft enquiry was always if there was any gold to be found there; and according to the information which they received concerning this particular, they determined either to quit the country or to fettle in it.

Of all thofe expenfive and uncertain projects, however, which bring bankruptcy upon the greater part of the people who engage in them, there is none perhaps more perfectly ruinous than the fearch after new filver and gold mines. It is perhaps the moft difadvantageous lottery in the world, or the one in which the gain of thofe who draw the prizes bears the leaft proportion to the lofs of thofe who draw the blanks: for though the prizes are few and the blanks many, the common price of a ticket is the whole fortune of a very rich man. Projects of mining, inftead of replacing the capital employed in them, together with the ordinary profits of ftock, commonly abforb both capital and profit. They are the projects, therefore, to which of all others a prudent law-giver, who defired to increafe the capital of his nation, would leaft chufe to give any extraordinary encouragement, or to turn

towards

OF COLONIES. 355

towards them a greater fhare of that capital than what would go to them of its own accord. Such in reality is the abfurd confidence which almoft all men have in their own good fortune, that wherever there is the leaft probability of fuccefs, too great a fhare of it is apt to go to them of its own accord.

But though the judgment of fober reafon and experience concerning fuch projects has always been extremely unfavourable, that of human avidity has commonly been quite otherwife. The fame paffion which has fuggefted to fo many people the abfurd idea of the philofopher's ftone, has fuggefted to others the equally abfurd one of immenfe rich mines of gold and filver. They did not confider that the value of thofe metals has, in all ages and nations, arifen chiefly from their fcarcity, and that their fcarcity has arifen from the very fmall quantities of them which nature has any where depofited in one place, from the hard and intractable fubftances with which fhe has almoft every where furrounded thofe fmall quantities, and confequently from the labour and expence which are every where neceffary, in order to penetrate to and get at them. They flattered themfelves that veins of thofe metals might in many places be found as large and as abundant as thofe which are commonly found of lead, or copper, or tin, or iron. The dream of Sir Walter Raleigh concerning the golden city and country of Eldorado, may fatisfy us, that even wife men are not always exempt from fuch ftrange delufions. More than

A A 2 a hun-

CHAP. VII.

OF COLONIES.

BOOK IV.

a hundred years after the death of that great man, the Jesuit Gumila was still convinced of the reality of that wonderful country, and expressed with great warmth, and I dare to say, with great sincerity, how happy he should be to carry the light of the gospel to a people who could so well reward the pious labours of their missionary.

In the countries first discovered by the Spaniards, no gold or silver mines are at present known which are supposed to be worth the working. The quantities of those metals which the first adventurers are said to have found there, had probably been very much magnified, as well as the fertility of the mines which were wrought immediately after the first discovery. What those adventurers were reported to have found, however, was sufficient to inflame the avidity of all their countrymen. Every Spaniard who sailed to America expected to find an Eldorado. Fortune too did upon this what she has done upon very few other occasions. She realized in some measure the extravagant hopes of her votaries, and in the discovery and conquest of Mexico and Peru (of which the one happened about thirty, the other about forty years after the first expedition of Columbus), she presented them with something not very unlike that profusion of the precious metals which they sought for.

A project of commerce to the East Indies, therefore, gave occasion to the first discovery of the West. A project of conquest gave occasion to all the establishments of the Spaniards in those

newly

OF COLONIES, 357

newly difcovered countries. The motive which C H A P. excited them to this conqueſt was a projeƈt of gold and filver mines ; and a courſe of accidents, which no human wifdom could forefee, rendered this projeƈt much more fuccefsful than the undertakers had any reafonable ground for expeƈting.

The firſt adventurers of all the other nations of Europe, who attempted to make ſettlements in America, were animated by the like chimerical views ; but they were not equally fuccefsful. It was more than a hundred years after the firſt ſettlement of the Brazils, before any filver, gold, or diamond mines were difcovered there. In the Englifh, French, Dutch, and Danifh colonies, none have ever yet been difcovered ; at leaſt none that are at prefent fuppofed to be worth the working. The firſt Englifh ſettlers in North America, however, offered a fifth of all the gold and filver which fhould be found there to the king, as a motive for granting them their patents. In the patents to Sir Walter Raleigh, to the London and Plymouth companies, to the council of Plymouth, &c. this fifth was accordingly referved to the Crown. To the expeƈtation of finding gold and filver mines, thofe firſt ſettlers too joined that of difcovering a north-weſt paffage to the Eaſt Indies. They have hitherto been difappointed in both.

A A 3   PART

OF COLONIES.

BOOK
IV.

PART SECOND.

Caufes of the Profperity of new Colonies.

THE colony of a civilized nation which takes possefion, either of a wafte country, or of one fo thinly inhabited, that the natives eafily give place to the new fettlers, advances more rapidly to wealth and greatnefs than any other human fociety.

The colonifts carry out with them a know- ledge of agriculture and of other ufeful arts, fuperior to what can grow up of its own accord in the courfe of many centuries among favage and barbarous nations. They carry out with them too the habit of fubordination, fome notion of the regular government which takes place in their own country, of the fyftem of laws which fupports it, and of a regular adminiftration of juftice ; and they naturally eftablifh fomething of the fame kind in a new fettlement. But among favage and barbarous nations, the natural progrefs of law and government is ftill flower than the natural progrefs of arts, after law and government have been fo far eftablifhed, as is neceffary for their protection. Every colonift gets more land than he can poffibly cultivate. He has no rent, and fcarce any taxes to pay. No landlord fhares with him in its produce, and the fhare of the fovereign is commonly but a trifle. He has every motive to render as great as pof- fible a produce, which is thus to be almoft en-

tirely

OF COLONIES. 359

tirely his own. But his land is commonly fo ex- C H A P. tenfive, that with all his own induftry, and with VII. all the induftry of other people whom he can get to employ, he can feldom make it produce the tenth part of what it is capable of producing. He is eager, therefore, to collect labourers from all quarters, and to reward them with the moft liberal wages. But thofe liberal wages, joined to the plenty and cheapnefs of land, foon make thofe labourers leave him, in order to become landlords themfelves, and to reward, with equal liberality, other labourers, who foon leave them for the fame reafon that they left their firft mafter. The liberal reward of labour encourages marriage. The children, during the tender years of infancy, are well fed and properly taken care of, and when they are grown up, the value of their labour greatly over-pays their maintenance. When arrived at ma-turity, the high price of labour, and the low price of land, enable them to eftablifh them-felves in the fame manner as their fathers did before them.

In other countries, rent and profit eat up wages, and the two fuperior orders of people opprefs the inferior one. But in new colonies, the intereft of the two fuperior orders obliges them to treat the inferior one with more gene-rofity and humanity; at leaft, where that in-ferior one is not in a ftate of flavery. Wafte lands of the greateft natural fertility, are to be had for a trifle. The increafe of revenue which the proprietor, who is always the undertaker,

A A 4 expects

BOOK IV.

expects from their improvement, conftitutes his profit ; which in thefe circumftances is commonly very great. But this great profit cannot be made without employing the labour of other people in clearing and cultivating the land ; and the difproportion between the great extent of the land and the fmall number of the people, which commonly takes place in new colonies, makes it difficult for him to get this labour. He does not, therefore, difpute about wages, but is willing to employ labour at any price. The high wages of labour encourage population. The cheapnefs and plenty of good land encourage improvement, and enable the proprietor to pay thofe high wages. In thofe wages confifts almoft the whole price of the land ; and though they are high, confidered as the wages of labour, they are low, confidered as the price of what is fo very valuable. What encourages the progrefs of population and improvement, encourages that of real wealth and greatnefs.

The progrefs of many of the ancient Greek colonies towards wealth and greatnefs, feems accordingly to have been very rapid. In the courfe of a century or two, feveral of them appear to have rivalled, and even to have furpaffed their mother cities. Syracufe and Agrigentum in Sicily, Tarentum and Locri in Italy, Ephefus and Miletus in Leffer Afia, appear by all accounts to have been at leaft equal to any of the cities of ancient Greece. Though pofterior in their eftablifhment, yet all the arts of refinement, philofophy, poetry, and eloquence, feem

to

OF COLONIES. 361

to have been cultivated as early, and to have C H A P. VII.
been improved as highly in them, as in any part
of the mother country. The fchools of the two
oldeft Greek philofophers, thofe of Thales and
Pythagoras, were eftablifhed, it is remarkable,
not in ancient Greece, but the one in an Afiatic,
the other in an Italian colony. All thofe colonies had eftablifhed themfelves in countries inhabited by favage and barbarous nations, who
eafily gave place to the new fettlers. They
had plenty of good land, and as they were altogether independent of the mother city, they
were at liberty to manage their own affairs in
the way that they judged was moft fuitable to
their own intereft.

The hiftory of the Roman colonies is by no
means fo brilliant. Some of them, indeed, fuch
as Florence, have, in the courfe of many ages,
and after the fall of the mother city, grown up
to be confiderable ftates. But the progrefs of
no one of them feems ever to have been very
rapid. They were all eftablifhed in conquered
provinces, which, in moft cafes, had been fully
inhabited before. The quantity of land affigned
to each colonift was feldom very confiderable,
and as the colony was not independent, they
were not always at liberty to manage their own
affairs in the way that they judged was moft fuitable to their own intereft.

In the plenty of good land, the European
colonies eftablifhed in America and the Weft
Indies refemble, and even greatly furpafs, thofe
of ancient Greece. In their dependency upon
the

OF COLONIES.

BOOK IV.

the mother ſtate, they reſemble thoſe of ancient Rome; but their great diſtance from Europe has in all of them alleviated more or leſs the effects of this dependency. Their ſituation has placed them leſs in the view and leſs in the power of their mother country. In purſuing their intereſt their own way, their conduct has, upon many occaſions, been overlooked, either becauſe not known or not underſtood in Europe; and upon ſome occaſions it has been fairly ſuffered and ſubmitted to, becauſe their diſtance rendered it difficult to reſtrain it. Even the violent and arbitrary government of Spain has, upon many occaſions, been obliged to recall or ſoften the orders which had been given for the government of her colonies, for fear of a general inſurrection. The progreſs of all the European colonies in wealth, population, and improvement, has accordingly been very great.

The crown of Spain, by its ſhare of the gold and ſilver, derived ſome revenue from its colonies, from the moment of their firſt eſtabliſhment. It was a revenue too, of a nature to excite in human avidity the moſt extravagant expectations of ſtill greater riches. The Spaniſh colonies, therefore, from the moment of their firſt eſtabliſhment, attracted very much the attention of their mother country; while thoſe of the other European nations were for a long time in a great meaſure neglected. The former did not, perhaps, thrive the better in conſequence of this attention; nor the latter the worſe in conſequence of this neglect. In proportion to the

extent

OF COLONIES.   363

extent of the country which they in fome mea- C H A P.
fure poffefs, the Spanifh colonies are confidered   VII.
as lefs populous and thriving than thofe of almoft
any other European nation.   The progrefs even
of the Spanifh colonies, however, in population
and improvement, has certainly been very rapid
and very great.   The city of Lima, founded
fince the conqueft, is reprefented by Ulloa, as
containing fifty thoufand inhabitants near thirty
years ago.   Quito, which had been but a miferable hamlet of Indians, is reprefented by the
fame author as in his time equally populous.
Gemelli Carreri, a pretended traveller, it is faid,
indeed, but who feems every where to have
written upon extreme good information, reprefents the city of Mexico as containing a hundred
thoufand inhabitants ; a number which, in fpite
of all the exaggerations of the Spanifh writers,
is, probably, more than five times greater than
what it contained in the time of Montezuma.
Thefe numbers exceed greatly thofe of Bofton,
New York, and Philadelphia, the three greateft
cities of the Englifh colonies.   Before the conqueft of the Spaniards there were no cattle fit
for draught, either in Mexico or Peru.   The
lama was their only beaft of burden, and its
ftrength feems to have been a good deal inferior
to that of a common afs.   The plough was unknown among them.   They were ignorant of
the ufe of iron.   They had no coined money,
nor any eftablifhed inftrument of commerce of
any kind.   Their commerce was carried on by
barter. A fort of wooden fpade was their princi-
                                        pal

BOOK IV. pal inftrument of agriculture. Sharp ftones ferved them for knives and hatchets to cut with; fifh bones and the hard finews of certain animals ferved them for needles to few with; and thefe feem to have been their principal inftruments of trade. In this ftate of things, it feems impoffible, that either of thofe empires could have been fo much improved or fo well cultivated as at prefent, when they are plentifully furnifhed with all forts of European cattle, and when the ufe of iron, of the plough, and of many of the arts of Europe, has been introduced among them. But the populoufnefs of every country muft be in proportion to the degree of its improvement and cultivation. In fpite of the cruel deftruction of the natives which followed the conqueft, thefe two great empires are, probably, more populous now than they ever were before: and the people are furely very different; for we muft acknowledge, I apprehend, that the Spanifh creoles are in many refpects fuperior to the ancient Indians.

After the fettlements of the Spaniards, that of the Portugueze in Brazil is the oldeft of any European nation in America. But as for a long time after the firft difcovery, neither gold nor filver mines were found in it, and as it afforded, upon that account, little or no revenue to the crown, it was for a long time in a great meafure neglected; and during this ftate of neglect, it grew up to be a great and powerful colony. While Portugal was under the dominion of Spain, Brazil was attacked by the Dutch, who

got

got poffeffion of feven of the fourteen provinces into which it is divided. They expected foon to conquer the other feven, when Portugal recovered its independency, by the elevation of the family of Braganza to the throne. The Dutch then, as enemies to the Spaniards, became friends to the Portugueze, who were likewife the enemies of the Spaniards. They agreed, therefore, to leave that part of Brazil, which they had not conquered, to the King of Portugal, who agreed to leave that part which they had conquered to them, as a matter not worth difputing about with fuch good allies. But the Dutch government foon began to opprefs the Portugueze colonifts, whò, inftead of amufing themfelves with complaints, took arms againft their new mafters, and by their own valour and refolution, with the connivance, indeed, but without any avowed affiftance from the mother country, drove them out of Brazil. The Dutch, therefore, finding it impoffible to keep any part of the country to themfelves, were contented that it fhould be entirely reftored to the crown of Portugal. In this colony there are faid to be more than fix hundred thoufand people, either Portugueze, or defcended from Portugueze, creoles, mulattoes, and a mixed race between Portugueze and Brazilians. No one colony in America is fuppofed to contain fo great a number of people of European extraction.

Towards the end of the fifteenth, and during the greater part of the fixteenth century, Spain and Portugal were the two great naval powers

366 OF COLONIES.

BOOK IV.

upon the ocean: for though the commerce of Venice extended to every part of Europe, its fleets had fcarce ever failed beyond the Mediterranean. The Spaniards, in virtue of the firft difcovery, claimed all America as their own; and though they could not hinder fo great a naval power as that of Portugal from fettling in Brazil, fuch was, at that time, the terror of their name, that the greater part of the other nations of Europe were afraid to eftablifh themfelves in any other part of that great continent. The French, who attempted to fettle in Florida, were all murdered by the Spaniards. But the declenfion of the naval power of this latter nation, in confequence of the defeat or mifcarriage of, what they called, their Invincible Armada, which happened towards the end of the fixteenth century, put it out of their power to obftruct any longer the fettlements of the other European nations. In the courfe of the feventeenth century, therefore, the Englifh, French, Dutch, Danes, and Swedes, all the great nations who had any ports upon the ocean, attempted to make fome fettlements in the New World.

The Swedes eftablifhed themfelves in New Jerfey; and the number of Swedifh families ftill to be found there, fufficiently demonftrates, that this colony was very likely to profper, had it been protected by the mother country. But being neglected by Sweden, it was foon fwallowed up by the Dutch colony of New York, which, again, in 1674, fell under the dominion of the Englifh.

2

The

OF COLONIES. 367

The fmall iflands of St. Thomas and Santa CHAP. Cruz are the only countries in the New World VII. that have ever been poffeffed by the Danes. Thefe little fettlements too were under the government of an exclufive company, which had the fole right, both of purchafing the furplus produce of the colonifts, and of fupplying them with fuch goods of other countries as they wanted, and which, therefore, both in its purchafes and fales, had not only the power of oppreffing them, but the greateft temptation to do fo. The government of an exclufive company of merchants is, perhaps, the worft of all governments for any country whatever. It was not, however, able to ftop altogether the progrefs of thefe colonies, though it rendered it more flow and languid. The late King of Denmark diffolved this company, and fince that time the profperity of thefe colonies has been very great.

The Dutch fettlements in the Weft, as well as thofe in the Eaft Indies, were originally put under the government of an exclufive company. The progrefs of fome of them, therefore, though it has been confiderable, in comparifon with that of almoft any country that has been long peopled and eftablifhed, has been languid and flow in comparifon with that of the greater part of new colonies. The colony of Surinam, though very confiderable, is ftill inferior to the greater part of the fugar colonies of the other European nations. The colony of Nova Belgia, now divided into the two provinces of New York and New Jerfey,

368   OF COLONIES.

BOOK Jerfey, would probably have foon become confi-
IV.   derable too, even though it had remained under
the government of the Dutch.   The plenty and
cheapnefs of good land are fuch powerful caufes
of profperity, that the very worft government
is fcarce capable of checking altogether the
efficacy of their operation.   The great diftance
too from the mother country would enable the
colonifts to evade more or lefs, by fmuggling,
the monopoly which the company enjoyed againft
them.   At prefent the company allows all Dutch
fhips to trade to Surinam upon paying two and a
half per cent. upon the value of their cargo for
a licence;   and only referves to itfelf exclufively
the direct trade from Africa to America, which
confifts almoft entirely in the flave trade.   This
relaxation in the exclufive privileges of the company, is probably the principal caufe of that degree of profperity which that colony at prefent
enjoys.   Curaçoa and Euftatia, the two principal iflands belonging to the Dutch, are free ports,
open to the fhips of all nations;   and this freedom, in the midft of better colonies whofe ports
are open to thofe of one nation only, has been
the great caufe of the profperity of thofe two
barren iflands.

The French colony of Canada was, during the
greater part of the laft century, and fome part
of the prefent, under the government of an exclufive company.   Under fo unfavourable an adminiftration its progrefs was neceffarily very flow
in comparifon with that of other new colonies;
but it became much more rapid when this
company

OF COLONIES.

company was diffolved after the fall of what is called the Miffiffippi fcheme. When the Englifh got poffeffion of this country, they found in it near double the number of inhabitants which Father Charlevoix had affigned to it between twenty and thirty years before. That Jefuit had travelled over the whole country, and had no inclination to reprefent it as lefs confiderable than it really was.

The French colony of St. Domingo was eftablifhed by pirates and free-booters, who, for a long time, neither required the protection, nor acknowledged the authority of France; and when that race of banditti became fo far citizens as to acknowledge this authority, it was for a long time neceffary to exercife it with very great gentlenefs. During this period the population and improvement of this colony increafed very faft. Even the oppreffion of the exclufive company, to which it was for fome time fubjected, with all the other colonies of France, though it no doubt retarded, had not been able to ftop its progrefs altogether. The courfe of its profperity returned as foon as it was relieved from that oppreffion. It is now the moft important of the fugar colonies of the Weft Indies, and its produce is faid to be greater than that of all the Englifh fugar colonies put together. The other fugar colonies of France are in general all very thriving.

But there are no colonies of which the progrefs has been more rapid than that of the Englifh in North America.

VOL. III. B B Plenty.

OF COLONIES.

Plenty of good land, and liberty to manage their own affairs their own way, seem to be the two great caufes of the profperity of all new colonies.

In the plenty of good land the Englifh colonies of North America, though, no doubt, very abundantly provided, are, however, inferior to thofe of the Spaniards and Portuguefe, and not fuperior to fome of thofe poffeffed by the French before the late war. But the political inftitutions of the Englifh colonies have been more favourable to the improvement and cultivation of this land, than thofe of any of the other three nations.

Firft, the engroffing of uncultivated land, though it has by no means been prevented altogether, has been more reftrained in the Englifh colonies than in any other. The colony law which impofes upon every proprietor the obligation of improving and cultivating, within a limited time, a certain proportion of his lands, and which, in cafe of failure, declares thofe neglected lands grantable to any other perfon; though it has not, perhaps, been very ftrictly executed, has, however, had fome effect.

Secondly, in Pennfylvania there is no right of primogeniture, and lands, like moveables, are divided equally among all the children of the family. In three of the provinces of New England the oldeft has only a double fhare, as in the Mofaical law. Though in thofe provinces, therefore, too great a quantity of land fhould fometimes be engroffed by a

particular

OF COLONIES. 371

particular individual, it is likely, in the courfe of a generation or two, to be fufficiently divided again. In the other Englifh colonies, indeed, the right of primogeniture takes place, as in the law of England. But in all the Englifh colonies the tenure of the lands, which are all held by free focage, facilitates alienation, and the grantee of any extenfive tract of land, generally finds it for his intereft to alienate, as faft as he can, the greater part of it, referving only a fmall quit-rent. In the Spanifh and Portuguefe colonies, what is called the right of Majorazzo * takes place in the fucceffion of all thofe great eftates to which any title of honour is annexed. Such eftates go all to one perfon, and are in effect en-tailed and unalienable. The French colonies, indeed, are fubject to the cuftom of Paris, which, in the inheritance of land, is much more favour-able to the younger children than the law of England. But, in the French colonies, if any part of an eftate, held by the noble tenure of chivalry and homage, is alienated, it is, for a li-mited time, fubject to the right of redemption, either by the heir of the fuperior or by the heir of the family; and all the largeft eftates of the country are held by fuch noble tenures, which neceffarily embarrafs alienation. But, in a new colony, a great uncultivated eftate is likely to be much more fpeedily divided by alienation than by fucceffion. The plenty and cheapnefs of good land, it has already been obferved, are the principal caufes of the rapid profperity of new

* Jus Majoratus.

B B 2

colonies.

372 OF COLONIES.

BOOK
IV.

colonies. The engroffing of land, in effect, de-ftroys this plenty and cheapnefs. The engroff-ing of uncultivated land, befides, is the greateft obftruction to its improvement. But the labour that is employed in the improvement and culti-vation of land affords the greateft and moft valu-able produce to the fociety. The produce of la-bour, in this cafe, pays not only its own wages, and the profit of the ftock which employs it, but the rent of the land too upon which it is em-ployed. The labour of the Englifh colonifts, therefore, being more employed in the improve-ment and cultivation of land, is likely to afford a greater and more valuable produce, than that of any of the other three nations, which, by the engroffing of land, is more or lefs diverted to-wards other employments.

Thirdly, the labour of the Englifh colonifts is not only likely to afford a greater and more valuable produce, but, in confequence of the moderation of their taxes, a greater proportion of this produce belongs to themfelves, which they may ftore up and employ in putting into mo-tion a ftill greater quantity of labour. The Englifh colonifts have never yet contributed any thing towards the defence of the mother coun-try, or towards the fupport of its civil govern-ment. They themfelves, on the contrary, have hitherto been defended almoft entirely at the expence of the mother country. But the ex-pence of fleets and armies is out of all propor-tion greater than the neceffary expence of civil government. The expence of their own civil

government

OF COLONIES.

government has always been very moderate. It
has generally been confined to what was neceffary for paying competent falaries to the governor, to the judges, and to fome other officers of
police, and for maintaining a few of the moft
ufeful public works. The expence of the civil
eftablifhment of Maffachufett's Bay, before the
commencement of the prefent difturbances, ufed
to be but about 18,000*l.* a year. That of New
Hampfhire and Rhode Ifland 3,500*l.* each.
That of Connecticut 4,000*l.* That of New
York and Pennfylvania 4,500*l.* each. That of
New Jerfey 1,200*l.* That of Virginia and South
Carolina 8,000*l.* each. The civil eftablifhments
of Nova Scotia and Georgia are partly fupported
by an annual grant of Parliament. But Nova
Scotia pays, befides, about 7,000*l.* a year towards
the public expences of the colony; and Georgia
about 2,500*l.* a year. All the different civil
eftablifhments in North America, in fhort, exclufive of thofe of Maryland and North Carolina, of which no exact account has been got,
did not, before the commencement of the prefent
difturbances, coft the inhabitants above 64,700*l.*
a year; an ever-memorable example at how
fmall an expence three millions of people may
not only be governed, but well governed. The
moft important part of the expence of government, indeed, that of defence and protection,
has conftantly fallen upon the mother country.
The ceremonial too of the civil government in
the colonies, upon the reception of a new governor, upon the opening of a new affembly, &c.

though

OF COLONIES.

BOOK IV.

though fufficiently decent, is not accompanied with any expenfive pomp or parade. Their ecclefiaftical government is conducted upon a plan equally frugal. Tithes are unknown among them; and their clergy, who are far from being numerous, are maintained either by moderate ftipends, or by the voluntary contributions of the people. The power of Spain and Portugal, on the contrary, derives fome fupport from the taxes levied upon their colonies. France, indeed, has never drawn any confiderable revenue from its colonies, the taxes which it levies upon them being generally fpent among them. But the colony government of all thefe three nations is conducted upon a much more expenfive plan, and is accompanied with a much more expenfive ceremonial. The fums fpent upon the reception of a new viceroy of Peru, for example, have frequently been enormous. Such ceremonials are not only real taxes paid by the rich colonifts upon thofe particular occafions, but they ferve to introduce among them the habit of vanity and expence upon all other occafions. They are not only very grievous occafional taxes, but they contribute to eftablifh perpetual taxes of the fame kind ftill more grievous; the ruinous taxes of private luxury and extravagance. In the colonies of all thofe three nations too, the ecclefiaftical government is extremely oppreffive. Tithes take place in all of them, and are levied with the utmoft rigour in thofe of Spain and Portugal. All of them befides are oppreffed with a numerous race of mendicant friars, whofe beggary being

OF COLONIES.

being not only licenfed, but confecrated by reli- CHAP.
gion, is a moft grievous tax upon the poor VII.
people, who are moft carefully taught that it is
a duty to give, and a very great fin to refufe
them their charity. Over and above all this,
the clergy are, in all of them, the greateft engroffers of land.

Fourthly, in the difpofal of their furplus
produce, or of what is over and above their own
confumption, the Englifh colonies have been
more favoured, and have been allowed a more
extenfive market, than thofe of any other European nation. Every European nation has endeavoured more or lefs to monopolize to itfelf
the commerce of its colonies, and, upon that account, has prohibited the fhips of foreign nations from trading to them, and has prohibited
them from importing European goods from any
foreign nation. But the manner in which this
monopoly has been exercifed in different nations
has been very different.

Some nations have given up the whole commerce of their colonies to an exclufive company,
of whom the colonies were obliged to buy all
fuch European goods as they wanted, and to
whom they were obliged to fell the whole of
their own furplus produce. It was the intereft
of the company, therefore, not only to fell the
former as dear, and to buy the latter as cheap as
poffible, but to buy no more of the latter, even
at this low price, than what they could difpofe of
for a very high price in Europe. It was their
intereft, not only to degrade in all cafes the

BB 4   value

BOOK IV. value of the furplus produce of the colony; but in many cafes to difcourage and keep down the natural increafe of its quantity. Of all the expedients that can well be contrived to ftunt the natural growth of a new colony, that of an exclufive company is undoubtedly the moft effectual. This, however, has been the policy of Holland, though their company, in the courfe of the prefent century, has given up in many refpects the exertion of their exclufive privilege. This too was the policy of Denmark till the reign of the late king. It has occafionally been the policy of France, and of late, fince 1755, after it had been abandoned by all other nations, on account of its abfurdity, it has become the policy of Portugal with regard at leaft to two of the principal provinces of Brazil, Fernambuco and Marannon.

Other nations, without eftablifhing an exclufive company, have confined the whole commerce of their colonies to a particular port of the mother country, from whence no fhip was allowed to fail, but either in a fleet and at a particular feafon, or, if fingle, in confequence of a particular licence, which in moft cafes was very well paid for. This policy opened, indeed, the trade of the colonies to all the natives of the mother country, provided they traded from the proper port, at the proper feafon, and in the proper veffels. But as all the different merchants, who joined their ftocks in order to fit out thofe licenfed veffels, would find it for their intereft to act in concert, the trade which was

carried

OF COLONIES.

carried on in this manner would neceffarily be conducted very nearly upon the fame principles as that of an exclufive company. The profit of thofe merchants would be almoft equally exorbitant and oppreffive. The colonies would be ill fupplied, and would be obliged both to buy very dear and to fell very cheap. This, however, till within thefe few years, had always been the policy of Spain, and the price of all European goods, accordingly, is faid to have been enormous in the Spanifh Weft Indies. At Quito, we are told by Ulloa, a pound of iron fold for about four and fixpence, and a pound of fteel for about fix and nine-pence fterling. But it is chiefly in order to purchafe European goods, that the colonies part with their own produce. The more, therefore, they pay for the one, the lefs they really get for the other, and the dearnefs of the one is the fame thing with the cheapnefs of the other. The policy of Portugal is in this refpect the fame as the ancient policy of Spain, with regard to all its colonies, except Fernambuco and Marannon, and with regard to thefe it has lately adopted a ftill worfe.

Other nations leave the trade of their colonies free to all their fubjects, who may carry it on from all the different ports of the mother country, and who have occafion for no other licence than the common difpatches of the cuftomhoufe. In this cafe the number and difperfed fituation of the different traders renders it impoffible for them to enter into any general combination, and their competition is fufficient to hinder them from

OF COLONIES.

BOOK IV.

from making very exorbitant profits. Under fo liberal a policy the colonies are enabled both to fell their own produce and to buy the goods of Europe at a reafonable price. But fince the diffolution of the Plymouth company, when our colonies were but in their infancy, this has always been the policy of England. It has generally too been that of France, and has been uniformly fo fince the diffolution of what, in England, is commonly called their Miffiffippi company. The profits of the trade, therefore, which France and England carry on with their colonies, though no doubt fomewhat higher than if the competition was free to all other nations, are, however, by no means exorbitant; and the price of European goods accordingly is not extravagantly high in the greater part of the colonies of either of thofe nations.

In the exportation of their own furplus produce too, it is only with regard to certain commodities that the colonies of Great Britain are confined to the market of the mother country. Thefe commodities having been enumerated in the act of navigation and in fome other fubfequent acts, have upon that account been called *enumerated commodities.* The reft are called *non-enumerated*; and may be exported directly to other countries, provided it is in Britifh or Plantation fhips, of which the owners and three-fourths of the mariners are Britifh fubjects.

Among the non-enumerated commodities are fome of the moft important productions of America

OF COLONIES. 379

rica and the Weſt Indies; grain of all forts, CHAP. VII. lumber, ſalt proviſions, fiſh, fugar, and rum.

Grain is naturally the firſt and principal ob-ject of the culture of all new colonies. By allowing them a very extenſive market for it, the law encourages them to extend this culture much beyond the conſumption of a thinly inhabited country, and thus to provide beforehand an ample ſubſiſtence for a continually increaſing population.

In a country quite covered with wood, where timber conſequently is of little or no value, the expence of clearing the ground is the principal obſtacle to improvement. By allowing the co-lonies a very extenſive market for their lumber, the law endeavours to facilitate improvement by raiſing the price of a commodity which would otherwiſe be of little value, and thereby enabling them to make ſome profit of what would other-wiſe be mere expence.

In a country neither half-peopled nor half-cultivated, cattle naturally multiply beyond the conſumption of the inhabitants, and are often upon that account of little or no value. But it is neceſſary, it has already been ſhewn, that the price of cattle ſhould bear a certain proportion to that of corn before the greater part of the lands of any country can be improved. By allowing to American cattle, in all ſhapes, dead and alive, a very extenſive market, the law endeavours to raiſe the value of a commodity of which the high price is ſo very eſſential to im-provement. The good effects of this liberty, however,

OF COLONIES.

however, muſt be ſomewhat diminiſhed by the 4th of George III. c. 15. which puts hides and ſkins among the enumerated commodities, and thereby tends to reduce the value of American cattle.

To increaſe the ſhipping and naval power of Great Britain, by the extenſion of the fiſheries of our colonies, is an objeƈt which the legiſlature ſeems to have had almoſt conſtantly in view. Thoſe fiſheries, upon this account, have had all the encouragement which freedom can give them, and they have flouriſhed accordingly. The New England fiſhery in particular was, before the late diſturbances, one of the moſt important, perhaps, in the world. The whale-fiſhery which, notwithſtanding an extravagant bounty, is in Great Britain carried on to ſo little purpoſe, that in the opinion of many people (which I do not, however, pretend to warrant) the whole produce does not much exceed the value of the bounties which are annually paid for it, is in New England carried on without any bounty to a very great extent. Fiſh is one of the principal articles with which the North Americans trade to Spain, Portugal, and the Mediterranean.

Sugar was originally an enumerated commodity which could be exported only to Great Britain. But in 1731, upon a repreſentation of the ſugar-planters, its exportation was permitted to all parts of the world. The reſtriƈtions, however, with which this liberty was granted, joined to the high price of ſugar in Great Britain, have

rendered

OF COLONIES.

rendered it, in a great meafure, ineffectual. Great Britain and her colonies ftill continue to be almoft the fole market for all the fugar produced in the Britifh plantations. Their confumption increafes fo faft, that, though in confequence of the increafing improvement of Jamaica, as well as of the Ceded Iflands, the importation of fugar has increafed very greatly within thefe twenty years, the exportation to foreign countries is faid to be not much greater than before.

Rum is a very important article in the trade which the Americans carry on to the coaft of Africa, from which they bring back negro flaves in return.

If the whole furplus produce of America in grain of all forts, in falt provifions, and in fifh, had been put into the enumeration, and thereby forced into the market of Great Britain, it would have interfered too much with the produce of the induftry of our own people. It was probably not fo much from any regard to the intereft of America, as from a jealoufy of this interference, that thofe important commodities have not only been kept out of the enumeration, but that the importation into Great Britain of all grain, except rice, and of falt provifions, has, in the ordinary ftate of the law, been prohibited.

The non-enumerated commodities could originally be exported to all parts of the world. Lumber and rice, having been once put into the enumeration, when they were afterwards taken out of it, were confined, as to the European market, to the countries that lie fouth of Cape Finifterre.

382 OF COLONIES.

BOOK IV.

Finifterre. By the 6th of George III. c. 52. all non-enumerated commodities were fubjected to the like reftriction. The parts of Europe which lie fouth of Cape Finifterre, are not manufacturing countries, and we were lefs jealous of the colony fhips carrying home from them any manufactures which could interfere with our own.

The enumerated commodities are of two forts: firft, fuch as are either the peculiar produce of America, or as cannot be produced, or at leaft are not produced, in the mother country. Of this kind are, melaffes, coffee, cocoa-nuts, tobacco, pimento, ginger, whale-fins, raw filk, cotton-wool, beaver and other peltry of America, indigo, fuftic, and other dying woods: fecondly, fuch as are not the peculiar produce of America, but which are and may be produced in the mother country, though not in fuch quantities as to fupply the greater part of her demand, which is principally fupplied from foreign countries. Of this kind are all naval ftores, mafts, yards, and bowfprits, tar, pitch, and turpentine, pig and bar iron, copper ore, hides and fkins, pot and pearl afhes. The largeft importation of commodities of the firft kind could not difcourage the growth or interfere with the fale of any part of the produce of the mother country. By confining them to the home market, our merchants, it was expected, would not only be enabled to buy them cheaper in the Plantations, and confequently to fell them with a better profit at home, but to eftablifh between the Plantations and foreign countries an advantageous carrying trade,

trade, of which Great Britain was neceffarily to be the center or emporium, as the European country into which thofe commodities were firft to be imported. The importation of commodities of the fecond kind might be fo managed too, it was fuppofed, as to interfere, not with the fale of thofe of the fame kind which were produced at home, but with that of thofe which were imported from foreign countries; becaufe, by means of proper duties, they might be rendered always fomewhat dearer than the former, and yet a good deal cheaper than the latter. By confining fuch commodities to the home market, therefore, it was propofed to difcourage the produce, not of Great Britain, but of fome foreign countries with which the balance of trade was believed to be unfavourable to Great Britain.

The prohibition of exporting from the colonies, to any other country but Great Britain, mafts, yards, and bowfprits, tar, pitch, and turpentine, naturally tended to lower the price of timber in the colonies, and confequently to increafe the expence of clearing their lands, the principal obftacle to their improvement. But about the beginning of the prefent century, in 1703, the pitch and tar company of Sweden endeavoured to raife the price of their commodities to Great Britain, by prohibiting their exportation, except in their own fhips, at their own price, and in fuch quantities as they thought proper. In order to counteract this notable piece of mercantile policy, and to render herfelf as much as poffible independent, not only of Sweden, but of all the other northern powers, Great Britain gave a bounty upon the importation of naval ftores from America, and the effect of this bounty was to raife the price of timber in America, much more than the confinement to the home market could lower it; and as both regulations were enacted at the fame time, their joint effect was rather to encourage than to difcourage the clearing of land in America.

Though pig and bar iron too have been put among the enumerated commodities, yet as, when imported from America, they are exempted from confiderable duties to which they are fubject when imported from any other country, the one part of the regulation contributes more to encourage the erection of furnaces in America, than the other to difcourage it. There is no manufacture which occafions fo great a confumption of wood as a furnace, or which can contribute fo much to the clearing of a country overgrown with it.

The tendency of fome of thefe regulations to raife the value of timber in America, and thereby to facilitate the clearing of the land, was neither, perhaps, intended nor underftood by the legiflature. Though their beneficial effects, however, have been in this refpect accidental, they have not upon that account been lefs real.

The moft perfect freedom of trade is permitted between the Britifh colonies of America and the Weft Indies, both in the enumerated and in the non-enumerated commodities. Thofe colonies are

now

OF COLONIES. 387

coarfe and houfehold manufactures, as a private CHAP.
family commonly makes for its own ufe, or for VII.
that of fome of its neighbours in the fame province.

To prohibit a great people, however, from
making all that they can of every part of their
own produce, or from employing their flock and
induftry in the way that they judge moft advantageous to themfelves, is a manifeft violation of
the moft facred rights of mankind. Unjuft,
however, as fuch prohibitions may be, they have
not hitherto been very hurtful to the colonies.
Land is ftill fo cheap, and, confequently, labour
fo dear among them, that they can import from
the mother country, almoft all the more refined
or more advanced manufactures cheaper than
they could make them for themfelves. Though
they had not, therefore, been prohibited from
eftablifhing fuch manufactures, yet in their prefent ftate of improvement, a regard to their own
intereft would, probably, have prevented them
from doing fo. In their prefent ftate of improvement, thofe prohibitions, perhaps, without cramp-
ing their induftry, or reftraining it from any employment to which it would have gone of its own
accord, are only impertinent badges of flavery
impofed upon them, without any fufficient reafon, by the groundlefs jealoufy of the merchants
and manufacturers of the mother country. In a
more advanced ftate they might be really oppreffive and infupportable.

Great Britain too, as fhe confines to her own
market fome of the moft important productions

c c 2 of

388   OF COLONIES.

BOOK of the colonies, fo in compenfation fhe gives to
IV.   fome of them an advantage in that market;
fometimes by impofing higher duties upon the
like productions when imported from other countries, and fometimes by giving bounties upon
their importation from the colonies. In the firft
way fhe gives an advantage in the home-market
to the fugar, tobacco, and iron of her own colonies, and in the fecond to their raw filk, to
their hemp and flax, to their indigo, to their
naval-ftores, and to their building-timber. This
fecond way of encouraging the colony produce
by bounties upon importation, is, fo far as I
have been able to learn, peculiar to Great Britain. The firft is not. Portugal does not content herfelf with impofing higher duties upon
the importation of tobacco from any other
country, but prohibits it under the feverest penalties.

With regard to the importation of goods from
Europe, England has likewife dealt more liberally with her colonies than any other nation.

Great Britain allows a part, almoft always the
half, generally a larger portion, and fometimes
the whole of the duty which is paid upon the importation of foreign goods, to be drawn back
upon their exportation to any foreign country.
No independent foreign country, it was eafy to
forefee, would receive them if they came to it
loaded with the heavy duties to which almoft all
foreign goods are fubjected on their importation
into Great Britain. Unlefs, therefore, fome
part of thofe duties was drawn back upon ex-
                                    portation,

OF COLONIES.

389

portation, there was an end of the carrying trade; a trade fo much favoured by the mercantile fyftem.

Our colonies, however, are by no means independent foreign countries; and Great Britain having affumed to herfelf the exclufive right of fupplying them with all goods from Europe, might have forced them (in the fame manner as other countries have done their colonies) to receive fuch goods, loaded with all the fame duties which they paid in the mother country. But, on the contrary, till 1763, the fame drawbacks were paid upon the exportation of the greater part of foreign goods to our colonies as to any independent foreign country. In 1763, indeed, by the 4th of Geo. III. c. 15. this indulgence was a good deal abated, and it was enacted, " That no part of the duty called the " old fubfidy fhould be drawn back for any " goods of the growth, production, or manu- " facture of Europe or the Eaft Indies, which " fhould be exported from this kingdom to any " Britifh colony or plantation in America; " wines, white callicoes and muflins excepted." Before this law, many different forts of foreign goods might have been bought cheaper in the plantations than in the mother country; and fome may ftill.

Of the greater part of the regulations concerning the colony trade, the merchants who carry it on, it muft be obferved, have been the principal advifers. We muft not wonder, there-

C C 3

fore,

BOOK IV.

fore, if in the greater part of them, their interest has been more considered than either that of the colonies or that of the mother country. In their exclusive privilege of supplying the colonies with all the goods which they wanted from Europe, and of purchasing all such parts of their surplus produce as could not interfere with any of the trades which they themselves carried on at home, the interest of the colonies was sacrificed to the interest of those merchants. In allowing the same drawbacks upon the re-exportation of the greater part of European and East India goods to the colonies, as upon their re-exportation to any independent country, the interest of the mother country was sacrificed to it, even according to the mercantile ideas of that interest. It was for the interest of the merchants to pay as little as possible for the foreign goods which they sent to the colonies, and consequently, to get back as much as possible of the duties which they advanced upon their importation into Great Britain. They might thereby be enabled to sell in the colonies, either the same quantity of goods with a greater profit, or a greater quantity with the same profit, and, consequently, to gain something either in the one way or the other. It was, likewise, for the interest of the colonies to get all such goods as cheap and in as great abundance as possible. But this might not always be for the interest of the mother country. She might frequently suffer both in her revenue, by giving back a

great

OF COLONIES.   391

great part of the duties which had been paid C H A P.
upon the importation of fuch goods; and in her   VII.
manufactures, by being underfold in the colony
market, in confequence of the eafy terms upon
which foreign manufactures could be carried
thither by means of thofe drawbacks. The
progrefs of the linen manufacture of Great Britain, it is commonly faid, has been a good deal
retarded by the drawbacks upon the re-exportation of German linen to the American colonies.

But though the policy of Great Britain with
regard to the trade of her colonies has been
dictated by the fame mercantile fpirit as that of
other nations, it has, however, upon the whole,
been lefs illiberal and oppreffive than that of any
of them.

In every thing, except their foreign trade, the
liberty of the Englifh colonifts to manage their
own affairs their own way is complete. It is
in every refpect equal to that of their fellow-
citizens at home, and is fecured in the fame
manner, by an affembly of the reprefentatives of
the people, who claim the fole right of impofing
taxes for the fupport of the colony government.
The authority of this affembly over-awes the
executive power, and neither the meaneft nor
the moft obnoxious colonift, as long as he obeys
the law, has any thing to fear from the refent-
ment, either of the governor, or of any other
civil or military officer in the province. The
colony affemblies, though, like the houfe of
commons in England, they are not always a very
equal reprefentation of the people, yet they ap-

        c c 4   proach

BOOK IV.

proach more nearly to that character; and as the executive power either has not the means to corrupt them, or, on account of the support which it receives from the mother country, is not under the neceffity of doing fo, they are perhaps in general more influenced by the inclinations of their conftituents. The councils, which, in the colony legiflatures, correfpond to the houfe of lords in Great Britain, are not compofed of an hereditary nobility. In fome of the colonies, as in three of the governments of New England, thofe councils are not appointed by the King, but chofen by the reprefentatives of the people. In none of the Englifh colonies is there any hereditary nobility. In all of them, indeed, as in all other free countries, the defcendant of an old colony family is more refpected than an upftart of equal merit and fortune: but he is only more refpected, and he has no privileges by which he can be troublefome to his neighbours. Before the commencement of the prefent difturbances, the colony affemblies had not only the legiflative, but a part of the executive power. In Connecticut and Rhode Ifland, they elected the governor. In the other colonies they appointed the revenue officers who collected the taxes impofed by thofe refpective affemblies, to whom thofe officers were immediately refponfible. There is more equality, therefore, among the Englifh colonifts than among the inhabitants of the mother country. Their manners are more republican, and their governments, thofe of three of the provinces of

New

OF COLONIES. 393

New England in particular, have hitherto been CHAP.
more republican too. VII.

The abfolute governments of Spain, Portugal, and France, on the contrary, take place in their colonies; and the difcretionary powers which fuch governments commonly delegate to all their inferior officers are, on account of the great diftance, naturally exercifed there with more than ordinary violence. Under all abfolute governments there is more liberty in the capital than in any other part of the country. The fovereign himfelf can never have either intereft or inclination to pervert the order of juftice, or to opprefs the great body of the people. In the capital his prefence over-awes more or lefs all his inferior officers, who in the remoter provinces, from whence the complaints of the people are lefs likely to reach him, can exercife their tyranny with much more fafety. But the European colonies in America are more remote than the moft diftant provinces of the greateft empires which had ever been known before. The government of the Englifh colonies is perhaps the only one which, fince the world began, could give perfect fecurity to the inhabitants of fo very diftant a province. The adminiftration of the French colonies, however, has always been conducted with more gentlenefs and moderation than that of the Spanifh and Portuguefe. This fuperiority of conduct is fuitable both to the character of the French nation, and to what forms the character of every nation. the nature of their government, which, though

arbitrary

394   OF COLONIES.

BOOK arbitrary and violent in comparifon with that of
IV. Great Britain, is legal and free in comparifon
with thofe of Spain and Portugal.

It is in the progrefs of the North American
colonies, however, that the fuperiority of the
Englifh policy chiefly appears. The progrefs
of the fugar colonies of France has been at leaft
equal, perhaps fuperior, to that of the greater
part of thofe of England; and yet the fugar
colonies of England enjoy a free government
nearly of the fame kind with that which takes
place in her colonies of North America. But
the fugar colonies of France are not difcouraged,
like thofe of England, from refining their own
fugar; and, what is of ftill greater importance,
the genius of their government naturally introduces a better management of their negro flaves.

In all European colonies the culture of the
fugar-cane is carried on by negro flaves. The
conftitution of thofe who have been born in the
temperate climate of Europe could not, it is fuppofed, fupport the labour of digging the ground
under the burning fun of the Weft Indies; and
the culture of the fugar-cane, as it is managed
at prefent, is all hand-labour, though, in the
opinion of many, the drill plough might be introduced into it with great advantage. But, as
the profit and fuccefs of the cultivation which
is carried on by means of cattle, depend very
much upon the good management of thofe cattle; fo the profit and fuccefs of that which is
carried on by flaves, muft depend equally upon
the good management of thofe flaves; and in the
good

OF COLONIES.   395

good management of their flaves the French CHAP.
planters, I think it is generally allowed, are VII.
fuperior to the Englifh.   The law, fo far as it
gives fome weak protection to the flave againft
the violence of his mafter, is likely to be better
executed in a colony where the government is
in a great meafure arbitrary, than in one where
it is altogether free.   In every country where
the unfortunate law of flavery is eftablifhed, the
magiftrate, when he protects the flave, inter-
meddles in fome meafure in the management of
the private property of the mafter; and, in a
free country, where the mafter is perhaps either
a member of the colony affembly, or an elector
of fuch a member, he dare not do this but with
the greateft caution and circumfpection.   The
refpect which he is obliged to pay to the mafter,
renders it more difficult for him to protect the
flave.   But in a country where the government
is in a great meafure arbitrary, where it is ufual
for the magiftrate to intermeddle even in the
management of the private property of individuals, and to fend them, perhaps, a lettre de
cachet if they do not manage it according to his
liking, it is much eafier for him to give fome
protection to the flave; and common humanity
naturally difpofes him to do fo.   The protection
of the magiftrate renders the flave lefs contemptible in the eyes of his mafter, who is
thereby induced to confider him with more regard, and to treat him with more gentlenefs.
Gentle ufage renders the flave not only more
faithful, but more intelligent, and therefore,

4   upon

BOOK IV.

upon a double account, more useful. He approaches more to the condition of a free fervant, and may poffefs fome degree of integrity and attachment to his mafter's intereft, virtues which frequently belong to free fervants, but which never can belong to a flave, who is treated as flaves commonly are in countries where the mafter is perfectly free and fecure.

That the condition of a flave is better under an arbitrary than under a free government, is, I believe, fupported by the hiftory of all ages and nations. In the Roman hiftory, the firft time we read of the magiftrate interpofing to protect the flave from the violence of his mafter, is under the emperors. When Vedius Pollio, in the prefence of Auguftus, ordered one of his flaves, who had committed a flight fault, to be cut into pieces and thrown into his fifh-pond in order to feed his fifhes, the emperor commanded him, with indignation, to emancipate immediately, not only that flave, but all the others that belonged to him. Under the republic no magiftrate could have had authority enough to protect the flave, much lefs to punifh the mafter.

The ftock, it is to be obferved, which has improved the fugar colonies of France, particularly the great colony of St. Domingo, has been raifed almoft entirely from the gradual improvement and cultivation of thofe colonies. It has been almoft altogether the produce of the foil and of the induftry of the colonifts, or, what comes to the fame thing, the price of that produce gradually accumulated by good management,

ment, and employed in raifing a ftill greater produce. But the ftock which has improved and cultivated the fugar colonies of England has, a great part of it, been fent out from England, and has by no means been altogether the produce of the foil and induftry of the colonifts. The profperity of the Englifh fugar colonies has been, in a great meafure, owing to the great riches of England, of which a part has overflowed, if one may fay fo, upon thofe colonies. But the profperity of the fugar colonies of France has been entirely owing to the good conduct of the colonifts, which muft therefore have had fome fuperiority over that of the Englifh; and this fuperiority has been remarked in nothing fo much as in the good management of their flaves.

Such have been the general outlines of the policy of the different European nations with regard to their colonies.

The policy of Europe, therefore, has very little to boaft of, either in the original eftablifhment, or, fo far as concerns their internal government, in the fubfequent profperity of the colonies of America.

Folly and injuftice feem to have been the principles which prefided over and directed the firft project of eftablifhing thofe colonies; the folly of hunting after gold and filver mines, and the injuftice of coveting the poffeffion of a country whofe harmlefs natives, far from having ever injured the people of Europe, had received the

firft

398   OF COLONIES.

BOOK firſt adventurers with every mark of kindneſs and
IV.   hoſpitality.

The adventurers, indeed, who formed ſome
of the later eſtabliſhments, joined, to the chimerical projeƈt of finding gold and ſilver mines,
other motives more reaſonable and more laudable; but even theſe motives do very little
honour to the policy of Europe.

The Engliſh puritans, reſtrained at home,
fled for freedom to America, and eſtabliſhed
there the four governments of New England,
The Engliſh catholics, treated with much greater
injuſtice, eſtabliſhed that of Maryland; the Quakers, that of Pennſylvania. The Portugueſe
Jews, perſecuted by the inquiſition, ſtript of
their fortunes, and baniſhed to Brazil, introduced, by their example, ſome ſort of order
and induſtry among the tranſported felons and
ſtrumpets, by whom that colony was originally
peopled, and taught them the culture of the
ſugar-cane. Upon all theſe different occaſions
it was, not the wiſdom and policy, but the diſ-
order and injuſtice of the European governments,
which peopled and cultivated America.

In effeƈtuating ſome of the moſt important of
theſe eſtabliſhments, the different governments
of Europe had as little merit as in projeƈting
them. The conqueſt of Mexico was the projeƈt,
not of the council of Spain, but of a governor
of Cuba; and it was effeƈtuated by the ſpirit of
the bold adventurer to whom it was entruſted,
in ſpite of every thing which that governor, who
foon

OF COLONIES.

foon repented of having trufted fuch a perfon, CHAP. VII. could do to thwart it. The conquerors of Chili and Peru, and of almoft all the other Spanifh fettlements upon the continent of America, carried out with them no other public encouragement, but a general permiffion to make fettlements and conquefts in the name of the King of Spain. Thofe adventures were all at the private rifk and expence of the adventurers. The government of Spain contributed fcarce any thing to any of them. That of England contributed as little towards effectuating the eftablifhment of fome of its moft important colonies in North America.

When thofe eftablifhments were effectuated, and had become fo confiderable as to attract the attention of the mother country, the firft regulations which fhe made with regard to them had always in view to fecure to herfelf the monopoly of their commerce; to confine their market, and to enlarge her own at their expence, and, confequently, rather to damp and difcourage, than to quicken and forward the courfe of their profperity. In the different ways in which this monopoly has been exercifed, confifts one of the moft effential differences in the policy of the different European nations with regard to their colonies. The beft of them all, that of England, is only fomewhat lefs illiberal and oppreffive than that of any of the reft.

In what way, therefore, has the policy of Europe contributed either to the firft eftablifhment, or to the prefent grandeur of the colonies

of

BOOK IV. of America? In one way, and in one way only, it has contributed a good deal. *Magna virûm Mater!* It bred and formed the men who were capable of atchieving fuch great actions, and of laying the foundation of fo great an empire; and there is no other quarter of the world of which the policy is capable of forming, or has ever actually and in fact formed fuch men. The colonies owe to the policy of Europe the education and great views of their active and enterprifing founders; and fome of the greateft and moft important of them, fo far as concerns their internal government, owe to it fcarce any thing elfe.

PART THIRD.

Of the Advantages which Europe has derived from the Difcovery of America, and from that of a Paffage to the Eaft - Indies by the Cape of Good Hope.

SUCH are the advantages which the colonies of America have derived from the policy of Europe.

What are thofe which Europe has derived from the difcovery and colonization of America?

Thofe advantages may be divided, firft, into the general advantages which Europe, confidered as one great country, has derived from thofe great events; and, fecondly, into the particular advantages which each colonizing country has derived from the colonies which particularly belong to it, in confequence of the authority or dominion which it exercifes over them.

3 The

OF COLONIES.

The general advantages which Europe, considered as one great country, has derived from the discovery and colonization of America, consist, first, in the increase of its enjoyments; and secondly, in the augmentation of its industry.

The surplus produce of America, imported into Europe, furnishes the inhabitants of this great continent with a variety of commodities which they could not otherwise have possessed, some for conveniency and use, some for pleasure, and some for ornament, and thereby contributes to increase their enjoyments.

The discovery and colonization of America, it will readily be allowed, have contributed to augment the industry, first, of all the countries which trade to it directly; such as Spain, Portugal, France, and England; and, secondly, of all those which, without trading to it directly, send, through the medium of other countries, goods to it of their own produce; such as Austrian Flanders, and some provinces of Germany, which, through the medium of the countries before mentioned, send to it a considerable quantity of linen and other goods. All such countries have evidently gained a more extensive market for their surplus produce, and must consequently have been encouraged to increase its quantity.

But, that those great events should likewise have contributed to encourage the industry of countries, such as Hungary and Poland, which may never, perhaps, have sent a single commo-

VOL. III. D D dity

BOOK IV.

dity of their own produce to America, is not, perhaps, altogether fo evident. That thofe events have done fo, however, cannot be doubted. Some part of the produce of America is confumed in Hungary and Poland, and there is fome demand there for the fugar, chocolate, and tobacco, of that new quarter of the world. But thofe commodities muft be purchafed with fomething which is either the produce of the induftry of Hungary and Poland, or with fomething which had been purchafed with fome part of that produce. Thofe commodities of America are new values, new equivalents, introduced into Hungary and Poland to be exchanged there for the furplus produce of thofe countries. By being carried thither they create a new and more extenfive market for that furplus produce. They raife its value, and thereby contribute to encourage its increafe. Though no part of it may ever be carried to America, it may be carried to other countries which purchafe it with a part of their fhare of the furplus produce of America; and it may find a market by means of the circulation of that trade which was originally put into motion by the furplus produce of America.

Thofe great events may even have contributed to increafe the enjoyments, and to augment the induftry of countries which, not only never fent any commodities to America, but never received any from it. Even fuch countries may have received a greater abundance of other commodities from countries of which the furplus produce

OF COLONIES. 403

produce had been augmented by means of the American trade. This greater abundance, as it muſt neceſſarily have increaſed their enjoyments, ſo it muſt likewiſe have augmented their induſtry. A greater number of new equivalents of ſome kind or other muſt have been preſented to them to be exchanged for the ſurplus produce of that induſtry. A more extenſive market muſt have been created for that ſurplus produce, ſo as to raiſe its value, and thereby encourage its increaſe. The maſs of commodities annually thrown into the great circle of European commerce, and by its various revolutions annually diſtributed among all the different nations comprehended within it, muſt have been augmented by the whole ſurplus produce of America. A greater ſhare of this greater maſs, therefore, is likely to have fallen to each of thoſe nations, to have increaſed their enjoyments, and augmented their induſtry.

The excluſive trade of the mother countries tends to diminiſh, or, at leaſt, to keep down below what they would otherwiſe riſe to, both the enjoyments and induſtry of all thoſe nations in general, and of the American colonies in particular. It is a dead weight upon the action of one of the great ſprings which puts into motion a great part of the buſineſs of mankind. By rendering the colony produce dearer in all other countries, it leſſens its conſumption, and thereby cramps the induſtry of the colonies, and both the enjoyments and the induſtry of all other countries, which both enjoy leſs when they pay more

CHAP.
VII.

DD 2

for

BOOK IV.

for what they enjoy, and produce lefs when they' get lefs for what they produce. By rendering the produce of all other countries dearer in the colonies, it cramps, in the fame manner, the induftry of all other countries, and both the enjoyments and the induftry of the colonies. It is a clog which, for the fuppofed benefit of fome particular countries, embarraffes the pleafures, and encumbers the induftry of all other countries; but of the colonies more than of any other. It not only excludes, as much as poffible, all other countries from one particular market; but it confines, as much as poffible, the colonies to one particular market: and the difference is very great between being excluded from one particular market, when all others are open, and being confined to one particular market, when all others are fhut up. The furplus produce of the colonies, however, is the original fource of all that increafe of enjoyments and induftry which Europe derives from the difcovery and colonization of America; and the exclufive trade of the mother countries tends to render this fource much lefs abundant than it otherwife would be.

The particular advantages which each colonizing country derives from the colonies which particularly belong to it, are of two different kinds; firft, thofe common advantages which every empire derives from the provinces fubject to its dominion; and, fecondly, thofe peculiar advantages which are fuppofed to refult from provinces of fo very peculiar a nature as the European colonies of America.

The

OF COLONIES. 405

The common advantages which every empire C H A P. derives from the provinces subject to its domi- VII. nion, consist, first, in the military force which they furnish for its defence; and, secondly, in the revenue which they furnish for the support of its civil government. The Roman colonies furnished occasionally both the one and the other. The Greek colonies, sometimes, furnished a military force; but seldom any revenue. They seldom acknowledged themselves subject to the dominion of the mother city. They were generally her allies in war, but very seldom her subjects in peace.

The European colonies of America have never yet furnished any military force for the defence of the mother country. Their military force has never yet been sufficient for their own defence; and in the different wars in which the mother countries have been engaged, the defence of their colonies has generally occasioned a very considerable distraction of the military force of those countries. In this respect, therefore, all the European colonies have, without exception, been a cause rather of weakness than of strength to their respective mother countries.

The colonies of Spain and Portugal only have contributed any revenue towards the defence of the mother country, or the support of her civil government. The taxes which have been levied upon those of other European nations, upon those of England in particular, have seldom been equal to the expence laid out upon them in time of peace, and never sufficient to defray that which

D D 3

406

OF COLONIES.

BOOK IV.

which they occafioned in time of war. Such colonies, therefore, have been a fource of expence and not of revenue to their refpective mother countries.

The advantages of fuch colonies to their refpective mother countries, confift altogether in thofe peculiar advantages which are fuppofed to refult from provinces of fo very peculiar a nature as the European colonies of America; and the exclufive trade, it is acknowledged, is the fole fource of all thofe peculiar advantages.

In confequence of this exclufive trade, all that part of the furplus produce of the Englifh colonies, for example, which confifts in what are called enumerated commodities, can be fent to no other country but England. Other countries muft afterwards buy it of her. It muft be cheaper therefore in England than it can be in any other country, and muft contribute more to increafe the enjoyments of England than thofe of any other country. It muft likewife contribute more to encourage her induftry. For all thofe parts of her own furplus produce which England exchanges for thofe enumerated commodities, fhe muft get a better price than any other countries can get for the like parts of theirs, when they exchange them for the fame commodities. The manufactures of England, for example, will purchafe a greater quantity of the fugar and tobacco of her own colonies, than the like manufactures of other countries can purchafe of that fugar and tobacco. So far, therefore, as the manufactures of England and
thofe

OF COLONIES.

thofe of other countries are both to be exchanged for the fugar and tobacco of the Englifh colonies, this fuperiority of price gives an encouragement to the former, beyond what the latter can in thefe circumftances enjoy. The exclufive trade of the colonies, therefore, as it diminifhes, or, at leaft, keeps down below what they would other-wife rife to, both the enjoyments and the induftry of the. countries which do not poffefs it; fo it gives an evident advantage to the countries which do poffefs it over thofe other countries.

This advantage, however, will, perhaps, be found to be rather what may be called a relative than an abfolute advantage; and to give a fuperiority to the country which enjoys it, rather by depreffing the induftry and produce of other countries, than by raifing thofe of that particular country above what they would naturally rife to in the cafe of a free trade.

The tobacco of Maryland and Virginia, for example, by means of the monopoly which England enjoys of it, certainly comes cheaper to England than it can do to France, to whom England commonly fells a confiderable part of it. But had France, and all other European countries been, at all times, allowed a free trade to Maryland and Virginia, the tobacco of thofe colonies might, by this time, have come cheaper than it actually does, not only to all thofe other countries, but likewife to England. The produce of tobacco, in confequence of a market fo much more extenfive than any which it has hitherto enjoyed, might, and probably would,

by

OF COLONIES.

BOOK IV.

by this time, have been fo much increafed as to reduce the profits of a tobacco plantation to their natural level with thofe of a corn plantation, which, it is fuppofed, they are ftill fomewhat above. The price of tobacco might, and probably would, by this time, have fallen fomewhat lower than it is at prefent. An equal quantity of the commodities either of England, or of thofe other countries, might have purchafed in Maryland and Virginia a greater quantity of tobacco than it can do at prefent, and, confequently, have been fold there for fo much a better price. So far as that weed, therefore, can, by its cheapnefs and abundance, increafe the enjoyments or augment the induftry either of England or of any other country, it would, probably, in the cafe of a free trade, have produced both thefe effects in fomewhat a greater degree than it can do at prefent. England, indeed, would not in this cafe have had any advantage over other countries. She might have bought the tobacco of her colonies fomewhat cheaper, and, confequently, have fold fome of her own commodities fomewhat dearer than fhe actually does. But fhe could neither have bought the one cheaper nor fold the other dearer than any other country might have done. She might, perhaps, have gained an abfolute, but fhe would certainly have loft a relative advantage.

In order, however, to obtain this relative advantage in the colony trade, in order to execute the invidious and malignant project of excluding as much as poffible other nations from any fhare

in

OF COLONIES. 409

In it, England, there are very probable reasons for believing, has not only sacrificed a part of the absolute advantage, which she, as well as every other nation, might have derived from that trade, but has subjected herself both to an absolute and to a relative disadvantage in almost every other branch of trade.

When, by the act of navigation, England assumed to herself the monopoly of the colony trade, the foreign capitals which had before been employed in it were necessarily withdrawn from it. The English capital, which had before carried on but a part of it, was now to carry on the whole. The capital which had before supplied the colonies with but a part of the goods which they wanted from Europe, was now all that was employed to supply them with the whole. But it could not supply them with the whole, and the goods with which it did supply them were necessarily sold very dear. The capital which had before bought but a part of the surplus produce of the colonies, was now all that was employed to buy the whole. But it could not buy the whole at any thing near the old price, and, therefore, whatever it did buy it necessarily bought very cheap. But in an employment of capital in which the merchant sold very dear and bought very cheap, the profit must have been very great, and much above the ordinary level of profit in other branches of trade. This superiority of profit in the colony trade could not fail to draw from other branches of trade a part of the capital which had before been employed in them. But this revulsion of capital, as it must have gradually increased

C H A P.
VII.

OF COLONIES.

BOOK IV.

increafed the competition of capitals in the colony trade, fo it muft have gradually diminifhed that competition in all thofe other branches of trade; as it muft have gradually lowered the profits of the one, fo it muft have gradually raifed thofe of the other, till the profits of all came to a new level, different from and fomewhat higher than that at which they had been before.

This double effect, of drawing capital from all other trades, and of raifing the rate of profit fomewhat higher than it otherwife would have been in all trades, was not only produced by this monopoly upon its firft eftablifhment, but has continued to be produced by it ever fince.

First, this monopoly has been continually drawing capital from all other trades to be employed in that of the colonies.

Though the wealth of Great Britain has increafed very much fince the eftablifhment of the act of navigation, it certainly has not increafed in the fame proportion as that of the colonies. But the foreign trade of every country naturally increafes in proportion to its wealth, its furplus produce in proportion to its whole produce; and Great Britain having engroffed to herfelf almoft the whole of what may be called the foreign trade of the colonies, and her capital not having increafed in the fame proportion as the extent of that trade, fhe could not carry it on without continually withdrawing from other branches of trade fome part of the capital which had before been employed in them, as well as withholding from them a great deal more which would otherwife have gone to them. Since the eftablifhment

of

OF COLONIES.

of the act of navigation, accordingly, the colony CHAP.
trade has been continually increafing, while VII.
many other branches of foreign trade, particularly of that to other parts of Europe, have been
continually decaying. Our manufactures for
foreign fale, inftead of being fuited, as before
the act of navigation, to the neighbouring market
of Europe, or to the more diftant one of the
countries which lie round the Mediterranean fea,
have, the greater part of them, been accommodated to the ftill more diftant one of the colonies,
to the market in which they have the monopoly,
father than to that in which they have many
competitors. The caufes of decay in other
branches of foreign trade, which, by Sir Matthew
Decker and other writers, have been fought for
in the excefs and improper mode of taxation, in
the high price of labour, in the increafe of
luxury, &c. may all be found in the over-growth
of the colony trade. The mercantile capital of
Great Britain, though very great, yet not being
infinite ; and though greatly increafed fince the
act of navigation, yet not being increafed in the
fame proportion as the colony trade, that trade
could not poffibly be carried on without withdrawing fome part of that capital from other
branches of trade, nor confequently without
fome decay of thofe other branches.

England, it muft be obferved, was a great
trading country, her mercantile capital was very
great and likely to become ftill greater and
greater every day, not only before the act of
navigation had eftablifhed the monopoly of the

colony

BOOK IV.

colony trade, but before that trade was very confiderable. In the Dutch war, during the government of Cromwel, her navy was fuperior to that of Holland; and in that which broke out in the beginning of the reign of Charles II. it was at leaft equal, perhaps fuperior, to the united navies of France and Holland. Its fuperiority, perhaps, would fcarce appear greater in the prefent times; at leaft if the Dutch navy was to bear the fame proportion to the Dutch commerce now which it did then. But this great naval power could not, in either of thofe wars, be owing to the act of navigation. During the firft of them the plan of that act had been but juft formed; and though before the breaking out of the fecond it had been fully enacted by legal authority; yet no part of it could have had time to produce any confiderable effect, and leaft of all that part which eftablifhed the exclufive trade to the colonies. Both the colonies and their trade were inconfiderable then in comparifon of what they are now. The ifland of Jamaica was an unwholefome defert, little inhabited, and lefs cultivated. New York and New Jerfey were in the poffeffion of the Dutch: the half of St. Chriftopher's in that of the French. The ifland of Antigua, the two Carolinas, Penfylvania, Georgia, and Nova Scotia, were not planted. Virginia, Maryland, and New England were planted; and though they were very thriving colonies, yet there was not, perhaps, at that time, either in Europe or America, a fingle perfon who forefaw or even fufpected the rapid progrefs which

OF COLONIES. 413

which they have fince made in wealth, popula- CHAP.
tion and improvement. The ifland of Barbadoes, VII.
in fhort, was the only Britifh colony of any confequence of which the condition at that time
bore any refemblance to what it is at prefent.
The trade of the colonies, of which England,
even for fome time after the act of navigation,
enjoyed but a part (for the act of navigation was
not very ftrictly executed till feveral years after
it was enacted), could not at that time be the
caufe of the great trade of England, nor of the
great naval power which was fupported by that
trade. The trade which at that time fupported
that great naval power was the trade of Europe,
and of the countries which lie round the Mediterranean fea. But the fhare which Great Britain at prefent enjoys of that trade could not
fupport any fuch great naval power. Had the
growing trade of the colonies been left free to
all nations, whatever fhare of it might have fallen
to Great Britain, and a very confiderable fhare
would probably have fallen to her, muft have
been all an addition to this great trade of which
fhe was before in poffeffion. In confequence of
the monopoly, the increafe of the colony trade
has not fo much occafioned an addition to the
trade which Great Britain had before, as a total
change in its direction.

Secondly, this monopoly has neceffarily contributed to keep up the rate of profit in all the
different branches of Britifh trade higher than
it naturally would have been, had all nations
been allowed a free trade to the Britifh colonies.
                                        The

BOOK IV.

The monopoly of the colony trade, as it neceſſarily drew towards that trade a greater proportion of the capital of Great Britain than what would have gone to it of its own accord; ſo by the expulſion of all foreign capitals it neceſſarily reduced the whole quantity of capital employed in that trade below what it naturally would have been in the caſe of a free trade. But, by leſſening the competition of capitals in that branch of trade, it neceſſarily raiſed the rate of profit in that branch. By leſſening too the competition of Britiſh capitals in all other branches of trade, it neceſſarily raiſed the rate of Britiſh profit in all thoſe other branches. Whatever may have been, at any particular period, ſince the eſtabliſhment of the act of navigation, the ſtate or extent of the mercantile capital of Great Britain, the monopoly of the colony trade muſt, during the continuance of that ſtate, have raiſed the ordinary rate of Britiſh profit higher than it otherwiſe would have been both in that and in all the other branches of Britiſh trade. If, ſince the eſtabliſhment of the act of navigation, the ordinary rate of Britiſh profit has fallen conſiderably, as it certainly has, it muſt have fallen ſtill lower, had not the monopoly eſtabliſhed by that act contributed to keep it up.

But whatever raiſes in any country the ordinary rate of profit higher than it otherwiſe would be, neceſſarily ſubjects that country both to an abſolute and to a relative diſadvantage in every branch of trade of which ſhe has not the monopoly.

It

It fubjects her to an abfolute difadvantage: becaufe in fuch branches of trade her merchants cannot get this greater profit, without felling dearer than they otherwife would do both the goods of foreign countries which they import into their own, and the goods of their own country which they export to foreign countries. Their own country muft both buy dearer and fell dearer; muft both buy lefs and fell lefs; muft both enjoy lefs and produce lefs, than fhe otherwife would do.

It fubjects her to a relative difadvantage; becaufe in fuch branches of trade it fets other countries which are not fubject to the fame abfolute difadvantage, either more above her or lefs below her than they otherwife would be. It enables them both to enjoy more and to produce more in proportion to what fhe enjoys and produces. It renders their fuperiority greater or their inferiority lefs than it otherwife would be. By raifing the price of her produce above what it otherwife would be, it enables the merchants of other countries to underfell her in foreign markets, and thereby to juftle her out of almoft all thofe branches of trade, of which fhe has not the monopoly.

Our merchants frequently complain of the high wages of Britifh labour as the caufe of their manufactures being underfold in foreign markets; but they are filent about the high profits of ftock. They complain of the extravagant gain of other people; but they fay nothing of their own. The high profits of Britifh ftock, however, may contribute towards raifing the price of Britifh manufactures in many cafes as much, and

in

416 OF COLONIES.

BOOK IV. in some perhaps more, than the high wages of British labour.

It is in this manner that the capital of Great Britain, one may justly say, has partly been drawn and partly been driven from the greater part of the different branches of trade of which she has not the monopoly; from the trade of Europe in particular, and from that of the countries which lie round the Mediterranean sea.

It has partly been drawn from those branches of trade; by the attraction of superior profit in the colony trade in consequence of the continual increase of that trade, and of the continual insufficiency of the capital which had carried it on one year to carry it on the next.

It has partly been driven from them; by the advantage which the high rate of profit, established in Great Britain, gives to other countries, in all the different branches of trade of which Great Britain has not the monopoly.

As the monopoly of the colony trade has drawn from those other branches a part of the British capital which would otherwise have been employed in them, so it has forced into them many foreign capitals which would never have gone to them, had they not been expelled from the colony trade. In those other branches of trade it has diminished the competition of British capitals, and thereby raised the rate of British profit higher than it otherwise would have been. On the contrary, it has increased the competition of foreign capitals, and thereby sunk the rate of foreign profit lower than it otherwise would have been. Both in the one way and in the other it must evidently have

OF COLONIES. 417

have fubjected Great Britain to a relative dif- CHAP.
advantage in all thofe other branches of trade. VII.

The colony trade, however, it may perhaps be
faid, is more advantageous to Great Britain than
any other; and the monopoly, by forcing into
that trade a greater proportion of the capital of
Great Britain than would otherwife have gone
to it, has turned that capital into an employment
more advantageous to the country than any
other which it could have found.

The moft advantageous employment of any
capital to the country to which it belongs, is
that which maintains there the greateft quantity
of productive labour, and increafes the moft the
annual produce of the land and labour of that
country. But the quantity of productive labour
which any capital employed in the foreign trade
of confumption can maintain, is exactly in proportion, it has been fhewn in the fecond book,
to the frequency of its returns. A capital of a
thoufand pounds, for example, employed in a
foreign trade of confumption, of which the
returns are made regularly once in the year, can
keep in conftant employment, in the country to
which it belongs, a quantity of productive labour
equal to what a thoufand pounds can maintain
there for a year. If the returns are made
twice or thrice in the year, it can keep in
conftant employment a quantity of productive
labour equal to what two or three thoufand
pounds can maintain there for a year. A foreign
trade of confumption carried on with a neighbouring, is, upon this account, in general, more

VOL. III.			E E			advan-

OF COLONIES.

BOOK IV.

advantageous than one carried on with a diftant country; and for the fame reafon a direct foreign trade of confumption, as it has likewife been fhewn in the fecond book, is in general more advantageous than a round-about one.

But the monopoly of the colony trade, fo far as it has operated upon the employment of the capital of Great Britain, has in all cafes forced fome part of it from a foreign trade of confumption carried on with a neighbouring, to one carried on with a more diftant country, and in many cafes from a direct foreign trade of confumption to a round-about one.

Firft, the monopoly of the colony trade has in all cafes forced fome part of the capital of Great Britain from a foreign trade of confumption carried on with a neighbouring, to one carried on with a more diftant country.

It has, in all cafes, forced fome part of that capital from the trade with Europe, and with the countries which lie round the Mediterranean fea, to that with the more diftant regions of America and the Weft Indies, from which the returns are neceffarily lefs frequent, not only on account of the greater diftance, but on account of the peculiar circumftances of thofe countries. New colonies, it has already been obferved, are always underftocked. Their capital is always much lefs than what they could employ with great profit and advantage in the improvement and cultivation of their land. They have a conftant demand, therefore, for more capital than they have of their own; and, in order to fupply the deficiency

OF COLONIES.

deficiency of their own, they endeavour to borrow as much as they can of the mother country, to whom they are, therefore, always in debt. The moſt common way in which the coloniſts contract this debt, is not by borrowing upon bond of the rich people of the mother country, though they ſometimes do this too, but by running as much in arrear to their correſpondents, who ſupply them with goods from Europe, as thoſe correſpondents will allow them. Their annual returns frequently do not amount to more than a third, and ſometimes not ſo great a proportion of what they owe. The whole capital, therefore, which their correſpondents advance to them is ſeldom returned to Britain in leſs than three, and ſometimes not in leſs than four or five years. But a Britiſh capital of a thouſand pounds, for example, which is returned to Great Britain only once in five years, can keep in conſtant employment only one-fifth part of the Britiſh induſtry which it could maintain if the whole was returned once in the year; and, inſtead of the quantity of induſtry which a thouſand pounds could maintain for a year, can keep in conſtant employment the quantity only which two hundred pounds can maintain for a year. The planter, no doubt, by the high price which he pays for the goods from Europe, by the intereſt upon the bills which he grants at diftant dates, and by the commiſſion upon the renewal of thoſe which he grants at near dates, makes up, and probably more than makes up, all the loſs which his correſpondent can ſuftain by this delay. But,

CHAP.
VII.

though

OF COLONIES.

though he may make up the loss of his correspondent, he cannot make up that of Great Britain. In a trade of which the returns are very diftant, the profit of the merchant may be as great or greater than in one in which they are very frequent and near; but the advantage of the country in which he refides, the quantity of productive labour conftantly maintained there, the annual produce of the land and labour muft always be much lefs. That the returns of the trade to America, and ftill more thofe of that to the Weft Indies, are, in general, not only more diftant, but more irregular, and more uncertain too, than thofe of the trade to any part of Europe, or even of the countries which lie round the Mediterranean fea, will readily be allowed, I imagine, by every body who has any experience of thofe different branches of trade.

Secondly, the monopoly of the colony trade has, in many cafes, forced fome part of the capital of Great Britain from a direct foreign trade of confumption, into a round-about one.

Among the enumerated commodities which can be fent to no other market but Great Britain, there are feveral of which the quantity exceeds very much the confumption of Great Britain, and of which a part, therefore, muft be exported to other countries. But this cannot be done without forcing fome part of the capital of Great Britain into a round-about foreign trade of confumption. Maryland and Virginia, for example, fend annually to Great Britain upwards of ninety-fix thoufand hogfheads of tobacco, and the

the confumption of Great Britain is faid not to
exceed fourteen thoufand. Upwards of eighty-
two thoufand hogfheads, therefore, muft be exported to other countries, to France, to Holland,
and to the countries which lie round the Baltic
and Mediterranean feas. But, that part of the
capital of Great Britain which brings thofe
eighty-two thoufand hogfheads to Great Britain,
which re-exports them from thence to thofe
other countries, and which brings back from
thofe other countries to Great Britain either
goods or money in return, is employed in a
round-about foreign trade of confumption; and
is neceffarily forced into this employment in
order to difpofe of this great furplus. If we would
compute in how many years the whole of this
capital is likely to come back to Great Britain,
we muft add to the diftance of the American
returns that of the returns from thofe other
countries. If, in the direct foreign trade of
confumption which we carry on with America,
the whole capital employed frequently does not
come back in lefs than three or four years; the
whole capital employed in this round-about one
is not likely to come back in lefs than four or
five. If the one can keep in conftant employment but a third or a fourth part of the domeftic
induftry which could be maintained by a
capital returned once in the year, the other can
keep in conftant employment but a fourth or a
fifth part of that induftry. At fome of the out-
ports a credit is commonly given to thofe
foreign correfpondents to whom they export

their

BOOK IV. their tobacco. At the port of London, indeed, it is commonly fold for ready money. The rule is, *Weigh and Pay.* At the port of London, therefore, the final returns of the whole round-about trade are more diftant than the returns from America by the time only which the goods may lie unfold in the warehoufe; where, however, they may fometimes lie long enough. But, had not the colonies been confined to the market of Great Britain for the fale of their tobacco, very little more of it would probably have come to us than what was neceffary for the home confumption. The goods which Great Britain purchafes at prefent for her own confumption with the great furplus of tobacco which fhe exports to other countries, fhe would, in this cafe, probably have purchafed with the immediate produce of her own induftry, or with fome part of her own manufactures. That produce, thofe manufactures, inftead of being almoft entirely fuited to one great market, as at prefent, would probably have been fitted to a great number of fmaller markets. Inftead of one great round-about foreign trade of confumption, Great Britain would probably have carried on a great number of fmall direct foreign trades of the fame kind. On account of the frequency of the returns, a part, and probably but a fmall part; perhaps not above a third or a fourth, of the capital which at prefent carries on this great round-about trade, might have been fufficient to carry on all thofe fmall direct ones, might have kept in conftant employment an equal quantity of Britifh induftry,

and

OF COLONIES.

423

and have equally supported the annual produce of the land and labour of Great Britain. All the purposes of this trade being, in this manner, answered by a much smaller capital, there would have been a large spare capital to apply to other purposes; to improve the lands, to increase the manufactures, and to extend the commerce of Great Britain; to come into competition at least with the other British capitals employed in all those different ways, to reduce the rate of profit in them all, and thereby to give to Great Britain, in all of them, a superiority over other countries still greater than what she at present enjoys.

The monopoly of the colony trade too has forced some part of the capital of Great Britain from all foreign trade of consumption to a carrying trade; and, consequently, from supporting more or less the industry of Great Britain, to be employed altogether in supporting partly that of the colonies, and partly that of some other countries.

The goods, for example, which are annually purchased with the great surplus of eighty-two thousand hogsheads of tobacco annually re-exported from Great Britain, are not all consumed in Great Britain. Part of them, linen from Germany and Holland, for example, is returned to the colonies for their particular consumption. But, that part of the capital of Great Britain which buys the tobacco with which this linen is afterwards bought, is necessarily withdrawn from supporting the industry of Great

CHAP.
VII.

E E 4

Britain,

424

OF COLONIES.

BOOK IV.

Britain, to be employed altogether in supporting, partly that of the colonies, and partly that of the particular countries who pay for this tobacco with the produce of their own induftry.

The monopoly of the colony trade befides, by forcing towards it a much greater proportion of the capital of Great Britain than what would naturally have gone to it, feems to have broken altogether that natural balance which would otherwife have taken place among all the different branches of Britifh induftry. The induftry of Great Britain, inftead of being accommodated to a great number of fmall markets, has been principally fuited to one great market. Her commerce, inftead of running in a great number of fmall channels, has been taught to run principally in one great channel. But the whole fyftem of her induftry and commerce has thereby been rendered lefs fecure; the whole ftate of her body politic lefs heathful, than it otherwife would have been. In her prefent condition, Great Britain refembles one of thofe unwholefome bodies in which fome of the vital parts are overgrown, and which, upon that account, are liable to many dangerous diforders fcarce incident to thofe in which all the parts are more properly proportioned. A fmall ftqp in that great blood-veffel, which has been artificially fwelled beyond its natural dimenfions, and through which an unnatural proportion of the induftry and commerce of the country has been forced to circulate, is very likely to bring on the

the moſt dangerous diforders upon the whole body politic. The expectation of a rupture with the colonies, accordingly, has ſtruck the people of Great Britain with more terror than they ever felt for a Spaniſh armada, or a French invaſion. It was this terror, whether well or ill grounded, which rendered the repeal of the ſtamp act, among the merchants at leaſt, a popular meaſure. In the total excluſion from the colony market, was it to laſt only for a few years, the greater part of our merchants uſed to fancy that they foreſaw an entire ſtop to their trade; the greater part of our maſter manufacturers, the entire ruin of their buſineſs; and the greater part of our workmen, an end of their employment. A rupture with any of our neighbours upon the continent, though likely too to occaſion ſome ſtop or interruption in the employments of ſome of all theſe different orders of people, is foreſeen, however, without any ſuch general emotion. The blood, of which the circulation is ſtopt in ſome of the ſmaller veſſels, eaſily diſgorges itſelf into the greater, without occaſioning any dangerous diforder; but, when it is ſtopt in any of the greater veſſels, convulſions, apoplexy, or death, are the immediate and unavoidable conſequences. If but one of thoſe overgrown manufactures, which by means either of bounties or of the monopoly of the home and colony markets, have been artificially raiſed up to an unnatural height, finds ſome ſmall ſtop or interruption in its employment, it frequently occaſions a mutiny and diforder alarming to government,

BOOK IV.

government, and embarraffing even to the deliberations of the legiflature. How great, therefore, would be the diforder and confufion, it was thought, which muft neceffarily be occafioned by a fudden and entire ftop in the employment of fo great a proportion of our principal manufacturers?

Some moderate and gradual relaxation of the laws which give to Great Britain the exclufive trade to the colonies, till it is rendered in a great meafure free, feems to be the only expedient which can, in all future times, deliver her from this danger, which can enable her or even force her to withdraw fome part of her capital from this overgrown employment, and to turn it, though with lefs profit, towards other employments; and which, by gradually diminifhing one branch of her induftry and gradually increafing all the reft, can by degrees reftore all the different branches of it to that natural, healthful, and proper proportion which perfect liberty neceffarily eftablifhes, and which perfect liberty can alone preferve. To open the colony trade all at once to all nations, might not only occafion fome tranfitory inconveniency, but a great permanent lofs to the greater part of thofe whofe induftry or capital is at prefent engaged in it. The fudden lofs of the employment even of the fhips which import the eighty-two thoufand hogfheads of tobacco, which are over and above the confumption of Great Britain, might alone be felt very fenfibly. Such are the unfortunate effects of all the regulations of the mercantile fyftem!

OF COLONIES.

427

fyftem! They not only introduce very dangerous diforders into the ftate of the body politic, but diforders which it is often difficult to remedy, without occafioning, for a time at leaft, ftill greater diforders. In what manner, therefore, the colony trade ought gradually to be opened; what are the reftraints which ought firft, and what are thofe which ought laft to be taken away; or in what manner the natural fyftem of perfect liberty and juftice ought gradually to be reftored, we muft leave to the wifdom of future ftatefmen and legiflators to determine.

CHAP. VII.

Five different events, unforefeen and unthought of, have very fortunately concurred to hinder Great Britain from feeling, fo fenfibly as it was generally expected fhe would, the total exclufion which has now taken place for more than a year (from the firft of December, 1774) from a very important branch of the colony trade, that of the twelve affociated provinces of North America. Firft, thofe colonies, in preparing themfelves for their non-importation agreement, drained Great Britain completely of all the commodities which were fit for their market: fecondly, the extraordinary demand of the Spanifh Flota has, this year, drained Germany and the North of many commodities, linen in particular, which ufed to come into competition, even in the Britifh market, with the manufactures of Great Britain: thirdly, the peace between Ruffia and Turkey has occafioned an extraordinary demand from the Turkey market, which, during the diftrefs of the country, and

while

BOOK while a Ruffian fleet was cruizing in the Archi-
IV. pelago, had been very poorly fupplied: fourthly,
the demand of the North of Europe for the manufactures of Great Britain, has been increafing
from year to year for fome time paft: and,
fifthly, the late partition and confequential
pacification of Poland, by opening the market
of that great country, have this year added an extraordinary demand from thence to the increafing demand of the North. Thefe events are all,
except the fourth, in their nature tranfitory and
accidental, and the exclufion from fo important
a branch of the colony trade, if unfortunately it
fhould continue much longer, may ftill occafion
fome degree of diftrefs. This diftrefs, however,
as it will come on gradually, will be felt much
lefs feverely than if it had come on all at once;
and, in the mean time, the induftry and capital
of the country may find a new employment and
direction, fo as to prevent this diftrefs from ever
rifing to any confiderable height.

The monopoly of the colony trade, therefore,
fo far as it has turned towards that trade a greater
proportion of the capital of Great Britain than
what would otherwife have gone to it, has in all
cafes turned it, from a foreign trade of confumption with a neighbouring, into one with a
more diftant country; in many cafes, from a
direct foreign trade of confumption, into a
round-about one; and in fome cafes, from all
foreign trade of confumption, into a carrying
trade. It has in all cafes, therefore, turned it,
from a direction in which it would have maintained

OF COLONIES.

tained a greater quantity of productive labour, into one, in which it can maintain a much smaller quantity. By suiting, besides, to one particular market only, so great a part of the industry and commerce of Great Britain, it has rendered the whole state of that industry and commerce more precarious and less secure, than if their produce had been accommodated to a greater variety of markets.

We muft carefully diftinguish between the effects of the colony trade and those of the monopoly of that trade. The former are always and necessarily beneficial; the latter always and necessarily hurtful. But the former are so beneficial, that the colony trade, though subject to a monopoly, and notwithstanding the hurtful effects of that monopoly, is still upon the whole beneficial, and greatly beneficial; though a good deal less so than it otherwise would be.

The effect of the colony trade in its natural and free state, is to open a great, though distant market for such parts of the produce of British industry as may exceed the demand of the markets nearer home, of those of Europe, and of the countries which lie round the Mediterranean sea. In its natural and free state, the colony trade, without drawing from those markets any part of the produce which had ever been sent to them, encourages Great Britain to increase the surplus continually, by continually presenting new equivalents to be exchanged for it. In its natural and free state, the colony trade tends to increase the quantity of productive labour in Great Britain,

CHAP.
VII.

BOOK IV.

Britain, but without altering in any refpect the direction of that which had been employed there before. In the natural and free ftate of the colony trade, the competition of all other nations would hinder the rate of profit from rifing above the common level either in the new market, or in the new employment. The new market, without drawing any thing from the old one, would create, if one may fay fo, a new produce for its own fupply; and that new produce would conftitute a new capital for carrying on the new employment, which in the fame manner would draw nothing from the old one.

The monopoly of the colony trade, on the contrary, by excluding the competition of other nations, and thereby raifing the rate of profit both in the new market and in the new employment, draws produce from the old market and capital from the old employment. To augment our fhare of the colony trade beyond what it other-wife would be, is the avowed purpofe of the monopoly. If our fhare of that trade were to be no greater with, than it would have been without the monopoly, there could have been no reafon for eftablifhing the monopoly. But whatever forces into a branch of trade of which the returns are flower and more diftant than thofe of the greater part of other trades, a greater proportion of the capital of any country, than what of its own accord would go to that branch, neceffarily renders the whole quantity of pro-ductive labour annually maintained there, the whole annual produce of the land and labour of that

OF COLONIES. 431

that country, lefs than they otherwife would be. CHAP.
It keeps down the revenue of the inhabitants of VII.
that country, below what it would naturally rife
to, and thereby diminifhes their power of accumulation. It not only hinders, at all times,
their capital from maintaining fo great a quantity of productive labour as it would otherwife
maintain, but it hinders it from increafing fo
faft as it would otherwife increafe, and confequently from maintaining a ftill greater quantity
of productive labour.

The natural good effects of the colony trade,
however, more than counterbalance to Great
Britain the bad effects of the monopoly, fo that,
monopoly and altogether, that trade, even as it
is carried on at prefent, is not only advantageous,
but greatly advantageous. The new market and
the new employment which are opened by the
colony trade, are of much greater extent than
that portion of the old market and of the old
employment which is loft by the monopoly.
The new produce and the new capital which has
been created, if one may fay fo, by the colony
trade, maintain in Great Britain a greater quantity of productive labour, than what can have
been thrown out of employment by the revulfion
of capital from other trades of which the returns
are more frequent. If the colony trade, however, even as it is carried on at prefent, is advantageous to Great Britain, it is not by means of
the monopoly, but in fpite of the monopoly.

It is rather for the manufactured than for the
rude produce of Europe, that the colony trade

4

opens

BOOK IV. opens a new market. Agriculture is the proper bufinefs of all new colonies; a bufinefs which the cheapnefs of land renders more advantageous than any other. They abound, therefore, in the rude produce of land, and inftead of importing it from other countries, they have generally a large furplus to export. In new colonies, agriculture either draws hands from all other employments, or keeps them from going to any other employment. There are few hands to fpare for the neceffary, and none for the ornamental manufactures. The greater part of the manufactures of both kinds, they find it cheaper to purchafe of other countries than to make for themfelves. It is chiefly by encouraging the manufactures of Europe, that the colony trade indirectly encourages its agriculture. The manufacturers of Europe, to whom that trade gives employment, conftitute a new market for the produce of the land; and the moft advantageous of all markets; the home market for the corn and cattle, for the bread and butcher's-meat of Europe; is thus greatly extended by means of the trade to America.

But that the monopoly of the trade of populous and thriving colonies is not alone fufficient to eftablifh, or even to maintain manufactures in any country, the examples of Spain and Portugal fufficiently demonftrate. Spain and Portugal were manufacturing countries before they had any confiderable colonies. Since they had the richeft and moft fertile in the world, they have both ceafed to be fo.

In

OF COLONIES.

In Spain and Portugal, the bad effects of the monopoly, aggravated by other caufes, have, perhaps, nearly overbalanced the natural good effects of the colony trade. Thefe caufes feem to be, other monopolies of different kinds; the degradation of the value of gold and filver below what it is in moft other countries; the exclufion from foreign markets by improper taxes upon exportation, and the narrowing of the home market, by ftill more improper taxes upon the tranfportation of goods from one part of the country to another; but above all, that irregular and partial adminiftration of juftice, which often protects the rich and powerful debtor from the purfuit of his injured creditor, and which makes the induftrious part of the nation afraid to prepare goods for the confumption of thofe haughty and great men, to whom they dare not refufe to fell upon credit, and from whom they are altogether uncertain of repayment.

In England, on the contrary, the natural good effects of the colony trade, affifted by other caufes, have in a great meafure conquered the bad effects of the monopoly. Thefe caufes feem to be, the general liberty of trade, which, notwithftanding fome reftraints, is at leaft equal, perhaps fuperior, to what it is in any other country; the liberty of exporting, duty free, almoft all forts of goods which are the produce of domeftic induftry, to almoft any foreign country; and what, perhaps, is of ftill greater importance, the unbounded liberty of tranfporting them from any one part of our own country

CHAP.
VII.

VOL. III.   F F   to

434   OF COLONIES.

BOOK
IV.
to any other, without being obliged to give any
account to any public office, without being liable
to queſtion or examination of any kind; but
above all, that equal and impartial adminiſtra-
tion of juſtice which renders the rights of the
meaneſt Britiſh ſubject reſpectable to the
greateſt, and which, by ſecuring to every man
the fruits of his own induſtry, gives the greateſt
and moſt effectual encouragement to every ſort
induſtry.

If the manufactures of Great Britain, however, have been advanced, as they certainly
have, by the colony trade, it has not been by
means of the monopoly of that trade, but in
ſpite of the monopoly. The effect of the monopoly has been, not to augment the quantity, but
to alter the quality and ſhape of a part of the
manufactures of Great Britain, and to accommodate to a market, from which the returns are
ſlow and diſtant, what would otherwiſe have been
accommodated to one from which the returns
are frequent and near. Its effect has conſequently been to turn a part of the capital of
Great Britain from an employment in which it
would have maintained a greater quantity of
manufacturing induſtry, to one in which it
maintains a much ſmaller, and thereby to diminiſh, inſtead of increaſing, the whole quantity
of manufacturing induſtry maintained in Great
Britain.

The monopoly of the colony trade, therefore,
like all the other mean and malignant expedients
of the mercantile ſyſtem, depreſſes the induſtry
of

OF COLONIES.

of all other countries, but chiefly that of the colonies, without in the leaft increafing, but on the contrary diminifhing, that of the country in whofe favour it is eftablifhed.

The monopoly hinders the capital of that country, whatever may at any particular time be the extent of that capital, from maintaining fo great a quantity of productive labour as it would otherwife maintain, and from affording fo great a revenue to the induftrious inhabitants as it would otherwife afford. But as capital can be increafed only by favings from revenue, the monopoly, by hindering it from affording fo great a revenue as it would otherwife afford, neceffarily hinders it from increafing fo faft as it would otherwife increafe, and confequently from main-taining a ftill greater quantity of productive labour, and affording a ftill greater revenue to the induftrious inhabitants of that country. One great original fource of revenue, therefore, the wages of labour, the monopoly muft neceffarily have rendered at all times lefs abundant than it otherwife would have been.

By raifing the rate of mercantile profit, the monopoly difcourages the improvement of land. The profit of improvement depends upon the difference between what the land actually pro-duces, and what, by the application of a certain capital, it can be made to produce. If this difference affords a greater profit than what can be drawn from an equal capital in any mercantile employment, the improvement of land will draw capital from all mercantile employments. If

F F 2

the

OF COLONIES.

BOOK IV.

the profit is lefs, mercantile employments will draw capital from the improvement of land. Whatever therefore raifes the rate of mercantile profit, either leffens the fuperiority or increafes the inferiority of the profit of improvement; and in the one cafe hinders capital from going to improvement, and in the other draws capital from it. But by difcouraging improvement, the monopoly neceffarily retards the natural increafe of another great original fource of revenue, the rent of land. By raifing the rate of profit too, the monopoly neceffarily keeps up the market rate of intereft higher than it otherwife would be. But the price of land in proportion to the rent which it affords, the number of years purchafe which is commonly paid for it, neceffarily falls as the rate of intereft rifes, and rifes as the rate of intereft falls. The monopoly, therefore, hurts the intereft of the landlord two different ways, by retarding the natural increafe, firft, of his rent, and fecondly, of the price which he would get for his land in proportion to the rent which it affords.

The monopoly, indeed, raifes the rate of mercantile profit, and thereby augments fomewhat the gain of our merchants. But as it obftructs the natural increafe of capital, it tends rather to diminifh than to increafe the fum total of the revenue which the inhabitants of the country derive from the profits of ftock; a fmall profit upon a great capital generally affording a greater revenue than a great profit upon a fmall one. The monopoly raifes the rate of profit, but it

hinders

OF COLONIES. 437

hinders the fum of profit from rifing fo high as it
otherwife would do.

All the original fources of revenue, the wages
of labour, the rent of land, and the profits of
ftock, the monopoly renders much lefs abundant,
than they otherwife would be. To promote the
little intereft of one little order of men in one
country, it hurts the intereft of all other orders
of men in that country, and of all men in all
other countries.

It is folely by raifing the ordinary rate of profit
that the monopoly either has proved or could
prove advantageous to any one particular order
of men. But befides all the bad effects to the
country in general, which have already been
mentioned as neceffarily refulting from a high
rate of profit; there is one more fatal, perhaps,
than all thefe put together, but which, if we may
judge from experience, is infeparably connected
with it. The high rate of profit feems every
where to deftroy that parfimony which in other
circumftances is natural to the character of the
merchant. When profits are high, that fober
virtue feems to be fuperfluous, and expenfive
luxury to fuit better the affluence of his fituation.
But the owners of the great mercantile capitals
are neceffarily the leaders and conductors of the
whole induftry of every nation, and their example
has a much greater influence upon the manners
of the whole induftrious part of it than that of
any other order of men, If his employer is attentive and parfimonious, the workman is very
likely to be fo too; but if the mafter is diffolute

F F 3   and

CHAP.
VII.

438 OF COLONIES.

BOOK IV. and diforderly, the fervant who-fhapes his work according to the pattern which his mafter prefcribes to him, will fhape his life too according to the example which he fets him. Accumulation is thus prevented in the hands of all thofe who are naturally the moft difpofed to accumulate; and the funds deftined for the maintenance of productive labour receive no augmentation from the revenue of thofe who ought naturally to augment them the moft. The capital of the country, inftead of increafing, gradually dwindles away, and the quantity of productive labour maintained in it grows every day lefs and lefs. Have the exorbitant profits of the merchants of Cadiz and Lifbon augmented the capital of Spain and Portugal? Have they alleviated the poverty, have they promoted the induftry of thofe two beggarly countries? Such has been the tone of mercantile expence in thofe two trading cities, than thofe exorbitant profits, far from augmenting the general capital of the country, feem fcarce to have been fufficient to keep up the capitals upon which they were made. Foreign capitals are every day intruding themfelves, if I may fay fo, more and more into the trade of Cadiz and Lifbon. It is to expel thofe foreign capitals from a trade which their own grows every-day more and more infufficient for carrying on, that the Spaniards and Portuguefe endeavour every day to ftraiten more and more the galling bands of their abfurd monopoly. Compare the mercantile manners of Cadiz and Lifbon with thofe of Amfterdam, and you will be fenfi-

ble

OF COLONIES.   **439**

ble how differently the conduct and character of C H A P.
merchants are affected by the high and by the   VII.
low profits of stock.   The merchants of London,
indeed, have not yet generally become such magnificent lords as thofe of Cadiz and Lifbon;
but neither are they in general fuch attentive
and parfimonious burghers as thofe of Amfterdam.
They are fuppofed, however, many of them, to
be a good deal richer than the greater part of the
former, and not quite fo rich as many of the latter. But the rate of their profit is commonly much
lower than that of the former, and a good deal
higher than that of the latter.   Light come light
go, fays the proverb; and the ordinary tone of expence feems every where to be regulated, not fo
much according to the real ability of fpending, as
to the fuppofed facility of getting money to fpend.

It is thus that the fingle advantage which the
monopoly procures to a fingle order of men, is in
many different ways hurtful to the general intereft of the country.

To found a great empire for the fole purpofe
of raifing up a people of cuftomers, may at firft
fight appear a project fit only for a nation of
fhopkeepers.   It is, however, a project altogether unfit for a nation of fhopkeepers; but
extremely fit for a nation whofe government is
influenced by fhopkeepers.   Such ftatefmen, and
fuch ftatefmen only, are capable of fancying
that they will find fome advantage in employing
the blood and treafure of their fellow-citizens,
to found and maintain fuch an empire.   Say
to a fhopkeeper, Buy me a good eftate, and I
fhall always buy my clothes at your fhop, even

F F 4   though

OF COLONIES.

BOOK IV.

though I should pay somewhat dearer than what I can have them for at other shops; and you will not find him very forward to embrace your proposal. But should any other person buy you such an estate, the shopkeeper would be much obliged to your benefactor if he would enjoin you to buy all your clothes at his shop. England purchased for some of her subjects, who found themselves uneasy at home, a great estate in a distant country. The price, indeed, was very small, and instead of thirty years purchase, the ordinary price of land in the present times, it amounted to little more than the expence of the different equipments which made the first discovery, reconnoitred the coast, and took a fictitious possession of the country. The land was good and of great extent, and the cultivators having plenty of good ground to work upon, and being for some time at liberty to sell their produce where they pleased, became in the course of little more than thirty or forty years (between 1620 and 1660) so numerous and thriving a people, that the shopkeepers and other traders of England wished to secure to themselves the monopoly of their custom. Without pretending, therefore, that they had paid any part, either of the original purchase-money, or of the subsequent expence of improvement, they petitioned the parliament that the cultivators of America might for the future be confined to their shop; first, for buying all the goods which they wanted from Europe; and, secondly, for selling all such parts of their own produce as those traders might find it convenient to buy. For they

OF COLONIES. 441

they did not find it convenient to buy every part C H A P. of it. Some parts of it imported into England VII. might have interfered with fome of the trades which they themfelves carried on at home. Thofe particular parts of it, therefore, they were willing that the colonifts fhould fell where they could; the farther off the better; and upon that account propofed that their market fhould be confined to the countries fouth of Cape Finifterre. A claufe in the famous act of navigation eftablifhed this truly fhopkeeper propofal into a law.

The maintenance of this monopoly has hitherto been the principal, or more properly perhaps the fole end and purpofe of the dominion which Great Britain affumes over her colonies. In the exclufive trade, it is fuppofed, confifts the great advantages of provinces, which have never yet afforded either revenue or military force for the fupport of the civil government, or the defence of the mother country. The monopoly is the principal badge of their dependency, and it is the fole fruit which has hitherto been gathered from that dependency. Whatever expence Great Britain has hitherto laid out in maintaining this dependency, has really been laid out in order to fupport this monopoly. The expence of the ordinary peace eftablifhment of the colonies amounted, before the commencement of the prefent difturbances, to the pay of twenty regiments of foot; to the expence of the artillery, ftores, and extraordinary provifions with which it was neceffary to fupply them; and to the expence

OF COLONIES.

BOOK
IV.

pence of a very considerable naval force which was constantly kept up, in order to guard, from the smuggling vessels of other nations, the immense coasts of North America, and that of our West Indian Islands. The whole expence of this peace establishment was a charge upon the revenue of Great Britain, and was, at the same time, the smallest part of what the dominion of the colonies has cost the mother country. If we would know the amount of the whole, we must add to the annual expence of this peace establishment the interest of the sums which, in consequence of her considering her colonies as provinces subject to her dominion, Great Britain has upon different occasions laid out upon their defence. We must add to it, in particular, the whole expence of the late war, and a great part of that of the war which preceded it. The late war was altogether a colony quarrel, and the whole expence of it, in whatever part of the world it may have been laid out, whether in Germany or the East Indies, ought justly to be stated to the account of the colonies. It amounted to more than ninety millions sterling, including not only the new debt which was contracted, but the two shillings in the pound additional land tax, and the sums which were every year borrowed from the sinking fund. The Spanish war which began in 1739, was pricipally a colony quarrel. Its principal object was to prevent the search of the colony ships which carried on a contraband trade with the Spanish main. This whole expence is, in reality, a bounty which has

been

OF COLONIES. 443

been given in order to fupport a monopoly. CHAP.
The pretended purpofe of it was to encourage VII.
the manufactures, and to increafe the commerce
of Great Britain. But its real effect has been to
raife the rate of mercantile profit, and to enable
our merchants to turn into a branch of trade, of
which the returns are more flow and diftant than
thofe of the greater part of other trades, a greater
proportion of their capital than they otherwife
would have done; two events which if a bounty
could have prevented, it might perhaps have
been very well worth while to give fuch a bounty.

Under the prefent fyftem of management,
therefore, Great Britain derives nothing but
lofs from the dominion which fhe affumes over
her colonies.

To propofe that Great Britain fhould voluntarily give up all authority over her colonies,
and leave them to elect their own magiftrates,
to enact their own laws, and to make peace and
war as they might think proper, would be to
propofe fuch a meafure as never was, and never
will be adopted, by any nation in the world.
No nation ever voluntarily gave up the dominion of any province, how troublefome foever it
might be to govern it, and how fmall foever the
revenue which it afforded might be in proportion to the expence which it occafioned. Such
facrifices, though they might frequently be agreeable to the intereft, are always mortifying to the
pride of every nation, and what is perhaps of ftill
greater confequence, they are always contrary to
the private intereft of the governing part of it,

3 who

BOOK IV. who would thereby be deprived of the difpofal of many places of truft and profit, of many opportunities of acquiring wealth and diftinction, which the poffeffion of the moft turbulent, and, to the great body of the people, the moft unprofitable province feldom fails to afford. The moft vifionary enthufiaft would fcarce be capable of propofing fuch a meafure, with any ferious hopes at leaft of its ever being adopted. If it was adopted, however, Great Britain would not only be immediately freed from the whole annual expence of the peace eftablifhment of the colonies, but might fettle with them fuch a treaty of commerce as would effectually fecure to her a free trade, more advantageous to the great body of the people, though lefs fo to the merchants, than the monopoly which fhe at prefent enjoys. By thus parting good friends, the natural affection of the colonies to the mother country, which, perhaps, our late diffenfions have well nigh extinguifhed, would quickly revive. It might difpofe them not only to refpect, for whole centuries together, that treaty of commerce which they had concluded with us at parting, but to favour us in war as well as in trade, and, inftead of turbulent and factious fubjects, to become our moft faithful, affectionate, and generous allies; and the fame fort of parental affection on the one fide, and filial refpect on the other, might revive between Great Britain and her colonies, which ufed to fubfift between thofe of ancient Greece and the mother city from which they defcended.

In

In order to render any province advantageous to the empire to which it belongs, it ought to afford, in time of peace, a revenue to the public fufficient not only for defraying the whole expence of its own peace eftablifhment, but for contributing its proportion to the fupport of the general government of the empire. Every province neceffarily contributes, more or lefs, to increafe the expence of that general government. If any particular province, therefore, does not contribute its fhare towards defraying this expence, an unequal burden muft be thrown upon fome other part of the empire. The extraordinary revenue too which every province affords to the public in time of war, ought, from parity of reafon, to bear the fame proportion to the extraordinary revenue of the whole empire which its ordinary revenue does in time of peace. That neither the ordinary nor extraordinary revenue which Great Britain derives from her colonies, bears this proportion to the whole revenue of the Britifh empire, will readily be allowed. The monopoly, it has been fuppofed, indeed, by increafing the private revenue of the people of Great Britain, and thereby enabling them to pay greater taxes, compenfates the deficiency of the public revenue of the colonies. But this monopoly, I have endeavoured to fhow, though a very grievous tax upon the colonies, and though it may increafe the revenue of a particular order of men in Great Britain, diminifhes inftead of increafing that of the great body of the people ; and confequently diminifhes inftead of increafing

446

OF COLONIES.

BOOK IV.

increasing the ability of the great body of the people to pay taxes. The men too whose revenue the monopoly increases, constitute a particular order, which it is both absolutely impossible to tax beyond the proportion of other orders, and extremely impolitic even to attempt to tax beyond that proportion, as I shall endeavour to shew in the following book. No particular resource, therefore, can be drawn from this particular order.

The colonies may be taxed either by their own assemblies, or by the parliament of Great Britain.

That the colony assemblies can ever be so managed as to levy upon their constituents a public revenue sufficient, not only to maintain at all times their own civil and military establishment, but to pay their proper proportion of the expence of the general government of the British empire, seems not very probable. It was a long time before even the parliament of England, though placed immediately under the eye of the Sovereign, could be brought under such a system of management, or could be rendered sufficiently liberal in their grants for supporting the civil and military establishments even of their own country. It was only by distributing among the particular members of parliament, a great part either of the offices, or of the disposal of the offices arising from this civil and military establishment, that such a system of management could be established even with regard to the parliament of England. But the distance of the colony assemblies from the eye of the Sovereign,

their

OF COLONIES. 447

their number, their difperfed fituation, and their various conftitutions, would render it very difficult to manage them in the fame manner, even though the fovereign had the fame means of doing it; and thofe means are wanting. It would be abfolutely impoffible to diftribute among all the leading members of all the colony affemblies fuch a fhare, either of the offices or of the difpofal of the offices arifing from the general government of the Britifh empire, as to difpofe them to give up their popularity at home, and to tax their conftituents for the fupport of that general government, of which almoft the whole emoluments were to be divided among people who were ftrangers to them. The unavoidable ignorance of adminiftration, befides, concerning the relative importance of the different members of thofe different affemblies, the offences which muft frequently be given, the blunders which muft conftantly be committed in attempting to manage them in this manner, feems to render fuch a fyftem of management altogether impracticable with regard to them.

The colony affemblies, befides, cannot be fuppofed the proper judges of what is neceffary for the defence and fupport of the whole empire. The care of that defence and fupport is not entrufted to them. It is not their bufinefs, and they have no regular means of information concerning it. The affembly of a province, like the veftry of a parifh, may judge very properly concerning the affairs of its own particular diftrict; but can have no proper means of judging

concerning

C H A P.
VII.

448   OF COLONIES.

BOOK concerning thofe of the whole empire. It can-
IV. not even judge properly concerning the proportion which its own province bears to the whole
empire; or concerning the relative degree of its
wealth and importance, compared with the other
provinces; becaufe thofe other provinces are not
under the infpection and fuperintendency of the
affembly of a particular province. What is neceffary for the defence and fupport of the whole
empire, and in what proportion each part ought
to contribute, can be judged of only by that
affembly which infpects and fuperintends the
affairs of the whole empire.

It has been propofed, accordingly, that the
colonies fhould be taxed by requifition, the parliament of Great Britain determining the fum
which each colony ought to pay, and the provincial affembly affeffing and levying it in the
way that fuited beft the circumftances of the
province. What concerned the whole empire
would in this way be determined by the affembly
which infpects and fuperintends the affairs of the
whole empire; and the provincial affairs of each
colony might ftill be regulated by its own
affembly. Though the colonies fhould in this
cafe have no reprefentatives in the Britifh parliament, yet, if we may judge by experience, there
is no probability that the parliamentary requifition would be unreafonable. The parliament
of England has not upon any occafion fhown the
fmalleft difpofition to overburden thofe parts of
the empire which are not reprefented in parliament. The iflands of Guernfey and Jerfey,
                                        without

OF COLONIES. 449

without any means of refifting the authority of parliament, are more lightly taxed than any part of Great Britain. Parliament in attempting to exercife its fuppofed right, whether well or ill grounded, of taxing the colonies, has never hitherto demanded of them any thing which even approached to a juft proportion to what was paid by their fellow-fubjects at home. If the contribution of the colonies, befides, was to rife or fall in proportion to the rife or fall of the land tax, parliament could not tax them without taking at the fame time its own conftituents, and the colonies might in this cafe be confidered as virtually reprefented in parliament.

Examples are not wanting of empires in which all the different provinces are not taxed, if I may be allowed the expreffion, in one mafs; but in which the fovereign regulates the fum which each province ought to pay, and in fome provinces affeffes and levies it as he thinks proper; while in others, he leaves it to be affeffed and levied as the refpective ftates of each province fhall determine. In fome provinces of France, the king not only impofes what taxes he thinks proper, but affeffes and levies them in the way he thinks proper. From others he demands a certain fum, but leaves it to the ftates of each province to affefs and levy that fum as they think proper. According to the fcheme of taxing by requifition, the parliament of Great Britain would ftand nearly in the fame fituation towards the colony affemblies, as the King of France does towards the ftates of thofe provinces which

VOL. III. G G

450 OF COLONIES.

BOOK IV.

which ftill enjoy the privilege of having ftates of their own, the provinces of France which are fuppofed to be the beft governed.

But though, according to this fcheme, the colonies could have no juft reafon to fear that their fhare of the public burdens fhould ever exceed the proper proportion to that of their fellow-citizens at home; Great Britain might have juft reafon to fear that it never would amount to that proper proportion. The parliament of Great Britain has not for fome time paft had the fame eftablifhed authority in the colonies, which the French King has in thofe provinces of France which ftill enjoy the privilege of having ftates of their own. The colony affemblies, if they were not very favourably difpofed (and unlefs more fkilfully managed than they ever have been hitherto, they are not very likely to be fo), might ftill find many pretences for evading or rejecting the moft reafonable requifitions of parliament. A French war breaks out, we fhall fuppofe; ten millions muft immediately be raifed, in order to defend the feat of the empire. This fum muft be borrowed upon the credit of fome parliamentary fund mortgaged for paying the intereft. Part of this fund parliament propofes to raife by a tax to be levied in Great Britain, and part of it by a requifition to all the different colony affemblies of America and the Weft indies. Would people readily advance their money upon the credit of a fund, which partly depended upon the good humour of all thofe affemblies, far diftant from the feat

of

OF COLONIES. 451

of the war, and fometimes, perhaps, thinking C H A P.
themfelves not much concerned in the event of VII.
it? Upon fuch a fund no more money would probably be advanced than what the tax to be levied
in Great Britain might be fuppofed to anfwer
for. The whole burden of the debt contracted
on account of the war would in this manner fall,
as it always has done hitherto, upon Great Britain; upon a part of the empire, and not upon
the whole empire. Great Britain is, perhaps,
fince the world began, the only ftate which, as it
has extended its empire, has only increafed its
expence without once augmenting its refources.
Other ftates have generally difburdened themfelves upon their fubject and fubordinate provinces of the moft confiderable part of the expence of defending the empire. Great Britain
has hitherto fuffered her fubject and fubordinate
provinces to difburden themfelves upon her of
almoft this whole expence. In order to put
Great Britain upon a footing of equality with
her own colonies, which the law has hitherto
fuppofed to be fubject and fubordinate, it feems
neceffary, upon the fcheme of taxing them by
parliamentary requifition, that parliament fhould
have fome means of rendering its requifitions immediately effectual, in cafe the colony affemblies
fhould attempt to evade or reject them; and
what thofe means are, it is not very eafy to conceive, and it has not yet been explained.

Should the parliament of Great Britain, at
the fame time, be ever fully eftablifhed in the
right of taxing the colonies, even independent of

G G 2   the

452 OF COLONIES.

BOOK
IV.
the confent of their own affemblies, the importance of thofe affemblies would from that
moment be at an end, and with it, that of all the
leading men of Britifh America. Men defire to
have fome fhare in the management of public
affairs chiefly on account of the importance
which it gives them. Upon the power which the
greater part of the leading men, the natural arif-
tocracy of every country, have of preferving or
defending their refpective importance, depends
the ftability and duration of every fyftem of free
government. In the attacks which thofe leading men are continually making upon the importance of one another, and in the defence of
their own, conflfts the whole play of domeftic
faction and ambition. The leading men of
America, like thofe of all other countries, defire
to preferve their own importance. They feel, or
imagine, that if their affemblies, which they are
fond of calling parliaments, and of confidering
as equal in authority to the parliament of Great
Britain, fhould be fo far degraded as to become
the humble minifters and executive officers of
that parliament, the greater part of their own
importance would be at an end. They have re-
jected, therefore, the propofal of being taxed by
parliamentary requifition, and like other ambitious and high-fpirited men, have rather chofen
to draw the fword in defence of their own importance.

Towards the declenfion of the Roman republic, the allies of Rome, who had borne the
principal burden of defending the ftate and extending

tending the empire, demanded to be admitted to all the privileges of Roman citizens. Upon being refufed, the focial war broke out. During the courfe of that war Rome granted thofe privileges to the greater part of them, one by one, and in proportion as they detached themfelves from the general confederacy. The parliament of Great Britain infifts upon taxing the colonies; and they refufe to be taxed by a parliament in which they are not reprefented. If to each colony, which fhould detach itfelf from the general confederacy, Great Britain fhould allow fuch a number of reprefentatives as fuited the proportion of what it contributed to the public revenue of the empire, in confequence of its being fubjected to the fame taxes, and in compenfation admitted to the fame freedom of trade with its fellow-fubjects at home; the number of its reprefentatives to be augmented as the proportion of its contribution might afterwards augment; a new method of acquiring importance, a new and more dazzling object of ambition would be prefented to the leading men of each colony. Inftead of piddling for the little prizes which are to be found in what may be called the paltry raffle of colony faction; they might then hope, from the prefumption which men naturally have in their own ability and good fortune, to draw fome of the great prizes which fometimes come from the wheel of the great ftate lottery of Britifh politics. Unlefs this or fome other method is fallen upon, and there feems to be none more obvious than this, of

preferving

454 OF COLONIES.

BOOK IV.

preferving the importance and of gratifying the ambition of the leading men of America, it is not very probable that they will ever voluntarily fubmit to us ; and we ought to confider that the blood which muft be fhed in forcing them to do fo, is, every drop of it, the blood either of thofe who are, or of thofe whom we wifh to have for our fellow-citizens. They are very weak who flatter themfelves that, in the ftate to which things have come, our colonies will be eafily conquered by force alone. The perfons who now govern the refolutions of what they call their continental congrefs, feel in themfelves at this moment a degree of importance which, perhaps, the greateft fubjects in Europe fcarce feel. From fhop-keepers, tradefmen, and attornies, they are become ftatefmen and legiflators, and are employed in contriving a new form of government for an extenfive empire, which, they flatter themfelves, will become, and which, indeed, feems very likely to become, one of the greateft and moft formidable that ever was in the world. Five hundred different people, perhaps, who in different ways act immediately under the continental congrefs; and five hundred thoufand, perhaps, who act under thofe five hundred, all feel in the fame manner a proportionable rife in their own importance. Almoft every individual of the governing party in America, fills, at prefent in his own fancy, a ftation fuperior, not only to what he had ever filled before, but to what he had ever expected to fill; and unlefs fome new object of ambition is prefented either to him or

to

to his leaders, if he has the ordinary fpirit of a man, he will die in defence of that ftation.

It is a remark of the Prefident Henaut, that we now read with pleafure the account of many little tranfactions of the Ligue, which when they happened were not perhaps confidered as very important pieces of news. But every man then, fays he, fancied himfelf of fome importance; and the innumerable memoirs which have come down to us from thofe times were, the greater part of them, written by people who took pleafure in recording and magnifying events in which, they flattered themfelves, they had been confiderable actors. How obftinately the city of Paris upon that occafion defended itfelf, what a dreadful famine it fupported rather than fubmit to the beft and afterwards to the moft beloved of all the French Kings, is well known. The greater part of the citizens, or thofe who governed the greater part of them, fought in defence of their own importance, which they forefaw was to be at an end whenever the ancient government fhould be re-eftablifhed. Our colonies, unlefs they can be induced to confent to a union, are very likely to defend themfelves againft the beft of all mother countries, as obftinately as the city of Paris did againft one of the beft of Kings.

The idea of reprefentation was unknown in ancient times. When the people of one ftate were admitted to the right of citizenfhip in another, they had no other means of exercifing that right but by coming in a body to vote. and deliberate

456 OF COLONIES.

BOOK IV.

deliberate with the people of that other ftate. The admiffion of the greater part of the inhabitants of Italy to the privileges of Roman citizens, completely ruined the Roman republic. It was no longer poffible to diftinguifh between who was and who was not a Roman citizen. No tribe could know its own members. A rabble of any kind could be introduced into the affemblies of the people, could drive out the real citizens, and decide upon the affairs of the republic as if they themfelves had been fuch. But though America were to fend fifty or fixty new reprefentatives to parliament, the door-keeper of the Houfe of Commons could not find any great difficulty in diftinguifhing between who was and who was not a member. Though the Roman conftitution, therefore, was neceffarily ruined by the union of Rome with the allied ftates of Italy, there is not the leaft probability that the Britifh conftitution would be hurt by the union of Great Britain with her colonies. That conftitution, on the contrary, would be completed by it, and feems to be imperfect without it. The affembly which deliberates and decides concerning the affairs of every part of the empire, in order to be properly informed, ought certainly to have reprefentatives from every part of it. That this union, however, could be eafily effectuated, or that difficulties and great difficulties might not occur in the execution, I do not pretend. I have yet heard of none, however, which appear infurmountable. The principal perhaps arife, not from the nature of things, but from the prejudices and opinions

of

OF COLONIES. 457

of the people both on this and on the other fide CHAP.
of the Atlantic. VII.

We, on this fide the water, are afraid left the
multitude of American reprefentatives fhould
overturn the balance of the conftitution, and increafe too much either the influence of the crown
on the one hand, or the force of the democracy
on the other. But if the number of American
reprefentatives were to be in proportion to the
produce of American taxation, the number of
people to be managed would increafe exactly in
proportion to the means of managing them;
and the means of managing, to the number of
people to be managed. The monarchical and
democratical parts of the conftitution would,
after the union, ftand exactly in the fame degree
of relative force with regard to one another as
they had done before.

The people on the other fide of the water are
afraid left their diftance from the feat of government might expofe them to many oppreffions.
But their reprefentatives in parliament, of which
the number ought from the firft to be confiderable, would eafily be able to protect them from
all oppreffion. The diftance could not much
weaken the dependency of the reprefentative
upon the conftituent, and the former would ftill
feel that he owed his feat in parliament, and all
the confequence which he derived from it, to the
good-will of the latter. It would be the intereft
of the former, therefore, to cultivate that good-
will by complaining, with all the authority of a
member of the legiflature, of every outrage which
                                              any

458   OF COLONIES.

BOOK any civil or military officer might be guilty of in
IV.   thofe remote parts of the empire.   The diftance
of America from the feat of government, befides,
the natives of that country might flatter themfelves, with fome appearance of reafon too,
would not be of very long continuance.   Such
has hitherto been the rapid progrefs of that
country in wealth, population and improvement,
that in the courfe of little more than a century,
perhaps, the produce of American might exceed
that of Britifh taxation.   The feat of the empire
would then naturally remove itfelf to that part
of the empire which contributed moft to the
general defence and fupport of the whole.

The difcovery of America, and that of a
paffage to the Eaft Indies by the Cape of Good
Hope, are the two greateft and moft important
events recorded in the hiftory of mankind.
Their confequences have already been very
great : but, in the fhort period of between two
and three centuries which has elapfed fince thefe
difcoveries were made, it is impoffible that the
whole extent of their confequences can have been
feen.   What benefits, or what misfortunes to
mankind may hereafter refult from thofe great
events, no human wifdom can forefee.   By
uniting, in fome meafure, the moft diftant parts
of the world, by enabling them to relieve one
another's wants, to encreafe one another's enjoyments, and to encourage one another's induftry,
their general tendency would feem to be beneficial.   To the natives, however, both of the
Eaft and Weft Indies, all the commercial benefits

OF COLONIES. 459

fits which can have refulted from thofe events CHAP. VII.
have been funk and loft in the dreadful misfortunes which they have occafioned. Thefe mif-
fortunes, however, feem to have arifen rather
from accident than from any thing in the nature
of thofe events themfelves. At the particular
time when thefe difcoveries were made, the
fuperiority of force happened to be fo great on
the fide of the Europeans, that they were enabled
to commit with impunity every fort of injuftice
in thofe remote countries. Hereafter, perhaps,
the natives of thofe countries may grow ftronger,
or thofe of Europe may grow weaker, and the
inhabitants of all the different quarters of the
world may arrive at that equality of courage and
force which, by infpiring mutual fear, can alone
overawe the injuftice of independent nations into
fome fort of refpect for the rights of one another.
But nothing feems more likely to eftablifh this
equality of force than that mutual communication
of knowledge and of all forts of improvements
which an extenfive commerce from all countries
to all countries naturally, or rather neceffarily,
carries along with it.

In the mean time one of the principal effects
of thofe difcoveries has been to raife the mercantile fyftem to a degree of fplendour and glory
which it could never otherwife have attained to.
It is the object of that fyftem to enrich a great
nation rather by trade and manufactures than by
the improvement and cultivation of land, rather
by the induftry of the towns than by that of the
country. But, in confequence of thofe difcoveries,

OF COLONIES.

BOOK IV.

coveries, the commercial towns of Europe, in-ftead of being the manufacturers and carriers for but a very fmall part of the world (that part of Europe which is wafhed by the Atlantic ocean, and the countries which lie round the Baltic and Mediterranean feas), have now become the manufacturers for the numerous and thriving cultivators of America, and the carriers, and in fome refpects the manufacturers too, for almoft all the different nations of Afia, Africa, and America. Two new worlds have been opened to their induftry, each of them much greater and more extenfive than the old one, and the market of one of them growing ftill greater and greater every day.

The countries which poffefs the colonies of America, and which trade directly to the Eaft Indies, enjoy, indeed, the whole fhew and fplen-dour of this great commerce. Other countries, however, notwithftanding all the invidious re-ftraints by which it is meant to exclude them, frequently enjoy a greater fhare of the real benefit of it. The colonies of Spain and Portu-gal, for example, give more real encouragement to the induftry of other countries than to that of Spain and Portugal. In the fingle article of linen alone the confumption of thofe colonies amounts, it is faid, but I do not pretend to warrant the quantity, to more than three millions fterling a year. But this great confumption is almoft entirely fupplied by France, Flanders, Holland, and Germany. Spain and Portugal furnifh but a fmall part of it. The capital which

OF COLONIES.

which fupplies the colonies with this great quantity of linen is annually diftributed among, and furnifhes a revenue to the inhabitants of thofe other countries. The profits of it only are fpent in Spain and Portugal, where they help to fupport the fumptuous profufion of the merchants of Cadiz and Lifbon.

Even the regulations by which each nation endeavours to fecure to itfelf the exclufive trade of its own colonies, are frequently more hurtful to the countries in favour of which they are eftablifhed than to thofe againft which they are eftablifhed. The unjuft oppreffion of the induftry of other countries falls back, if I may fay fo, upon the heads of the oppreffors, and crufhes their induftry more than it does that of thofe other countries. By thofe regulations, for example, the merchant of Hamburgh muft fend the linen which he deftines for the American market to London, and he muft bring back from thence the tobacco which he deftines for the German market; becaufe he can neither fend the one directly to America, nor bring back the other directly from thence. By this reftraint he is probably obliged to fell the one fomewhat cheaper, and to buy the other fomewhat dearer than he otherwife might have done; and his profits are probably fomewhat abridged by means of it. In this trade, however, between Hamburgh and London, he certainly receives the returns of his capital much more quickly than he could poffibly have done in the direct trade to America, even though we fhould fuppofe, what

462

OF COLONIES.

BOOK IV.

what is by no means the cafe, that the payments of America were as punctual as thofe of London. In the trade, therefore, to which thofe regulations confine the merchant of Hamburgh, his capital can keep in conftant employment a much greater quantity of German induftry than it poffibly could have done in the trade from which he is excluded. Though the one employment, therefore, may to him perhaps be lefs profitable than the other, it cannot be lefs advantageous to his country. It is quite otherwife with the employment into which the monopoly naturally attracts, if I may fay fo, the capital of the London merchant. That employment may, perhaps, be more profitable to him than the greater part of other employments, but, on account of the flownefs of the returns, it cannot be more advantageous to his country.

After all the unjuft attempts, therefore, of every country in Europe to engrofs to itfelf the whole advantage of the trade of its own colonies, no country has yet been able to engrofs to itfelf any thing but the expence of fupporting in time of peace and of defending in time of war the oppreffive authority which it affumes over them. The inconveniencies refulting from the poffeffion of its colonies, every country has engroffed to itfelf completely. The advantages refulting from their trade it has been obliged to fhare with many other countries.

At firft fight, no doubt, the monopoly of the great commerce of America, naturally feems to be an acquifition of the higheft value. To the

undif-

OF COLONIES. 463

undifcerning eye of giddy ambition, it naturally CHAP. prefents itfelf amidft the confufed fcramble of VII. politics and war, as a very dazzling object to fight for. The dazzling fplendour of the object, however, the immenfe greatnefs of the commerce, is the very quality which renders the monopoly of it hurtful, or which makes one employment, in its own nature neceffarily lefs advantageous to the country than the greater part of other employments, abforb a much greater proportion of the capital of the country than what would otherwife have gone to it.

The mercantile ftock of every country, it has been fhewn in the fecond book, naturally feeks, if one may fay fo, the employment moft advantageous to that country. If it is employed in the carrying trade, the country to which it belongs becomes the emporium of the goods of all the countries whofe trade that ftock carries on. But the owner of that ftock neceffarily wifhes to difpofe of as great a part of thofe goods as he can at home. He thereby faves himfelf the trouble, rifk, and expence, of exportation, and he will upon that account be glad to fell them at home, not only for a much fmaller price, but with fomewhat a fmaller profit than he might expect to make by fending them abroad. He naturally, therefore, endeavours as much as he can to turn his carrying trade into a foreign trade of confumption. If his ftock again is employed in a foreign trade of confumption, he will, for the fame reafon, be glad to difpofe of at home as great a part as he can of the home goods, which

he

464   OF COLONIES.

BOOK he collects in order to export to some foreign
IV. market, and he will thus endeavour, as much as
he can, to turn his foreign trade of confumption
into a home trade. The mercantile ftock of
every country naturally courts in this manner
the near, and fhuns the diftant employment;
naturally courts the employment in which the
returns are frequent, and fhuns that in which
they are diftant and flow; naturally courts the
employment in which it can maintain the greateft
quantity of productive labour in the country to
which it belongs, or in which its owner refides,
and fhuns that in which it can maintain there
the fmalleft quantity. It naturally courts the
employment which in ordinary cafes is moft
advantageous, and fhuns that which in ordinary
cafes is leaft advantageous to that country.

But if in any of thofe diftant employments,
which in ordinary cafes are lefs advantageous
to the country, the profit fhould happen to rife
fomewhat higher than what is fufficient to
balance the natural preference which is given to
nearer employments, this fuperiority of profit
will draw ftock from thofe nearer employments,
till the profits of all return to their proper level.
This fuperiority of profit, however, is a proof
that, in the actual circumftances of the fociety,
thofe diftant employments are fomewhat underftocked in proportion to other employments, and
that the ftock of the fociety is not diftributed in
the propereft manner among all the different
employments carried on in it. It is a proof that
fomething is either bought cheaper or fold dearer
than

OF COLONIES.   465

than it ought to be, and that fome particular C H A P.
clafs of citizens is more or lefs oppreffed either ___VII.
by paying more or by getting lefs than what is
fuitable to that equality, which ought to take
place, and which naturally does take place among
all the different claffes of them. Though the
fame capital never will maintain the fame quantity of productive labour in a diftant as in a
near employment, yet a diftant employment may
be as neceffary for the welfare of the fociety as a
near one; the goods which the diftant employment deals in being neceffary, perhaps, for carrying on many of the nearer employments. But
if the profits of thofe who deal in fuch goods are
above their proper level, thofe goods will be fold
dearer than they ought to be, or fomewhat above
their natural price, and all thofe engaged in the
nearer employments will be more or lefs oppreffed by this high price. Their intereft, therefore, in this cafe requires that fome ftock fhould
be withdrawn from thofe nearer employments,
and turned towards that diftant one, in order to
reduce its profits to their proper level, and the
price of the goods which it deals in to their
natural price. In this extraordinary cafe, the
public intereft requires that fome ftock fhould
be withdrawn from thofe employments which
in ordinary cafes are more advantageous, and
turned towards one which in ordinary cafes is
lefs advantageous to the public: and in this
extraordinary cafe, the natural interefts and inclinations of men coincide as exactly with the
public intereft as in all other ordinary cafes,

VOL. III.   H H   and

466   OF COLONIES.

BOOK and lead them to withdraw stock from the near,
IV. and to turn it towards the distant employment.

It is thus that the private interests and passions
of individuals naturally dispose them to turn
their stock towards the employments which in
ordinary cases are most advantageous to the society. But if from this natural preference they
should turn too much of it towards those employments, the fall of profit in them and the
rise of it in all others immediately dispose them
to alter this faulty distribution. Without any
intervention of law, therefore, the private interests and passions of men naturally lead them to
divide and distribute the stock of every society,
among all the different employments carried on
in it, as nearly as possible in the proportion
which is most agreeable to the interest of the
whole society.

All the different regulations of the mercantile system, necessarily derange more or less this
natural and most advantageous distribution of
stock. But those which concern the trade to
America and the East Indies derange it perhaps
more than any other; because the trade to those
two great continents absorbs a greater quantity
of stock than any two other branches of trade.
The regulations, however, by which this derangement is effected in those two different
branches of trade are not altogether the same.
Monopoly is the great engine of both: but it is
a different sort of monopoly. Monopoly of one
kind or another, indeed, seems to be the sole
engine of the mercantile system.

                                                    ; In

OF COLONIES. 467

In the trade to America every nation endeavours to engrofs as much as poffible the whole
market of its own colonies, by fairly excluding
all other nations from any direct trade to them.
During the greater part of the fixteenth century,
the Portuguefe endeavoured to manage the trade
to the Eaft Indies in the fame manner, by
claiming the fole right of failing in the Indian
feas, on account of the merit of having firft
found out the road to them. The Dutch ftill
continue to exclude all other European nations
from any direct trade to their fpice iflands.
Monopolies of this kind are evidently eftablifhed
againft all other European nations, who are
thereby not only excluded from a trade to which
it might be convenient for them to turn fome
part of their ftock, but are obliged to buy the
goods which that trade deals in fomewhat dearer,
than if they could import them themfelves directly
from the countries which produce them.

But fince the fall of the power of Portugal,
no European nation has claimed the exclufive
right of failing in the Indian feas, of which the
principal ports are now open to the fhips of all
European nations. Except in Portugal, however, and within thefe few years in France, the
trade to the Eaft Indies has in every European
country been fubjected to an exclufive company.
Monopolies of this kind are properly eftablifhed
againft the very nation which erects them. The
greater part of that nation are thereby not only
excluded from a trade to which it might be con-

CHAP.
VII.

H H 2 venient

468   OF COLONIES.

BOOK venient for them to turn fome part of their ftock,
IV.   but are obliged to buy the goods which that
trade deals in, fomewhat dearer that if it was
open and free to all their countrymen. Since
the eftablifhment of the Englifh Eaft India company, for example, the other inhabitants of
England, over and above being excluded from
the trade, muft have paid in the price of the Eaft
India goods which they have confumed, not
only for all the extraordinary profits which the
company may have made upon thofe goods in
confequence of their monopoly, but for all the
extraordinary wafte which the fraud and abufe,
infeparable from the management of the affairs
of fo great a company, muft neceffarily have
occafioned. The abfurdity of this fecond kind
of monopoly, therefore, is much more manifeft
than that of the firft.

Both thefe kinds of monopolies derange more
or lefs the natural diftribution of the ftock of
the fociety: but they do not always derange
it in the fame way.

Monopolies of the firft kind always attract
to the particular trade in which they are eftablifhed, a greater proportion of the ftock of the
fociety than what would go to that trade of its
own accord.

Monopolies of the fecond kind may fometimes attract ftock towards the particular trade
in which they are eftablifhed, and fometimes
repel it from that trade according to different
circumftances. In poor countries they naturally
                                    attract

OF COLONIES.

attract towards that trade more stock than would otherwise go to it. In rich countries they naturally repel from it a good deal of stock which would otherwise go to it.

Such poor countries as Sweden and Denmark, for example, would probably have never sent a single ship to the East Indies, had not the trade been subjected to an exclusive company. The establishment of such a company necessarily encourages adventurers. Their monopoly secures them against all competitors in the home market, and they have the same chance for foreign markets with the traders of other nations. Their monopoly shows them the certainty of a great profit upon a considerable quantity of goods, and the chance of a considerable profit upon a great quantity. Without such extraordinary encouragement, the poor traders of such poor countries would probably never have thought of hazarding their small capitals in so very distant and uncertain an adventure as the trade to the East Indies must naturally have appeared to them.

Such a rich country as Holland, on the contrary, would probably, in the case of a free trade, send many more ships to the East Indies than it actually does. The limited stock of the Dutch East India company probably repels from that trade many great mercantile capitals which would otherwise go to it. The mercantile capital of Holland is so great that it is, as it were, continually overflowing, sometimes into the public funds of foreign countries, sometimes into loans

HH 3

to

BOOK IV.

to private traders and adventurers of foreign countries, fometimes into the moft round-about foreign trades of confumption, and fometimes into the carrying trade. All near employments being completely filled up, all the capital which can be placed in them with any tolerable profit being already placed in them, the capital of Holland neceffarily flows towards the moft diftant employments. The trade to the Eaft Indies, if it were altogether free, would probably abforb the greater part of this redundant capital. The Eaft Indies offer a market both for the manufactures of Europe and for the gold and filver as well as for feveral other productions of America, greater and more extenfive than both Europe and America put together.

Every derangement of the natural diftribution of ftock is neceffarily hurtful to the fociety in which it takes place; whether it be by repelling from a particular trade the ftock which would otherwife go to it, or by attracting towards a particular trade that which would not otherwife come to it. If, without any exclufive company, the trade of Holland to the Eaft Indies would be greater than it actually is, that country muft fuffer a confiderable lofs by part of its capital being excluded from the employment moft convenient for that part. And in the fame manner, if, without any exclufive company, the trade of Sweden and Denmark to the Eaft Indies would be lefs than it actually is, or, what perhaps is more probable, would not exift at all, thofe two countries muft likewife fuffer a confiderable

OF COLONIES. 471

fiderable lofs by-part of their capital being C H A P.
drawn into an employment which muft be more VII.
or lefs unfuitable to their prefent circumftances.
Better for them, perhaps, in their prefent circumftances, to buy Eaft India goods of other
nations, even though they fhould pay fomewhat
dearer, than to turn fo great a part of their fmall
capital to fo very diftant a trade, in which the
returns are fo very flow, in which that capital
can maintain fo fmall a quantity of productive
labour at home, where productive labour is fo
much wanted, where fo little is done, and where
fo much is to do.

Though without an exclufive company, therefore, a particular country fhould not be able to
carry on any direct trade to the Eaft Indies, it
will not from thence follow that fuch a company
ought to be eftablifhed there, but only that fuch
a country ought not in thefe circumftances to
trade directly to the Eaft Indies. That fuch
companies are not in general neceffary for carrying on the Eaft India trade, is fufficiently demonftrated by the experience of the Portuguefe, who
enjoyed almoft the whole of it for more than a
century together without any exclufive company.

No private merchant, it has been faid, could
well have capital fufficient to maintain factors
and agents in the different ports of the Eaft
Indies, in order to provide goods for the fhips
which he might occafionally fend thither; and
yet, unlefs he was able to do this, the difficulty
of finding a cargo might frequently make his
fhips lofe the feafon for returning, and the ex-

H H 4   pence

OF COLONIES.

BOOK IV.

pence of fo long a delay would not only eat up the whole profit of the adventure but frequently occafion a very confiderable lofs. This argument, however, if it proved any thing at all, would prove that no one great branch of trade could be carried on without an exclufive company, which is contrary to the experience of all nations. There is no great branch of trade in which the capital of any one private merchant is fufficient, for carrying on all the fubordinate branches which muft be carried on, in order to carry on the principal one. But when a nation is ripe for any great branch of trade, fome merchants naturally turn their capitals towards the principal, and fome towards the fubordinate branches of it; and though all the different branches of it are in this manner carried on, yet it very feldom happens that they are all carried on by the capital of one private merchant. If a nation, therefore, is ripe for the Eaft India trade, a certain portion of its capital will naturally divide itfelf among all the different branches of that trade. Some of its merchants will find it for their intereft to refide in the Eaft Indies, and to employ their capitals there in providing goods for the fhips which are to be fent out by other merchants who refide in Europe. The fettlements which different European nations have obtained in the Eaft Indies, if they were taken from the exclufive companies to which they at prefent belong, and put under the immediate protection of the fovereign, would render this refidence both fafe and eafy, at leaft to the mer-

chants

OF COLONIES.   473

chants of the particular nations to whom thofe C H A P.
fettlements belong. If at any particular time ___VII.___
that part of the capital of any country which of
its own accord tended and inclined, if I may fay
fo, towards the Eaft India trade, was not fufficient for carrying on all thofe different branches
of it, it would be a proof that, at that particular
time, that country was not ripe for that trade,
and that it would do better to buy for fome
time, even at a higher price, from other European nations, the Eaft India goods it had occafion for, than to import them itfelf directly
from the Eaft Indies. What it might lofe by
the high price of thofe goods could feldom be
equal to the lofs which it would fuftain by the
diftraction of a large portion of its capital from
other employments more neceffary, or more ufeful, or more fuitable to its circumftances and
fituation, than a direct trade to the Eaft Indies.

Though the Europeans poffefs many confiderable fettlements both upon the coaft of
Africa and in the Eaft Indies, they have not
yet eftablifhed in either of thofe countries fuch
numerous and thriving colonies as thofe in the
iflands and continent of America. Africa, however, as well as feveral of the countries comprehended under the general name of the Eaft Indies, are inhabited by barbarous nations. But
thofe nations were by no means fo weak and
defencelefs as the miferable and helplefs Americans; and in proportion to the natural fertility
of the countries which they inhabited, they were
befides much more populous. The moft barba-
                                                    rous

474 OF COLONIES.

BOOK IV. rous nations either of Africa or of the Eaſt Indies were ſhepherds; even the Hottentots were ſo. But the natives of every part of America, except Mexico and Peru, were only hunters; and the difference is very great between the number of ſhepherds and that of hunters whom the ſame extent of equally fertile territory can maintain. In Africa and the Eaſt Indies, therefore, it was more difficult to diſplace the natives, and to extend the European plantations over the greater part of the land of the original inhabitants. The genius of excluſive companies, beſides, is unfavourable, it has already been obſerved, to the growth of new colonies, and has probably been the principal cauſe of the little progreſs which they have made in the Eaſt Indies. The Portugueſe carried on the trade both to Africa and the Eaſt Indies without any excluſive companies, and their ſettlements at Congo, Angola, and Benguela on the coaſt of Africa, and at Goa in the Eaſt Indies, though much depreſſed by ſuperſtition and every ſort of bad government, yet bear ſome faint reſemblance to the colonies of America, and are partly inhabited by Portugueſe who have been eſtabliſhed there for ſeveral generations. The Dutch ſettlements at the Cape of Good Hope and at Batavia, are at preſent the moſt conſiderable colonies which the Europeans have eſtabliſhed either in Africa or in the Eaſt Indies, and both theſe ſettlements are peculiarly fortunate in their ſituation. The Cape of Good Hope was inhabited by a race of people almoſt as barbarous and quite as inca-

pable

OF COLONIES.

475

pable of defending themfelves as the natives of America. It is befides the half-way houfe, if one may fay fo, between Europe and the Eaft Indies, at which almoft every European fhip makes fome ftay both in going and returning. The fupplying of thofe fhips with every fort of frefh provifions, with fruit and fometimes with wine, affords alone a very extenfive market for the furplus produce of the colonifts. What the Cape of Good Hope is between Europe and every part of the Eaft Indies, Batavia is between the principal countries of the Eaft Indies. It lies upon the moft frequented road from Indof-tan to China and Japan, and is nearly about mid-way upon that road. Almoft all the fhips too that fail between Europe and China touch at Batavia ; and it is, over and above all this, the center and principal mart of what is called the country trade to the Eaft Indies ; not only of that part of it which is carried on by Europeans, but of that which is carried on by the native Indians; and veffels navigated by the inhabitants of China and Japan, of Tonquin, Malacca, Cochin-China, and the ifland of Celebes, are frequently to be feen in its port. Such advantageous fituations have enabled thofe two colonies to furmount all the obftacles which the oppreffive genius of an exclufive company may have occafionally oppofed to their growth. They have enabled Batavia to furmount the additional difadvantage of perhaps the moft unwholefome climate in the world.

CHAP.
VII.

The

476   OF COLONIES.

BOOK   The Englifh and Dutch companies, though
  IV.   they have eftablifhed no confiderable colonies,
except the two above mentioned, have both
made confiderable conquefts in the Eaft Indies.
But in the manner in which they both govern
their new fubjects, the natural genius of an exclufive company has fhown itfelf moft diftinctly.
In the fpice iflands the Dutch are faid to burn
all the fpiceries which a fertile feafon produces
beyond what they expect to difpofe of in Europe with fuch a profit as they think fufficient.
In the iflands where they have no fettlements,
they give a premium to thofe who collect the
young bloffoms and green leaves of the clove
and nutmeg trees which naturally grow there,
but which this favage policy has now, it is faid,
almoft completely extirpated.   Even in the
iflands where they have fettlements they have
very much reduced, it is faid, the number of
thofe trees.   If the produce even of their own
iflands was much greater than what fuited their
market, the natives, they fufpect, might find
means to convey fome part of it to other nations; and the beft way, they imagine, to fecure
their own monopoly, is to take care that no
more fhall grow than what they themfelves carry
to market.   By different arts of oppreffion they
have reduced the population of feveral of the
Moluccas nearly to the number which is fufficient to fupply with frefh provifions and other
neceffaries of life their own infignificant garri-
fons, and fuch of their fhips as occafionally come
                                    there

OF COLONIES.

477

there for a cargo of fpices. Under the govern-ment even of the Portuguefe, however, thofe iflands are faid to have been tolerably well inhabited. The Englifh company have not yet had time to eftablifh in Bengal fo perfectly deftructive a fyftem. The plan of their government, however, has had exactly the fame tendency. It has not been uncommon, I am well affured, for the chief, that is, the firft clerk of a factory, to order a peafant to plough up a rich field of poppies, and fow it with rice or fome other grain. The pretence was, to prevent a fcarcity of provifions; but the real reafon, to give the chief an opportunity of felling at a better price a large quantity of opium, which he happened then to have upon hand. Upon other occafions the order has been reverfed; and a rich field of rice or other grain has been ploughed up, in order to make room for a plantation of poppies; when the chief forefaw that extraordinary profit was likely to be made by opium. The fervants of the company have upon feveral occafions attempted to eftablifh in their own favour the monopoly of fome of the moft important branches, not only of the foreign, but of the inland trade of the country. Had they been allowed to go on, it is impoffible that they fhould not at fome time or another have attempted to reftrain the production of the particular articles of which they has thus ufurped the monopoly, not only to the quantity which they themfelves could purchafe, but to that which they could expect to fell with fuch a profit as they might think fufficient. In the

C H A P.
VII.

478　　　　　　　　　OF COLONIES.

BOOK
IV.

the courfe of a century or two, the policy of the English company would in this manner have probably proved as completely deftructive as that of the Dutch.

Nothing, however, can be more directly contrary to the real intereft of thofe companies, confidered as the fovereigns of the countries which they have conquered, than this deftructive plan. In almoft all countries the revenue of the fovereign is drawn from that of the people. The greater the revenue of the people, therefore, the greater the annual produce of their land and labour, the more they can afford to the fovereign. It is his intereft, therefore, to increafe as much as poffible that annual produce. But if this is the intereft of every fovereign, it is peculiarly fo of one, whofe revenue, like that of the fovereign of Bengal, arifes chiefly from a land-rent. That rent muft neceffarily be in proportion to the quantity and value of the produce, and both the one and the other muft depend upon the extent of the market. The quantity will always be fuited with more or lefs exactnefs to the confumption of thofe who can afford to pay for it, and the price which they will pay will always be in proportion to the eagernefs of their competition. It is the intereft of fuch a fovereign, therefore, to open the moft extenfive market for the produce of his country, to allow the moft perfect freedom of commerce, in order to increafe as much as poffible the number and the competition of buyers; and upon this account to abolifh, not only all monopolies, but

all

OF COLONIES. 479

all reftraints upon the tranfportation of the home produce from one part of the country to another, upon its exportation to foreign countries, or upon the importation of goods of any kind for which it can be exchanged. He is in this manner moft likely to increafe both the quantity and value of that produce, and confequently of his own fhare of it, or of his own revenue.

But a company of merchants are, it feems, incapable of confidering themfelves as fovereigns, even after they have become fuch. Trade, or buying in order to fell again, they ftill confider as their principal bufinefs, and b a ftrange abfurdity, regard the character of the fovereign as but an appendix to that of the merchant, as fomething .which ought to be made fubfervient to it, or by means of which they may be enabled to buy cheaper in India, and thereby to fell with a better profit in Europe. They endeavour for this purpofe to keep out as much as poffible all competitors from the market of the countries which are fubject to their government, and confequently to reduce, at leaft, fome part of the furplus produce of thofe countries to what is barely fufficient for fupplying their own demand, or to what they can expect to fell in Europe with fuch a profit as they may think reafonable. Their mercantile habits draw them in this manner, almoft neceffarily, though perhaps infenfibly, to prefer upon all ordinary occafions the little and tranfitory profit of the monopolift to the great and permanent

CHAP.
VII.

revenue

BOOK IV.

revenue of the sovereign, and would gradually lead them to treat the countries subject to their government nearly as the Dutch treat the Moluccas. It is the interest of the East India company, considered as sovereigns, that the European goods which are carried to the Indian dominions, should be sold there as cheap as possible; and that the Indian goods which are brought from thence should bring there as good a price, or should be sold there as dear as possible. But the reverse of this is their interest as merchants. As sovereigns, their interest is exactly the same with that of the country which they govern. As merchants, their interest is directly opposite to that interest.

But if the genius of such a government, even as to what concerns its direction in Europe, is in this manner essentially and perhaps incurably faulty, that of its administration in India is still more so. That administration is necessarily composed of a council of merchants, a profession no doubt extremely respectable, but which in no country in the world carries along with it that sort of authority which naturally over-awes the people, and without force commands their willing obedience. Such a council can command obedience only by the military force with which they are accompanied, and their government is therefore necessarily military and despotical. Their proper business, however, is that of merchants. It is to sell, upon their masters' account, the European goods consigned to them, and to buy in return Indian goods for the European

OF COLONIES.

European market. It is to fell the one as dear and to buy the other as cheap as poffible, and confequently to exclude as much as poffible all rivals from the particular market where they keep their fhop. The genius of the adminiftration, therefore, fo far as concerns the trade of the company, is the fame as that of the direction. It tends to make government fubfervient to the intereft of monopoly, and confequently to ftunt the natural growth of fome parts at leaft of the furplus produce of the country to what is barely fufficient for anfwering the demand of the company.

All the members of the adminiftration, befides, trade more or lefs upon their own account, and it is in vain to prohibit them from doing fo. Nothing can be more completely foolifh than to expect that the clerks of a great counting-houfe at ten thoufand miles diftance, and confequently almoft quite out of fight, fhould, upon a fimple order from their mafters, give up at once doing any fort of bufinefs upon their own account, abandon for ever all hopes of making a fortune, of which they have the means in their hands, and content themfelves with the moderate falaries which thofe mafters allow them, and which, moderate as they are, can feldom be augmented, being commonly as large as the real profits of the company trade can afford. In fuch circumftances, to prohibit the fervants of the company from trading upon their own account, can have fcarce any other effect than to enable the fuperior fervants, under pretence of executing their mafters' order, to opprefs fuch of the inferior ones

CHAP. VII.

VOL. III. I I as

OF COLONIES.

BOOK IV.

as have had the misfortune to fall under their displeasure. The servants naturally endeavour to establish the same monopoly in favour of their own private trade as of the public trade of the company. If they are suffered to act as they could wish, they will establish this monopoly openly and directly, by fairly prohibiting all other people from trading in the articles in which they chuse to deal; and this, perhaps, is the best and least oppressive way of establishing it. But if by an order from Europe they are prohibited from doing this, they will, notwithstanding, endeavour to establish a monopoly of the same kind, secretly and indirectly, in a way that is much more destructive to the country. They will employ the whole authority of government, and pervert the administration of justice, in order to harass and ruin those who interfere with them in any branch of commerce which, by means of agents, either concealed, or at least not publicly avowed, they may chuse to carry on. But the private trade of the servants will naturally extend to a much greater variety of articles than the public trade of the company. The public trade of the company extends no further than the trade with Europe, and comprehends a part only of the foreign trade of the country. But the private trade of the servants may extend to all the different branches both of its inland and foreign trade. The monopoly of the company can tend only to stunt the natural growth of that part of the surplus produce which, in the case of a free trade, would be exported to Europe. That of the servants tends to stunt the natural growth of

every

OF COLONIES. 483

every part of the produce in which they chufe to deal, of what is deftined for home confumption, as well as of what is deftined for exportation; and confequently to degrade the cultivation of the whole country, and to reduce the number of its inhabitants. It tends to reduce the quantity of every fort of produce, even that of the neceffaries of life, whenever the fervants of the company chufe to deal in them, to what thofe fervants can both afford to buy and expeci to fell with fuch a profit as pleafes them.

From the nature of their fituation too the fervants muft be more difpofed to fupport with rigorous feverity their own intereft againft that of the country which they govern, than their mafters can be to fupport theirs. The country belongs to their mafters, who cannot avoid having fome regard for the intereft of what belongs to them. But it does not belong to the fervants. The real intereft of their mafters, if they were capable of underftanding it, is the fame with that of the country*, and it is from ignorance chiefly, and the meannefs of mercantile prejudice, that they ever opprefs it. But the real intereft of the fervants is by no means the fame with that of the country, and the moft perfeci information would not neceffarily put an end to their oppreffions. The regulations accordingly which have been fent out from Europe, though they have been frequently weak, have upon moft occafions been

* The intereft of every proprietor of India Stock, however, is by no means the fame with that of the country in the government of which his vote gives him fome influence. See Book V. Chap. i. Part 3d.

I I 2 well-

CHAP. VII.

BOOK IV.

well-meaning. More intelligence, and perhaps less good meaning, has fometimes appeared in thofe eftablifhed by the fervants in India. It is a very fingular government, in which every member of the adminiftration wifhes to get out of the country, and confequently to have done with the government, as foon as he can, and to whofe intereft, the day after he has left it, and carried his whole fortune with him, it is perfectly indifferent though the whole country was fwallowed up by an earthquake.

I mean not, however, by any thing which I have here faid, to throw any odious imputation upon the general character of the fervants of the Eaft India company, and much lefs upon that of any particular perfons. It is the fyftem of government, the fituation in which they are placed, that I mean to cenfure; not the character of thofe who have acted in it. They acted as their fituation naturally directed, and they who have clamoured the loudeft againft them would, probably, not have acted better themfelves. In war and negociation, the councils of Madras and Calcutta have upon feveral occafions conducted themfelves with a refolution and decifive wifdom which would have done honour to the Senate of Rome in the beft days of that republic. The members of thofe councils, however, had been bred to profeffions very different from war and politics. But their fituation alone, without education, experience, or even example, feems to have formed in them all at once the great qualities which it required, and to have infpired them both with abilities and virtues which they

I   themfelves

OF COLONIES.

themfelves could not well know that they pof- CHAP.
feffed. If upon fome occafions, therefore, it has VII.
animated them to actions of magnanimity which
could not well have been expected from them,
we fhould not wonder if upon others it has
prompted them to exploits of fomewhat a different nature.

Such exclufive companies, therefore, are nui-
fances in every refpect; always more or lefs inconvenient to the countries in which they are
eftablifhed, and deftructive to thofe which have
the misfortune to fall under their government.

CHAP. VIII.

Conclufion of the Mercantile Syftem..

THOUGH the encouragement of exporta- CHAP.
tion, and the difcouragement of importa- VIII.
tion, are the two great engines by which the
mercantile fyftem propofes to enrich every country, yet with regard to fome particular commodities, it feems to follow an oppofite plan : to
difcourage exportation, and to encourage importation. Its ultimate object, however, it pretends, is always the fame, to enrich the country
by an advantageous balance of trade. It difcourages the exportation of the materials of manufacture, and of the inftruments of trade, in
order to give our own workmen an advantage,
and to enable them to underfell thofe of other
nations in all foreign markets : and by reftrain-

ing,

486   CONCLUSION OF THE MERCANTILE SYSTEM.

BOOK IV.

ing, in this manner, the exportation of a few commodities, of no great price, it propofes to occafion a much greater and more valuable exportation of others. It encourages the importation of the materials of manufacture, in order that our own people may be enabled to work them up more cheaply, and thereby prevent a greater and more valuable importation of the manufactured commodities. I do not obferve, at leaft in our Statute Book, any encouragement given to the importation of the inftruments of trade. When manufactures have advanced to a certain pitch of greatnefs, the fabrication of the inftruments of trade becomes itfelf the object of a great number of very important manufactures. To give any particular encouragement to the importation of fuch inftruments, would interfere too much with the intereft of thofe manufactures. Such importation, therefore, inftead of being encouraged, has frequently been prohibited. Thus the importation of wool cards, except from Ireland, or when brought in as wreck or prize goods, was prohibited by the 3d of Edward IV.; which prohibition was renewed by the 39th of Elizabeth, and has been continued and rendered perpetual by fubfequent laws.

The importation of the materials of manufacture has fometimes been encouraged by an exemption from the duties to which other goods are fubject, and fometimes by bounties.

The importation of fheep's wool from feveral different countries, of cotton wool from all countries, of undreffed flax, of the greater part of

dying

CONCLUSION OF THE MERCANTILE SYSTEM. 487

dying drugs, of the greater part of undreffed
hides from Ireland or the Britifh colonies, of feal
fkins from the Britifh Greenland fifhery, of pig
and bar iron from the Britifh colonies, as well
as of feveral other materials of manufacture, has
been encouraged by an exemption from all
duties, if properly entered at the cuftom-houfe.
The private interefts of our merchants and manufacturers may, perhaps, have extorted from
the legiflature thefe exemptions, as well as the
greater part of our other commercial regulations.
They are, however, perfectly juft and reafonable, and if, confiftently with the neceffities of
the ftate, they could be extended to all the other
materials of manufacture, the public would certainly be a gainer.

The avidity of our great manufacturers, however, has in fome cafes extended thefe exemptions a good deal beyond what can juftly be confidered as the rude materials of their work. By
the 24 Geo. II. chap. 46. a fmall duty of only
one penny the pound was impofed upon the importation of foreign brown linen yarn, inftead of
much higher duties to which it had been fubjected before, viz. of fixpence the pound upon
fail yarn, of one fhilling the pound upon all
French and Dutch yarn, and of two pounds
thirteen fhillings and fourpence upon the hundred weight of all fpruce or Mufcovia yarn. But
our manufacturers were not long fatisfied with
this reduction. By the 29th of the fame King,
chap. 15. the fame law which gave a bounty upon
the exportation of Britifh and Irifh linen of

CHAP. VIII.

I I 4   which

488   CONCLUSION OF THE MERCANTILE SYSTEM.

BOOK which the price did not exceed eighteen pence
IV. the yard, even this fmall duty upon the importation of brown linen yarn was taken away. In the
different operations, however, which are neceffary for the preparation of linen yarn, a good
deal more induftry is employed, than in the fubfequent operation of preparing linen cloth from
linen yarn. To fay nothing of the induftry of the
flax-growers and flax-dreffers, three or four fpinners, at leaft, are neceffary, in order to keep one
weaver in conftant employment ; and more than
four-fifths of the whole quantity of labour, neceffary for the preparation of linen cloth, is employed in that of linen yarn ; but our fpinners
are poor people, women commonly fcattered
about in all different parts of the country, without fupport or protection. It is not by the fale of
their work, but by that of the complete work of
the weavers, that our great mafter manufacturers make their profits. As it is their intereft
to fell the complete manufacture as dear, fo is
it to buy the materials as cheap as poffible. By
extorting from the legiflature bounties upon the
exportation of their own linen, high duties upon
the importation of all foreign linen, and a total
prohibition of the home confumption of fome
forts of French linen, they endeavour to fell
their own goods as dear as poffible. By encouraging the importation of foreign linen
yarn, and thereby bringing it into competition
with that which is made by our own people,
they endeavour to buy the work of the poor
fpinners as cheap as poffible. They are as intent

CONCLUSION OF THE MERCANTILE SYSTEM. 489

CHAP. VIII.

tent to keep down the wages of their own weavers as the earnings of the poor fpinners, and it is by no means for the benefit of the workman, that they endeavour either to raife the price of the complete work, or to lower that of the rude materials. It is the induftry which is carried on for the benefit of the rich and the powerful, that is principally encouraged by our mercantile fyftem. That which is carried on for the benefit of the poor and the indigent, is too often either neglected or oppreffed.

Both the bounty upon the exportation of linen, and the exemption from duty upon the importation of foreign yarn, which were granted only for fifteen years, but continued by two different prolongations, expire with the end of the feffion of parliament which fhall immediately follow the 24th of June 1786.

The encouragement given to the importation of the materials of manufacture by bounties, has been principally confined to fuch as were imported from our American plantations.

The firft bounties of this kind were thofe granted about the beginning of the prefent century, upon the importation of naval ftores from America. Under this denomination were comprehended timber fit for mafts, yards, and bowfprits; hemp, tar, pitch, and turpentine. The bounty, however, of one pound the ton upon mafting-timber, and that of fix pounds the ton upon hemp, were extended to fuch as fhould be imported into England from Scotland. Both thefe bounties continued without any variation,

at

490 CONCLUSION OF THE MERCANTILE SYSTEM.

BOOK
IV.

at the fame rate, till they were feverally allowed to expire; that upon hemp, on the 1ft of January 1741, and that upon mafting-timber at the end of the feffion of parliament immediately following the 24th June 1781.

The bounties upon the importation of tar, pitch, and turpentine underwent, during their continuance, feveral alterations. Originally that upon tar was four pounds the ton; that upon pitch the fame; and that upon turpentine, three pounds the ton. The bounty of four pounds the ton upon tar was afterwards confined to fuch as had been prepared in a particular manner; that upon other good, clean, and merchantable tar, was reduced to two pounds four fhillings the ton. The bounty upon pitch was likewife reduced to one pound; and that upon turpentine to one pound ten fhillings the ton.

The fecond bounty upon the importation of any of the materials of manufacture, according to the order of time, was that granted by the 21 Geo. II. chap. 30. upon the importation of indigo from the Britifh plantations. When the plantation indigo was worth three-fourths of the price of the beft French indigo, it was by this act entitled to a bounty of fixpence the pound. This bounty, which, like moft others, was granted only for a limited time, was continued for feveral prolongations, but was reduced to four pence the pound. It was allowed to expire with the end of the feffion of parliament which followed the 25th March 1781.

The third bounty of this kind was that granted
(much

CONCLUSION OF THE MERCANTILE SYSTEM. 491

(much about the time that we were beginning C H A P. fometimes to court and fometimes to quarrel VIII. with our American colonies) by the 4 Geo. III. chap. 26. upon the importation of hemp, or un-dreffed flax, from the Britifh plantations. This bounty was granted for twenty-one years, from the 24th June 1764, to the 24th June 1785. For the firft feven years it was to be at the rate of eight pounds the ton, for the fecond at fix pounds, and for the third at four pounds. It was not extended to Scotland, of which the climate (although hemp is fometimes raifed there, in fmall quantities and of an inferior quality,) is not very fit for that produce. Such a bounty upon the importation of Scotch flax into England would have been too great a dif-couragement to the native produce of the fouthern part of the United Kingdom.

The fourth bounty of this kind, was that granted by the 5 Geo. III. chap. 45. upon the im-portation of wood from America. It was granted for nine years, from the 1ft January 1766, to the 1ft January 1775. During the firft three years, it was to be for every hundred and twenty good deals, at the rate of one pound; and for every load containing fifty cubic feet of other fquared timber at the rate of twelve fhillings. For the fecond three years, it was for deals to be at the rate of fifteen fhillings, and for other fquared timber, at the rate of eight fhillings; and for the third three years, it was for deals to be at the rate of ten fhillings, and for other fquared timber, at the rate of five fhillings.

The

492 CONCLUSION OF THE MERCANTILE SYSTEM.

BOOK
IV.

The fifth bounty of this kind, was that granted by the 9 Geo. III. chap. 38. upon the importation of raw filk from the Britifh plantations. It was granted for twenty-one years, from the 1ft January 1770, to the 1ft January 1791. For the firft feven years it was to be at the rate of twenty-five pounds for every hundred pounds value ; for the fecond, at twenty pounds ; and for the third, at fifteen pounds. The management of the filk-worm, and the preparation of filk, requires fo much hand labour; and labour is fo very dear in America, that even this great bounty, I have been informed, was not likely to produce any confiderable effect.

The fixth bounty of this kind, was that granted by 11 Geo. III. chap. 50. for the importation of pipe, hogfhead, and barrel ftaves and heading, from the Britifh plantations. It was granted for nine years, from 1ft January 1772, to the 1ft January 1781. For the firft three years, it was for a certain quantity of each, to be at the rate of fix pounds; for the fecond three years, at four pounds; and for the third three years, at two pounds.

The feventh and laft bounty of this kind, was that granted by the 19 Geo. III. chap. 37. upon the importation of hemp from Ireland. It was granted in the fame manner as that for the importation of hemp and undreffed flax from America, for twenty-one years, from the 24th June 1779, to the 24th June 1800. This term is divided, likewife, into three periods of feven years each ; and in each of thofe periods, the

rate

CONCLUSION OF THE MERCANTILE SYSTEM. 493

rate of the Irish bounty is the same with that CHAP. of the American. It does not, however, like VIII. the American bounty, extend to the importation of undreffed flax. It would have been too great a difcouragement to the cultivation of that plant in Great Britain. When this laft bounty was, granted, the British and Irish legiflatures were not in much better humour with one another, than the British and American had been before. But this boon to Ireland, it is to be hoped, has been granted under more fortunate aufpices, than all thofe to America.

The fame commodities upon which we thus gave bounties, when imported from America, were fubjected to confiderable duties when imported from any other country. The intereft of our American colonies was regarded as the fame with that of the mother country. Their wealth was confidered as our wealth. Whatever money was fent out to them, it was faid, came all back to us by the balance of trade, and we could never become a farthing the poorer, by any expence which we could lay out upon them. They were our own in every refpect, and it was an expence laid out upon the improvement of our own property, and for the profitable employment of our own people. It is unneceffary, I apprehend, at prefent to fay any thing further, in order to expofe the folly of a fyftem, which fatal experience has now fufficiently expofed. Had our American colonies really been a part of Great Britain, thofe bounties might have been confidered as bounties upon production, and would

ftill

494   CONCLUSION OF THE MERCANTILE SYSTEM.

BOOK ftill have been liable to all the objections to which
 IV. fuch bounties are liable, but to no other.

The exportation of the materials of manufacture is fometimes difcouraged by abfolute prohibitions, and fometimes by high duties.

Our woollen manufacturers have been more fuccefsful than any other clafs of workmen, in perfuading the legiflature that the profperity of the nation depended upon the fuccefs and extenfion of their particular bufinefs. They have not only obtained a monopoly againft the confumers by an abfolute prohibition of importing woollen cloths from any foreign country; but they have likewife obtained another monopoly againft the fheep farmers and growers of wool by a' fimilar prohibition of the exportation of live fheep and wool. The feverity of many of the laws which have been enacted for the fecurity of the revenue is very juftly complained of, as impofing heavy penalties upon actions which, antecedent to the ftatutes that declared them to be crimes, had always been underftood to be innocent. But the cruelleft of our revenue laws, I will venture to affirm, are mild and gentle, in comparifon of fome of thofe which the clamour of our merchants and manufacturers has extorted from the legiflature, for the fupport of their own abfurd and oppreffive monopolies. Like the laws of Draco, thefe laws may be faid to be all written in blood.

By the 8th of Elizabeth, chap. 3. the exporter of fheep, lambs, or rams, was for the firft offence to forfeit all his goods for ever, to fuffer a year's imprifonment, and then to have his left hand cut

4   off

CONCLUSION OF THE MERCANTILE SYSTEM. 495

off in a market town upon a market day, to be there nailed up; and for the fecond offence to be adjudged a felon, and to fuffer death accordingly. To prevent the breed of our fheep from being propagated in foreign countries, feems to have been the object of this law. By the 13th and 14th of Charles II. chap. 18. the exportation of wool was made felony, and the exporter fubjected to the fame penalties and forfeitures as a felon.

For the honour of the national humanity, it is to be hoped that neither of thefe ftatutes were ever executed. The firft of them, however, fo far as I know, has never been directly repealed, and Serjeant Hawkins feems to confider it as ftill in force. It may however, perhaps, be confidered as virtually repealed by the 12th of Charles II. chap. 32. fect. 3. which, without exprefsly taking away the penalties impofed by former ftatutes, impofes a new penalty, viz. That of twenty fhillings for every fheep exported, or attempted to be exported, together with the forfeiture of the fheep and of the owner's fhare of the fhip. The fecond of them was exprefsly repealed by the 7th and 8th of William III. chap. 28. fect. 4. By which it is declared that, " Whereas " the ftatute of the 13th and 14th of King " Charles II. made againft the exportation of " wool, among other things in the faid act men- " tioned, doth enact the fame to be deemed " felony; by the feverity of which penalty the " profecution of offenders hath not been fo ef- " fectually put in execution : Be it therefore " enacted by the authority forefaid, that fo
" much

C H A P.
VIII.

496　CONCLUSION OF THE MERCANTILE SYSTEM.

BOOK IV.

" much of the faid act, which relates to the " making the faid offence felony, be repealed " and made void."

The penalties, however, which are either impofed by this milder ftatute, or which, though impofed by former ftatutes, are not repealed by this one, are ftill fufficiently fevere. Befides the forfeiture of the goods, the exporter incurs the penalty of three fhillings for every pound weight of wool either exported or attempted to be exported, that is about four or five times the value. Any merchant or other perfon convicted of this offence, is difabled from requiring any debt or account belonging to him from any factor or other perfon. Let his fortune be what it will, whether he is, or is not able to pay thofe heavy penalties, the law means to ruin him completely. But as the morals of the great body of the people are not yet fo corrupt as thofe of the contrivers of this ftatute, I have not heard that any advantage has ever been taken of this claufe. If the perfon convicted of this offence is not able to pay the penalties within three months after judgment, he is to be tranfported for feven years, and if he returns before the expiration of that term, he is liable to the pains of felony, without benefit of clergy. The owner of the fhip, knowing this offence, forfeits all his intereft in the fhip and furniture. The mafter and mariners, knowing this offence, forfeit all their goods and chattels, and fuffer three months imprifonment. By a fubfequent ftatute the mafter fuffers fix months imprifonment.

In

CONCLUSION OF THE MERCANTILE SYSTEM. 497

CHAP. VIII.

In order to prevent exportation, the whole inland commerce of wool is laid under very burdenfome and oppreffive reftrictions. It cannot be packed in any box, barrel, cafk, cafe, cheft, or any other package, but only in packs of leather or pack-cloth, on which muft be marked on the outfide the words *wool* or *yarn*, in large letters not lefs than three inches long, on pain of forfeiting the fame and the package, and three fhillings for every pound weight, to be paid by the owner or packer. It cannot be loaden on any horfe or cart, or carried by land within five miles of the coaft, but between fun-rifing and fun-fetting, on pain of forfeiting the fame, the horfes and carriages. The hundred next adjoining to the fea coaft, out of or through which the wool is carried or exported, forfeits twenty pounds, if the wool is under the value of ten pounds ; and if of greater value, then treble that value, together with treble cofts, to be fued for within the year. The execution to be againft any two of the inhabitants, whom the feffions muft re-imburfe, by an affeffment on the other inhabitants, as in the cafes of robbery. And if any perfon compounds with the hundred for lefs than this penalty, he is to be imprifoned for five years ; and any other perfon may profecute. Thefe regulations take place through the whole kingdom.

But in the particular counties of Kent and Suffex the reftrictions are ftill more troublefome. Every owner of wool within ten miles of the fea-coaft muft give an account in writing, three days

VOL. III.   K K   after

498 CONCLUSION OF THE MERCANTILE SYSTEM.

BOOK IV.

after shearing to the next officer of the customs, of the number of his fleeces, and of the places where they are lodged. And before he removes any part of them he must give the like notice of the number and weight of the fleeces, and of the name and abode of the person to whom they are sold, and of the place to which it is intended they should be carried. No person within fifteen miles of the sea, in the said counties, can buy any wool, before he enters into bond to the King, that no part of the wool which he shall so buy shall be sold by him to any other person within fifteen miles of the sea. If any wool is found carrying towards the sea-side in the said counties, unless it has been entered and security given as aforesaid, it is forfeited, and the offender also forfeits three shillings for every pound weight. If any person lays any wool, not entered as aforesaid, within fifteen miles of the sea, it must be seized and forfeited; and if, after such seizure, any person shall claim the same, he must give security to the Exchequer, that if he is cast upon trial he shall pay treble costs, besides all other penalties.

When such restrictions are imposed upon the inland trade, the coasting trade, we may believe, cannot be left very free. Every owner of wool who carrieth or causeth to be carried any wool to any port or place on the sea-coast, in order to be from thence transported by sea to any other place or port on the coast, must first cause an entry thereof to be made at the port from whence it is intended to be conveyed, containing the weight,

CONCLUSION OF THE MERCANTILE SYSTEM. 499

CHAP.
VIII.

weight, marks, and number of the packages before he brings the fame within five miles of that port; on pain of forfeiting the fame, and alfo the horfes, carts, and other carriages; and alfo of fuffering and forfeiting, as by the other laws in force againft the exportation of wool. This law, however, (1 Will. III. chap. 32.) is fo very indulgent as to declare, that " this fhall not
" hinder any perfon from carrying his wool
" home from the place of fhearing, though it be
" within five miles of the fea, provided that in
" ten days after fhearing, and before he remove
" the wool, he do under his hand certify to the
" next officer of the cuftoms, the true number
" of fleeces, and where it is houfed; and do not
" remove the fame, without certifying to fuch
" officer, under his hand, his intention fo to do,
" three days before." Bond muft be given that the wool to be carried coaft-ways is to be landed at the particular port for which it is entered out-wards; and if any part of it is landed without the prefence of an officer, not only the forfeiture of the wool is incurred as in other goods, but the ufual additional penalty of three fhillings for every pound weight is likewife incurred.

Our woollen manufacturers, in order to juftify their demand of fuch extraordinary reftrictions and regulations, confidently afferted, that Eng-lifh wool was of a peculiar quality, fuperior to that of any other country; that the wool of other countries could not, without fome mixture of it, be wrought up into any tolerable manufacture; that fine cloth could not be made without it;

K K 2

that

CONCLUSION OF THE MERCANTILE SYSTEM.

BOOK
IV.

that England, therefore, if the exportation of it could be totally prevented, could monopolize to herfelf almoft the whole woollen trade of the world; and thus, having no rivals, could fell at what price fhe pleafed, and in a fhort time acquire the moft incredible degree of wealth by the moft advantageous balance of trade. This doctrine, like moft other doctrines which are confidently afferted by any confiderable number of people, was, and ftill continues to be, moft implicitly believed by a much greater number; by almoft all thofe who are either unacquainted with the woollen trade, or who have not made particular enquiries. It is, however, fo perfectly falfe, that Englifh wool is in any refpect neceffary for the making of fine cloth, that it is altogether unfit for it. Fine cloth is made altogether of Spanifh wool. Englifh wool cannot be even fo mixed with Spanifh wool as to enter into the compofition without fpoiling and degrading, in fome degree, the fabric of the cloth.

It has been fhown in the foregoing part of this work, that the effect of thefe regulations has been to deprefs the price of Englifh wool, not only below what it naturally would be in the prefent times, but very much below what it actually was in the time of Edward III. The price of Scots wool, when in confequence of the union it became fubject to the fame regulations, is faid to have fallen about one half. It is obferved by the very accurate and intelligent author of the Memoirs of Wool, the Reverend Mr. John Smith, that the price of the beft Englifh wool in

England

England is generally below what wool of a very inferior quality commonly fells for in the market of Amſterdam. To depreſs the price of this commodity below what may be called its natural and proper price, was the avowed purpoſe of thoſe regulations; and there ſeems to be no doubt of their having produced the effect that was expected from them.

This reduction of price, it may perhaps be thought, by diſcouraging the growing of wool, muſt have reduced very much the annual produce of that commodity, though not below what it formerly was, yet below what, in the preſent ſtate of things, it probably would have been, had it, in conſequence of an open and free market, been allowed to riſe to the natural and proper price. I am, however, diſpoſed to believe, that the quantity of the annual produce cannot have been much, though it may perhaps have been a little, affected by theſe regulations. The growing of wool is not the chief purpoſe for which the ſheep farmer employs his induſtry and ſtock. He expects his profit, not ſo much from the price of the fleece, as from that of the carcaſe; and the average or ordinary price of the latter, muſt even, in many caſes, make up to him whatever deficiency there may be in the average or ordinary price of the former. It has been obſerved in the foregoing part of this work, that " Whatever regulations tend to ſink the " price, either of wool or of raw hides, below " what it naturally would be, muſt, in an im-" proved and cultivated country, have ſome

" tendency

502 CONCLUSION OF THE MERCANTILE SYSTEM.

BOOK IV.

" tendency to raife the price of butchers' meat.
" The price both of the great and fmall cattle
" which are fed on improved and cultivated
" land, muft be fufficient to pay the rent which
" the landlord, and the profit which the farmer
" has reafon to expect from improved and cul-
" tivated land. If it is not, they will foon ceafe
" to feed them. Whatever part of this price,
" therefore, is not paid by the wool and the
" hide, muft be paid by the carcafe. The lefs
" there is paid for the one, the more muft be
" paid for the other. In what manner this
" price is to be divided upon the different parts
" of the beaft, is indifferent to the landlords and
" farmers, provided it is all paid to them. In
" an improved and cultivated country, there-
" fore, their intereft as landlords and farmers
" cannot be much affected by fuch regulations,
" though their intereft as confumers may, by
" the rife in the price of provifions." According to this reafoning, therefore, this degradation
in the price of wool is not likely, in an improved
and cultivated country, to occafion any diminution in the annual produce of that commodity;
except fo far as, by raifing the price of mutton,
it may fomewhat diminifh the demand for, and
confequently the production of, that particular
fpecies of butchers' meat. Its effect, however,
even in this way, it is probable, is not very confiderable.

But though its effect upon the quantity of the
annual produce may not have been very confiderable, its effect upon the quality, it may
perhaps

CONCLUSION OF THE MERCANTILE SYSTEM. 503

CHAP.
VIII.

perhaps be thought, muſt neceſſarily have been very great. The degradation in the quality of Engliſh wool, if not below what it was in former times, yet below what it naturally would have been in the preſent ſtate of improvement and cultivation, muſt have been, it may perhaps be ſuppoſed, very nearly in proportion to the degradation of price. As the quality depends upon the breed, upon the paſture, and upon the management and cleanlineſs of the ſheep, during the whole progreſs of the growth of the fleece, the attention to theſe circumſtances, it may naturally enough be imagined, can never be greater than in proportion to the recompence which the price of the fleece is likely to make for the labour and expence which that attention requires. It happens, however, that the goodneſs of the fleece depends, in a great meaſure, upon the health, growth, and bulk of the animal ; the ſame attention which is neceſſary for the improvement of the carcaſe, is, in ſome reſpects, ſufficient for that of the fleece. Notwithſtanding the degradation of price, Engliſh wool is ſaid to have been improved conſiderably during the courſe even of the preſent century. The improvement might perhaps have been greater if the price had been better ; but the lowneſs of price, though it may have obſtructed, yet certainly it has not altogether prevented that improvement.

The violence of theſe regulations, therefore, ſeems to have affected neither the quantity nor the quality of the annual produce of wool ſo

K K 4

much

BOOK IV.

much as it might have been expected to do (though I think it probable that it may have affected the latter a good deal more than the former); and the intereft of the growers of wool, though it muft have been hurt in fome degree, feems, upon the whole, to have been much lefs hurt than could well have been imagined.

Thefe confiderations, however, will not juftify the abfolute prohibition of the exportation of wool. But they will fully juftify the impofition of a confiderable tax upon that exportation.

To hurt in any degree the intereft of any one order of citizens, for no other purpofe but to promote that of fome other, is evidently contrary to that juftice and equality of treatment which the Sovereign owes to all the different orders of his fubjects. But the prohibition certainly hurts, in fome degree, the intereft of the growers of wool, for no other purpofe but to promote that of the manufacturers.

Every different order of citizens is bound to contribute to the fupport of the fovereign or commonwealth. A tax of five, or even of ten fhillings upon the exportation of every ton of wool, would produce a very confiderable revenue to the fovereign. It would hurt the intereft of the growers fomewhat lefs than the prohibition, becaufe it would not probably lower the price of wool quite fo much. It would afford a fufficient advantage to the manufacturer, becaufe, though he might not buy his wool altogether fo cheap as under the prohibition, he would ftill buy it, at leaft, five or ten fhillings cheaper than

any

any foreign manufacturer could buy it, befides CHAP. faving the freight and infurance, which the other would be obliged to pay. It is fcarce poffible to devife a tax which could produce any confiderable revenue to the Sovereign, and at the fame time occafion fo little inconveniency to any body.

The prohibition, notwithftanding all the penalties which guard it, does not prevent the exportation of wool. It is exported, it is well known, in great quantities. The great difference between the price in the home and that in the foreign market, prefents fuch a temptation to fmuggling, that all the rigour of the law cannot prevent it. This illegal exportation is advantageous to nobody but the fmuggler. A legal exportation fubject to a tax, by affording a revenue to the Sovereign, and thereby faving the impofition of fome other, perhaps, more burdenfome and inconvenient taxes, might prove advantageous to all the different fubjects of the ftate.

The exportation of fuller's earth, or fuller's clay, fuppofed to be neceffary for preparing and cleanfing the woollen manufactures, has been fubjected to nearly the fame penalties as the exportation of wool. Even tobacco-pipe clay, though acknowledged to be different from fuller's clay, yet, on account of their refemblance, and becaufe fuller's clay might fometimes be exported as tobacco-pipe clay, has been laid under the fame prohibitions and penalties.

By

CONCLUSION OF THE MERCANTILE SYSTEM.

BOOK IV.

By the 13th and 14th of Charles II. chap. 7. the exportation, not only of raw hides, but of tanned leather, except in the fhape of boots, fhoes, or flippers, was prohibited; and the law gave a monopoly to our boot-makers and fhoemakers, not only againft our graziers, but againft our tanners. By fubfequent ftatutes, our tanners have got themfelves exempted from this monopoly, upon paying a fmall tax of only one fhilling on the hundred weight of tanned leather, weighing one hundred and twelve pounds. They have obtained likewife the drawback of two-thirds of the excife duties impofed upon their commodity, even when exported without further manufacture. All manufactures of leather may be exported duty free; and the exporter is befides entitled to the drawback of the whole duties of excife. Our graziers ftill continue fubject to the old monopoly. Graziers feparated from one another, and difperfed through all the different corners of the country, cannot, without great difficulty, combine together for the purpofe either of impofing monopolies upon their fellow-citizens, or of exempting themfelves from fuch as may have been impofed upon them by other people. Manufacturers of all kinds, collected together in numerous bodies in all great cities, eafily can. Even the horns of cattle are prohibited to be exported; and the two infignificant trades of the horner and comb-maker enjoy, in this refpect, a monopoly againft the graziers.

Reftraints,

CONCLUSION OF THE MERCANTILE SYSTEM. 507

CHAP.
VIII.

Reftraints, either by prohibitions or by taxes, upon the exportation of goods which are partially, but not completely manufactured, are not peculiar to the manufacture of leather. As long as any thing remains to be done, in order to fit any commodity for immediate ufe and confumption, our manufacturers think that they themfelves ought to have the doing of it. Woollen yarn and worfted are prohibited to be exported under the fame penalties as wool. Even white cloths are fubject to a duty upon exportation, and our dyers have fo far obtained a monopoly againft our clothiers. Our clothiers would probably have been able to defend themfelves againft it, but it happens that the greater part of our principal clothiers are themfelves likewife dyers. Watch-cafes, clock-cafes, and dial-plates for clocks and watches, have been prohibited to be exported. Our clock-makers and watchmakers are, it feems, unwilling that the price of this fort of workmanfhip fhould be raifed upon them by the competition of foreigners.

By fome old ftatutes of Edward III., Henry VIII., and Edward VI., the exportation of all metals was prohibited. Lead and tin were alone excepted; probably on account of the great abundance of thofe metals; in the exportation of which, a confiderable part of the trade of the kingdom in thofe days confifted. For the encouragement of the mining trade, the 5th of William and Mary, chap. 17. exempted from this prohibition, iron, copper, and mundic metal made from Britifh ore. The exportation of all

forts

508   CONCLUSION OF THE MERCANTILE SYSTEM.

BOOK
IV.

forts of copper bars, foreign as well as Britifh, was afterwards permitted by the 9th and 10th of William III. chap. 26. The exportation of un-manufactured brafs, of what is called gun-metal, bell-metal, and fhroff-metal, ftill continues to be prohibited. Brafs manufactures of all forts may be exported duty free.

The exportation of the materials of manufac-ture, where it is not altogether prohibited, is in many cafes fubjected to confiderable duties.

By the 8th George I. chap. 15., the exporta-tion of all goods, the produce or manufacture of Great Britain, upon which any duties had been impofed by former ftatutes, was rendered duty free. The following goods, however, were ex-cepted: Allum, lead, lead ore, tin, tanned lea-ther, copperas, coals, wool cards, white wool-len cloths, lapis calaminaris, fkins of all forts, glue, coney hair or wool, hares wool, hair of all forts, horfes, and litharge of lead. If you except horfes, all thefe are either materials of manufacture, or incomplete manufactures (which may be confidered as materials for ftill further manufacture), or inftruments of trade. This ftatute leaves them fubject to all the old duties which had ever been impofed upon them, the old fubfidy and one per cent. outwards.

By the fame ftatute a great number of foreign drugs for dyers ufe, are exempted from all duties upon importation. Each of them, how-ever, is afterwards fubjected to a certain duty, not indeed a very heavy one, upon exportation. Our dyers, it feems, while they thought it for

their

CONCLUSION OF THE MERCANTILE SYSTEM. 509

their intereft to encourage the importation of thofe drugs, by an exemption from all duties, thought it likewife for their intereft to throw fome fmall difcouragement upon their exportation. The avidity, however, which fuggefted this notable piece of mercantile ingenuity, moft probably difappointed itfelf of its object. It neceffarily taught the importers to be more careful than they might otherwife have been, that their importation fhould not exceed what was neceffary for the fupply of the home market. The home market was at all times likely to be more fcantily fupplied; the commodities were at all times likely to be fomewhat dearer there than they would have been, had the exportation been rendered as free as the importation.

By the above-mentioned ftatute, gum, fenega, or gum arabic, being among the enumerated dying drugs, might be imported duty free. They were fubjected, indeed, to a fmall poundage duty, amounting only to three pence in the hundred weight upon their re-exportation. France enjoyed, at that time, an exclufive trade to the country moft productive of thofe drugs, that which lies in the neighbourhood of the Senegal; and the Britifh market could not be eafily fupplied by the immediate importation of them from the place of growth. By the 25th Geo. II. therefore, gum fenega was allowed to be imported (contrary to the general difpofitions of the act of navigation), from any part of Europe. As the law, however, did not mean to encourage this

510   CONCLUSION OF THE MERCANTILE SYSTEM.

BOOK IV.

this fpecies of trade, fo contrary to the general principles of the mercantile policy of England, it impofed a duty of ten fhillings the hundred weight upon fuch importation, and no part of this duty was to be afterwards drawn back upon its exportation. The fuccefsful war which began in 1755 gave Great Britain the fame exclufive trade to thofe countries which France had enjoyed before. Our manufacturers, as foon as the peace was made, endeavoured to avail themfelves of this advantage, and to eftablifh a monopoly in their own favour, both againft the growers, and againft the importers of this commodity. By the 5th Geo. III. therefore, chap. 37. the exportation of gum fenega from His Majefty's dominions in Africa was confined to Great Britain, and was fubjected to all the fame reftrictions, regulations, forfeitures and penalties, as that of the enumerated commodities of the Britifh colonies in America and the Weft Indies. Its importation, indeed, was fubjected to a fmall duty of fix-pence the hundred weight, but its re-exportation was fubjected to the enormous duty of one pound ten fhillings the hundred weight. It was the intention of our manufacturers that the whole produce of thofe countries fhould be imported into Great Britain, and in order that they themfelves might be enabled to buy it at their own price, that no part of it fhould be exported again, but at fuch an expence as would fufficiently difcourage that exportation. Their avidity, however, upon this, as well as upon many other occafions, difappointed itfelf of its objeƈt.

CONCLUSION OF THE MERCANTILE SYSTEM. 511

object. This enormous duty prefented fuch a temptation to fmuggling, that great quantities of this commodity were clandeftinely exported, probably to all the manufacturing countries of Europe, but particularly to Holland, not only from Great Britain but from Africa. Upon this account, by the 14 Geo. III. chap. 10. this duty upon exportation was reduced to five fhillings the hundred weight.

In the book of rates, according to which the old fubfidy was levied, beaver fkins were efti-mated at fix fhillings and eight-pence a-piece, and the different fubfidies and impofts, which before the year 1722 had been laid upon their importation, amounted to one-fifth part of the rate, or to fixteen-pence upon each fkin; all of which, except half the old fubfidy, amounting only to two-pence, was drawn back upon export-ation. This duty upon the importation of fo important a material of manufacture had been thought too high, and, in the year 1722, the rate was reduced to two fhillings and fix-pence, which reduced the duty upon importation to fix-pence, and of this only one half was to be drawn back upon exportation. The fame fuccefsful war put the country moft productive of beaver under the dominion of Great Britain, and beaver fkins being among the enumerated commodities, their ex-portation from America was confequently con-fined to the market of Great Britain. Our manu-facturers foon bethought themfelves of the advan-tage which they might make of this circumftance, and in the year 1764, the duty upon the importa-tion

512 CONCLUSION OF THE MERCANTILE SYSTEM.

BOOK IV.

tion of beaver-fkin was reduced to one penny, but the duty upon exportation was raifed to feven-pence each fkin, without any drawback of the duty upon importation. By the fame law, a duty of eighteen-pence the pound was impofed upon the exportation of beaver-wool or wombs, without making any alteration in the duty upon the importation of that commodity, which, when imported by Britifh and in Britifh fhipping, amounted at that time to between four-pence and five-pence the piece.

Coals may be confidered both as a material of manufacture and as an inftrument of trade. Heavy duties, accordingly, have been impofed upon their exportation, amounting at prefent (1783) to more than five fhillings the ton, or to more than fifteen fhillings the chaldron, Newcaftle meafure; which is in moft cafes more than the original value of the commodity at the coal pit, or even at the fhipping port for exportation.

The exportation, however, of the inftruments of trade, properly fo called, is commonly reftrained, not by high duties, but by abfolute prohibitions. Thus by the 7th and 8th of William III. chap. 20. fect. 8. the exportation of frames or engines for knitting gloves or ftockings is prohibited under the penalty, not only of the forfeiture of fuch frames or engines, fo exported, or attempted to be exported, but of forty pounds, one half to the King, the other to the perfon who fhall inform or fue for the fame. In the fame manner by the 14th Geo. III. chap. 71. the exportation to foreign

4   parts,

CONCLUSION OF THE MERCANTILE SYSTEM. 513

parts, of any utenfils made ufe of in the cotton, linen, woollen and filk manufactures, is prohibited under the penalty, not only of the forfeiture of fuch utenfils, but of two hundred pounds, to be paid by the perfon who fhall offend in this manner, and likewife of two hundred pounds to be paid by the mafter of the fhip who fhall knowingly fuffer fuch utenfils to be loaded on board his fhip.

When fuch heavy penalties were impofed upon the exportation of the dead inftruments of trade, it could not well be expected that the living inftrument, the artificer, fhould be allowed to go free. Accordingly, by the 5 Geo. I. chap. 27. the perfon who fhall be convicted of enticing any artificer of, or in any of the manufactures of Great Britain, to go into any foreign parts, in order to practife or teach his trade, is liable for the firft offence to be fined in any fum not exceeding one hundred pounds, and to three months imprifonment, and until the fine fhall be paid; and for the fecond offence, to be fined in any fum at the difcretion of the court, and to imprifonment for twelve months, and until the fine fhall be paid. By the 23 Geo. II. chap. 13. this penalty is increafed for the firft offence to five hundred pounds for every artificer fo enticed, and to twelve months imprifonment, and until the fine fhall be paid; and for the fecond offence, to one thoufand pounds, and to two years imprifonment, and until the fine fhal be paid.

VOL. III. L L By

CONCLUSION OF THE MERCANTILE SYSTEM.

BOOK IV.

By the former of thofe two ftatutes, upon proof that any perfon has been enticing any artificer, or that any artificer has promifed or contracted to go into foreign parts for the purpofes aforefaid, fuch artificer may be obliged to give fecurity at the difcretion of the court, that he fhall not go beyond the feas, and may be committed to prifon until he give fuch fecurity.

If any artificer has gone beyond the feas, and is exercifing or teaching his trade in any foreign country, upon warning being given to him by any of His Majefty's Minifters or Confuls abroad, or by one of His Majefty's Secretaries of State for the time being, if he does not, within fix months after fuch warning, return into this realm, and from thenceforth abide and inhabit continually within the fame, he is from thenceforth declared incapable of taking any legacy devifed to him within this kingdom, or of being executor or adminiftrator to any perfon, or of taking any lands within this kingdom by defcent, devife, or purchafe. He likewife forfeits to the King all his lands, goods and chattels, is declared an alien in every refpect, and is put out of the King's protection.

It is unneceffary, I imagine, to obferve, how contrary fuch regulations are to the boafted liberty of the fubject, of which we affect to be fo very jealous; but which, in this cafe, is fo plainly facrificed to the futile interefts of our merchants and manufacturers.

The

CONCLUSION OF THE MERCANTILE SYSTEM.

CHAP.
VIII.

The laudable motive of all thefe regulations, is to extend our own manufactures, not by their own improvement, but by the depreffion of thofe of all our neighbours, and by putting an end, as much as poffible, to the troublefome compe- tition of fuch odious and difagreeable rivals. Our mafter manufacturers think it reafonable, that they themfelves fhould have the monopoly of the ingenuity of all their countrymen. Though by reftraining, in fome trades, the number of apprentices which can be employed at one time, and by impofing the neceffity of a long ap- prenticefhip in all trades, they endeavour, all of them, to confine the knowledge of their re- fpective employments to as fmall a number as poffible: they are unwilling, however, that any part of this fmall number fhould go abroad to inftruct foreigners.

Confumption is the fole end and purpofe of all production; and the intereft of the producer ought to be attended to, only fo far as it may be neceffary for promoting that of the confumer. The maxim is fo perfectly felf-evident, that it would be abfurd to attempt to prove it. But in the mercantile fyftem, the intereft of the con- fumer is almoft conftantly facrificed to that of the producer; and it feems to confider produc- tion, and not confumption, as the ultimate end and object of all induftry and commerce.

In the reftraints upon the importation of all foreign commodities which can come into com- petition with thofe of our own growth, or manu- facture, the intereft of the home-confumer is

L L 2 evidently

516 CONCLUSION OF THE MERCANTILE SYSTEM.

BOOK IV.

evidently facrificed to that of the producer. It is altogether for the benefit of the latter, that the former is obliged to pay that enhancement of price which this monopoly almoſt always occaſions.

It is altogether for the benefitof the producer that bounties are granted upon the exportation of ſome of his productions. The home-conſumer is obliged to pay, firſt, the tax which is necef-ſary for paying the bounty, and ſecondly, the ſtill greater tax which neceſſarily ariſes from the enhancement of the price of the commodity in the home market.

By the famous treaty of commerce with Por-tugal, the conſumer is prevented by high duties from purchaſing of a neighbouring country, a commodity which our own climate does not produce, but is obliged to purchaſe it of a diſtant country, though it is acknowledged, that the commodity of the diſtant country is of a worſe quality than that of the near one. The home-conſumer is obliged to ſubmit to this in-conveniency, in order that the producer may import into the diſtant country ſome of his pro-ductions upon more advantageous terms than he would otherwiſe have been allowed to do. The conſumer, too, is obliged to pay whatever en-hancement in the price of thoſe very produc-tions, this forced exportation may occaſion in the home market.

But in the ſyſtem of laws which has been eſtabliſhed for the management of our American and Weſt Indian colonies, the intereſt of the

2

home-

CONCLUSION OF THE MERCANTILE SYSTEM. 517

home-confumer has been facrificed to that of
the producer with a more extravagant profufion
than in all our other commercial regulations.
A great empire has been eftablifhed for the fole
purpofe of raifing up a nation of cuftomers who
fhould be obliged to buy from the fhops of our
different producers, all the goods with which
thefe could fupply them. For the fake of that
little enhancement of price which this monopoly
might afford our producers, the home-con-
fumers have been burdened with the whole expence of maintaining and defending that empire.
For this purpofe, and for this purpofe only, in
the two laft wars, more than two hundred millions have been fpent, and a new debt of more
than a hundred and feventy millions has been
contracted over and above all that had been expended for the fame purpofe in former wars.
The intereft of this debt alone is not only greater
than the whole extraordinary profit, which, it
ever could be pretended, was made by the monopoly of the colony trade, but than the whole
value of that trade, or than the whole value of
the goods, which at an average have been
annually exported to the colonies.

It cannot be very difficult to determine who
have been the contrivers of this whole mercantile fyftem; not the confumers, we may believe,
whofe intereft has been entirely neglected; but
the producers, whofe intereft has been fo carefully attended to; and among this latter clafs
our merchants and manufacturers have been by

CHAP.
VIII.

L L 3 far

518   CONCLUSION OF THE MERCANTILE SYSTEM.

BOOK
IV.

far the principal architects. In the mercantile regulations, which have been taken notice of in this chapter, the interest of our manufacturers has been most peculiarly attended to ; and the interest, not so much of the consumers as that of some other sets of producers, has been sacrificed to it.

APPENDIX.

THE two following Accounts are subjoined in order to illustrate and confirm what is said in the Fifth Chapter of the Fourth Book, concerning the Tonnage bounty to the White Herring Fishery. The Reader, I believe, may depend upon the accuracy of both Accounts.

An Account of Busses fitted out in Scotland for Eleven Years, with the Number of Empty Barrels carried out, and the Number of Barrels of Herrings caught; also the Bounty at a Medium on each Barrel of Seasteeks, and on each Barrel when fully packed.

Years.	Number of Busses	Empty Barrels carried out.	Barrels of Herrings caught.	Bounty paid on the Busses.		
				£	s.	d.
1771	29	5948	2832	2085	0	0
1772	168	41316	22237	11055	7	6
1773	190	42333	42055	12510	8	6
1774	248	59303	56365	16952	2	6
1775	275	69144	52879	19315	15	0
1776	294	76329	51863	21290	7	6
1777	240	62679	43313	17592	2	6
1778	220	56390	40958	16316	2	6
1779	206	55194	29367	15287	0	0
1780	181	48315	19885	13445	12	6
1781	135	33992	16593	9613	12	6
Total,	2186	550943	378347	155463	11	0

Seasteeks

APPENDIX.

Seafteeks 378347   Bounty at a medium for each barrel of feafteeks, £ 0 8 2¼

But a barrel of feafteeks being only reckoned two-thirds of a barrel fully packed, one-third is deducted, which brings the bounty to £ 0 12 3¼

⅓ deducted 126115⅔

Barrels full } packed, } 252231⅓

And if the herrings are exported, there is befides a premium of - 0 2 8

So that the bounty paid by Government in money for each barrel, is - - - £ 0 14 11¾

But if to this, the duty of the falt ufually taken credit for as expended in curing each barrel, which at a medium is of foreign, one bufhel and one-fourth of a bufhel at 10s. a bufhel, be added, viz. 0 12 6

The bounty on each barrel would amount to - - - - £ 1 7 5¾

If

APPENDIX.

If the herrings are cured with Britiſh ſalt, it will
ſtand thus, viz.

Bounty as before   -   -   £0 14 11¾
—but if to this bounty the duty on
two buſhels of Scots ſalt at 1s. 6d.
per buſhel, ſuppoſed to be the
quantity at a medium uſed in cur-
ing each barrel is added, to wit,   0   3   0
_____

The bounty on each barrel will
amount to   -   -   -   £0 17 11¾

And,

When buſs herrings are entered for home conſumption in Scotland, and pay the ſhilling a
barrel of duty, the bounty ſtands thus, to wit as
before   -   -   -   £0 12 3¾
From which the 1s. a barrel is
to be deducted   -   -   0   1   0
_____
0 11 3¾

But to that there is to be added
again, the duty of the foreign ſalt
uſed in curing a barrel of herrings,
viz.   -   -   -   - 0 12 6
_____

So that the premium allowed for
each barrel of herrings entered for
home conſumption is   -   -   £1   3   9¾
_____

If

APPENDIX.

If the herrings are cured with British falt, it will ftand as follows, viz.

Bounty on each barrel brought in by the buffes as above - - £ 0 12 3¼

From which deduct the 1s. a barrel paid at the time they are entered for home confumption - 0 1 0

£ 0 11 3¾

But if to the bounty the duty on two bufhels of Scots falt, at 1s. 6d. per bufhel, fuppofed to be the quantity at a medium ufed in curing each barrel, is added, to wit, - 0 3 0

The premium for each barrel entered for home confumption will be £ 0 14 3¾

Though the lofs of duties upon herrings exported cannot, perhaps, properly be confidered as bounty; that upon herrings entered for home confumption certainly may.

An

APPENDIX. 523

An Account of the Quantity of Foreign Salt imported into Scotland, and of Scots Salt delivered Duty free from the Works there for the Fishery, from the 5th of April 1771 to the 5th of April 1782, with a Medium of both for one Year.

PERIOD.	Foreign Salt imported.	Scots Salt delivered from the Works.
	Bushels.	Bushels.
From the 5th of April 1771, to the 5th of April 1782.	936974	168226
Medium for one Year	$85179\frac{5}{11}$	$15293\frac{3}{11}$

It is to be observed that the Bushel of Foreign Salt weighs 84lb. that of British Salt 56lb. only.

END OF THE THIRD VOLUME.

Strahan and Preston,
Printers Street, London.

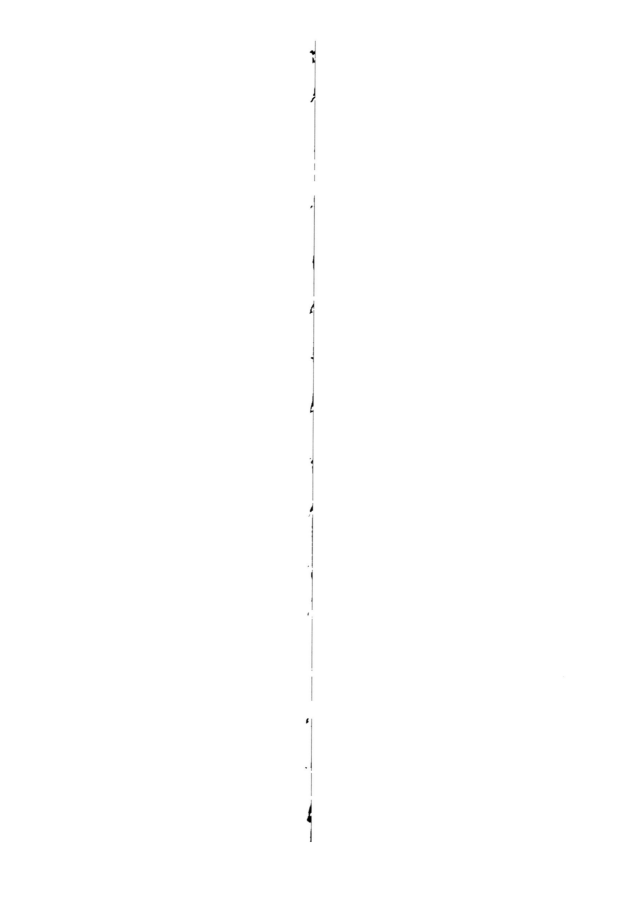

CPSIA information can be obtained at www.ICGtesting.com
Printed in the USA
LVOW052039240512

283181LV00013B/160/P